Encyclopedia of
WAR MACHINES

Encyclopedia of WAR MACHI

INES

an historical survey of the world's great weapons

Edited by **Daniel Bowen**

PEERAGE BOOKS

Contents

Air

THE WAR KITES	6
BALLOONS FOR THE MILITARY	13
SHIPS OF THE AIR	26
THE INVENTION OF THE AEROPLANE	40
AIR POWER BECOMES THE CRUCIAL FACTOR	50

Sea

THE EARLY SEAFARERS	134
THE PENTEKONTER & THE RAM	138
THE TRIREME RULES THE SEA	140
THE FORMIDABLE FIRE-SHIP	142
THE DROMON—A COASTAL RUNNER	146
GREEK FIRE HALTS THE SARACEN	148
THE VIKING LONGSHIP	150
THE STURDY MEDIEVAL COG	152
GUNPOWDER—THE GREAT DIVIDE	156
THE GALEASS AND THE GUN	156
ARTILLERY ADAPTS TO THE SEA	158

Land

THE FIRST DEVICES OF WAR	254
THE WAR CHARIOT	258
THE EARLIEST SIEGE MACHINES	260
FRONTIERS AGAINST INVASION	264
THE GREEK PHALANX	266
THE LEGIONS OF ROME	268
A THOUSAND YEARS OF SIEGE DEVICES	272
THE MOUNTED KNIGHT	274
THE DEADLY QUARREL OF THE CROSSBOW	282
THE CLOTHYARD SHAFT OF THE LONGBOW	284
SWISS PIKES AND MERCENARIES	286
THE MEDIEVAL CASTLE	288
GUNPOWDER BREAKTHROUGH	294
THE GREAT CANNON	296

ADDING STRENGTH AND SPEED	66	ADAPTING THE BOMB	92
FIGHTERS OF THE SECOND WORLD WAR	72	WARNING AND GUIDANCE	100
THE LONG RANGE FIGHTERS	80	THE HELICOPTER	104
THE BOMBER OFFENSIVE	82	JET POWER	111
THE ATOMIC BOMB	90	DEVELOPMENT OF THE MISSILE	116

THE GALLEON—WARSHIP OF AN ERA	160	THE REVOLVING GUN TURRET	190
THE DUTCH THREAT	166	BIRTH OF THE BATTLESHIP	194
THE RISING FRENCH NAVY	168	TORPEDO AND MINE	198
SHIPS-OF-THE-LINE	170	TORPEDO BOAT DESTROYERS	202
THE CARRONADE 'SMASHER'	172	WARFARE BENEATH THE WAVES—THE SUBMARINE	204
THE FRIGATE—LIGHT & FAST	174	BREAKTHROUGH ON THE POWDER FRONT	216
A NEW FORM OF POWER	176	DREADNOUGHT OR DINOSAUR	222
STEAM TAKES TO SEA	178	BATTLECRUISERS AT SPEED	224
HIGH EXPLOSIVE SHELLS	182	THE WASHINGTON TREATY: A LIMIT TO POWER	232
SHELLS, GUNS AND SHRAPNEL	184	THE AIRCRAFT CARRIER: A NEW DIMENSION	238
THE MIGHTY IRONCLAD	186	NUCLEAR POWER—WEAPONS FOR THE FUTURE	252

CANNON FOR EVERY PURPOSE	298	MINES AND BOOBY TRAPS	350
MORTARS: THE BARRAGE FROM ABOVE	304	BRIDGING THE GAP	352
FROM BOMBARDELLI TO FLINTLOCK	306	THE TERROR OF FIRE	354
THE MODERN RIFLE TAKES SHAPE	312	BIOLOGICAL AND CHEMICAL WARFARE	356
RAPID FIRE FROM THE REVOLVER	316	MISSILES ON TARGET	358
MACHINE GUNS FOR MASSACRE	318	COMMUNICATIONS AND COMPUTERS	360
PORTABLE FIREPOWER	324	INDEX	362
THE BIG GUNS	326		
ARMOURED FIGHTING VEHICLES	330		
THE TANK TAKES TO THE FIELD	334		
SPECIAL DUTY TANKS	337		
THE TANK DESTROYERS	342		
AIMED AT THE SKY	346		
WAR ON RAILS	348		

First published by Octopus Books Ltd

This edition published by Peerage Books
59 Grosvenor Street
London W1

© 1977 Octopus Books Ltd

Reprinted 1984

ISBN 0 907408 40 0

Printed in Hong Kong

WAR IN THE AIR

THE WAR KITES

The development of the aeroplane, and consequently the great aerial war machine of the 20th Century, was dependent on, among other things, an object we normally regard as a child's toy – the kite. In this chapter we shall look at the kite as an aerial war machine in its own right, and as the necessary precursor to the fighters and bombers that first saw action in the First World War. For we must remember that it was the aerodynamic lessons learnt from kites that enabled the construction of a practicable aeroplane; indeed the first aeroplanes were often nothing more than free-floating, powered kites. This was a principle that Alexander Graham Bell, a keen investigator of the aerodynamic properties of kites (as well as the telephone), saw very clearly: 'A properly constructed flying-machine should be capable of being flown as a kite and, conversely, a properly constructed kite should be capable of use as a flying-machine when driven by its own power.'

First of all, what is a kite and where did it originate? Clive Hart in his invaluable book, *The Kite*, defines it as a 'heavier-than-air machine held to earth by means of a flexible line and capable of rising to a positive angle with the horizon as a result of the forces created by wind pressure'. The first kites originated in Asia as far back as the 4th or 5th Centuries B.C. In China games were played with them; kite festivals were long held in Korea and Japan; in Melanesia and Polynesia kites were used as aids in fishing. However, they also had a military significance. As early as 196 B.C., one source reports, a Chinese general used kites on a kind of reconnaissance mission. By flying a kite over enemy fortifications he was able to establish the length of the tunnel which would have to be dug in order to get in.

With time, the military use of kites became more sophisticated. By the 6th Century, they were an important strategic weapon, as the following report shows (quoted in J. Needham's *Science and Civilization in China*, published by the Cambridge University Press).

Early war kites were often brilliantly painted in order to terrify the enemy

'In the Thai-Ching reign period (547–549) . . . Houching rebelled and besieged Thai-chheng (Nanking), isolating it from loyal forces far and near. Chien Wen . . . and the crown prince . . . decided to use many kites flying in the sky to communicate knowledge of the emergency to army leaders at a distance.'

Dr. Needham interprets this as an account of the use of kites for signalling purposes, with carrier pigeons being used to send out despatches. Kites were similarly used for signalling in 781, when a besieged general sent out messages to fellow-commanders, informing them of his plight. This worked successfully, and the siege was eventually lifted.

We also have an example of kites being used as a propaganda tool. In the 13th Century the Mongols besieged the Chin Tartars in their capital. Chin officers hit on the idea of using kites to drop messages to those of their men who had been taken prisoner by the Mongols, encouraging them to rise up and return to their own side.

Kites in the Far East eventually reached man-carrying proportions. Marco Polo reported the use of man-lifters by fishermen and a Japanese manuscript hints at the use of them in a reconnaissance capacity during a military operation.

The kites used in the Far East were, and still are, greatly varied, depending on their purpose. Animal-shaped kites were used during religious festivals, big rectangular ones with the cord smeared with cut glass or porcelain fought in kite wars, while children happily flew tiny pear-shaped kites with tails. The form of the kite developed considerably over the centuries, resulting in some of the most aerodynamically sound kites ever produced.

The Chinese, for instance, were producing cambered (i.e. curved) wing kites as early as the 10th Century. As we now know, the cambered aerofoil is a lot more efficient than a flat one. A typical Chinese cambered kite would be three feet broad and eleven feet long. A bridle was attached to the centre of one side and a retaining rope on the other. Here again, the Chinese had made important advances, for the use of the bridle greatly increased control of the kite in the fore-and-aft direction. They also experimented with two-cord kites in order to control the kite's angle of attack, depending on the strength of the wind. The frame was usually of bamboo set at a dihedral angle (again insuring greater stability) with the fabric of either silk or paper.

The Japanese 'war kite' could extend up to 15 feet in height and 10 feet across with a harness of seven bridles. It required a strong wind and, unlike the Chinese kite, could not fly without a tail. (Incidentally, a tail is used in flat kites to increase air resistance and thus lift.) The Koreans developed a versatile fighter kite. Rectangular in shape, it was 32 by 28 inches with a bamboo frame and silk covering. A hole was cut in the centre of the fabric about 11 inches in diameter, which enabled the kite to achieve equilibrium in strong winds.

Finally, a word about the Malay kite which was rediscovered by an American, Eddy, in the late 19th Century and used on a number of occasions for aerial photography. The framework consisted of a dorsal spine, slightly curved, across which two horizontal sticks, the same length as the spine, were fitted, one-fifth of the distance along the spine from either end. These sticks were bent, as in a bow, by a piece of cord nine-tenths the length of the spine. Varnished string connected the six points of the kite

Beautifully shaped kites were traditionally flown in China on the ninth day of the ninth month

framework, but the fabric (either cloth or paper) only covered the central rectangular piece. The Eddy kite differed from this in having the total framework covered. The great advantage of the Malay or Eddy kite was that it introduced to the west a stable kite that could fly tailless. It opened the door for further developments in kites; among other things, in their military use.

The Kite Revolution

European kites were probably derived from the Roman *dracones*, dragon-shaped wind-sock standards carried by Roman forces around the 2nd Century A.D. They were quite alarming creatures made by attaching a large, dragon-faced head to the top of a pole. Behind it, billowing in the wind, was a long tube of cloth. These were used for signalling, to identify ranks, but primarily to strike terror into the hearts of the enemy.

The dragon standard continued in use throughout the Middle Ages. At one point it was discovered that it would seem even more frightening if a burning torch was placed in the mouth, thus making the dragon look as if it were belching forth fire and smoke. The Polish historian Drugosz described one such effect:

The kite-carriage was a fanciful idea of 1827

'Among other standards there was, in the Tartar army, an immense banner . . . And at the top of the enemy banner was the representation of a hideous, jet-black head with a bearded chin. During the pursuit on the slopes . . . the standard-bearer began with all his strength to shake the head which was on top of a spear, and from it there poured forth vile-smelling steam, smoke and fumes, which engulfed the whole Polish army. Because of the horrible and intolerable fumes, the Polish warriors, nearly unconscious and half dead, were weak and unable to fight.'

By the end of the 16th Century, however, the popularity of the dragon-shaped kite had dwindled, giving way to the simpler pear- and diamond-shaped designs. At the same time, the military possibilities of the kite were overlooked. It had been relegated to the status of a mere plaything, and it was to be almost 300 years before it was again taken seriously.

Interest is Renewed

The man who paved the way for the kite flying rennaissance was a Bristol schoolteacher by the name of George Pocock. Pocock had the idea of harnessing a large arch-topped kite to a horse-less carriage, and with this contraption he made a successful run along the Bristol-Marlborough road. He also claimed that by means of a similar kite he had actually succeeded in lifting his daughter, Martha, into the air.

The idea of man-lifting kites now began to gain considerable popularity, especially in military circles, where it was quickly realized that they might be very useful for observation purposes. Captain B. F. S. Baden-Powell (the brother of the founder of the Boy Scout movement) was the first European to work seriously on man-lifting kites. In January, 1894, he lifted a man 10 feet off the ground. The kite was hexagonally shaped and 36 feet high. It covered an area of 500 square feet with a sheet of cambric stretched on a bamboo framework. The kite was flown on two lines from which a basket was suspended. With similar kites arranged in tandem he eventually lifted a man 200 feet off the ground. He used the kites for reconnaissance purposes during the Boer War and, with his kites, aided Marconi to set up a wireless service on the battlefield.

The man who really revolutionized kite flying was Lawrence Hargrave, a modest Australian who, in 1893, invented the box-kite. The box-kite was remarkably simple, yet very stable: it had great lifting ability and was almost immediately recognized as far superior to all previous kite configurations.

The kite was made by arranging two cells, or shallow boxes with the bottoms and tops removed, one behind the other. They were held together by variously placed struts and booms, usually diagonal. These were necessary to support the structure but hindered efficiency by adding weight and head resistance. The vertical sides of the box-kite provided lateral stability while the space between the cells provided fore-and-aft stability. Hargrave, himself, was lifted 16 feet by a train of four of these kites arranged in two pairs in tandem.

An American lieutenant, H. D. Wise, using a similar configuration, achieved 50 feet. At the junction of the two lines a pulley was attached with a rope running through it by means of which a 'boatswain's chair', carrying the passenger, was lifted. The main line was wound on a windlass. The kites were made of spruce framework and covered with cotton cloth. The areas of the kites were $22\frac{1}{2}$, 40, 90, and 166 square feet – a total area of $312\frac{1}{2}$ square feet. The main line was a half inch manilla rope.

Lt. Wise also devised a mobile aerial photographic kite kit to be used under battle conditions. It contained eight Eddy folding kites, 6,000 feet of cord, 1 field windlass, rings, pulleys and so on, 1 Wise Universal pointing camera and support, 1 Wise automatic operator for the camera, and 16 regulation signal flags with code staff. Field tests were provisionally successful but Wise's scheme was never implemented.

Cody's Man Lifter

The most successful of all man-lifters were the famous Cody 'War Kites'. Cody was a flamboyant American expatriate living in Britain: a cowboy and showman, and a brilliant and original engineer. For his man-lifters, he adopted the basic structure of the Hargrave box-kite, but he so modified it as to produce, in effect, an entirely new species of kite.

Large wings were built out at the top of the kite, and horn-like structures projected from the sides. These were larger on the front cell and smaller on the back. The wings and, indeed, the entire fabric covering of the cells could be tautened or slackened off as necessary, by means of a special set of controls which also could be

F. S. Cody, on the left, and his famous 'War Kite', taking

used to true the kite.

Perhaps more ingenious than the kites themselves was the way Cody assembled them to do the work of man-lifting. He invented a system that resembled the cable-car operations we see up the sides of mountains – only, the top of Cody's cable was fixed to a large kite which hung in the sky. This was the *pilot* kite, and it gave stability and guidance to the entire system. However, it did not provide the main lifting force: this was done by a series of *lifter* kites, usually from two to six, depending on the weather and the weight

part in the first international kite camp on June 25, 1903, on England's South Downs, in Sussex

to be lifted. Each lifter kite took its place at a specific station on the main cable.

Last of all was the *carrier* kite, which had suspended beneath it a passenger basket. When all the other kites were properly positioned the carrier would ascend to the height required. We may note that the aeronaut being lifted could control from his basket the movement of the carrier kite, by means of an elaborate system of lines and pulleys. That is, he could ascend and descend at will; he could also effectively brake when necessary.

With his apparatus Cody could lift a man thousands of feet, and maintain him in the air securely and steadily – an achievement that totally outclassed anything that had ever been accomplished with kites before.

In 1903, the Royal Navy bought four sets of Cody 'War Kites'. The War Office, not to be outdone, in 1905 acquired both the kites and Cody, who was officially installed as 'Chief Kite Instructor' at the Balloon School in Farnborough, later to be known as the Royal Aircraft Establishment.

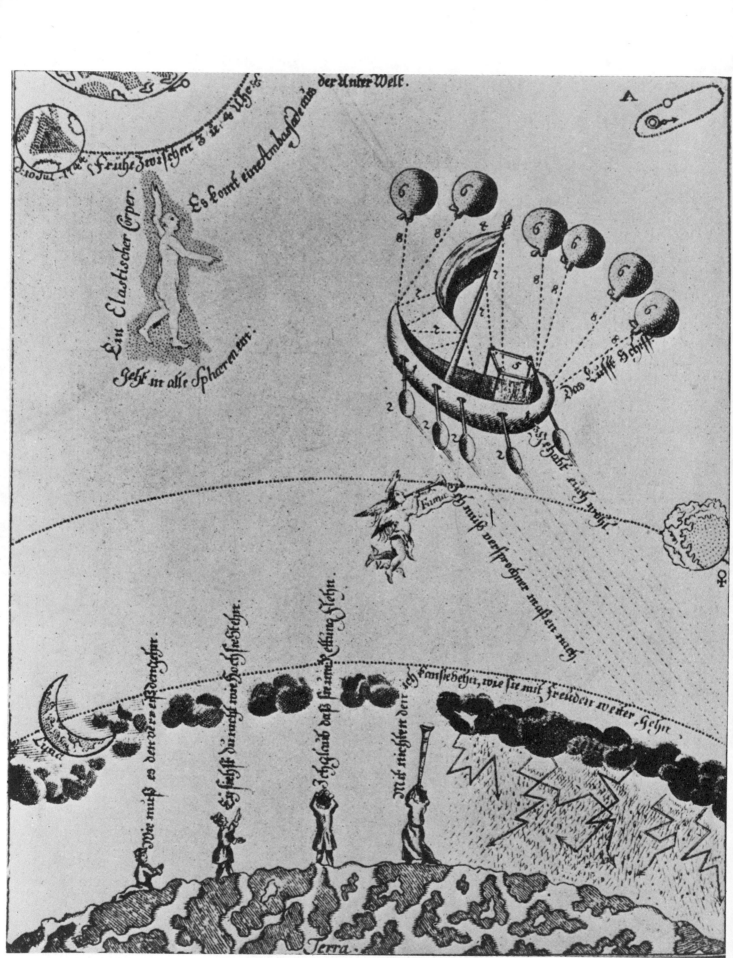

De Lana's impractical flying machine, supported by copper spheres, sets off for another planet, from an engraving of 1744

BALLOONS FOR THE MILITARY

With help of the balloon, man finally succeeded in cutting the cords that bound him to earth. And, with its help, he learned his first lessons in aerial warfare.

A balloon defies gravity because it is lighter than the air it displaces. Roger Bacon, a 13th-Century scholar and scientist, understood this principle and imagined a huge globe, constructed of very thin metal and 'filled with the thin air of the upper atmosphere, or with liquid fire, thus rising into the heavens'. It would take the mass of humanity another six centuries to catch up with this vision.

In the meantime, some four hundred years later, a Jesuit priest, father Francesco de Lana-Terzi, began to take an interest in the latest scientific discoveries. Among them were the findings by Pascal and Toricelli that the atmosphere has a measurable density; also the discovery by Otto van Guericke, that a vacuum can be artificially created.

Inspired by these ideas, de Lana designed a flying machine, which was to be borne aloft by four great copper spheres from which the air had been evacuated. The Jesuit insisted, however, that this design was a theoretical exercise only – which was just as well, since his copper globes would have been instantly crushed by atmospheric pressure had he attempted to put his idea into practice. De Lana had decided that it was safer for man to stay on the ground as God had intended him to. He foresaw with chilling accuracy the possibility of aerial warfare: 'Where is the man who can fail to see that no city would be proof against surprise . . . houses, fortresses and cities could thus be destroyed, with the certainty that the aerial ship could come to no harm, as the missiles could be hurled from a great height'.

If ballooning was ever to be practical, scientists had to discover a substance that was lighter than air. This was achieved in 1776 by Henry Cavendish, who called his discovery 'phlogiston' or 'inflammable air'. The great French scientist Lavoisier, in 1790, named this light and very dangerous gas hydrogen. Meanwhile, in Birmingham, Dr. Joseph Priestley, a chemist and physician, continued the research started by Cavendish and, in 1774, he published his findings in a work entitled *Experiments and Observations on Different Kinds of Air*. With this publication and the increasing pace of enquiry the stage was set for the great era of the balloons.

Henry Cavendish discovered a gas lighter than air
Dr Priestley experimented with 'different kinds of air'

The Montgolfièr

Priestley's work aroused considerable scientific interest in Europe. It fired the imagination of Joseph Montgolfièr, a 36-year-old French paper manufacturer. Joseph immediately began to speculate upon the possibilities of hydrogen as a lifting agent and, with this in mind, he carried out a number of experiments. He learned how to produce the gas and with it he attempted to inflate a small paper globe. The attempt was a failure, since the hydrogen passed through the paper like water through a sieve.

Nothing daunted, Joseph changed his line of attack, turning his attention to the possibilities of hot air. He constructed a small silken balloon and lit a fire beneath it. The balloon immediately rose to the ceiling in the most gratifying manner imaginable and Joseph was jubilant. This emotion must have been communicated to his brother, Etienne, who saw the experiment and became a full partner in the pioneer balloon work.

Montgolfier had no real understanding of the principle behind his hot-air balloon: namely, that air expands when heated and so becomes less dense than the surrounding atmosphere. Instead, he imagined that in the product of combustion – the fumes given off by the fire – he had discovered a new gas. He then spent many months laboriously experimenting with various foul-smelling and unlikely substances, including wet straw, wool, old shoes, decomposed meat and even cow dung – in an effort to find the combination that to his mind produced the lightest form of the gas.

The news of the Montgolfièr balloon spread

across the country like wildfire and in Paris it caused a great sensation among members of the Academy of Science. These learned men, not to be outdone by a provincial paper manufacturer, commissioned one of their members, a physicist named Charles, to build a balloon on their behalf.

Charles was convinced that there was only one gas – hydrogen – which would provide suitable lift for a balloon. Working with two brothers called Robert, who had invented a way of coating silk with rubber so as to make it impervious to hydrogen, and so contain the gas, he constructed the envelope for his balloon.

The Charles balloon, launched in August, 1783, was a great success, and totally outclassed the performance of the Montgolfièr, as the hot-air balloon had come to be called, in terms of the height it attained and the time and distance it travelled. Although the Montgolfièr brothers continued to work on and improve their balloons, it was soon established that the hydrogen balloon was a vastly superior craft. The initial and only advantage of the Montgolfièr was that it could be speedily and easily inflated, in the days when hydrogen generation was a difficult and costly process. However, as techniques for producing and storing hydrogen improved, this advantage was lost.

The first manned balloon ascent took place in November, 1783. The craft used was a large Montgolfièr. Soon afterwards, a manned flight was made in a hydrogen balloon.

Above: Alexandre Charles and Ainée Robert step out of their decorated craft after the first manned flight in a hydrogen-filled balloon. The flight was made from the garden of the Tuileries on December 1, 1783

Right: Charles's first unmanned hydrogen balloon reached almost 3,000 feet above Paris in August, 1783. But when it landed terrified villagers destroyed it with pitchforks, believing that they were being attacked by some strange, shapeless and dreadful monster

Early Military Balloons

As we have seen, the military value of the balloon was quickly appreciated by its inventors. Benjamin Franklin, the American diplomat and writer, also understood its usefulness for 'elevating an Engineer to take a view of an Enemy's Army, Works &c; conveying Intelligence into, or out of, a besieged Town, giving Signals to Distant Places or the like'. He also saw the possibility of large-scale aerial attack:

'Five thousand balloons, capable of raising two men each, could not cost more than Five Ships of the Line; and where is the Prince who can afford so to cover his Country with Troops for its Defense, as that Ten Thousand Men descending from the Clouds might not in many places do an infinite deal of mischief before a Force could be brought together to repel them?'

From theory to practice was a short step. In the wake of the French Revolution, it was suggested that balloons should be used by the French army for observation; and so, in 1794, *L'Entreprenant,* the world's first military balloon, was constructed. This balloon was made especially strong, as it was meant to withstand the wind rather than float freely with it. It was held captive by two cables attached to its equator – the band about its circumference.

L'Entreprenant was manned by a crew of two: one to do the actual observation, and one to handle the controls. Messages were signalled to

Benjamin Franklin foresaw large-scale aerial warfare

the ground with flags, and written reports sent down in small sand-bags attached to the cables.

A demonstration ascent was made for members of the Scientific Commission, who were so impressed by the performance of the balloon that they recommended the formation of the world's first 'air force': the Aerostatic Corps of the Artillery Service. The balloon, together with a company of these *Aerostiers*, was then sent to join the French army at Maubeuge, where it immediately proved its worth in reconnaissance.

From Maubeuge, *L'Entreprenant* and the balloon corps moved on to their greatest triumph, at the battle of Fleurus. This engagement lasted for some ten hours, and during this entire period the balloon – manned by its two observers, Brevet-Captain Coutelle, commander of the balloon corps, and General Morlot of the army – remained aloft. The French army was at all times effectively directed from the air. The result was a resounding French victory, the first ever won on the strength of aerial superiority.

Encouraged by this success, the French built three more military balloons. These were completed in 1796, and each was sent to a different front, together with its own corps of Aerostiers. But, in 1799, Napoleon disbanded the force, for in his own conception of military strategy – a highly mobile *land* force – there was no room for a static object like the balloon.

French military balloons being used as observation posts

American balloon unit inflating a reconnaissance balloon with hydrogen (1862)

The American Civil War

The next serious and large-scale military use of balloons occurred during the Civil War in America. From the beginning, a number of well-known aeronauts had volunteered to do observation work for the Union forces. These early efforts, however, were not successful for a variety of reasons. In the first place, there were problems with the balloons, which were not designed for military use. There were technical difficulties involved in getting the balloons inflated and transporting them in this state to the field. But worst of all was the fact that the aeronauts received very little co-operation or support from the conservative military bureaucracy, which had no experience of ballooning and tended to regard the whole thing as a new-fangled nuisance.

John La Mountain, in 1861, made the first really successful ascent of the Civil War. From a height of 1,400 feet, he spotted two concealed Confederate camps at Fortress Monroe. Later, he used barges on the James River as aircraft carriers, from which he rose 2,000 feet. But his most spectacular achievements were the free flights he made over Confederate territory, relying on a favourable east wind near ground level to carry him across enemy lines, and then discharging ballast and returning with the prevailing westerly currents at higher altitudes. La Mountain repeated this courageous feat not once but many times.

The most important aerial contribution to the Union war effort was made by Thaddeus Lowe. Lowe was an inspired organiser and inventive genius who was eventually befriended by President Lincoln. He was subsequently appointed as a balloonist with General McClellan's Army of the Potomac, and made several captive ascents in his own balloon, the *Enterprise*.

His first major breakthrough was the installation of telegraph equipment in the car of the *Enterprise*, leading the wires down along a cable. On 18 June, 1861, Lowe transmitted his first message to President Lincoln, as follows:

'To the President of the United States

'Sir, This point of observation commands an area nearly 50 miles in diameter. The city, with its girdle of encampments, presents a superb scene. I have pleasure in sending you this first despatch ever telegraphed from an aerial station, and in acknowledging indebtedness for your encouragement for the opportunity of demonstrating the availability of the science of aeronautics in the military service of the country, T. D. C. Lowe.'

Lowe went on to design a new military balloon, the *Union* which he also equipped with telegraph apparatus. In this balloon he made many successful observation ascents. He scored another 'first' on September 24, 1861, when, using his telegraph, he directed the artillery to fire on Confederate forces assembled at Falls Church. Never before had aerial technology been used so successfully.

In all, Lowe constructed seven military balloons. He designed an aircraft carrier (a converted coal barge) for use with them and, on one occasion, a balloon was towed for 13 miles, carrying an aeronaut, at 1,000 feet, making continuous observations.

Another important innovation was – finally – the introduction of a 'portable' field generator. These generators were enormous and cumbersome affairs mounted on horse-wagons, but they did serve the purpose for which they were intended. Balloons were no longer exposed to needless risks by being dragged, fully inflated, across the countryside. With the new generators it was possible to fill an average sized balloon in approximately two and a half hours.

The balloons played crucial roles in at least two battles which would otherwise have ended in crushing Union defeats: at Four Oaks and Gaine's Hill. But perhaps their most important contribution was strategic – they hampered enemy movements and made enforced concealment a necessity, so that the Rebel troops had to expend a great deal of energy in avoiding surveillance.

'I have often wondered,' wrote the Confederate General Alexander after the war, 'why the enemy abandoned the use of military balloons early in 1863.'

The reason was the unsympathetic attitude of top army officers. This reached a pitch when General Cyrus B. Comstock was put in charge of balloon operations. Comstock showed so little interest and understanding of the balloonists' efforts that the exasperated Lowe resigned. Deprived of his leadership, the entire balloon corps soon crumbled.

The Confederates made some attempts to utilize balloons, but these were sporadic efforts only. A single Montgolfièr was used for observation by the Confederate General Johnston. However, its practical value was severely limited because it carried no stove and could therefore remain aloft for only a few minutes at a time. It was replaced by a gas-balloon made in Savannah and known as the 'silk-dress' balloon because its envelope was made of bolts of silk of differing colours and patterns. This balloon was captured by Union forces shortly after it was completed.

Undaunted by this set-back, the Rebels built yet another 'silk-dress' balloon. This was flown for almost a year until in July, 1873, it escaped from its moorings in a gust of high wind, and was blown over enemy lines, The Confederates never built another balloon, presumably because by that time the Unionists' balloon operations had been suspended.

Above: Preparing a balloon at the Gare du Nord, Paris, to carry dispatches (left) out of the besieged city

The Paris Airlift

We now turn to one of the most spectacular stories of military ballooning history. The scene is Paris, 1870; the Prussians have besieged the city. All surface communications between the capital and the rest of the country have been cut.

During the early stages of the Franco-Prussian war the French government had shown no interest in military balloons. However, the situation in Paris was now desperate, and when a number of aeronauts approached the head of the Post Office, in September, 1870, with a proposal that balloons be used to maintain contact with Gambetta, who was organizing resistance in the provinces, he could not refuse.

On September 23, the professional aeronaut Jules Drurof took off from the Place St. Pierre, with 223 pounds of mail. Some three hours later he landed safely behind enemy lines. It was the start of one of the most astonishing air-lifts in history.

A pigeon-fancier solved the problem of how to get mail back into the city by volunteering the services of his gallant birds. Shortly afterwards, the Parisian photographer Dagron developed special micro-film techniques, which enabled a pigeon to carry film representing 5,000 letters.

Clearly there were not enough balloons or balloonists in the city to sustain the operation for any length of time. And so two great railway stations, the Gare du Nord and the Gare d'Orleans, were transformed into impromptu balloon factories, with hundreds of workers turning out balloons with unprecedented speed. The balloons were large, strong and constructed as cheaply and simply as possible since they were not meant to be used more than once. A number of sailors then in the city were given brief training courses in balloon management. With these fearless men as pilots, the airlift continued.

Naturally enough, the balloons soon attracted the unwelcome attentions of Prussian rifles. These guns were of considerable range and fire power, making it unsafe for balloons at anything less than 3,500 feet. After several narrow escapes, the authorities ruled that in future all ascents would be made by night.

Altogether a total of 66 flights were made, carrying about ten tons of mail, 155 human beings, over 400 pigeons and five dogs. Fifty-eight of these flights were recorded as successful, landing safely in friendly territory. Of the others, two drifted to sea, and a small number had the bad luck to land in enemy territories. The last balloon to leave Paris, on January 28, 1871, carried orders to French shipping to proceed to Dieppe – and news of the French capitulation.

The Paris airlift caused most European powers to sit up and take note. Henceforth, aerial superiority would be of vital importance, and none of the great powers could afford to fall behind. Soon there were balloon schools and balloon corps flourishing in Austria, Germany, France, Russia and England.

British Balloons at War

Captain J. L. B. Templer, a skilled and enthusiastic amateur, was the guiding genius of British military ballooning. Templer's career as a military balloonist started in 1878, when he was granted £150 ($750 at that time) to construct the *Crusader*, Britain's first military balloon. During the course of that career, he developed a balloon corps in Britain that was second to none in the world.

Templer introduced a number of innovations that were essential for effective and practical military operations. For example, the problem of providing gas for balloons in the field had still not been solved to his satisfaction. Templer

Signal arms spread on a British balloon

rejected the 'portable' generators designed by Lowe as being much too cumbersome and slow in action. He finally arrived at a better solution: pressurized steel cylinders in which the gas could be stored until it was required.

Templer also developed a new method for producing hydrogen. The standard procedure for obtaining the gas was through the chemical interaction of zinc and sulphuric acid; this, Templer felt, was unsatisfactory because the gas so generated contained traces of acid which tended to corrode balloon envelopes. Templer therefore evolved an electrolytic process – breaking down water into its component elements – which produced a gas much more free from impurities.

Another outstanding breakthrough was in the construction of the balloons themselves. Previously, all balloon envelopes had been made from fabric – whether silk or simple cambric – which was 'doped' or varnished to prevent any leakage of the hydrogen. As far as Templer was concerned, none of the various varnishes then in use would render cloth sufficiently impervious for his purposes. He therefore started making his balloons from something else – gold beater's skin.

Gold beater's skin is one of the strongest and lightest materials known to man. It is also remarkably impervious. It is made from the lining of the *caecum*, or blind gut, of an ox, each animal supplying only a square foot or so of the

British troops moving an observation balloon in the Transvaal

precious membrane. Because of its expense and relative scarcity, it had hitherto been used only for toys and, significantly, model balloons. Templer and his workers evolved methods for obtaining, cleaning, processing and finally joining many pieces together to form an almost perfect sphere.

By 1899, as a result of these improvements, the British had the most compact and useful military balloon in history. It was remarkably small and economical of hydrogen, without sacrificing any of the lift necessary for observation purposes. The war in Africa provided a golden opportunity for the balloon to prove its worth.

The Boer War was fought on several different fronts simultaneously. One consequence of this was that no less than four separate balloon corps each made vital contributions to the British effort. In fact, the scale and influence of balloon operations during this was has never been equalled.

The Second Balloon Section, which was the first to leave Britain for Africa, arrived at Durban, in Natal. From Durban, this section dashed to Ladysmith, where it gave valuable service: locating and observing Boer movements before battle and, during the fight, directing artillery. As it happened, the British lost this battle and Ladysmith was besieged. The Second Balloon Section was trapped – cut off from vital supplies of hydrogen – so, after a month's work,

operations had to be suspended.

However, this was not the end of military ballooning in the area. A balloon section was scraped together outside the besieged town, and this improvised band of irregulars played a decisive role in the battles leading to the lifting of the siege.

One commentator has described these men as 'just about the finest military balloonists that have ever existed'. They kept the Boers under almost constant surveillance, not only following their movements but also seriously undermining their morale.

The Boers retaliated by trying to shoot down the unwelcome observers, but in spite of their unquestionable skill as gunners their efforts were wasted. The balloons proved themselves to be virtually invulnerable. Not only were they very difficult to hit, but they had to be hit many times before they could be brought down.

Two other balloon sections – the First and the Third – also played active roles in the war, in the western area, and their contributions were also invaluable. The balloons continually reported enemy positions and directed artillery during the battle.

It is perhaps ironic that at the point at which balloons reached their highest military development, they were already foredoomed. By the time the war was over, in 1902, the airship had taken their place as the primary aerial weapon.

The French were pioneers of balloon and dirigible flight. Above and below: Aspects of Meusnier's design for a dirigible balloon shaped like a cigar Another Frenchman, Giffard, actually made an airship powered by steam (right).

SHIPS OF THE AIR

With the advent of balloons, the dream of flight was only partially fulfilled. Balloons could rise, and they could lift useful loads, but they were helplessly at the mercy of the winds.

Almost from the beginning, ambitious aeronauts tried to 'steer' their gasbags through the heavens, by attaching sails or oars or flapping wings to them. Needless to say, these attempts were failures.

But in 1784 (just one year after the first balloon flights by the Montgolfièrs and Charles) a Frenchman by the name of Meusnier submitted a design for a dirigible ('directable' or 'steerable') balloon to the French Academy of Sciences. This design called for a cigar-shaped airship, to be driven by three propellers, and it incorporated the revolutionary idea of a *ballonnet*.

Meusnier correctly understood that the spherical shape of the traditional balloon was not suitable for directed flight: that to move forward

through the air, the craft should be elongated or streamlined. He also understood that the airship would maintain this shape only because of constant pressure within the envelope – and if gas were lost, the ship might buckle or crumple in mid-air.

To counteract this tendency – and also as a means of regulating the altitude reached – Meusnier introduced the ballonnet: a small balloon within the main envelope which could be pumped up with pressurized air. As the airship rose and the hydrogen within it expanded, air from the ballonnet would be forced out through a safety valve. Similarly, as the hydrogen contracted (or if it were lost through leakage) air would be pumped into the ballonnet. Such an arrangement, Meusnier pointed out, would also result in the conservation of ballast and of precious hydrogen.

Meusnier's design was unworkable, as he

Santos-Dumont used his No. 9 dirigible to travel above the streets of Paris

himself realized, mainly because of the lack of a suitable power-source. In the years that followed, interest in the idea of dirigibility remained high, but success ultimately depended on the development of an engine which was both light and powerful enough.

During the 1840's, several model airships were built and actually flew, propelled by clockwork or small steam engines. Airship pioneers realized that clockwork could never power a full scale ship. By about 1850, many were seriously investigating the steam engine.

The credit for the first full-sized steerable airship goes to another Frenchman, Henri Giffard. His cumbersome engine, which drove a three-bladed propeller, weighed about 350 pounds and managed to develop 3 horse-power. During its maiden flight – made under almost perfect conditions of no wind – the airship achieved an

average speed of 5 miles an hour. It landed safely 17 miles from its starting place.

Giffard himself realized that his machine was seriously underpowered, so much so that, if there had been a wind, the airship would have floated with it just like any other balloon. But a more powerful motor would have meant one that weighed much more, and the craft was already far too heavy.

In 1884, two French Army engineers, Charles Renard and Arthur Krebs completed the construction of their airship, *La France*. This ship was the most advanced and sophisticated to date. Its design was slim and streamlined, coming to a point at either end, and it incorporated such technical refinements as a rudder and elevator, as well as ballonnets. *La France* was powered by an electric motor and developed $8\frac{1}{2}$ horse-power. However, the power-weight ratio was still a piti-

The basket of Woelfert's airship Deutschland, *with the internal combustion engine that drove it*

ful 210 pounds per horse-power because of the weight of the electrical batteries.

The first flight of *La France* was a great triumph. The ship faithfully answered her controls and, successfully defying the winds, made a circular five-mile trip that lasted some 23 minutes – and exhausted the batteries! It was clear that for further progress to be made a still more suitable power source had to be developed.

The answer was not long in coming: the petrol-fuelled internal combustion engine. The first to take this engine aloft was a German named Karl Woelfert, but Woelfert's effort ended in disaster. Hydrogen is an alarmingly combustible gas. Woelfert kept his primitive engine ignited with an open-flame burner. As the ship ascended to 3,000 feet and vented gas – in an instant it was a blazing inferno which fell to earth, killing Woelfert and his engineer, Robert Knabe.

It was left to a wealthy young Brazilian, newly arrived in Paris, to show that the internal combustion engine could indeed successfully power a dirigible balloon. Alberto Santos-Dumont had courage, determination, great mechanical ability and, equally important, plenty of money. He built a series of small pressure airships – each an improvement over the last – whose primary features were their simplicity and lightness. Their design was based, to a large extent, on the work of predecessors making use of, for example, such features as the ballonnet. But Santos' dirigibles were the first to be truly practicable and they turned him, overnight, into the rage of Paris.

His *No. 6* won the Deutsch prize offered for the first flight from St. Cloud, round the Eiffel Tower and back in less than thirty minutes. He used *No. 9,* his smallest ship, as a runabout around Paris – 'dropping in' at his favourite cafés, and

so forth. The Brazilian's exploits, above all, popularized the notion of 'dirigibility' in the French capital.

The next major advance in airship design was the work of the Lebaudy brothers. Their ship, the *Lebaudy I* (nicknamed 'le Jaune' because of its yellow envelope) made its maiden flight in 1902. Strapped to the belly of the craft was an elliptical underframe of steel tubing, which served both to maintain the shape of the airship and as a surface from which to suspend the gondola (or car).

The *Lebaudy I* was therefore, the first semi-rigid airship. It could reach speeds of up to 25 m.p.h., and set several distance records for dirigibles. *Lebaudy I* was damaged in 1903 and rebuilt as *Lebaudy II*. She was eventually acquired by the French army, and became the successful prototype of a series of military airships which served in France and in several other countries.

Left: Santos-Dumont rounding the Eiffel Tower, Paris. Above left: A nasty crash at Saint Cloud. Above right: A cartoon of Santos-Dumont, published in the magazine Vanity Fair, *in November, 1901. Right: The skeleton of the Lebaudy airship, showing the balloon underframe of steel tubing*

Von Zeppelin and the Rigid Airship

The rigid airship owed its existence to two important technological advances made in the 19th Century. The first was, as we have seen, the invention of the internal combustion engine. The second was the discovery of aluminium, the new 'silver made from clay'. This substance, strong yet light, proved to be the ideal building material for the framework of an airship.

The first rigid airship built from aluminium was the brainchild of David Schwarz, a Hungarian engineer. His ship was a total loss. After numerous mechanical difficulties she landed hard and crumpled like an old tin can. Miraculously, her pilot jumped free and did not sustain any injuries.

With the exception of the Lebaudy ships the dirigible had so far shown little practical utility. The small craft of Santos-Dumont and others were not suitable for carrying heavy loads or for making sustained flights. What was needed was something much larger, for experiments had shown that the range and carrying capacity of an airship was in direct proportion to its dimensions. Yet there were limits to the possible size of a ship with a cloth envelope and there was the

Above: Count Zeppelin. Below: David Schwartz's aluminium airship of 1893

constant difficulty of maintaining the lifting bag's smooth contour by internal pressure alone. There was also an ever-present danger that the bag would spring a leak.

The man who found the solution to all these problems was an aristocratic German soldier whose name will always be linked with the rigid craft he pioneered – Count Ferdinand August Adolf von Zeppelin.

According to the tradition of his times, Zeppelin embarked on a career in the army early in life. He was always keenly aware of the military potential of the dirigible, and the launching of *La France* by Renard and Krebs, seriously disturbed him. He was alarmed by the possibility that France might pull ahead in the arms race, leaving Germany lagging far behind. And so he began to work on plans for a rigid airship.

In 1890, after a characteristic clash with Kaiser Wilhelm of Prussia, the hot-headed Zeppelin, now a Lieutenant-General, was asked for his resignation. This meant that the old soldier – he was fifty-two – could henceforth devote himself full-time to his dreams of German aerial superiority.

In 1893, the Count submitted a design for an airship to the German War Ministry, but faults were found with his proposal and it was turned down. Zeppelin remained undaunted and proceeded to work on a second design. This became the prototype for all the future rigid airships – or zeppelins – that came to be built. In 1898 the construction of the ship was commenced.

The basic framework of the dirigible was a skeleton of lightweight aluminium girders, 24 longitudinal beams which connected 16 transverse rings. The interior was thus divided into 17 compartments, each of which was occupied by a hydrogen cell made of rubberized cotton. Each individual cell had an automatic release valve at the bottom, and some had valves at the top which could be operated from the control car. The outer covering was made from impregnated cotton designed to reduce skin friction. The ship measured about 400 feet from bow to stern.

Two open gondolas, connected by a flimsy catwalk, were slung from the bottom of the ship. Each carried a Daimler engine weighing 850 pounds. These engines developed about 15 horsepower, and, for the weight of the ship, it was clear

Zeppelin's giant airship Hindenburg *blazes before crumpling to earth*

that she was underpowered.

The *LZ 1* (Luftschiff Zeppelin 1) made her maiden flight in July, 1902 – a flight which lasted about a quarter of an hour. The ship was very unstable and she barely responded to her controls. She was hauled back to her hangar for repair work but, after just two more flights, she was admitted to be a failure and was broken up.

With determined optimism the Count persisted in his dreams. By 1905, he had got enough financial backing to start work on *LZ 2*. Despite many improvements to its structure, *LZ 2* was doomed to disaster. After her first and only flight she was destroyed by a storm.

Zeppelin doggedly went on to build *LZ 3* which, to the amazement of all concerned, was an unqualified success. The military authorities even went so far as to express an interest in the Count's work, and the army declared that it would purchase an airship if it could make an uninterrupted 24-hour flight. Zeppelin was awarded half a million marks and with this money he constructed *LZ 4*.

LZ 4 made several highly successful flights, but she was jinxed by the bad luck that had plagued Zeppelin's earlier creations. After an attempt at a 24-hour cruise, which was troubled by minor mechanical failures, the ship was

In the night sky, a giant Zeppelin receives a fatal hit

moored in a field for repairs. A sudden thunderstorm struck – there was a burst of flame – and within moments the ship was a charred ruin.

This latest tragedy should have broken the 70-year-old Count's spirit, but by now there was a great deal of public interest in the huge airships. When news of the disaster broke, the German people literally flooded the old warrior with telegrams, letters of sympathy, and most important of all, money – more than six million marks. The German people had decreed that work on the Zeppelins should continue. The Zeppelin factory, therefore, went on turning out airships and the German army acquired *LZ 3* and

LZ 5. By 1911, the navy had also decided to invest in the dirigibles.

Zeppelins in Action

The German people saw the Zeppelins as the 'secret weapon' that would win the war for them. The military authorities had rather less faith. When the war broke out in 1914, the army owned eight airships and the navy, after two losses, just one. The Admiralty therefore embarked on a crash expansion programme.

At the beginning, the army's airships did very

poorly, thus confirming the worst fears of the War Office. They were too heavy, with insufficient lift and low speeds – and were thus horribly vulnerable to ground fire. After two months of battle, four of the eight ships were lost. As a result, their reconnaissance role was abandoned and their operations confined to strategic bombing missions. By late autumn, with the addition of four more ships to the fleet, the army had at its disposal an effective air force that could carry 2,000 pounds of bombs as far as London or Paris. Army Zeppelins made routine attacks on enemy bases, railway yards, and the like. On December 25, 1914, the French towns of Dunkirk, Nancy and Verdun were raided.

By February, 1915, the navy had acquired 10 airships, which they used for scouting and patrol work. The German Admiralty had anticipated that the Royal Navy would establish a close blockade of the North Sea coast, as they had done during the Napoleonic Wars. Instead, a distant blockade was imposed and the German battleships found themselves on the defensive, with all too few vessels available for necessary patrol work. The Zeppelins were drafted to do the job of observing the movements of enemy surface vessels and submarines.

However, the officers of both the army and the navy had dreams of greater things – namely, the bombing of London. They were convinced that if the English capital was raided, the hated Islanders would soon be demoralized and sue for peace. The Kaiser was at first opposed to this plan. He was worried about the 'historic monuments' of London, and he had a tender solicitude for the safety of his 'Royal Cousins', the British King and Queen. Eventually he consented to the bombing of docks and military establishments on the Lower Thames – so long as great pains were taken to spare historic buildings, private property, and 'above all . . . royal palaces'.

The services vied with each other for the honour of conducting the first raid on England. It fell to the Admiralty, which made a totally

The great size of the Zeppelin shows clearly as it hovers above the German fleet at anchor

abortive attempt on January 13, 1915, and another on January 19, in which an insignificant amount of damage was done.

Throughout the late spring and summer the airships of both services attacked Britain. But the raids were not overwhelmingly successful, due mainly to navigational problems – the Zeppelins, flying by night, could not properly find the cities that were supposed to be their targets. Electronic aids, now taken for granted, were of course non-existent; and for better or for worse, most airship commanders had to rely on a 'sixth sense' to get their bearings. Nevertheless, in 1915, 27 of the 47 ships that had set out for England actually made successful attacks.

In the years that followed, the dirigibles made more raids but they did less damage at increasingly higher cost. The aeroplane, in 1914 a primitive craft of limited military value, became more effective and anti-aircraft guns became deadlier and more accurate. The vulnerable Zeppelins were forced to climb higher and higher

The Zeppelin Hindenburg *joins in a Nuremburg rally*

in their efforts to avoid the new British fighters, resulting in a loss of efficiency and a lowering of the load that they could usefully carry.

On September 2, 1916, the German army sustained serious losses in the biggest air-raid on London yet attempted. This marked the end of their offensive use of airships.

The Height Climbers

The Admiralty, however, was not so easily discouraged. It retaliated with the development of 'height climbers', which made their appearance early in 1917.

These 'height climbers', with a capacity of two million cubic feet, could reach the unprecedented ceiling of 20,000 feet. They were the ultimate development of the Zeppelin as a weapon of war. With them, the entire British defence system was at once rendered obsolete. After their introduction the British only managed to shoot down two of the ships before the armistice. However, it must be pointed out that the 'height climbers' brought more problems to the Germans than had been anticipated. They used up enormous quantities of hydrogen (which was becoming increasingly difficult to supply) and their navigation was made more uncertain because they operated mostly above cloud level. At great heights, the speed of the dirigibles was greatly reduced, due to strong gales and currents which were much more frequent than at lower levels. Also, crews suffered horribly from cold and lack of oxygen.

All this, combined with the fact that airships were in constant demand for scouting missions, resulted in raids over London becoming much less frequent, although they were continued until 1918. But they had little more than nuisance value. The dream of bombing Britain into submission was over.

It had been suggested that the navy Zeppelins would have been put to far better use had the Admiralty simply used them as scouts and in conjunction with U-boats, rather than risking them in attack on London. Yet the airships were of some value, if only for the demoralizing effect they had on the British, who dedicated considerable resources and energy to battling the huge marauders.

Nevertheless, by 1918 the lumbering machines were totally discredited as a weapon, even in Germany where no less than 106 had been built. They had failed to win the war.

Blimps on Patrol

None of the belligerents of the First World War had put as much faith and resources into the airship as Germany. However, in 1914, most European powers were uneasily aware of the military potential of the machine and felt it their duty at least to attempt to put the airship to work.

Although Britain had experimented with airships from the beginning of the century, she had only a few small vessels in service at the outbreak of war. These were immediately posted to coastal patrol duties. When, early in 1915, threats of German submarines became particularly alarming, the Admiralty ordered the construction of a large number of quick, inexpensive, non-rigid airships for patrol work (type B-limp, soon known as 'the blimp'). Eventually, airship bases were set up all along the British coast, their crews patiently waiting for the tell-tale signs of U-boats.

In 1917, the airships were assigned another job, that of accompanying convoys of merchant ships. The presence of the blimps forced enemy submarines to be on the alert at all times, and also to travel submerged, thus reducing their speed and the length of time they could remain at sea. In short, they played a vital role in the crucial task of keeping Britain's life-lines open. Altogether, nearly 400 blimps were produced in Britain during the years of combat.

France, the United States and Italy also employed airships. In France, where the army possessed about 15 non-rigid dirigibles, early efforts to use them for dropping bombs on enemy targets were plagued by trigger-happy French gunners, who persisted in mistaking them for enemy craft. Eventually, all missions had to be flown by night, since the low ceiling of the ships made them such easy targets.

By 1916, although the French army airships had carried out a fair number of successful raids, it was clear that German anti-aircraft defences were more than a match for them. So the French army suspended operations and handed whatever craft they had left over to the army.

Since the beginning of 1916, the French navy had assembled an airship fleet which they, like the British, were using for coastal patrol duties. Like the British, they found the ships useful for U-boat reconnaissance and eventually assigned them to merchant convoys.

In America, blimps were also used for coastal patrol and actually succeeded in twice sighting

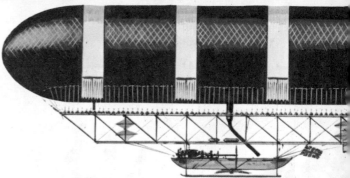

U-boats just outside New York harbour. However, no American airships were ever posted in Europe.

Italy was the only other nation to use airships during the war. Although some of her ships were used for anti-submarine patrols, most were used by the army for bombing and reconnaissance missions across the Austrian lines. These missions were little better than suicidal for they were flown in broad daylight, and the dirigibles were targets for Austrian anti-aircraft gunners. By the end of the war, Italy had lost the majority of her airships and their crews.

A few words should be said about the aftermath of the Great War. Clearly, dirigibles would

Above: British naval coastal patrol airship on convoy escort duty, 1914–18 war. Far left: 'Nulli Secundus', 1907. first British military dirigible balloon. Left: Classic Good Year, U.S. Naval Blimp, a highly developed airship (not to scale with 'Nulli Secundus'

never again be used as primary weapons of combat. However, in America at least, naval authorities had not forgotten the usefulness of the small blimp for reconnaissance and patrol duties. In 1942, and thereafter until the end of World War II, blimps were used, as they had been in the First War, as coastal patrols and convoy escorts. So effective were they that the U.S. authorities claimed that no convoy escorted by a blimp was ever lost to the enemy throughout World War II.

The blimps eventually mastered the procedure of landing on an aircraft carrier, replenishing supplies, and carrying on with their patrols. This came to be a standard practice.

After World War II, United States airship operations were greatly reduced, but the blimps did continue throughout the 1950s and into the 1960s as part of the North American defence chain, employed, as usual, for submarine spotting and as part of the Distant Early Warning radar service, to extend the radar service well out over the Atlantic.

However, by 1962, the American Ballistic Missile Early Warning radar chain was complete. There were no longer any gaps in it for the useful blimp to stop. And so, in 1964, the last airship squadron of the U.S. Navy was decommissioned. Another phase of the air war was over and another machine relegated to the past.

THE INVENTION OF THE AEROPLANE

Leonardo da Vinci has long been recognized as a magnificent artist and a scientist of high achievements. His interest in aviation, however, was discovered only in the late 19th Century. Nevertheless, we now know that this remarkable man produced countless sketches and ideas for flying machines, some of them very complex indeed. Unfortunately, Leonardo, like his less brilliant predecessors, concentrated most of his energy on ornithopters, or flapping-wing designs. To this end, he spent a great deal of time in careful study of the flight of birds. In 1505, he published his observations in the form of a treatise, *Sul Volo degli Ucelli*.

As it turned out, most of Leonardo's notions about the mechanics of birds' flight were fundamentally incorrect. He supposed, for example, that birds supported themselves in the air by a 'downward and backward' motion, akin to a swimming or rowing action. We now know, in fact, that birds are not able to beat their wings in a purely backward motion.

The result was that Leonardo produced a great many designs for flying machines, most of them meant to be borne aloft by human muscle-power. Clearly, however, none of the flapping contraptions would ever have been able to get off the ground.

Experts suppose that Leonardo must have built models of many of his designs and perhaps full-scale versions of one or two. However, it is certain that Leonardo never made any public attempt at flight.

Nevertheless, Leonardo has to his credit a remarkable series of sketches, including several varieties of ornithopters, one of which was even powered by a spring motor. Another was a partial glider, having fixed wings with flapping panels attached to the outer edges. His wing designs, in particular, were elaborate and amazingly life-like.

Leonardo also produced several machines which might be categorized as flying chariots, also certain wing-testing and flight control apparatus.

From our point of view, his most interesting and original inventions were those of the parachute and the helicopter. Leonardo's parachute was a pyramid-shaped affair. Although the design was never practicable, it is nonetheless a true fore-runner of today's parachute, which was 're-invented' some three hundred years later.

His screw helicopter is perhaps the most famous and impressive of his aeronautical designs, meant to rise by means of a helical, or spiral, screw. It was not a workable idea, although there are suggestions that Leonardo may actually have built and flown a model. But this machine owes its greatest importance to the fact that it represents Leonardo's first, and perhaps only, departure from the idea that successful human flight must be based on a detailed imitation of nature. Many historians of flight regret that Leonardo did not pursue this helicopter design, but devoted himself, instead, to his flapping-wing machines. In the end da Vinci's main contribution was to provoke later interest and thought in flying.

The Problems of Flight

Sir George Cayley (1773–1857) was the founder of the modern science of aerodynamics. It was he who first really understood why and how birds fly, and why and how heavier-than-air machines could be made to. He defined the problem of mechanical flight in the following words: 'To make a surface support a given weight by the application of power to the resistance of air.'

Below and right: Leonardo da Vinci's designs for a flying machine were based on the workings of a bird's wing. Pulleys were intended to work the joints.

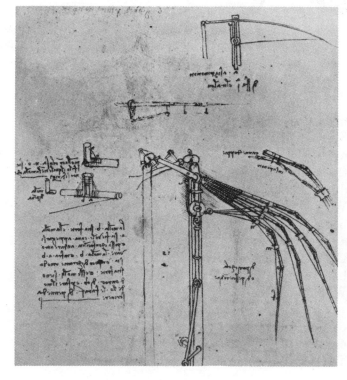

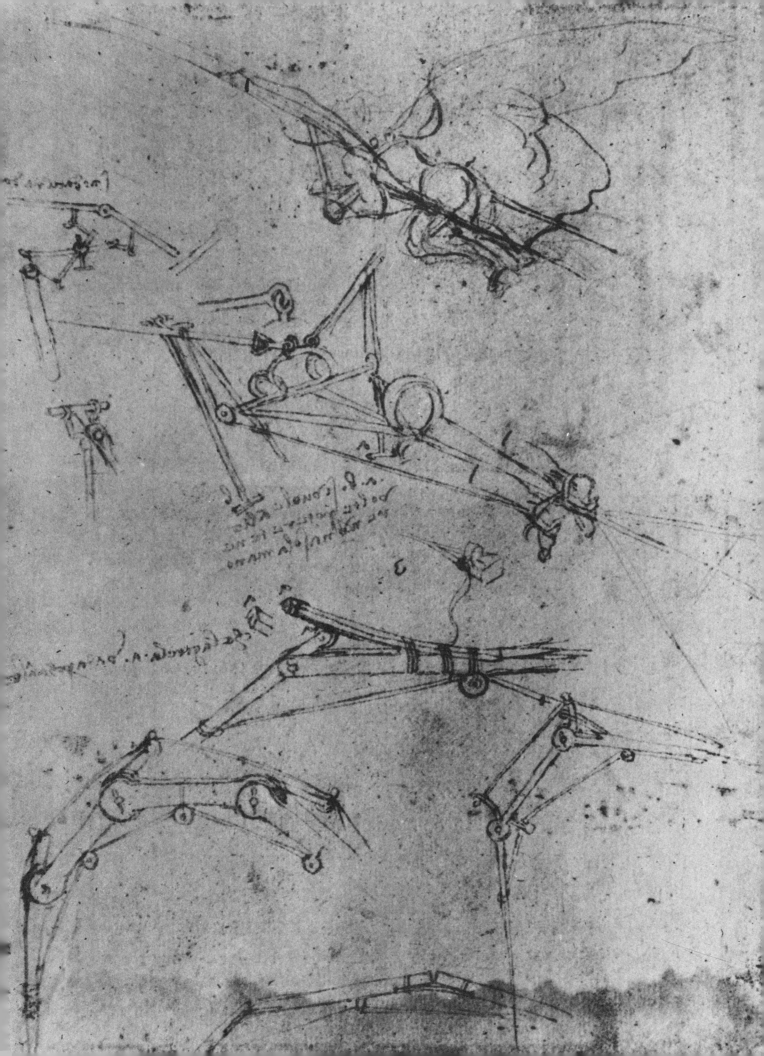

Cayley saw that for the purposes of heavier-than-air flight the forces of *lift* and *propulsion* had to be separated: problems of lift would be solved by the unique properties of the *aerofoil*.

He knew that certain flat-shaped structures, or aerofoils, would support themselves in the air if only they could be made to move fast enough. This principle is appreciated by anyone who has ever skipped stones across the surface of a lake. Cayley understood that *lift* was the result of differential air pressure on the aerofoil. That is, when the aerofoil is travelling through the air, because of its shape a low-pressure area (or partial vacuum) is created on its top surface and, at the same time, a high pressure area is created on the bottom surface. The aerofoil rises, simultaneously 'pushed' and 'sucked' upwards.

Cayley built many gliders and model aeroplanes which successfully illustrated the proper-ties of aerofoils. He soon realized that a *cambered*, or somewhat arched aerofoil would produce the maximum lift.

There is at present in the Science Museum in London a silver disc engraved by Cayley in 1799. On one side of it he illustrated, for the first time, the forces acting on a wing, clearly distinguishing between lift, thrust, and drag. On the other side is Cayley's sketch of a fixed-wing glider, which incorporated such features as a boat-like fuselage and a tail unit with various control surfaces.

Between 1804 and 1853, the Yorkshireman carried our numerous experiments with gliders, and eventually established the basic configuration of the aeroplane as we know it today. His gliders and models featured such innovations as forward main planes, fuselage, adjustable fin and tail planes – in short, they were capable of con-trolled flight. He also proposed that wings be

superposed, one over the other: thus originating the biplane, triplane etc. Many modern flight historians feel that if an adequate source of power had existed in his time, Cayley might have been the first to achieve powered flight.

The Pioneers

Cayley's work influenced many other thinkers in the world of aviation. In the 1840's, two Englishmen, John Stringfellow and William Henson, designed an 'Aerial Steam Carriage' which incorporated many of the Yorkshireman's basic notions and became the prototype for the monoplane. Later, Stringfellow built a model triplane, which was directly derived from Cayley's work.

From 1850, interest in the idea of heavier-than-air flight gained increasing popularity, especially

Above: William Henson's Aerial Steam Carriage, as it might have appeared in flight. Right: Sir George Cayley.

Langley's steampowered Aerodrome No. 5 flew for more than a minute in May 1895, and landed safely

in France. A French naval officer called Felix du Temple built history's first successful powered model aeroplane, using first clockwork and then steam power. This machine could make short hops and land safely. Many years later he built a full-sized version which also leapt a short distance into the air after a downhill run.

Another Frenchman, Alphonse Pénaud, experimented with aeroplane models, and it is to him that we owe the tradition of powering them with twisted elastic bands. Pénaud also did much to illustrate Cayley's notions on the inherent stability of aircraft.

Clement Ader, an electrical engineer, achieved the distinction of actually leaving level ground in a powered aeroplane. Ader's hop, make in 1890, is not generally considered a real flight, because he had absolutely no control of his craft in the air. His machine, called the *Eole*, was a bat-winged monoplane powered by a steam engine which drove a front-mounted propeller. It had no control surfaces.

Sir Hiram Maxim, the expatriate American who is famous for his invention of the Maxim machine-gun, also took an interest in aviation. Maxim constructed a huge biplane with twin steam-driven propellers, which was to run on rails. The machine was tested, barely lifted itself a few feet clear of the tracks, and came down again, fouling the guard-rails. It was the end of Maxim's work in aviation: an experiment that succeeded in proving very little.

The American S. P. Langley built a number of steampowered models which he called *aerodromes*. These models flew successfully, and Langley was encouraged to build a full-sized machine. However, like many of the men we have discussed in this section, Langley never really studied the problem of control in the air; he concentrated mainly on the question of lift. His full-sized machine was a failure.

Sacrifices Must Be Made

The German Otto Lilienthal was the first to perceive the importance of gaining practical experience in the air. His ultimate goal was

Otto Lilienthal prepares for another dramatic flight

powered flight but he realized that a successful aviator had to be able to control his machine in the air before he gave it the benefit of power. He wrote, in 1896:

'One can get a proper insight into the practice of flying only by actual flying experiments . . . The manner in which we have to meet the irregularities of the wind, when soaring in the air, can only be learnt by being in the air itself . . . The only way which leads us to a quick development in human flight is a systematic and energetic practice in actual flying experiments.'

And so Lilienthal built and tested a number of fixed-wing gliders. He constructed five types of monoplane gliders and two biplane types. His first experiments were made from a springboard near his home, but later he moved his test locations to hills in the surrounding country. Eventually he had his own artificial hill constructed.

Lilienthal's machines were all hang-gliders. That is, he supported himself in them with his arms, leaving his torso and legs dangling free.

He could thus twist and move his body in any desired direction, and so he achieved a measure of control and stability.

His most successful glider was his No. 11 monoplane. He called it his *Normal-Segelapparat* (standard sailing-machine) and in it he could make controlled glides of up to 1,150 feet. He built several replicas of this craft, which he distributed to other aspiring aviators.

In 1895, he began experimenting with methods of flight-control other than body-swinging, and he produced plans for several different control methods. Alas, Lilienthal was never to bring his plans to fruition. In 1896 he crashed on a glide in his No. 11 monoplane. His spine was broken and he died the next day. His last words were reported to be *'Opfer mussen gebracht werden'* ('Sacrifices must be made').

Most authorities are convinced that, had he lived, Lilienthal would have achieved powered flight well before the Wright brothers' triumph of 1903. As it was, Lilienthal directly inspired the Wrights.

The Wrights' Triumph

December 17, 1903, will always remain the greatest date in the history of aviation. For on that date Wilbur and Orville Wright, two bicycle makers from Dayton, Ohio, were the first men ever to achieve powered, sustained, and controlled flight.

The Wright brothers drew much of their early inspiration from the work of Lilienthal. Like Lilienthal, they were determined to gain mastery and control in the air by practising with gliders before committing themselves to powered flight.

In 1899, after having studied all the material on aviation then available, the brothers commenced their experiments. Their first craft was a biplane kite which utilized the technique of wing-warping, or twisting, to achieve lateral (sideways) stability.

The technique proved effective and the

Left: Wilbur Wright at the controls in full flight

brothers used it in their first glider, built in 1900. This No. 1 glider greatly resembled their kite. It was also a biplane, on which the pilot lay prone to reduce head-resistance. The glider was transported to the Kill Devil Hills, south of Kitty Hawk, North Carolina, and the brothers made their first tests.

The results were encouraging and led to the production of a No. 2 glider, but they had many problems with this machine. They guessed that the calculations which they had relied upon (made by Lilienthal and others) were faulty; so they started on a programme of intensive research and study. They even built a wind-tunnel for the testing of wings.

By September, 1902, they had built a fully practical glider, the No. 3. With this craft they made almost a thousand perfectly controlled glides. They were now ready to build their aeroplane.

Since they were unable to find a suitable engine for their machine, the brothers took it upon themselves to design and construct their own: a four cylinder water-cooled motor that developed 12 horsepower. They also did basic research on propellers in order to produce their own highly efficient design.

At last the brothers were ready to test their *Flyer*. On December 14, 1903. Wilbur made the first attempt, but he ploughed into some sand dunes. Three days later, it was Orville's turn: he took off into the wind and flew for 12 seconds, covering about 500 feet in air distance. Three more flights were made on that day – the longest lasted 59 seconds and covered over half a mile in air distance. The aeroplane had finally arrived.

Bleriot's record-breaking aeroplane was the first to fly the English Channel

The Wright Brothers' first flight lasted only 12 seconds. Orville is lying at the controls

In 1904, the Wrights built *Flyer No. II*, and in it they made many brief flights; the longest was about five minutes.

Flyer No. III, 'the first practical powered aeroplane in history' was built in 1905. This machine was fully manoeuvrable: it could bank and turn, perform figures of eight, and remain airborn for over half an hour at a time. The pilot lay prone on it, as was the case with the other Wright Flyers.

An interesting feature of the Wright aircraft was that inherent instability was designed into them, so that the pilot had to 'fly' the machine constantly, righting it after every disturbance, no matter how small, in much the same way that the driver must constantly control his automobile. This policy was eventually seen to be a mistake. European aeroplane designers rejected it, opting for a compromise between inherent stability and sensitivity of controls.

In 1908, Wilbur Wright went to France to demonstrate the brothers' achievements. It is fair to say that this occasion brought about a revolution in the history of European flight.

In Europe, aviation had been more or less moribund since the death of Lilienthal in 1896. When the first garbled reports of the Wrights' work started coming in, a number of Europeans, mostly Frenchmen, were spurred into action. However, none of them grasped the significance of the Wrights' pioneering work with gliders, or the reason for the inherent instability of their machines (i.e. to make constant control necessary). And so, in general, they achieved very little. A few aeroplanes were built but they greatly lacked manoeuvrability, suffering in particular from the lack of lateral controls and from inefficient propellers. It was not until 1907 that any European could stay in the air for even a full minute or begin to describe a tentative circle.

Needless to say, the French were dumbfounded by Wilbur Wright's display of aerial prowess in

Right: Farman flew the first circular kilometre in this plane

1908. The French pioneer, Leon Delagrange spoke for his fellow aviators when he said: *'Eh bien, nous sommes battus! Nous n'existons pas!'* ('Well, we are beaten! We just don't exist.')

The Europeans were at once shamed into a prodigious amount of activity; from 1908, aviation developed rapidly. By the end of 1909, the aeroplane had come of age. This was signified by two events in particular: the historic cross-Channel flight by Louis Bleriot in a frail monoplane he called No. XI, and the great air-show at Reims.

At this airshow, the biplane developed by Henri Farman was particularly prominent. It was a light, rotary-engine powered craft, which used large ailerons instead of wing-warping for lateral control, and achieved an attractive combination of Wright-like manoeuvrability with inherent stability.

Cayley's dream had finally been realized: the era of the aeroplane had begun. Man, at last, had some control over the air.

AIR POWER BECOMES THE CRUCIAL FACTOR

At the outbreak of the First World War, aerial war machines and, specifically, heavier-than-air craft, formed an insignificant part of the armouries of the major world powers. Flying was the realm of a small group of dedicated enthusiasts and was generally frowned upon by the military establishment. Yet within four years air power was well on the way to becoming the crucial factor in warfare – a tremendous upheaval in such a short space of time.

The reason for that upheaval was, simply, the ravenous hunger of total war for any and all sorts of war machines, whatever might obtain that slight but all important advantage over the enemy. Kites, balloons and gliders had all been

Above: A Bristol Box-kite prepares for a flight

German Taube: a monoplane of the First World War

used in warfare, so why not these new-fangled contraptions? Thus it came about that the fragile pre-war aeroplanes underwent an almost magical transformation into sleek and powerful weapons screeching through the skies at unheard of speeds and into heavy, ponderous machines carrying death dealing bombs into the heart of the enemy's territory.

As the war opened the major powers had done little to further the cause of military aviation. The military establishments were conservative in the extreme and refused to acknowledge that the new machines could be of real significance. At best, it was thought, they might serve as extensions of the cavalry scout.

'Aviation is good sport, but for the Army it is useless', declared the French General Foch.

'Experience has shown that a real combat in the air, such as journalists and romancers have described, should be considered a myth. The duty of the aviator is to see, not to fight,' reported the

German General Staff in September, 1914.

'See, Not Fight'

The 'see, not fight' attitude on the part of the authorities resulted in a policy of neither protecting nor arming aircraft. All that was required of the aeroplane was the ability to take off, fly for a reasonable length of time and land safely, specifications that were easily met by the host of aeroplane manufacturers in Great Britain, France and Germany.

The machines used at the outbreak of war were a varied collection culled from civilian manufacturers. Common sights at the front were the various pre-war biplanes like the Maurice Farman M.F.7 'Longhorn', an odd-looking craft with a complicated forward structure. The Bristol Box-kite, so named because of its shape, trained many men to fly. The German Taube, of Austrian design, was a twin-seater monoplane controlled by differential warping of the trailing edges of the wings. Another popular monoplane was the French Morane-Saulnier Type 'L' parasol scout. But whatever the plane, the pilots were confined to a simple observatory role.

In short term policy the authorities were correct. The really important contributions of aircraft to the war effort were in reconnaissance and artillery spotting missions. Thus by spotting

Below: The French Morane-Saulnier, mounting a single gun

Above left: The Fokker E.III, with interruptor mechanism, was master of the air. Below left: The French Nieuport

Russian troop movements before the Battle of Tannenburg the Germans were able to prepare a victorious counter-offensive. Hindenburg wrote in his memoirs that 'without airmen there would have been no Tannenburg'.

The French showed that they too could use aircraft successfully. On September 3, 1914, French airmen noticed a growing gap between the German First and Second Armies near the Marne. Knowledge of that fatal opening led to the Allied victory in the subsequent battle.

As more and more aircraft took to the skies it was inevitable that pilots and observers should begin to arm themselves with pistols, rifles, hand grenades and even machine guns. The flyers soon found that their impromptu armament was unwieldy and difficult to operate. The demand grew for an aeroplane that could operate as a steady gun platform, and it became rapidly clear that whichever side produced the required warplane would gain the ascendancy in the air.

On the Offensive

Until the development of the ultra-sophisticated radar equipment of the 1950s and 1960s the fighter was basically a flying gun platform. The most efficient means of destroying enemy aircraft was by aiming the plane 'down the barrel'. The problem designers were faced with in 1914–1915 was how to fit a forward firing machine gun in the tractor planes (those with front propellers) of the day.

The first breakthrough came at the beginning of 1915. A French pilot, Roland Garros, asked Raymon Saulnier, the aircraft manufacturer, to fit an interrupter gear into his plane. The idea of the interrupter gear was to stop the machine gun firing when the propeller moved into its line of fire. Saulnier had been working on an interrupter gear for a number of years but had been frustrated by the tendency of machine guns of the day to hang-fire; that is, not to fire at a steady rate.

was also used by British aces with great success. Above: This De Havilland DH2 had a pusher propeller

Discouraged, Saulnier began experiments along a different line. Instead of trying to interrupt the machine gun fire, why not protect the propeller against damage?

The result was armoured plates attached to the propeller blade to deflect those bullets that would otherwise hit the propeller. The armoured plates were subsequently attached to Garros' Moran-Saulnier airscrew. The result was phenomenal. Within two weeks Garros had shot down five enemy aircraft, an incredible achievement in those days. The deflector plates had made the aeroplane a powerful *fighting* weapon. The offensive capabilities of the aeroplane could no longer be doubted. A war machine was born, and with it the great aerial arms race.

Interrupter Gear

The deflector plates had proved a point but also became a dead-end line with no potential for de-velopment. It was an interim mechanism only in use until the real thing could be perfected. And the real thing was the interrupter gear.

On April 19, 1915, Garros was shot down behind enemy lines and, before he could destroy his plane, the Germans had seized it. The very next day the armoured airscrew was being studied in Anthony Fokker's workshop. Within a few months the Fokker team had come up with a prototype fighter (then known as a scout) embodying a new Parabellum machine gun firing forward through the airscrew by means of an interrupter mechanism. By the middle of the summer 11 German pilots were supplied with the new fighter, the Fokker Eindekker 1.

The Fokker Scourge

The effect of Fokker's invention can best be gauged by the epithet given to those winter months of 1915–1916, when Fokker Eindekkers I,

II and III reigned supreme – the Fokker scourge. The Germans were hitting back and with a vengeance. For nine months the Fokker gave the Germans undisputed mastery of the air and it was not until the spring of 1916 that the legend of Fokker invincibility began to crumble under the impact of a second generation of improved Allied war planes.

Until the Fokker appeared over the skies of Europe pilots believed that they were invulnerable to enemy aircraft bearing directly down on them. It was inconceivable that fire power should come through the propeller. Surprise was therefore a major factor in the success of the Fokkers, but as aeroplanes they had their disadvantages. They were structurally mediocre. The E.1. was underpowered by its 100 horsepower Oberursel engine; the bracings on the single wing were vulnerable to hostile fire and the wing itself could not stand up to excessive strain.

The Allies Hit Back

The Fokker scourge was eventually stemmed by the introduction of a better class of machine. The British sent in their two-seater Vickers Gun Bus and the single seater pusher DH2. The rear-mounted engine on the DH2 gave a clear forward field of fire for the Lewis gun, which, because it did not shoot through the propeller, had an unrestricted rate of fire.

The French adapted their Nieuport Bébé and came up with the Nieuport 17, armed with a synchronized Vickers gun in addition to the Lewis mounted on the top plane and operated by a Bowden cable. The Nieuports were favourites with the British aces and Albert Ball and James McCudden scored some of their most impressive kills in the French machines.

The first British forward-firing fighter was the graceful two-seater Sopwith 1½ Strutter. The 1½ Strutter was fitted with a Vickers machine gun linked to a Ross interrupter gear. The observer was equipped with a Lewis gun. The 1½ Strutter was undoubtedly the best fighter/reconnaissance plane of its time. Development, however, moved at a rapid pace in wartime and the Strutter was soon outclassed by the German Albatros D series of fighters.

The Albatros Outguns All

The old pusher style DH2, the Nieuports and the

Sopwith 1½ Strutter gave the Allies the necessary fighting power to wrest control of the skies from the Germans. But the Allied supremacy was very short-lived for the Germans had been experimenting with a new series of fighting machines: the Albatros D.

The Albatros D series produced some of the finest fighter planes of the war. The biplane structure was fitted with a powerful 160 horse-

Planes of the First World War. Top: Fokker D-VII. Right: Pfalz D-XII. Bottom: Nieuport 28

power water-cooled Mercedes engine (in later marks, the Albatros D reached 118 miles an hour). In addition to its fine flying capabilities the Albatros had formidable fire power in its twin forward-firing Spandau machine guns. As a result the biplane had the highest firing rate (1,000 rounds per minute as opposed to 300 for the Sopwith 1½ Strutter) of any warplane then available. In sum, the Albatros D could out-

manoeuvre, outfly and outgun any comparable machine.

Hunting Squadrons

A weapon in itself does not make a great war machine; its proper use does. Fighter efficiency was increased by forming the fighters into *Jagdstaffeln* (*Jastas* for short) hunting squadrons.

German fighter ace, Max Immelmann

Fighting techniques developed by the great German aces, Max Immelmann and Oswald Boelcke, during the Fokker scourge, were refined and applied to formation fighting. The Jastas became the most lethal aerial war machines of their day. Unconstrained by the escort and observation duties which were expected of their opposite numbers, the Jastas roamed the skies with one mission–to seek and destroy enemy aircraft.

The Red Baron Strikes

The squadron leader of Jasta 11 was a young (23), arrogant Prussian officer, with ten kills to his credit and a growing reputation when, in 1916, he met his toughest challenge–Major Lanoe G. Hawker, British ace and holder of the Victoria Cross. The Prussian was Manfred von Richthofen,

later to become famous as the Red Knight or Baron, the greatest ace of the First World War.

Hawker, flying a DH2, had been instrumental in stemming the Fokker onslaught of 1915–1916. But the DH2 was totally outclassed by late 1916, when the skies began to fill with the sleek and vicious Albatros, with their deadly twin Spandaus. Hawker had been cornered a number of times by German pilots and it was only due to his amazing skill that he escaped. Twice he was shot down, once wounded. Yet he continued to go out on patrols with the 24th Squadron.

On November 23, 1916, Hawker ran into a German scout. The scout was an Albatros but Hawker had the advantage of height. He pointed the nose of his DH2 downwards and threw it into a dive, hoping to catch the German from behind (the fatal blind spot). At 10,000 feet Hawker eased out of the dive, passing the Albatros with guns blazing. He failed to destroy the plane and lost his sole advantage.

From then on the DH2 and the Albatros looped round and round, each trying to get behind the other. But the Albatros was the superior machine. It could turn tighter and fly faster than its opponent. The hunter now became the hunted. The best that Hawker could hope for was a small slip on the part of the German that would let him escape. But Richthofen was too clever. This was to be a duel to the finish.

'Round and round we go in circles, like two madmen, playing ring-around-a-rosie almost two miles above the earth,' wrote Richthofen in his

The Albatros D.VA. The Albatros D series completely outclassed Allied machines

combat report. For twenty minutes the two parried and counter-parried but, in the end, the better machine told. 'My machine,' continued Richthofen, 'gave me an advantage by being able to climb better and faster. This enabled me at last to break the circle and manoeuvre into a position behind and above him.' By this time the two had lost so much height that they were skimming the tops of trees and farmhouses.

In a last endeavour to foil his enemy, Hawker gave full reign to the left rudder in an attempt to meet Richthofen head on. The attempt failed. At fifty yards the German opened fire, splattering bullets across the fuselage of the DH2. One bullet hit home, smashing through Hawker's skull. The pilotless craft plunged earthwards. Richthofen remarked that Hawker was a 'brave man, a sportsman and a fighter' but, against a superior war machine, Hawker was helpless.

It was incredible he managed to survive as long as he did. His fellow pilots did not fare so well – their average life expectancy was 11 days.

The Albatros scourge was far, far worse than anything experienced previously. It culminated in the Bloody April of 1917. Then the Allies began to produce machines that could match the Germans. Among these was the Sopwith Camel.

The Sopwith Camel

The biplane Camel was built around an air-cooled rotary engine (130 horsepower Clerget). It called for a great deal of skill in handling.

The Camel, built to challenge the German Albatros

Armed with twin Vickers guns mounted in the fuselage, the Camel had both firepower and manoeuvrability. It could climb to 10,000 feet in 10·5 minutes and maintained a maximum speed at that height of 112·5 miles an hour. The Camel was the classic rotary engine fighter of the war.

The War's Top Fighter

The Camel, the SE 5 and the SE 5A, the Spad XIII were the machines that put an end to the Albatros supremacy. The war, however, was not over and, twice before, the Germans had proved that they could wrest control of the skies from the Allies with superior war machines. In late 1917 and early 1918 they made one last stab at producing the ultimate fighter aeroplane. Draft specifications were submitted and trials held.

The new Fokker biplane completely outperformed all its rivals. A single-seater with a slim fuselage built around a 160 horsepower Mercedes engine, it was able to fly at 118 miles an hour and climb to 10,000 feet in 9·5 minutes. Its most amazing asset, however, was its uncanny ability to hang on its propeller and fire straight upwards, a manoeuvre that caused Allied planes to stall. The Fokker D VII was certainly the war's best fighter but came too late to revive the failing fortunes of the German Air Force.

Overleaf: A bombing formation of British D.H.4s close up to beat off a fierce attack of biplanes and Fokker triplanes with concentrated machine gun fire. A painting by G. H. Davies

The Flying Circus

As the war dragged on, the lonely ace scouring the skies for an unsuspecting enemy gave way to large fighter formations. The Germans had taken the lead with the establishment of Jastas but the British, Americans and French soon followed suit. The French took particular pride in their *Escadrille de Chasse* (Hunting Squadrons) and chief among these were the élite squadrons of *Les Cigognes* and *Les Sportifs*.

The Germans responded by regrouping their Jastas into larger formations known as *Jagdgeschwader*. The Geschwaders were sent in at critical points on the front and moved up and down the lines of their own transport units. Their garishly painted aeroplanes (leading the Allies to dub them 'flying circuses') presented a formidable aspect in the air. And for a time they gained local tactical superiority. But the overwhelming Allied numbers, their increasingly efficient organisation and the improved quality of the Allied machines left no doubt as to the final outcome.

The Germans lost the war but not for lack of superior aerial war machines. In technological and tactical development the Germans were far ahead of the Allies. It was the Germans who discovered that the true aerial war machine was a combination of plane and tightly formed unit and, with their war machines, they won astounding air victories. It is instructive to look at the casualty figures for the war: the German Air Force lost 5,853 men killed, 7,302 wounded and 2,751 missing and taken prisoner as well as 3,128 aeroplanes. The British Air Force alone lost 6,166 men killed, 7,245 wounded and 3,212 missing and taken prisoner.

Air Power and Bombs

Even while fighters and fighter tactics showed an increasing sophistication, important developments were taking place in other areas of aerial warfare. It must be remembered that fighters were produced in the first place to provide protection for reconnaissance and bomber aircraft. We have already noted the effects and early successes of reconnaissance missions. The future of air power lay, however, in the concept of strategic bombing.

Almost from the beginning of man's dream of flight, he had envisaged the hostile purposes to which aeroplanes could be put. It needed little imagination to realize the destructive potential of missiles hurled from high places. Once warfare

developed beyond the primitive hand-to-hand fighting, missiles of one form or another, from arrows to the latest in military cannon, dominated the battlefield.

The idea of dropping bombs on the enemy from aircraft was, in many ways, an extension of artillery bombardment. But there was one crucial difference – the bomber could penetrate far behind enemy lines, the so-called 'third dimension'. It was on this crucial difference that military thinkers after the First World War

Far left: Igor Sikorsky was a pioneer in three different aeronautical fields: multi-engined aircraft, trans-oceanic flying boats and helicopters.
Below: Sikorsky's four-engined Ilya Mourometz was used for bombing raids.
Left: The Italian Caproni Ca series proved useful bombers. This is a Ca3.

developed the concept of strategic bombing, an idea that was, eventually, to have a tremendous influence in the creation of massive bombing war machines. But we are getting ahead of our story. In 1914, the real problem was a technological one, for the effective bomber aircraft did not exist.

Gavotti's Raid

Even before the war there were precedents for bombing raids. An Italian, Lt. Gavotti, an observer in the aeroplane, dropped four bombs on enemy targets (Turkish) in the Libyan war of 1911. The bombs were Swedish grenades adapted for aerial use. They caused a limited amount of damage and a great deal of consternation; it was a severe shock to discover the enemy attacking well behind the front lines.

Despite Gavotti's example the introduction of an aircraft specifically built as a bomber had to wait upon the war, which gave the necessary impetus to the development of that machine. By 1918, mammoth four engine machines were capable of carrying substantial payloads over considerable distances.

The Bomber

The first moves towards the true bomber were made in Russia, when Igor Sikorsky constructed the first four-engined aeroplane, the *Ilya Mourometz*. The *Mourometz* was sent on bombing raids against Poland in 1915, but internal crises prevented further innovations.

The Italians developed a highly successful bomber in 1915, the Caproni Ca series. The Ca 1 was a biplane with a wing span of nearly 73 feet. Powered by a 100 horse-power Fiat water-cooled engine it attained a maximum speed of 72 miles

an hour, had a ceiling of 13,100 feet, and carried a 1,000 pound payload. A central nacelle held the crew of two pilots and one observer/bombardier/gunner. The Capronis were used in tactical air raids on Austrian positions in the Adriatic. One raid, on February 18, 1916, dropped four tons of bombs on Ljubljana.

The Germans turned to bombing raids early, with the use of the Zeppelin airship. The Zeppelin, however, proved much too vulnerable as a military craft, so the Germans, working furiously to find an effective replacement, came up with the Gotha.

The Gotha was a twin-engined pusher biplane with a wing span of about 77 feet. It operated at a

Left: The Gotha, a formidable bomber.
Below: The Handley Page 0/400, with wings folded for transport, and in flight

The Handley Page V/1500 super-bomber; too late to bomb Berlin

ceiling of 15,000 feet, putting it out of reach of most fighters, and it carried a load of up to six 112-pound bombs for raids on England.

The Gotha was closely followed by the Giant, a larger and faster aeroplane. This had a maximum speed of 84 miles an hour, a ceiling of 14,170 feet, and endurance of up to 10 hours.

The Gotha and Giant raids on England were carried out from May, 1917, through to May, 1918, causing extensive damage. As weapons the Gothas and Giants were formidable, but they were not employed in sufficient concentrations to have a serious effect on the course of the war.

However, to a public unused to this kind of aerial warfare, the bombing raids were terrifying. A public outcry resulted in two very important decisions. The first, on the recommendations of the Smuts committee, led to the establishment of the Royal Air Force, as a separate military service, on April 1, 1918. The second decision was stimulated by the cry for revenge – the construction of heavy bombers to raid Germany and pay the Germans back.

The British had already been experimenting with heavy bombers. In 1916 Frederick Handley Page was told to build a 'bloody paralyser', and he did – the Handley Page 0/100. With a wing span of 100 feet, it was the largest plane to go into action on the British side. It was powered by the new Rolls-Royce Eagle Mk II engines which gave it a speed of 85 miles an hour at 7,000 feet and a range of 700 miles. The 0/100 weighed 14,000 pounds fully laden and carried up to 16 112-pound bombs. It proved itself an effective tactical bomber in attacks on railway junctions and the Saar Steel works.

By the end of the war the British had constructed three new super-bombers – the Handley Page V/1500. The 126 feet wide V/1500s were powered by four Rolls-Royce 375 horse-power

Eagle engines and reached a maximum speed of 97 miles an hour at 8,750 feet. They could carry up to 7,500 pounds of bombs, and stay in the air for 14 hours. They were the biggest and best the war had produced, and were all set to carry out bombing raids on Berlin when the war ended.

Though they began in 1915, bombing raids did not become really effective until late in the war. In the early years both sides were groping for the most effective means of deploying bombers. It was only through the experience of war that the policy of formation flying and concentrated bombing on strategic targets was formulated. Once these aims were realized the bomber force became a powerful machine of war. But by that time the war was near its end. The real fruits of strategic bombing would only be reaped in the Second World War.

The war had seen a tremendous development in military aircraft. The motley collection of 1914 planes had become, by 1918, highly specialized war machines. Fighters carried twin machine guns firing at a rate of 1,000 rounds a minute, whereas at the beginning of the war aeroplanes went unarmed. Reconnaissance craft were flying almost twice as fast as their 1914 precursors, and a completely new class of plane had arrived on the scene – the heavy bomber. By the end of the war the large bombers, with a tail as big as single seater fighters, were carrying bomb loads of up to four tons to enemy targets 800 miles away.

Beyond the immediate innovations lay the massive experience gained by manufacturers and pilots in building and handling aircraft. Experiments were carried out on various forms of planes, from semi-monocoque monoplanes to the extremely manoeuvrable triplane. It was this experience which laid the foundation for the revolutionary developments of the inter-war years.

The inter-war years was an heroic age in aviation history. From the sport of the wealthy, aviation became a multi-billion pound industry. In those years the great airliners were established and the great aviator-explorers set their mark on the world. The names of Alcock and Brown, Charles Lindbergh, Richard Byrd, Amelia Earhart and Charles Kingsford Smith became household words, fearless aviators who blazed pioneering trails across the skies. A host of technical innovations made aircraft bigger, faster and safer.

In the military field, the inter-war years were important for the work of Trenchard in Britain, Colonel 'Billy' Mitchell in the United States, and Brigadier-General Giulio Douhet in Italy. To the point of sacrificing their careers, they advocated the importance of air power in any future war – specifically, long range strategic bombing.

Trenchard was more concerned with the preservation of an independent air force in the face of pressure for its return to army control. Douhet and, to a lesser extent, Mitchell, were responsible for the concept of the self-defending bomber. They assumed that such a bomber could effectively break through all opposition and reach its target, thus gaining advantage in the war. Their ideas led to the development of the long range, self-defending strategic bombers: Blenheims and Wellingtons in Britain, and the B-17, B-24 and B-29 in the United States.

The ideas of strategic bombing were beginning to be formulated even during the First World War. The problem at that time was that the technical requirements to carry out such a policy did not exist. The great developments in aircraft design over the next 20 years made possible what was previously only a dream.

Streamlining the Fighter

Much of the impetus of post-war design was towards streamlining. Practical experiments and scientific theory made the aviation world aware of the extreme importance of streamlining for improved performance.

As early as 1894, the English theorist, F. W. Lanchester, had shown scientifically that the drag of a perfectly streamlined aeroplane was no more than that caused by the friction of the air moving over its surface plus the drag necessary

to sustain it in the air. The German aerodynamicist, Ludwig Prandtl, arrived at similar conclusions independently. However, the significance of the Lanchester-Prandtl theory was not fully realized until after the First World War, chiefly due to the lack of suitable aeroplane material. Advances in metallurgy and the perfection of the *cantilever* monoplane (with the wings attached to fuselage without any external support or bracing) went a long way towards fulfilling the vision of the fully streamlined aeroplane.

The Fokker D-VII; once Germany's most famous fighter

The first tentative steps in that direction were made by the Germans. Their most famous fighter of the war, the Fokker D VII, incorporated thick-section cantilever wings. Earlier, in 1915, Junkers designed an all-steel cantilever monoplane. It did not fly well because the steel skin carried all the stresses, which it was not built to do. Platz, the Fokker designer, used plywood, which at that time was more suitable as it was inherently lighter. The Junkers monoplane had low set wings at a pronounced dihedral angle, while the Fokker monoplane wings were laid horizontally across the top of the fuselage. The introduction of retractable undercarriages, another forward step in the streamlining process, proved the Junkers design more efficient, for it allowed a shorter and lighter undercarriage.

Stressed Skin for Strength

The problem that Junker faced in the construction of his monoplane – inordinate stress on the

Boeing 247, made more efficient by the variable pitch propeller

steel skin – was resolved by another German, Dr Adolph Rohrbach. Over a 10 year period Dr. Rohrbach experimented with and perfected a new mode of aircraft construction, the stressed-skin method. Rohrbach's revolutionary concept was to have the skin of the aeroplane carry the primary structural loads. He achieved the desired result by building his wing around a central box section girder of thick duralumin sheet.

Rohrbach's work was extended by a colleague, Dr. H. Wagner. Dr. Wagner discovered that sheet metal could carry an increased load after it had buckled. Until Wagner formulated his theory designers automatically assumed that their designs were a failure if the sheet metal buckled. A lot of effort and money was expended to avoid this 'fault'. Wagner's theory of the diagonal-tension field team formed the basis for aeroplane structures from the mid-1930s. Basically, the theory postulated that sheet metal skin carried its greatest stresses diagonally, and if it were supported by stiffeners around the edges the skin would increase its loading capacity after buckling. In fact, tests showed that buckled skin carried up to 85 per cent greater load.

By the mid-1930s the all-metal, stressed-skin, cantilever monoplane began to replace the wood and fabric planes with their complex systems of struts and braces. The new type of plane displayed a greater efficiency and had a longer life than the conventional aircraft of the period. An American governmental report on 'Those new types of machine' stated that 'because of their structural permanency, their high load carrying capacity, and their maximum speed, they will undoubtedly be the airplanes of the future'. Not only did they become the new aeroplanes of the future, but also the new war machines of the future.

Engine Cowling Reduces Drag

Streamlining took another major step forward with the invention of engine cowlings. One of the great problems with the air-cooled radial engine, which in the inter-war years began to replace the rotary engine, was that it produced an enormous drag on the aeroplane. Efforts to reduce the drag were complicated by fears that enclosing the engine would hinder its cooling. Rotary engines had been cowled but because, with the rotary, the engine itself moved in a circular motion, cooling was not a major problem.

In England, H. L. Townsend of the British National Physical Laboratory found that a ring mounted round a radial engine reduced drag. In the United States, the National Advisory Committee for Aeronautics conducted tests which showed that a complete cowling system reduced drag far more effectively than the Townsend ring, without, in any way, hindering engine cooling. The NACA cowling was quickly adopted by various commercial airliners, which proved its value by increasing their performance and reducing their operating costs.

The introduction of slotted flaps and the variable pitch propeller were two further funda-

Handley Page 32 Hamlet, with wing flaps

mental innovations which helped transform aeroplanes into the efficient transport and military machines that they became.

As its name implies, the variable pitch propeller is one where the pitch (the blade angle with respect to airflow) of each blade can be varied. The propeller could thus adapt itself to changing airflow conditions enabling it to make full use of engine power.

The first practical variable pitch propeller to go into regular operation, the Hamilton-Standard, was invented by F. W. Caldwell in 1930. He used a hydraulically operated system to change the pitch of the drop-forged aluminium blades. Installed in the Boeing 247 in 1933 the variable-pitch propeller reduced normal take-off run by 20 per cent, increased the aeroplane's rate of climb by 22 per cent and doubled its maximum altitude on one engine from 2,000 to 4,000 feet, a successful demonstration of the aerodynamic properties of the variable-pitch propeller.

The Caldwell system was followed by the Turnbull propeller which used an electric motor to operate the propeller. During the Second World War production of the Turnbull propeller became so great that, for a while, the United States government refused to pay royalties, considering the payments excessive.

Soon afterwards the invention of the constant speed propeller enabled the pilot to maintain a constant engine speed under any flying conditions. This was effected by automatic changes of propeller pitch.

Slots and Flaps

The aerodynamic properties of wing flaps and slotted wings had been known before they were put into general use. As with the variable pitch propeller they were only suitable for monoplanes, and thus had to wait for the development of the cantilever monoplane.

The lifting power of the slotted wing was first discovered by a young German pilot, G. V. Lachmann. While recovering from an air crash Lachmann pondered on the problem of the stall (the point at which the lifting power of air is inadequate to support the aeroplane). Since a stall always occurs when the aircraft is operating at a high angle of incidence (the angle at which the wing hits the airflow), Lachmann reasoned that, by slotting the wing, each section would act as a separate wing operating at a normal angle of incidence. After much difficulty he convinced Prandtl to test his theory. The tests were a great success. Lift on slotted wings was increased by 63 per cent.

At the same time Handley Page, working from wind tunnel tests, had discovered the impact of the slotted wing. Lachmann joined the Handley Page organization and soon they had developed the multi-retractable slats which increased lift by more than 300 per cent – an enormous advance in aeroplane design.

The slotted flap followed on naturally from the slotted wing. In its simplest form the flap is a hinged section of the trailing edge of the wing.

When hinged downward there was a notable increase in lift (useful for take-off and in near-stall conditions) and drag (useful for landing). The efficiency of the flap was increased by adding a slot at its leading edge where it connects with the major portion of the wing.

The combination of slotted wings and flaps was an enormous advance in aeroplane design, and increased speed and wing loading on aircraft. Fighters were the planes that benefited most from the invention of the flap for they were more prone to stalling in the extreme conditions in which they were flown.

Other developments which were of great importance but not directly connected with aeroplane design were the invention and refinement of navigational aids such as the horizontal gyro, which indicated the pitching and banking movements of the aircraft, and the directional gyro, which indicated the heading of the aircraft. These blind flying instruments released the pilot from having to make reference to landmarks, an especial advantage under the rigours of wartime flying.

One of the Great Warplanes

One aeroplane which incorporated many of the new design features enumerated above was the

DC-3 (also known as the *Dakota* and C-47). The DC-3 has been called the finest aircraft ever built. When production ceased in 1945 some 13,000 aircraft of this model had been completed. It served as a commercial transport aeroplane and, during the Second World War, was one of America's finest troop transport machines.

The DC-3 was powered by two Cyclone engines (1,000 and 1,200 horse-power) and the wings were constructed on Northrop's multi-cellular design. It was an extremely durable aeroplane and displayed amazing performances during the war. It could continue to fly even after huge chunks of wing had been shot off or when riddled with holes. The DC-3 was, undoubtedly, one of the great warplanes. The basis for that greatness lay in the revolutionary changes in aircraft design in the 1920s and 1930s.

As the 1930s drew to a close it seemed more and more likely that, once again, the world would be at war. The great powers turned their attention to developing military aircraft which would give them the advantage. The dominance of air power in the Second World War rested completely on the great developments of the previous 20 years. Without them there would have been no aerial war machines.

Below: The sturdy Douglas C-47

In his *History of Warfare* General Montgomery wrote: 'When I myself rose to high command in 1942, I laid it down as an axiom that you must win air battles before embarking on the land or sea battle'. Military thought had come a long way from the early days of the First World War when Foch had declared aviation good sport, but useless in war. It was now, going to the other extreme, acclaimed as the single most important factor in warfare. The reason for the aeroplane's great importance as a war machine was the revolutionary developments in aircraft design discussed in the previous chapter. On the basis of that revolution were built the great aerial fighting machines of the Second World War.

As with the First World War the demands of wartime led to rapid escalations in fighter efficiency and power. Both the Allies and the Axis powers were involved in a deadly arms race searching for the big breakthrough that would give mastery of the air. That breakthrough did come, but not till the end of the war. The introduction of jet aircraft would have given, with time, air superiority to the Germans. Fortunately, that potentiality was underestimated by Hitler. In the meantime, the piston-engined aircraft was extended to its very limits.

The Top Fighters

At the outbreak of war the twin-engined fighter-bomber was thought to be effective. But, gradually, the comparatively slow speeds of these machines led them to be withdrawn to the role of night fighter. Very quickly the single engined monoplane became the most effective machine: Spitfire, Hurricane, Me-109, Fw 190 and the P-47 Thunderbolt are examples of these.

One drawback found by the Germans during the Battle of Britain, and by the Allies over Germany, was that these aircraft had limited flight endurance. For the Allies, this meant that the fighters, when operating from Britain before D Day, could escort the bombers only as far as Aachen in Germany. Drop tanks were developed to overcome this problem, but they reduced the manoeuvrability of the fighter and proved highly inflammable, despite experimentation with various types. The introduction of the P-51 Mustang, a long range fighter with a speed of over 400 miles an hour, was very important and, in a sense, the end of a line of development, which had

started in the late 1930s with slow twin-engined fighters like the Fw 189.

In this section we examine some of those key fighters of the war.

The Messerschmitt Bf-109

In 1939 Germany had one of the most efficient and best equipped airforces in the world. The combination of Luftwaffe fighters and bombers with the Panzer divisions led to the brilliant Blitzkrieg victories in Poland and western Europe. The mainstay of the German fighter force in the early years of the war was the incomparable Messerschmitt Bf-109 (also typed the Me-109).

The Bf-109 was designed in 1935 by Willy Messerschmitt for the Bayerische Flugzeug-

werke at a time when most fighter pilots were still enthusing over the biplane. The fighter pilots, basing their views on First World War experience of aerial combat, held that the most important characteristics of a fighter plane were manoeuvrability (with emphasis on an extremely short radius of turn) and rate of climb. The monoplane, with its higher wing loading, would not turn as sharply as the biplane, though it more than made up for this by speed, rate of climb and sturdiness.

Messerschmitt believed in the monoplane as the design of the future. Without any experience in fighter design, Messerschmitt entered a competition for a new monoplane fighter with the leading biplane fighter manufacturers, Heinkel, Arado and Focke-Wulf. Messerschmitt worked on the principle of joining the most powerful engine available to the lightest and cleanest airframe that it could take. In his design he utilized all the latest technological innovations, from stressed-skin metal frame to Handley Page slots. At the test trials at Travemunde, the Bf-109VI flew circles around its competitors. Powered by a Kestrel V engine of 695 horse-power, is attained a maximum speed of 292 miles an hour at an altitude of 13,000 feet with a maximum ceiling of 26,300 feet. By 1939, the Bf-109's amazing performance in international competitions created a legend.

The first production model of the Bf-109 was the Bf-109B-1 powered by the Jumo 210D engine of 635 horse-power, giving a maximum speed of

Below: The Me-109, a fighter with a reputation

Above: German Stukas in formation. Below: A Spitfire banks sharply

292 miles an hour at 13,100 feet and a top ceiling of 26,575 feet. Armament consisted of three MG 17 machine guns.

One point in which Messerschmitt had not modernised his plane was the wooden fixed pitch propeller. Complaints led to the installation of the Hamilton-Standard two-bladed variable pitch prop which vastly increased performance. Note how important it was for a modern fighter to utilize all the latest technological inventions in order not to fall behind in the race for power. A poor climb rate was deadly in the face of enemy attack (the variable pitch prop always provided a better rate of climb than the old style propellers), for height was one of the chief advantages in a dog fight, enabling the attacker to dive on his opponent out of the sun.

The Bf-109B-2 was an up-engined version of

Close formation flying by two Hurricanes of the R.A.F.

the B-1 and it was used to great advantage by the Kondor Legion in the Spanish Civil War.

Prelude to War

The Bf-109 was the first fighter plane to incorporate the revolutionary breakthroughs of the inter-war years; it became, in the words of Adolph Galland, German ace and Luftwaffe Inspector-General of Fighters, 'at the time (1935–1941) the best fighter plane in the world.' In its first battle test the Bf-109 proved beyond a shadow of a doubt that a new age in aerial warfare had arrived.

The Spanish Civil War (1936–1939) was a prelude to the greater war to come. It was on the battlefields and in the skies over Spain that the Germans and Italians tested out their new weapons of war. The Germans especially were eager to test out the might of their rejuvenated war machine.

By 1937, it was a well-known 'secret' that the Germans had sent the Kondor Legion, under General Sperrle, to fight with Franco. The German pilots were, initially, flying the Heinkel 51 biplanes, but ran into unexpected difficulties against the Soviet-built I-15 and I-16 fighters. The call went out for the Bf-109. In the spring, the first two squadrons of *Jagdgruppe 88* were equipped with the Bf-109. In July, 1937, the surprise appearance of the Bf-109s turned a major Republican offensive at the Battle of Brunette into a costly stalemate which the Republicans could not afford. One Republican pilot wrote after the event: 'We lost one hundred and four Republican airplanes and approximately twenty-five thousand men. The Nationalists of Franco lost only twenty-three aircraft and about ten thousand men.' The balance of power had shifted dramatically.

The fighter pilots had inherited from the First World War fighter tactics based on the capabilities of their old style machines. The development of the modern fighter necessitated a change of tactics. From the close formation adopted at the end of the First World War the German pilots evolved a loose 'finger-four' pattern, fighters grouped in pairs with a lead fighter and a wingman. The responsibility of the wingman was to protect the leader from a rear attack, his vulnerable point. Two pairs formed the finger-four (so called because it resembled the layout on the human hand).

As was pointed out earlier, it is the combination of superior weapons and proper tactics that make for a victorious war machine. The Germans had both. The combination of the finger-four and the Bf-109 made the Luftwaffe the supreme aerial fighting machine in Europe for two years.

By 1945, some 33,000 of the Bf-109 series were built – more than any other fighter in the war. But, by 1940, advanced Allied designs were creating machines that could more than match the Bf-109. Some of the first to debunk the myth of the Bf-109's invincibility were the British Supermarine Spitfire and the Hurricane, the two fighters that helped to win the Battle of Britain.

The Spitfire

The Spitfire had its origins in the Schneider Trophy races – the most prestigious aeronautic meeting in the twenties. R. J. Mitchell, chief designer for the Supermarine Aviation Works, was determined to build a craft that would sweep the races. In doing so he laid the foundations for the future fighter.

The prototype Spitfire, serial number K5054, began to take shape in 1935. It was built around the powerful new Rolls-Royce Merlin engine (bore – 5·4 inches, 6-inch stroke, and 27-litre capacity). The Spitfire Mk I achieved a take-off power of 880 horse-power and a maximum of 1,030 horse-power. It climbed to 20,000 feet in 9·5 minutes, and reached a maximum speed of 362 miles an hour at 18,500 feet. It had a ceiling of almost 32,000 feet. Combat range was 400 miles. The Spitfire was armed with eight ·303 inch Browning machine guns mounted in the wings. Later models replaced some of the machine guns

with 20 mm Hispano cannon. The test on March 5, 1936, surpassed all existing British specifications for fighter aircraft. As a result, in June of that year, the first production orders for the Spitfire were issued.

Like all modern fighters, the Spitfire was a cantilever monoplane with stressed-skin wings and a monocoque fuselage. The two-bladed wooden propeller of the prototype was soon replaced by a three blade, two pitch, de Havilland prop. Later still combat experience showed that the German Bf-109 had the edge in rate of climb. This was due to its VDM three blade, constant speed airscrew. The Spitfires were converted to a similar system.

The Spitfire was a wonderful machine, received enthusiastically by R.A.F. pilots, who revelled in its light, sensitive touch. In 1939 there were 400 Spitfires in service, ready to combat the German menace.

The Battle of Britain

In July, 1940, Hitler drew up plans for an invasion of Britain, code-named, 'Operation Sea Lion'. The first step in the proposed invasion was a command to Goering, Commander in Chief of the

The four-bladed propellers of these later Spitfires provided even better performance

Luftwaffe, 'to overcome the British air force with all means at its disposal and as soon as possible'. Goering, bloated with pride in his air force, misled by intelligence reports, and under-estimating the strength of his rivals, predicted that the British would be brought to their knees within a matter of days. That his boast did not come true was due above all to his stupidity in transferring Luftwaffe attacks from R.A.F. bases to civilian centres of population. It was also due to the morale of the English people, the radar installations set up prior to the war, and the pilots of the R.A.F. flying Hurricanes and Spitfires.

As long as the Luftwaffe concentrated on R.A.F. airfields and aircraft factories they were on a winning track. British losses were high; German ones comparatively low. In August the R.A.F. lost 338 Hurricanes and Spitfires in combat and 104 badly damaged; the Germans lost 177 Bf-109s and 24 badly damaged. Hitler, however, kept pressing Goering for a quick and victorious end to the air operations in order that Operation Sea Lion, the invasion of Britain, could get under way. A harried Goering decided that a change of tactics was called for. He directed the Luftwaffe bombers to attack London and other major

population centres. This was to be his undoing, for the shift in targets enabled the R.A.F. to recoup its losses and thus hold a strong defensive line against the German raids.

September 15 is remembered annually as Battle of Britain Day, a crucial turning point in the air battle. On that warm Sunday morning in 1940, Mr. and Mrs. Churchill visited the underground operations headquarters of 11 Group. Girl plotters of the W.A.A.F. read out the increasing number of enemy aircraft crossing the Channel. By 11 a.m. there were 250 German bombers and fighters intent on destroying London. Air Marshall Keith Park sent two squadrons of Spitfires to engage the enemy over Kent, followed by three additional squadrons and the remainder of 11 Group. Five squadrons of 12 Group led by Group Captain Douglas Bader joined the fray. A total of 200 British fighters were ready to grapple with the enemy.

The fierce determination of the British to fight for every inch of sky slowed the German advance. The bombers were neither able to mass not to concentrate their bombing. To make matters worse the short-range Bf-109 escort planes had to turn back shortly after arriving over English soil. In the end the Germans were forced to drop their loads wherever they could, scattered over miles of London's southern suburbs, and to beat a hasty retreat. The first wave ended in disaster for the aggressor but the assault was not yet broken.

Two hours later a second stream of German bombers and fighters came storming over the Channel. This time over 300 British fighters were sent aloft to stem the tide. Park committed his total force. There were no reserves to throw in at the eleventh hour. Appraising the situation, Churchill remarked, 'Never has so much been owed by so many to so few.'

It was not long before the two forces engaged in combat, and for 10 minutes the fate of England hung in the balance. Tracers zipped through the air; aircraft, billowing black smoke, plummetted to the ground; others disintegrated in mid-air. A confused mass of aircraft ducked in and out of formation or looped round and round in desperate struggle. Slowly, the German formation began to crumble. The German fighters, running low on fuel, turned, one by one, back to the mainland. Suddenly the storm was over. The sky cleared of enemy aircraft. The back of the assault was broken and London was saved. Operation Sea Lion was postponed indefinitely.

P-51 Mustang

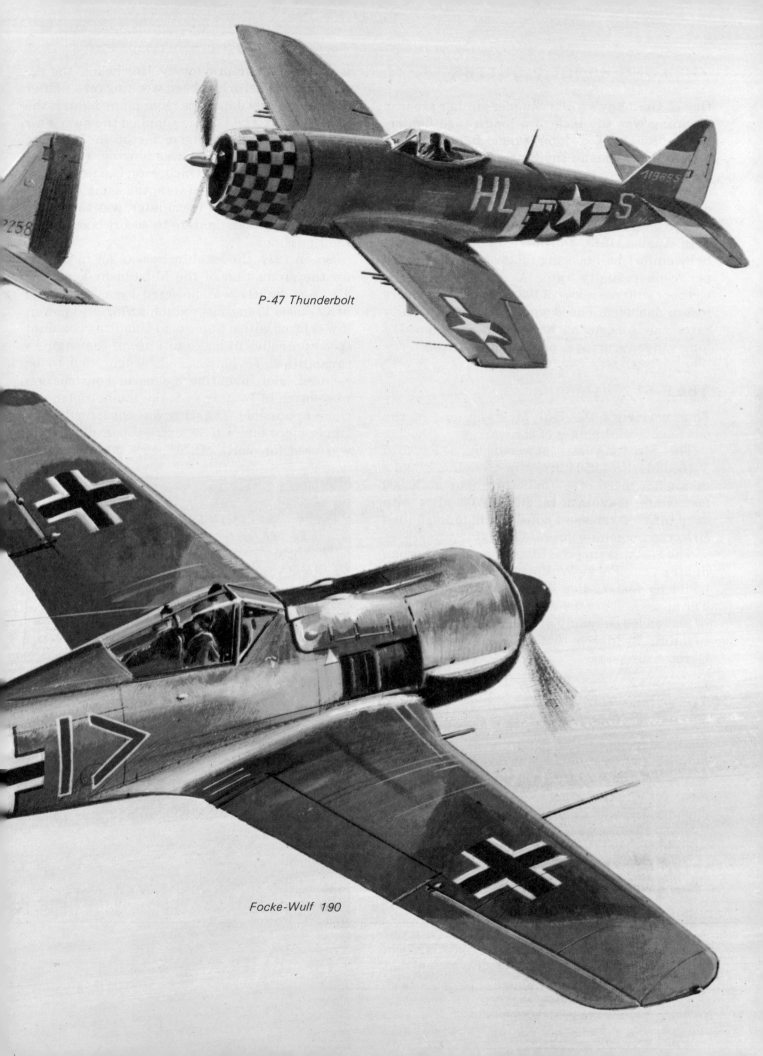

P-47 Thunderbolt

Focke-Wulf 190

THE LONG RANGE FIGHTERS

One of Germany's great blunders in her pre-war planning was the lack of a long range fighter. The absence of a long range fighter escort proved disastrous in the Battle of Britain. With the beginning of the strategic bombing offensive against Germany the British, too, felt the effects of the absence of long range fighters, as did the American air force.

In August, 1943, an American air raid on the Schweinfort ball-bearing factories suffered a 16 per cent casualty rate. A follow-up raid in October suffered a loss of 198 (out of 291) bombers lost or damaged. Faced with increasing casualty rates the Americans halted the raids until a long range escort was put into production.

The P-51 Mustang

Thus was born the P-51 Mustang, one of the most successful planes of the war.

The Mustang was powered by a Packard V-1650-Merlin 1,650 horse-power engine. It had a maximum speed of 440 miles an hour at 30,000 feet, and a maximum range of 2,200 miles with drop tanks. Armament consisted of four 0·5-inch Browning machine guns.

The P-51 was superior to its equivalent German fighters, the Focke-Wulfe 100 and the Bf-109. It could fly faster, dive deeper, and turn tighter. The appearance of the P-51 in the opening months of 1944 ended Germany's last hopes for dominance in the air. By March, 1944, the P-51 had conquered German airspace.

The Mitsubishi Zero

Towards the end of 1943 the Americans had finally developed the potential of long range fighters, fighters that meant death to the Luftwaffe. Yet the long range fighter was not a new idea, for on the other side of the world the Japanese had produced an aircraft which gave them, in the first years of the war, undoubted air superiority over the Pacific – the Mitsubishi Zero.

'Of all the elements,' writes one historian, 'in the vast Japanese war machine that brought to pass that country's astonishing success, no single item was more important than the Zero.'

Until 1935 most of the Japanese aircraft industry was based on European and American designs. At that time, however, it was felt that the Japanese had gained enough experience to go

it alone. A year previously Horikoshi, the designer of the Zero, had been working on a fighter design, the first Japanese monoplane fighter, the A5M Claude. The Claude supplied the navy's air forces and was a decisive factor in Japanese victories over the Chinese during the Sino-Japanese War of 1937. One lesson learned during the war against the Chinese, the same one that the Europeans would learn later, was the necessity of long range fighters to escort bombers on their missions.

So, in 1937, the machinery was set in motion for the production of the Mitsubishi Type OO. The new fighter was powered by a Mitsubishi MK2 Zuisei 13 engine producing 875 horse-power. It was fitted with a Sumitomo-Hamilton constant speed propeller to make full use of the engine's capabilities. To gain speed, weight had to be reduced, and inventive means of construction were brought to bear to make the aeroplane as clean as possible. The wing was constructed of a single piece and a new 'extra-super' duralumin was used for many of the parts that went into

the new plane.

The Zero was designed with one specification – to attack and to destroy. To save even more weight and to increase manoeuvrability, the Japanese pilots forwent the usual protective devices – self-sealing fuel tanks, armour plating, and parachutes. Armament consisted of two 7·7mm machine guns firing through the propeller and two 20mm cannon on the wings.

The Battle of Chungking

The Zeros first saw action in China in the late summer of 1940. They ran escort for bomber missions to Chungking, seat of Chiang Kai Shek's Nationalist government. For three weeks the Zeros and the bombers flew to their target without a challenge. The bombers roared over the city and dropped their payload, daily pounding the buildings into rubble. The Zero pilots were anxious to test their new planes in combat and did all they could to tease their opponents into the air, without success.

Finally, on September 13, after the daily bombing mission had been completed, 13 Zero pilots received word of a number of Chinese pilots preparing to land at their home fields. The Zeros turned about rapidly and began to climb to gain the all important advantage of height. High above the city with the sun behind them they waited. When they pounced on the Chinese, they took the Chinese fighters (flying Soviet-built I-15 biplanes and I-16 monoplanes) completely by surprise. Within a half hour all the Chinese fighters had been shot down. The Japanese suffered no losses.

The pattern for the Zero success story was established. For four long years the Zero dominated the skies over the Pacific. Three years before the P-51, the Zero achieved long distance performance. Without the Zero fighter it is doubtful whether the Japanese advance over the Pacific world could have been so swift and destructive. The Zero was to the Japanese what the Bf-109 was to the Germans, and the Spitfire to the British – a great plane and a great fighter.

A Mitsubishi Navy Type Zero. These planes dominated the Pacific War for four years

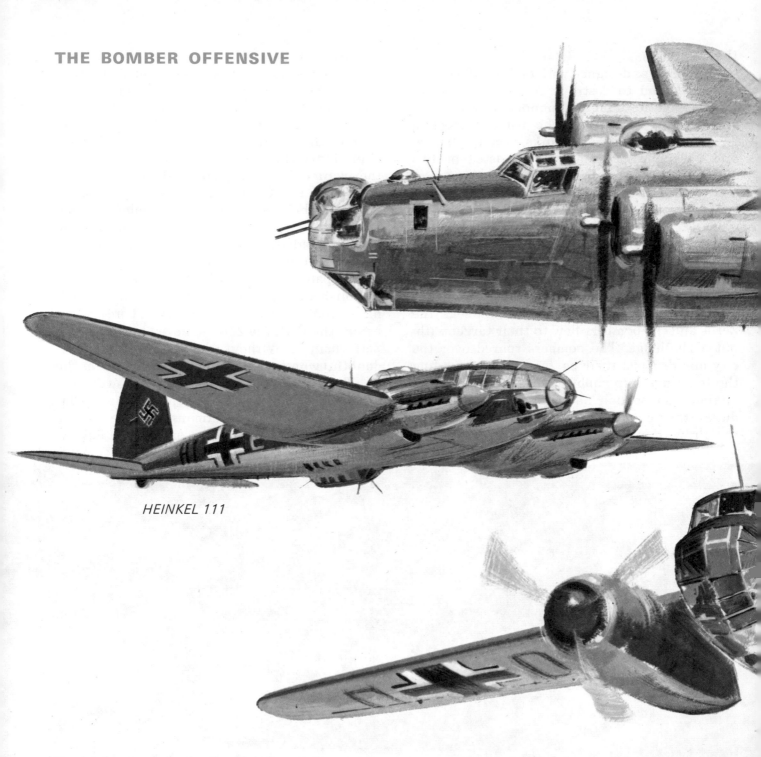

HEINKEL 111

The fighters were the heroes of the air war in their sleek, fast monoplanes, twirling and turning in the sky. It was difficult not to be captivated by their skill and showmanship.

Yet the fighters purpose was secondary, a tactical rather than strategical weapon. Ground attack and escort missions were the stuff of their life. The strategic importance of the aeroplane as a war machine was, it was claimed, to be found in the bomber offensive.

The German bombers were basically designed to support advancing ground forces (the Americans adopted this tactic for the Pacific war). The

Stuka dive bomber is one example of this concept, but the He-111 and Do-217 were also close-support bombers. They were used in a strategic role over Britain, but were not designed for this and proved ineffective.

The British aimed to use their twin-engined Wellingtons, Blenheims, Hampdens etc. in daylight raids. They quickly found that they were too lightly defended and too slow. So the British adopted night-bombing techniques. When the four-engined Lancaster came into service in 1942 it was used in this role, after a few abortive attempts at daylight raids. One drawback with

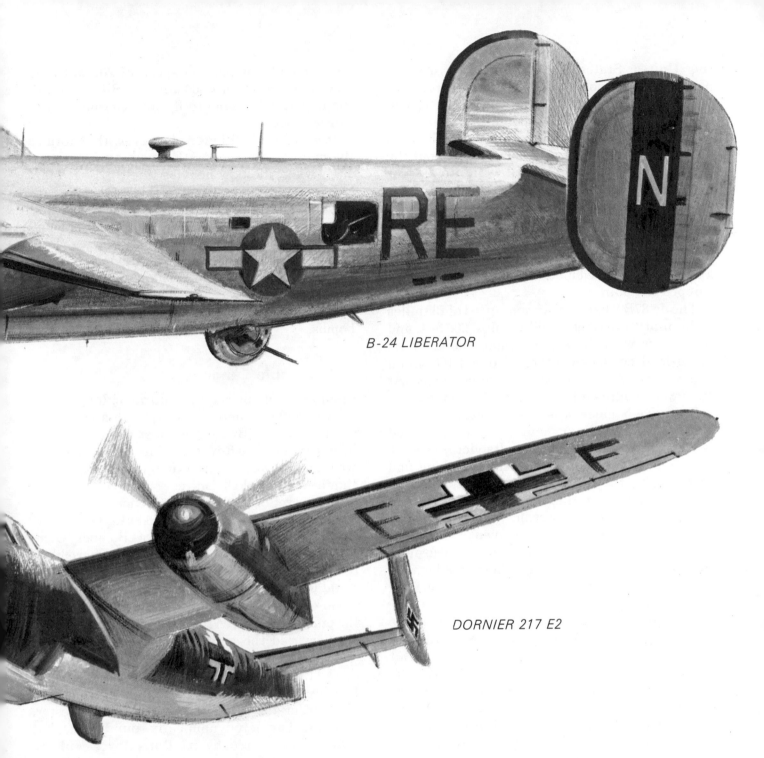

B-24 LIBERATOR

DORNIER 217 E2

the British machines was that their ·303 machine guns were outclassed by the 20mm cannon of the Fw 190s.

The Americans developed the self-defending bombers, such as the B-17, B-24 and B-29. After heavy losses over Germany in 1943 they had to abandon deep penetration raids without fighter escort (and therefore tacitly admit that the self-defending bomber was a myth). They did, however, normally attack during the day.

Another difference between the American and British over Germany was that the British carried out 'area bombing' (i.e. aiming at the centre of towns), whereas the Americans claimed to carry out 'precision bombing' against factories and military targets only. Despite their claims, accuracy in navigation and bomb aiming was a constant problem for both British and American airman, though results improved with the development of radar aids.

The Trumpets of Jericho

Curiously enough, the German dive-bomber force had its origins in a visit by Ernst Udet, First World War ace and Luftwaffe general, to the United States, where he witnessed the performance of some Curtiss 'Hell Divers'. Udet was very impressed by their performance, and convinced Goering of their potential. The attraction of the dive-bomber lay in its ability to achieve pin-point accurate bombing without the aid of bombsights, which until well into the war were of very poor quality. Under Goering's prodding the German aircraft industry hastened to produce their own version of dive-bombers. By the spring of 1937 the first Junkers Ju 87A Stukas were on the production lines. A year later, a new and improved model, the Ju 87B was being shipped to Spain.

The Ju 87B-2 had a maximum speed of 238 miles an hour at 13,400 feet, a ceiling of 26,200 feet, and was armed with three 7·9mm machine guns. Its bomb load consisted either of one 1,100-pound bomb or one 550- and four 110-pound bombs. At maximum loading it had a range of 370 miles.

The dive-bomber was a new weapon and it achieved extraordinary successes in Spain and in the early stages of the war. Its victories were due to a combination of accurate bombing and surprise. To the uninitiated, the Stuka, diving out of the sky at enormous speeds and producing a shrill, high-pitched scream ('the trumpets of Jericho'), was a frightening event. The noise produced a kind of panic reaction among ground troops. So, in the early days, the Stuka bombed merrily away without much interference from anti-aircraft fire.

In Spain, during the Civil War, and in the Blitzkrieg, the Ju 87 built up an extraordinary myth of durability and destructive power. But once the initial surprise had been overcome the Stuka proved to be very vulnerable. During the Battle of Britain the Stuka suffered such heavy losses that it had to be withdrawn from the battle. This was because they were not designed for aerial battle. They continued to be used extensively in other theatres of war, especially Russia, as effective *blitzkrieg* weapons. Yet in its day the Stuka had been one of Germany's most powerful war machines.

Blenheim and Wellington

The R.A.F. entered the war with the twin-engined Blenheim. It was an all-metal monoplane with retractable undercarriage powered by two 920-horsepower Bristol Mercury radial engines. Armaments consisted of ·303 machine guns in a dorsal turret and a 1,000-pound bomb

load. It had a maximum speed of 262 miles an hour and a range of 1,800 miles. A Blenheim was the first R.A.F. plane to fly into Germany after war was declared.

It was the Wellington, however, that formed the mainstay of the R.A.F. bombing force until 1941, when the new heavies, the Stirling, Manchester and Halifax, came off the production line.

The Wellington was characterized by an amazing ability to endure a great deal of punishment. The secret lay in the geodetic (lattice-work) construction. The six-man-crew bomber had a range of 1,325 miles and a maximum speed of 255 miles an hour. It was armed with six ·303 Browning machine guns and up to 6,000 pounds of bombs.

The Durable Lancaster

England, in its pursuit of a durable, long range, heavy bomber, finally came up with a winner in the Lancaster. 'By far the most effective heavy bomber which the Royal Air Force despatched on war operations,' in the judgement of Group Captain Leonard Cheshire.

The secret of the Lancaster's success lay in its durability. As Air Chief Marshall Sir Arthur Harris, Commander-in-Chief of Bomber Command, wrote in 1947: 'Its efficiency was incredible, both in performance and in the way in which it could be saddled with ever increasing loads.'

No other British bomber could have survived the pummelling given to the Lancaster, nor could have carried the enormous new, armour penetrating bombs designed by Barnes Wallis.

The Lancaster was designed by Roy Chadwicke for the Avroe Aviation Company. It was developed from the two-engined Avro-Manchester, which had an aerodynamically sound frame, but was underpowered by its Rolls-Royce Vulture engines. By refitting the frame with four reliable Merlin engines the Lancaster was born.

The Lancaster was built of light alloy, and powered by Four Rolls-Royce Merlin XX engines delivering 1,280 horse-power each. Fully loaded it attained a maximum speed of 275 miles an hour at 15,000 feet, with a ceiling of 19,000 feet. It had a maximum range of 2,530 miles decreasing to 1,550 miles with a 22,000 pound load. Its armament consisted of a Frazer-Nash nose turret with two ·303-inch Brownings, a mid-upper turret with two ·303s, a tail turret with four ·303s, and a ventral turret with one ·303. The first production model flew in October, 1941.

Two sturdy British bombers of the early war years. Above: Wellington. Below: Blenheim

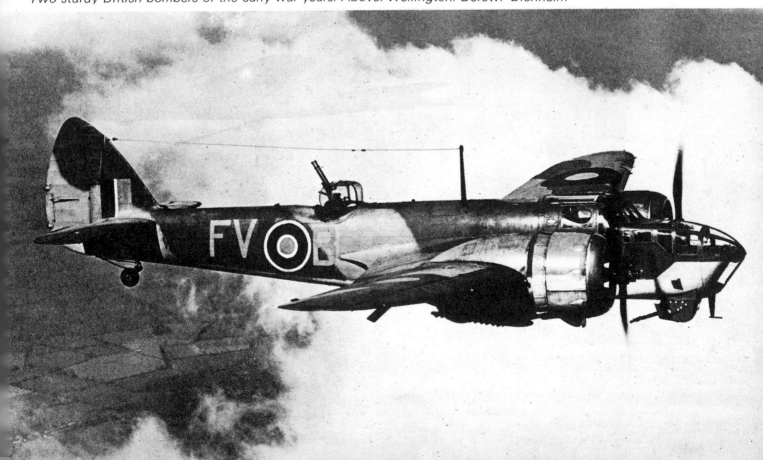

Above left: Sir Arthur Harris, who praised the Lancaster. Above right: Waiting in the half light before a raid

Above: Load capacity and toughness were the mark of the Lancaster. Below: A Fortress of Coastal Command

The B-29 Superfortress

If the Lancaster was the queen of the heavy bombers then the B-29 Superfortress was the king, the supreme bomber of the Allied offensive.

In the autumn of 1939 the Kilner-Lindbergh report, commissioned by General Arnold of the Army Air Corps, recommended the development of long range medium and heavy bombers. The outbreak of the European war in September added urgency to the report, and in November the first studies were conducted on the feasibility of a very long range heavy bomber. Thus was born the B-29.

Specifications were sent to four companies for bids. Boeing won. A year later the prototype B-29 was completed. This embodied a number of radical design changes which astonished the aviation world. Faced with the problem of building a bomber of almost twice the weight (98,000 pounds) of the B-17 Flying Fortress, with a 30 per cent increase in speed and only an 80 per cent increase in horse-power, the engineers came up with a revolutionary thin, low drag wing.

Construction methods were improved to make the B-29 an aerodynamically clean aeroplane. Thus, all rivets were flush, and the landing gear folded flat into the wing. Improvements of this

Clean lines helped to give the heavy B-29 Superfortress outstanding range capacity

nature made the bomber a tidy, streamlined, aeroplane.

Another new feature of the B-29 was the pressurized cabin which maintained an atmosphere equivalent to 8,000 feet at an actual altitude of 30,000 feet. The front and rear pressurized portions of the warplane were connected by means of a tube placed over the large bomb bay doors.

The B-29 was powered by four Wright R-3350 engines developing 2,200 horse-power each. It had a maximum speed of 365 miles an hour at 25,000 feet, a cruising speed of 220 miles an hour and a range of 5,830 miles. It was armed with 10–12

·5-inch machine guns and one 20mm cannon. Bomb load varied between 8,000 and 16,000 pounds.

By the spring of 1944 the Superfortress was ready to enter into action. Based in Chengtu, in eastern China, the 20th Bomber Command launched strikes against Japanese occupied China and the Japanese home islands.

The capture of the Marianas Islands in the summer of 1944 meant that a base could be established for a regular bomber offensive against Japan. The offensive culminated with the dropping of atomic bombs on Hiroshima and Nagasaki.

The devastating blast of a post-war nuclear test

THE ATOMIC BOMB

On July 16, 1945, President Truman was informed that an atomic bomb had been successfully detonated in the New Mexico desert. The greatest weapon in human history had been created. After much thought Truman decided that the new weapon must be used to bring a hasty end to the war. Orders were given for a squadron of B-29s to be modified to carry the new bomb.

The modifications were limited to the bomb bay, and included a new bomb frame, hoist, sway braces, and release unit. Tests on the modified B-29 had been going on since February, 1944 and were completed by the following August.

In the summer of 1944 a special squadron, the 509th Composite Wing, was formed to drop the bombs. The squadron leader was Colonel Paul W. Tibbets, Jr. For the next few months, until the bomb was ready, the unit spent long hours practising dummy runs, simulating precision bombing, and practising overwater navigation. In July, 1945, the 509th was moved to Tinian, an island in the Marianas group. Last minute testings continued until August 4, two days before the first drop.

The first atomic strike took place on August 6, 1945, in a B-29 commanded by Tibbets. Tibbets had named his craft the *Enola Gay*, in honour of his mother. A little before three in the morning of the 6th Tibbets and his crew assembled on the airfield. The ground crew had already prepared the *Enola Gay* for take-off. The *Enola Gay* carried the 'Little Boy' bomb, as the atomic weapon was called, weighing about 9,000 pounds. The bomb was not assembled until the plane was airborne in case the plane crashed on take-off.

At 9.15 a.m. Tibbets was over Hiroshima. He had not met with any opposition. The release button was triggered, the bomb bay doors opened, and the bomb, with a parachute attached to it, toggled free. Within minutes 78,000 people were dead, another 51,000 injured. The most destructive weapon in recorded history had been unleashed.

A second drop on August 9 – this time on Nagasaki – convinced the Japanese of the futility of further resistance. The Second World War was over, and the B-29 Superfortress had been instrumental in bringing it to its conclusion.

Above: Destruction caused at Hiroshima by the atomic bomb   *Below: 'Fatman' nuclear bomb, used on Nagasaki*

Below: A Grand Slam leaving a Lancaster during the attack on the viaduct at Arnsberg

Above: A 12,000 pound bomb is made ready for loading

ADAPTING THE BOMB

It was not only bombers that were becoming bigger and better as the war progressed, but the load they carried as well. Right to the Second World War bombs remained small and fairly primitive. The growing concern with strategic bombing offensive meant that attention was directed toward the weapons that had to do the job. The end of the war saw an enormous variety of bombs – incendiaries, high explosives, personnel fragmentation bombs, armour piercing bombs, smoke bombs etc. Of these bombs a few stand out for their ingenuity, size or deadliness.

Tallboy and Grandslam

In 1941, Dr. Barnes Wallis, controller of Armament Research at Vickers-Armstrong, began to work on a high capacity armour piercing bomb. He reasoned correctly that the enemy's resources would be moved to underground concrete bunkers, against which the conventional bomb was useless. Barnes Wallis proposed to combine armour piercing capabilities with a high capacity explosive bomb. The result was Grand Slam, an 11 ton bomb carrying six to seven tons of high explosive in a sleek casing. When released from 40,000 feet the bomb could penetrate 135 feet of sand, exploding subterraneously. But the Grand Slam was too enormous a concept to grasp in the early stages of the war, and a scaled down version, Tallboy, saw action before its parent bomb.

Tallboy was a 6 ton missile, 21·5 feet long and three feet in diameter. One of its most notable successes was the sinking of the *Tirpitz*, Germany's greatest battleship.

Operation Paravane

The *Tirpitz* was the sister ship to the *Bismarck*, a massive fortress of 45,000 tons of guns and armour plate. Attempts to destroy her by mini

93

submarines and torpedoes had failed. On November 12, 1944, 38 Lancasters of 617 squadron were despatched on a mission to sink the *Tirpitz*. The great battleship was located at Haak Island, near Tromsö in Norway, just within reach of a Scottish base.

The Lancasters left their base, Lossiemouth, at three in the morning. Six hours later they arrived over the *Tirpitz*. The ship was taken completely by surprise. The big bombers zoomed in on their targets and dropped their lethal load. Twenty-eight Tallboys were dropped, two of them direct hits. The *Tirpitz* could not withstand the assault of the super bombs. She jack-knifed and sank in the shallow waters.

The Dam Buster

Barnes Wallis was a busy man during the war. Aside from aircraft design and the creation of the two largest bombs in the war, he invented one of the most unusual bombs of the war – the skip bomb. The skip bomb was purpose-built to destroy vital German dams in the Ruhr.

The skip bomb was a drum shaped device containing about three tons of high explosive. It was meant to be dropped spinning from a height of 60 feet onto the reservoir. The bomb would then skip to the dam, sink and explode at the base.

The story of the dam buster squadron, the 617,

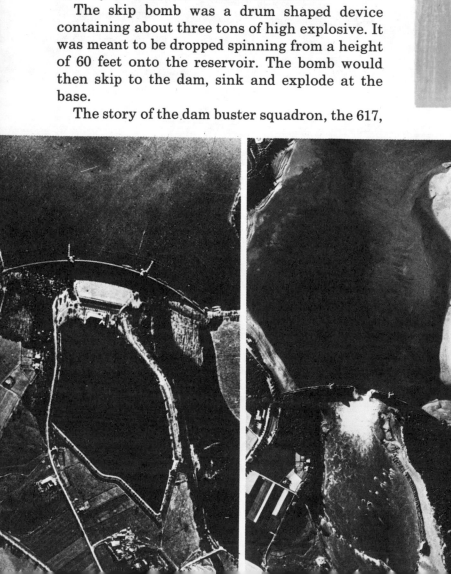

The Barnes Wallis 9,500 lb. bouncing bomb which destroyed the Moehne Dam (seen before and after the attack, below left) was held inside the bomb bay by a special mechanism which caused it to revolve in an anti-clockwise direction. This gave it spinning momentum, making it bounce as it struck the water from a height of 60 feet — pinpointed by search lights fore and aft of the plane which converged when the plane was at the right height. The bomb bounced over the torpedo nets and exploded against the dam wall.

Left: The Moehne Dam before and after

under the leadership of Wing Commander Guy Gibson, is too well known to go into here in detail. Let it suffice to say that, under the most gruelling conditions, the Moehne and Eder Dams were breached causing extensive flooding and costing 1,000 lives. Great though the achievement of Barnes Wallis and squadron 617 was, in the end the Germans were able to repair the damage quite quickly, thus showing the limitations of the aeroplane as a war machine.

Every Kind of Bomb

General purpose high-explosive bombs (HE) made up the majority of the two million odd tons of ordnance dropped during the war. Carried by bombers and dropped in freefall, they varied in weight from 100 to 3,000 pound. About half the weight was explosive charge. The HE's operated on blast effect (a 500 pound bomb would carve a crater 30 feet in diameter and about 15 feet deep,

in an average estimate; the actual impact depended naturally on the nature of the terrain being bombed). To be effective the bombs had to hit the target directly or very close by as even simple shelters provided protection at a 70 yard range.

Fragmentation bombs were similar to the general purpose HE bombs, but carried only 14 per cent by weight of explosive charge. The remainder was taken up by wire wrapping to increase the shrapnel effect. Fragmentation bombs were used in anti-personnel attacks, and on sensitive targets like truck convoys.

Cluster bombs were developed to achieve uniform coverage over a large area (a problem not solved by making the standard bombs larger). Small bomblets were packaged into a single canister. The canister was blown open, usually by compressed gas, just above ground level, spreading the bomblets over a radius of several hundred feet. In later developments of the

Bombs on target, photographed through the bomb bay doors

Above: A viaduct destroyed by Lancasters. Below: The dramatic effect of napalm in the jungle

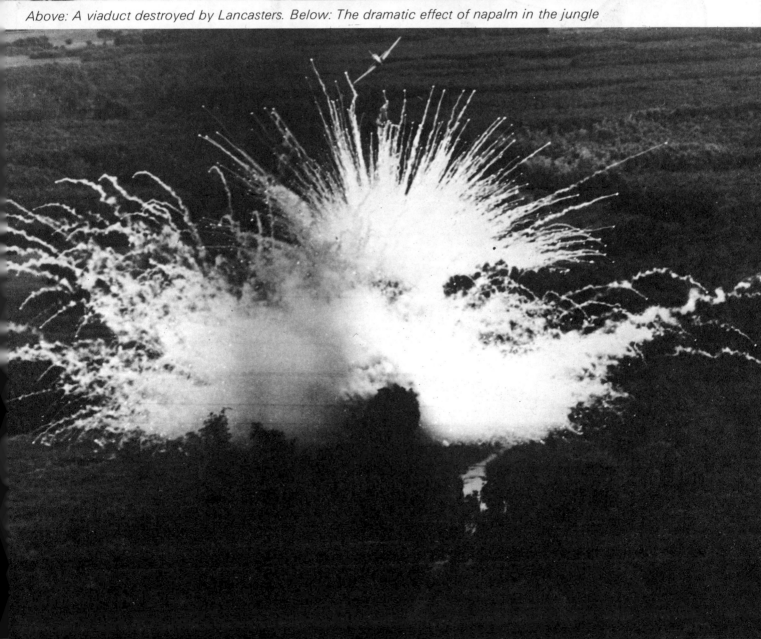

cluster bomb, 600 bomblets, each holding 2 ounces of explosive and 300 steel pellets, were fitted into a single canister. The fuses on the bomblets could be set to explode on impact or operate on a time-delay mechanism. Targets, as in fragmentation bombs, were personnel or vulnerable equipment.

One of the most vicious incendiary bombs developed was the napalm bomb. Napalm – gasoline jellied by mixing it with soap powder – placed in thin containers was dropped over the target. A central core surrounded by white phosphorous detonated on impact throwing the napalm over distances of 100 feet. The phosphorous ignited spontaneously thus lighting the highly inflammable napalm. Napalm burns with a very hot flame and is very difficult to extinguish. It is a sticky substance and attempts to brush it off only succeed in spreading it.

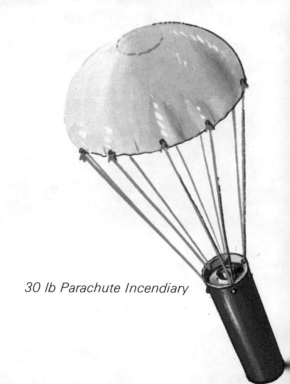

30 lb Parachute Incendiary

12,000 lb HC

12,000 lb 'Tallboy'

98

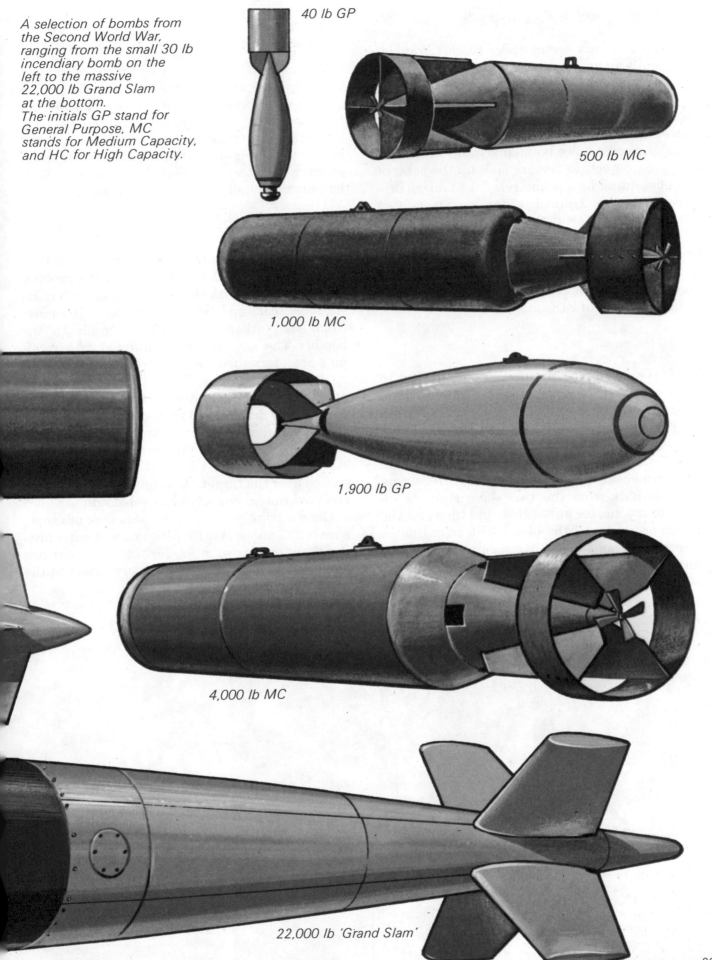

A selection of bombs from the Second World War, ranging from the small 30 lb incendiary bomb on the left to the massive 22,000 lb Grand Slam at the bottom.
The initials GP stand for General Purpose, MC stands for Medium Capacity, and HC for High Capacity.

40 lb GP

500 lb MC

1,000 lb MC

1,900 lb GP

4,000 lb MC

22,000 lb 'Grand Slam'

WARNING AND GUIDANCE

In 1936 a research group under Robert Watson-Watts built an experimental radar device, and in so doing opened a new era in air warfare. Not only could radar detect invading aircraft, but it also enabled the British bombers to develop greater accuracy in their bombing missions.

Radar operates by bouncing radio beams off any given object. Receivers pick up the echo of the rebounding beams and relay it to an oscilloscope where a trained radar operative can calculate how far away the unidentified object is.

By 1939 a perimeter of 20 early warning radar ground stations were established in the southeast of England. Without these stations it is likely that the Germans would have been successful in the Battle of Britain.

The Gee System

The Gee system was the first one developed to aid bombers on their missions. Three ground stations, at a distance of 200 miles from each other, transmitted pulses to the bomber. There was one master station and two subsidiary, 'slave' stations. The navigator on board the bomber, measured the time difference in receiving transmissions from the two slave stations relative to the master pulse. He could then plot the Gee co-ordinates of the plane. The co-ordinates were printed as a grid on a special Gee map of Europe. By checking the calculated Gee co-ordinates with the map, the navigator got a fix on the aircraft's position.

The margin of error varied between one half to five miles and effective radius of the Gee system was about 300 miles, enough to take the bombers into the Ruhr valley. Gee's most important contribution was as an aid to dead-reckoning navigation, finding the way into the enemy's territory and getting out again. More helpful as a blind bomb sight was Oboe.

Cat and Mouse

The accuracy of bombing in anything but perfect weather was dismal. One way round the problem was introduced with the Oboe system. Two radar stations, 'cat' and 'mouse', at about 100 miles from each other, transmitted signals to the bomber. The 'cat' station maintained the aircraft on a predetermined course by radioing a series of dash and dot impulses. The aircraft radar showed dots if the aircraft deviated to one side of the course, and dashes if to the other side.

When the aircraft was direct on course the radar emitted a steady beam. The 'mouse' station, meanwhile, signalled the aircraft as it passed over the target. As soon as the signal was received the bombs would be released.

Oboe's principal limitation was lack of range, a mere 275 miles. As the Allies moved eastwards it did not matter so much for the radar stations could be established progressively closer to the main strategic targets.

Below: GEE indicator unit and controls. Below centre: A typical 'Chain Home' Station

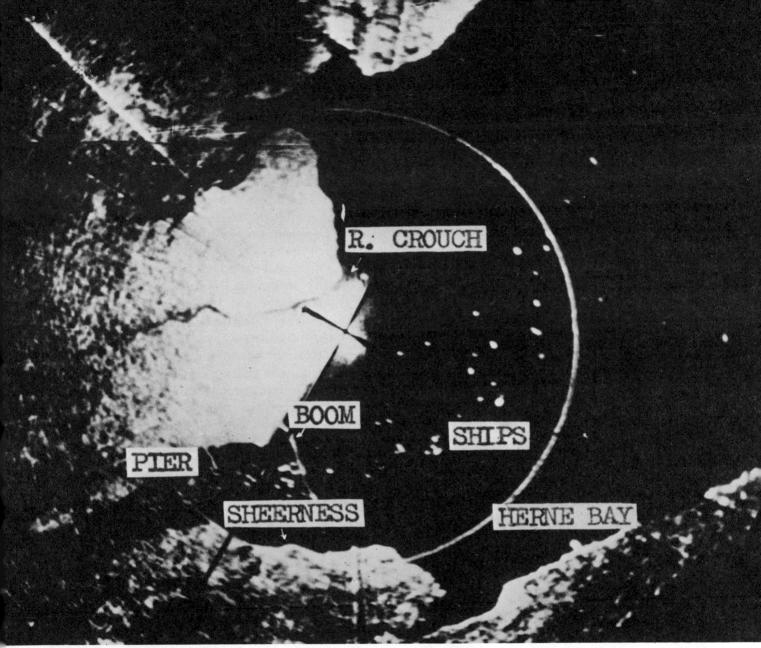

R. CROUCH

BOOM

SHIPS

PIER

SHEERNESS

HERNE BAY

Above: Night radar picture of Thames estuary. Below right: General view of Fighter Direction Station

Another limitation was that the home radar stations could only handle a limited number of bombers at any given time. Eventually Oboe found its principal use in Pathfinder Force. The Pathfinder Force was a kind of 'follow the leader' tactic. The lead aircraft, generally a Mosquito, was zeroed in on the target where it dropped a marker bomb or flare. The rest of the bombing force, following closely behind, released their load as they passed over the flare.

Mapping the Route with H2S

H2S was a radar system that did not depend on ground control stations. It used the varying intensity of echoing radar beams to map out the terrain the bomber over-flew. The radar map indicated differences between built up areas and open country, moutains and valleys, the sea and land. The aircraft was equipped with a downward-looking rotating radar transmitter which scanned the countryside, building up a map reading. By comparing H2S readings with known data, the navigator received a pretty accurate fix on the aircraft's position. At the time of the Battle of Berlin more than 90 per cent of Bomber Command was equipped with the H2S device.

A Window for Bombs

One of the most unusual weapons of war ever created were the bundles of long, thin strips of aluminium foil known as 'window'. It is strange that something so seemingly innocuous resulted in the first successful fire-bombing raid of the war.

The reason for the mystery lay in window's ability to confuse German radar. By dropping thousands of bundles of the stuff it blotted out other echoes on the German radar system.

On July 24/25, 1943, a massive Bomber Command force raided Hamburg. That they were able to do so was thanks to the window, which confused German defences. The raid on Hamburg was one of the most destructive of the war causing, over a week, enormous fire-storms which gutted the city and killed 42,000 people.

Oboe system with cat station to direct bomber's path and mouse station to direct bomb on target.

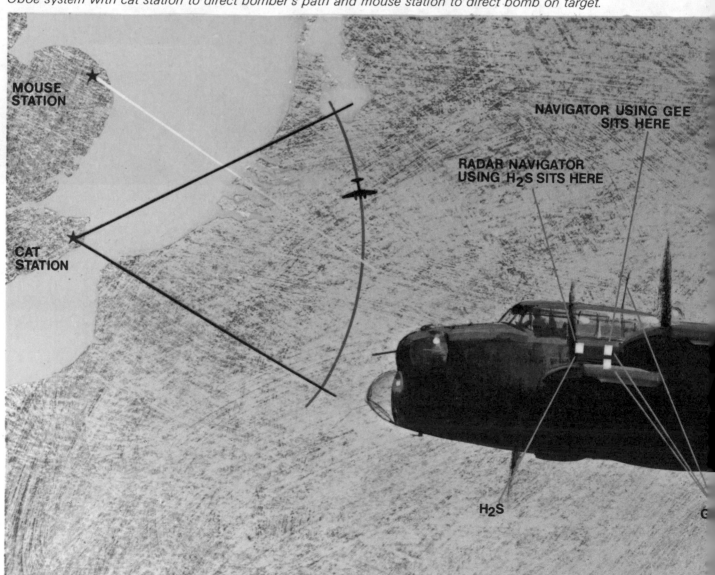

MOUSE STATION

NAVIGATOR USING GEE SITS HERE

RADAR NAVIGATOR USING H2S SITS HERE

CAT STATION

H2S

Above. 'Window' dropped from a Lancaster over Essen, to interfere with radar

H2S

H2S SCANNER

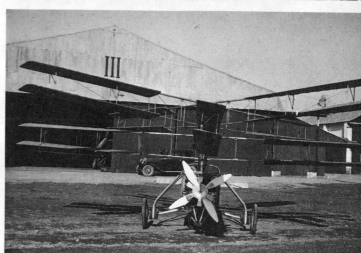

Top: Paul Cornu was the first to take off. Above left: 1925 Autogiro. Above right: Pescara 4S. Below: Fa-61

THE HELICOPTER

In the age of limited wars, that often take the form of guerrilla activity, new types of war machines have been developed or adapted to cope with the situation. Vietnam, in particular, showed the helplessness of traditional types of aircraft in close jungle combat. Airspace was unquestionably controlled by the Americans, but fighters could act as ground support only with difficulty, and the heavy transport planes could not supply troops to the front lines. It was at this point that a slow, ungainly creature took over the functions of the aeroplane. That creature was the helicopter – the latest of the powerful aerial war machines.

The helicopter works on the same principle as the aeroplane. The rotating blades of the rotor act in the same way as an aeroplane wing. At great speeds the airflow will provide the lift necessary to raise the aircraft above ground. The crucial difference, of course, is that the aeroplane as a whole must pick up speed to create the lifting forces on its fixed wings, whereas, in the helicopter, the rotor creates the airflow and thus its own lift. This is the reason why helicopters can rise vertically while aeroplanes cannot.

However, the whirling blades also limit the performance of the helicopter (and it is one of the reasons why it took so much longer to develop than the fixed wing aeroplane). The helicopter suffers from an effect called *dissymmetry of lift*. The term refers to the unequal forces on the rotor blades. The blade passes through a 360 degree circle of rotation. A blade is thus advancing forward against the airflow, or retreating.

The advancing blade naturally has the additional lift of thrust (forward motion), as well as the lift produced by the rotation of the blades. Thus the advancing blade will tend to flap up, and the retreating one down. The flapping effect compensates for dissymetry of lift by changing the angle of advancing and retreating blades.

The retreating blade has a sharper angle of attack, thus increasing its lift, and vice versa for the advancing blade. However, the greater the speed of the helicopter, the greater the flapping effect. Eventually this flapping effect results in serious and dangerous vibrations in the craft. The helicopter's speed is thus limited.

Experiments Take Shape

The principles of rotational flight had been understood for centuries. Experiments had been going on from the earliest days in man's dream of flight, but it was not until the 20th Century that the means were found to fulfil this vision.

Igor Sikorsky at the controls of one of his successful models — the VS-300

The first free flight of a helicopter was made in 1907 by Paul Cornu. His helicopter was powered by a 24 horse-power Antoinette engine, and had two rotors mounted in tandem. The flight lasted about 20 seconds, in which time the craft rose six feet in the air.

Another Frenchman, Louis Breguet, constructed a helicopter powered by a 55 horse-power Renault engine, and supplied with two 25-foot rotors. It rose to a height of 15 feet, and then crashed.

In Russia, a young designer turned his attention to helicopters. Igor Sikorsky's attempts to build a workable rotating wing craft in 1909 ended in failure. Thirty years later Sikorsky returned to his first love and created the prototype of all modern helicopters.

A major step forward was taken in 1924. The Marquis Raul Pateras Pescara designed a helicopter that could move forward, as well as up. Pescara mounted two co-axial rotors on the same mast. Each rotor was on two levels, eight blades per level, 16 blades on a rotor, 32 blades all together – whirling crazily around, driven by a 180 horsepower Hispano-Suiza engine.

Pescara's design enabled the pilot to change the pitch of the blades for added lift (collective pitch control). In addition the craft had a primitive cyclical pitch control whereby the pitch of the blades were changed in cycles creating unequal lifting forces. This allowed the pilot to turn the craft in any direction he wanted.

Despite advances in theory and methods of construction, rotating wing aircraft were still in their infancy by the end of the 1920s. Then a Spaniard, working from a different perspective, created an aircraft from which solved the helicopter's problems.

The Autogiro

Juan de la Cierva was fascinated with the idea of a craft independent of forward motion, and thus less likely to stall. The answer he came up with was an aircraft with free spinning rotor blades – the autogiro. Once an autogiro had obtained some speed the blades would rotate on their own, creating additional lift. If the engine stalled or cut out altogether the free spinning rotors would continue their merry chase round, undisturbed by the lack of an active mechanical motor. Nature takes care of its own, and the airflow from underneath would ensure a gliding descent for the craft.

Top left: Helicopters armed with machine guns flying into action in Vietnam.
Centre left: The modern 'cowboy' of the air.
Bottom left: Whirlwind helicopter of the Royal Navy.
Above: Sioux helicopters in formation at a display in Britain.
Right: Sikorsky HH53 helicopter, armed with rockets, an impressive strike weapon

Cierva experimented with various aircraft in the late 1920s, but they all showed a similar fault. Once airborne, the craft evinced dangerous tendencies to roll. It took some time before Cierva hit on the answer and the solution. The problem was dissymmetry of lift. The solution was a flapping hinge to give the blades enough freedom to straighten themselves out. Later a vertical hinge was added to the hub of the rotor. The vertical hinge released massive pressures on the blade root by allowing it to lag, forward or rearward, in the rotor disc. In time these improvements evolved into the *fully articulated hub*, one where the blades are allowed as much freedom of movement as possible.

The military soon became interested in these autogiros. The United States Navy considered using it in an undeclared war in Nicaragua. The still primitive autogiro could not, however, compete with the Marine biplane.

When, in the mid-1930s, the autogiro took off on its first vertical flight (by means of attaching the rotor to a motor while on the ground, and disengaging once airborne), the helicopter engineers stood up and took note. The autogiro had established and proved all the basic elements necessary for creating a practical helicopter. In 1935 the first such helicopter was flown. The honoured man – Louis Breguet.

The Breguet machine was given lift by two rotors mounted one atop the other on the same mast with the drive shaft turning inside another. It was necessary to have the rotors moving in counter directions to offset the torque (turning force) of the motor. The natural tendency of a single rotor machine would be to twist the machine in the opposite direction to the rotor.

The Breguet helicopter featured all the design innovations developed in the previous few years, from articulated hub and cyclic pitch control to collective pitch and differential collective system. In the differential system the collective pitch of just one rotor can be altered, increasing the torque of that rotor. The ship could then turn round on its vertical axis.

Within a year the Breguet was overshadowed by the Focke-Acheglis Fa-61, the finest helicopter design in 1936. The Fa-61 had two rotors mounted on outriggers on either side of the vessel.

The best helicopter of the Second World War was Anton Flettner's 'synchropter'. The synchropter derived its name from the closely inter-

2·75 inch rockets streak forward from a Huey Cobra, capable of firing more than 2,000 pounds of mixed weaponry

meshed and synchronised rotors on the ship.

In 1939, Sikorsky turned his hand to helicopter design and emerged with the VS-300. He revolutionized design by his simplicity. For his helicopter rotors he utilized a penny farthing shape – a large rotor up front and a small anti-torque motor to the rear.

Helicopters developed further after the war, finding their first military use in the Korean conflict, foretaste to come of helicopter service in Vietnam. Helicopters played an enormously important role in the Vietnamese jungle, rescuing sick and wounded, landing troops when and where needed and running reconnaissance missions.

The Huey Cobra

The most effective form of close ground support in guerrilla conditions was found to be the gunship, a natural role for the helicopter. The first helicopter specifically built for that purpose was the Bell AH-1 Huey Cobra.

Its narrow (four foot) fuselage made it a much more difficult target for ground fire, and at a maximum speed of 219 miles an hour it could move quickly away if things got too hot. The AH-1 is powered by a 1,400 horse-power Lycoming T53-L-13 turboshaft engine. Its main rotor diameter is 44 feet, it has a gross weight of nine and a half thousand pounds and a range of 387 miles. But the main feature lay in its armament: a chin turret mounting two 7·62mm six barrel Miniguns and two 40mm grenade launchers; and racks under the stub wings for four rocket packs. The Miniguns can fire at a rate of 1,600 rounds per minute increasing to 4,000 rounds per minute.

The two-man Huey Cobra entered service in Vietnam in 1967 and preparations are under way for a twin-engined version.

CH-54A transport helicopter of the U.S. Army

The Gloster E28/39 powered by a Whittle jet. The jet fighter did not come into its own until the last year of the war

JET POWER

By the end of the Second World War piston engined aircraft had gone about as far as they could go. Horsepower could not be increased without greatly increasing engine weight and if this could have been done there existed another serious problem – the 'sonic barrier'. As an aeroplane approached the speed of sound the drag increased enormously. Propellers could not cope with that kind of drag and lost all their efficiency. It thus seemed that man was limited to a speed of 400–500 an hour.

In 1928 a young R.A.F. cadet, Frank Whittle, wrote an article for the college paper on the possibility of jet propulsion by means of the gas turbine. The idea was ridiculed at the time, yet in that youthful paper was set the foundation for a profound revolution in aviation.

Sir Frank Whittle and his successful jet engine

Gas turbines had been around since the turn of the century. Many aviators had even thought of adapting the turbine for aeroplane use, but at the time it was still too clumsy, and aviators only thought of using it to run a conventional propeller. There was no interest in that. Whittle asked, why not use the thrust of the hot gases of the gas turbine to propel the aeroplane? The jet, after all, operates on the same principle as the rocket – Newton's Third Law: 'To every action there is an equal and opposite reaction.'

After many trials and tribulations, Whittle managed to have a prototype engine built in 1937, nine years after the idea was first propounded.

The Whittle engine was compounded of three parts. The compressor at the intake end sucked in air and compressed it by means of centrifugal chambers. The middle part was the combustion chamber where the fuel was mixed with the air and ignited. The outlet end contained the gas turbine, a fast-spinning, bladed wheel. A shaft joined the gas turbine and the compressor. The

78, the world's first jet- propelled aeroplane. Below: The Me-262, which Hitler failed to use to best advantage

turbine used the energy of the hot gases to provide useful work. The rest of the hot gases were released through a tiny opening, to increase exit velocity, and, in consequence, thrust.

Four years after the prototype Whittle engine had been built, a Gloster W28/39 took-off from Cranwell airfield – the first British jet.

Although Whittle was the first to propose the idea of the turbojet, the Germans were the first to exploit it. Hans von Ohain had, in the mid-1930s, independently reached similar conclusions as Whittle. But unlike the British pioneer, Ohain did not have to struggle to get a hearing for his ideas. Heinkel, the big aeroplane manufacturer took him in for the express purpose of building a jet aircraft. The result was the Heinkel He 178, the world's first jet aeroplane.

The Menace of the Messerschmitt

Although early development work was being undertaken before the war, the jet fighter did not come into its own until the last year of the conflict. The most important and menacing jet of the Second World War was the Messerschmitt Me 262. It was powered by two Jumo engines developing nearly 2,000 pounds of thrust each. Other radical design features included swept back low wings.

The straight wings of conventional aircraft performed smoothly enough at average propeller speed, but would not do for jets. Experimentation pointed to swept back, thin wings as the solution. The swept back wing provided greater efficiency at higher altitudes and greater speeds, but at a cost – a loss in lift and drag. This meant that jet pilots had to accept a higher take-off and landing speed, and a longer runway.

The Me 262 was intended as a fighter, and as such could have created havoc among Allied Air Forces. With a speed of 525 miles an hour it was at least 75 to 100 miles an hour faster than its nearest rival. Furthermore, armaments consisted of a formidable array of 30mm guns. Happily, Hitler, obsessed with bombing the enemy, ordered the conversion of the whole stock of Me 262s into bombers.

The Turbofan

After the war, jet engined aircraft replaced the conventional armed aeroplanes. In the B-52 Stratofortress, America created the largest bomber and transport jet in existence. The 1961,

B-52 H model had a gross weight of 488,000 pounds with 18,000-pound thrust turbofan engines.

The turbofan engine was thought of in the 1930s, but not developed till much later. The basic idea was the same as the turbojet. Greater power, however, was siphoned off by the gas turbine to drive a large diameter fan at the front of the engine. The fan could be run at a lower spin rate than the turbine by means of a reducing gearing system. The turbofan increased air intake and thrust over the ordinary turbojet, without greatly increasing drag and fuel consumption.

The Soviet answer to the B-52 was the Tu-22 bomber with a thrust of 26,000 to 28,000 pounds and a maximum speed of 1,000 miles an hour.

The Supremacy of the Sabre

Fighters were the aircraft that benefited most

Above: Victor tanker refuelling Lightning in flight. Below: R.A.F. Avro Vulcan bomber

from the jet revolution. Just five years after the end of the Second World War, the United States was at war again. This time the U.S. maintained air supremacy by means of a fleet of F-86 Sabre jets. Swept back wings and a thrust of 3,750 pounds made the Sabre one of the best fighters in Korea.

The Phantom in Vietnam

This jet from the McDonnell-Douglas Corporation, together with the Republic F-105 Thunderchief, formed the workhorse of the Vietnam air war. Powered by two General Electric J79 engines (changed in the British version to Rolls-Royce Spey turbofans) the F-4 reaches a maximum speed of 1,386 miles an hour at 36,000 feet. It has a tactical radius of 550 miles and in addition to a 20mm cannon it can also carry a bomb load of 8 tons.

The Republic F-105 Thunderchief

The F-105 is powered by 26,500-pound Pratt & Whitney afterburning turbojet engine. It has a maximum speed of 1,485 miles an hour at 36,000 feet and a combat radius of 920 miles. Armament consists of a 20mm cannon and a 14,000-pound bomb capacity load. The F-105D were modernized with a new electronic integral bombing system.

Vertical Take Off

One bonus advantage of the invention of jets has been a closer look at Vertical and Short Take-Off and Landing vehicles. The helicopter, though useful, is too slow and cumbersome. It was found that by directing the nozzle of a jet the aircraft could be manoeuvred in the opposite direction. This became the basis of modern research into V/STOL. Turbofans fitted with variable pitch blades can vary the pitch so as to produce a reverse thrust. By adjusting thrust conditions jet aircraft can be made to land vertically and yet maintain their incredibly fast speeds while airborne. The Hawker Siddeley Harrier is at the moment the most famous V/STOL strike fighter in existence. It is, however, still in the initial stages of development. Its full potential is yet to be explored.

DEVELOPMENT OF THE MISSILE

The Launching of V-2 rockets towards the end of the Second World War heralded a new era in warfare. The ability of the V-2 to drop on a given target at a speed of 3,500 miles an hour, just minutes after launching, precluding any possibility of interception and defence, was more than impressive. It pointed to the rise of a revolutionary war machine. The subsequent growth in sophistication of rocketry and the addition of sensitive guidance systems ensured that the guided ballistic missile would, if not completely supersede, at least dominate all aspects of war in the future.

Strangely enough, the newest of war machines has a history stretching back hundreds of years to medieval China.

Chinese War Rockets

When or how gunpowder was invented is shrouded in the mists of time. It is known, however, that by the early 11th Century the Chinese were well acquainted with the substance. Soon after, records indicate, gunpowder was being used to propel primitive rocket devices.

The first rockets were of a simple construction – basically metal tubes filled with gunpowder and attached to arrows. But these had in common with the V-2 the basic principle of rocketry, Newton's Third Law of Motion: 'To every action there is an equal and opposite reaction.' In the rocket, the hot gases created by exploding the powder propel the projectile in a direction opposite to the thrust of the gases.

By the 13th Century, batteries of rocket arrows were being built to combat foreign invaders. One of the first recorded instances of the military value of rockets concerns the battle of K'ai Fung-fu in 1232.

The Battle of K'ai Fung-fu

For months the Mongols had besieged the Chinese city of K'ai Fung-fu, just north of the Yellow River. The townsmen had resisted valiantly, but they could certainly not survive another concerted assault by the seasoned Mongol veterans.

Firing a rocket in the early 17th Century

At this point someone must have suggested to the governor of the town that gunpowder might be used to project incendiary rockets against the Mongol horde. Scores of rockets were hurriedly made and fixed into batteries. When the Mongols next attacked, the Chinese were ready and waiting. The fiery (and noisy) rockets were released against the on-rushing enemy, wreaking

Above left: A British naval rocket brigade in 1868. Above right: Rockets firing from HMS Monarch, *1882*

havoc in their flanks. The Mongols feared these fire arrows with their 'thunder that shakes the heavens' more than any other foe. The rockets halted the assault and the city was saved.

The Battle of Seringapatam

The use of the rocket rapidly spread throughout the world, but despite its widespread presence the military value of the rocket went into a decline so that by the 17th Century the main use of the rocket was in fireworks.

The rebirth of the military rocket was inspired, once again, by events in the East. Towards the end of the 18th Century the British fought two campaigns against the ruler of Mysore, Tippoo Sultan. The unusual feature of these engagements was that, in his army, Tippoo Sultan had established a rocketry division of 5,000 men. The Sultan's rockets varied in size, up to 10 inches long and about 2·5 inches in diameter. They had a range of about 1,000 feet. To increase the damage inflicted by the rockets the guiding stick was replaced on some of them by a sword blade three feet in length.

At the Battle of Seringapatam the rockets were no more than of nuisance value (although one English officer wrote of 'the shower of rockets . . . causing death, wounds, and dreadful lacerations.' What Tippoo's rockets did do was focus attention on their military potential. The challenge of designing an effective war rocket was taken up by an Englishman, William Congreve.

The Rockets' Red Glare

Colonel (later Sir) William Congreve was much intrigued by reports of the Indian rockets. His interest in the rockets led to a series of experiments at the Royal Laboratory of Woolwich Arsenal. The result was a 32-pound, incendiary rocket with a range of 2,000 yards. The rocket was an iron cylinder three and a half feet long and four inches in diameter. Clips fitted to the cylinder made it easy to attach the 15-foot guiding stick.

The Congreve rocket got its first trial in the autumn of 1806, during the Napoleonic wars. A British flotilla anchored outside Boulogne, ready to bombard the city. In the space of half an hour, over 2,000 rockets were unleashed on the hapless city. Congreve wrote at the time:

'The dismay and astonishment of the enemy were complete – not a shot was returned – and in less than ten minutes the town was discovered to be on fire.' The following year a fantastic barrage of 25,000 Congreve rockets on Copenhagen caused severe fires and a great deal of destruction.

The Congreve rocket proved itself to be an awesome machine of war. The Europeans hurried to stock their arsenals with this latest weapon. The French, the Italians, the Austrians and even the Russians used them. The British, however, were the rocketeers *par excellence*. They used rockets successfully in numerous campaigns, one of the most famous being the bombardment of Fort McHenry, near Baltimore, in the War of 1812. A young lawyer, Francis Scott Key Parkinson, witnessed the barrage and was inspired to write a verse which told of the 'rockets' red glare'. That verse is now a part of the United States national anthem.

Spinning for Stability

The success of the war rockets led a number of men to seek ways of improving on the Congreve model. An obvious area of improvement was in guidance. Congreve's large guiding sticks were clumsy and inefficient. But what was to replace the stick? A Frenchman, Frezier, experimented with fin-stabilized rockets, but the fins proved little better than the sticks. At about that time rifling was being introduced into artillery to increase range and accuracy. The rifled gun or cannon imparted a spin to the projectile which accounted for the enormous increase in efficiency. Why not do the same for rockets? The trouble was, how could it be done?

An Englishman, William Hale, found the solution. He realized that the exhaust gases of a rocket could be utilized to impart a spin to the rocket. From theory, Hale went on to build the first practical spin-stabilized rocket. He built movable vanes in the tail of the rocket. The exhaust gases forced the vanes to move round

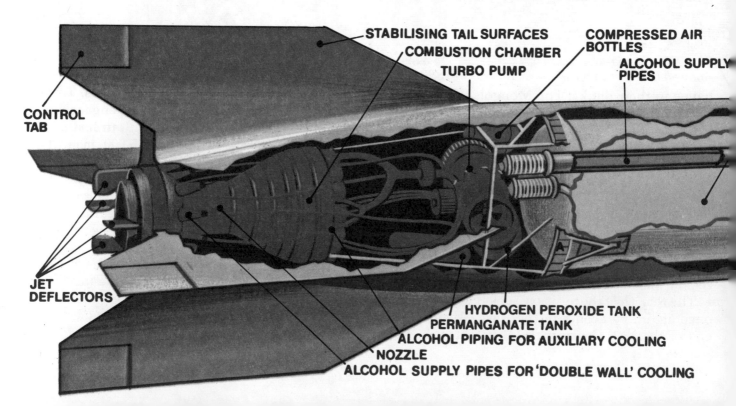

CONTROL TAB

JET DEFLECTORS

STABILISING TAIL SURFACES
COMBUSTION CHAMBER
TURBO PUMP

COMPRESSED AIR BOTTLES
ALCOHOL SUPPLY PIPES

HYDROGEN PEROXIDE TANK
PERMANGANATE TANK
ALCOHOL PIPING FOR AUXILIARY COOLING
NOZZLE
ALCOHOL SUPPLY PIPES FOR 'DOUBLE WALL' COOLING

and the vanes in turn spun the rocket.

The Hale rocket replaced Congreve's design and saw action in a number of engagements the most notable of which was the American-Mexican War.

The Mexican War

In 1846, the United States declared war on Mexico. Major General Winfield Scott commanded the U.S. forces. Among the troops shipped to Mexico was a contingent of rocketeers. The rocketeers were sent to besiege the city of Vera Cruz. By the end of March, 1847, the city was surrounded. The American rocketeers bombarded the city with two-and-a-quarter inch six-pound Hale rockets. After five days the city surrendered. The rocket showed that it continued to be an outstanding war machine, but its days were numbered.

The development of improved artillery in the mid-19th Century outclassed rockets in all respects. The decline of the military rocket in the 19th Century was as swift as its rise. But it was not the end of the story of rockets. At the turn of this century, men driven by visions of inter-planetary space travel gave a new lease of life to the rocket.

The Birth of Modern Rocketry

In 1865, Jules Verne wrote a fictional account of a voyage to the moon, *De La Terre A La Lune* ('From the Earth to the Moon'). Little did he realize that his work would inspire the dream of space travel in three men, a Russian, a German and an American – three men who established the science of rocketry as we know it today.

The Russian, Konstantin Eduardovitch Tsiolkovsky, was born in 1857, in the town of Izhevshoye. In 1878, he settled in Borovsk to teach and commence his life's work on the theoretical principle of modern rocketry. In 1883, he made the discovery that would eventually initiate the space age – that reaction flight, as used by rockets, was not dependent on the atmosphere. Tsiolkovsky also postulated that the multi-stage rocket would provide the means of escape from the Earth's gravitational pull.

Tsiolkovsky was concerned with inter-planetary space travel. He would perhaps have been horrified to know that his theories also formed the basis for the latest and most powerful war machines in existence.

The American, Professor Robert H. Goddard, is today acknowledged to be the father of modern rocketry. In addition to a substantial body of theoretical work Goddard initiated experiments with the objective of developing a practical rocket.

On March 16, 1926, Goddard launched the world's first liquid-fuelled rocket. (The fuel was liquid oxygen.) The 10-foot rocket accelerated to 60 miles an hour and flew 184 feet. The first step had been taken. Over the next 15 years Goddard continued his experiments in New Mexico. He worked in comparative isolation from the mainstream of the aviation and scientific world. But

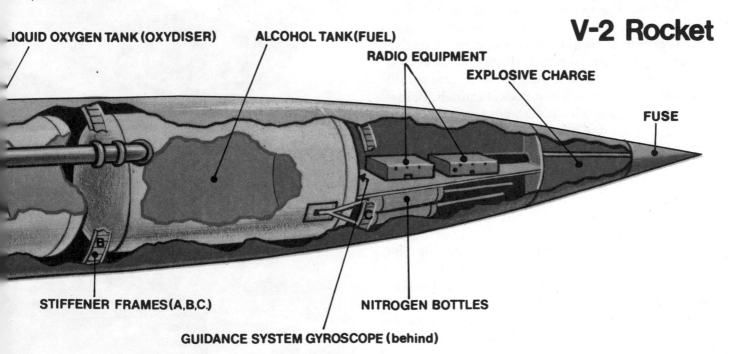

V-2 Rocket

LIQUID OXYGEN TANK (OXYDISER) ALCOHOL TANK (FUEL) RADIO EQUIPMENT EXPLOSIVE CHARGE FUSE

STIFFENER FRAMES (A,B,C.) NITROGEN BOTTLES

GUIDANCE SYSTEM GYROSCOPE (behind)

the Second World War renewed interest in the military application of rockets and, by the beginning of 1942, Goddard's group was working on the problems of jet assisted take-off and rocket-propelled missiles.

In Germany, there was a greater public interest in rocketry. Hermann Oberth was a great publicist for the idea of interplanetary space travel and was a prime mover in the establishment of the *Verein für Raumschiffahrt* (Society for Space Travel). His ideas followed along the same lines as Goddard. The VfR formed the basis for Germany's lead in rocket technology during the war.

In the early 1930s the VfR had been experimenting with various rocket engines, with a view to space travel. When Hitler came to power in 1933, the energy of the nation was diverted towards rearmament. No one was excluded from the injunction to make Germany strong. The VfR was disbanded and its chief scientist, Werner von Braun, was attached to the army, with instructions to produce a viable war rocket. In 1937, a rocket base was established at Peenemunde, an isolated peninsula on the Baltic coast. War made the invention of a suitable rocket-launched warhead a matter of urgency. The result was the A-4 liquid propelled rocket, later redesignated V-2 (V for *Vergeltungswaffen*, or revenge weapon).

V-2s on London

Of all the rocket weapons produced during the war, none was more advanced than the V-2. Just under 47 feet long the rocket was made up of four sections. The nose was a conical warhead constructed of quarter-inch thick mild steel and filled with Amatol, a high explosive that could withstand the stresses of a rocket launch. Below the warhead was the instrument section, containing the guidance and control mechanisms. The main body of the rocket was occupied by the two fuel tanks, alcohol on top, liquid oxygen on the bottom. The tail section held the rocket motor, the burning cups, vanes to impart spin, and the *venturi*, the narrow opening in the tail through which the jet of hot gases passed. The principle of the *venturi* was based on the theory that the narrower the opening the stronger the thrust.

For firing, the V-2 was placed on a massive steel ring (the firing table) and below this was placed a blast deflector. After the British bombing raids on Peenemunde in August, 1943, the V-2s were made mobile by preparing launching sites on railway cars and on trucks.

The rocket motor was ignited by a simple pinwheel device running horizontally inside the motor. The pinwheel, in turn, was ignited electrically by an outside cable which was disconnected just prior to firing. When the pinwheel was lit (by sparks showering through the exhaust nozzle) valves were opened to allow the fuel to flow into the motor under gravitational pull. If the fuel ignited successfully (giving, incidentally, a thrust of seven tons, not enough to lift the 14-ton rocket), the fuel pumps were activated and fed the alcohol and oxygen into the motor under great pressure. The pressure-fed motor produced a thrust of 27 tons, which was then sufficient to launch the rocket on its course. Every second, the rocket lost 260 pounds of weight in fuel consumed. The lighter the rocket

120

the faster it accelerated, until it reached burn-out stage and began its rapid descent to earth.

The first successful V-2 launch, covering a distance of 119·3 miles, took place at Peenemunde on October 3, 1942. For Werner von Braun it meant the fulfilment of years of effort and struggle and the first concrete step in placing man on the moon. To Hitler and the army generals it meant revenge, a great machine that would reverse the failing fortunes of war. Both von Braun and Hitler were right. The V-2 became the basis for all future space travel, but it also formed the basis for all modern guided missile systems.

By September, 1944, the first V-2s were ready for launching against the enemies of the Reich. The first two missiles were directed at Paris and fired on September 6. They had little success. Two days later the V-2 campaign shifted its focus onto England. From September through to March of the following year about 1,500 V-2s were sent hurtling across the Channel in a last desperate attempt to halt the closing of the noose around Germany's neck. By the end of the campaign over two and a half thousand people had been killed and almost six and a half thousand people seriously injured.

This was a mere dent compared to the effects of the Blitz, yet it did have the effect of causing plans to be drawn up for the evacuation of London – something which had not been done in the Blitz. The V-2 was a great breakthrough in military technology but, like the jet, it came too late to change substantially the course of the war. There was neither time to concentrate the V-2 bombings, nor to refine the rocket's guidance system.

Mobile launcher raising a V-2 into the firing position

A captured Yokosuka MXY-7 Okha

Katyusha, Okha and Bazooka

Though the Germans were undoubtedly in the lead in rocketry, experiments were being conducted in other countries. Three of the most deadly lesser rocket weapons to come out of the war were the Katyusha, the Okha and bazooka.

The Soviets have always been secretive about their military technology. Information about rocketry development is especially hard to come by, but it is known that they had been working on rocket-powered missiles as early as the 1930s. The most famous and the most numerous of the Soviet war rockets was the Katyusha, a solid-propellant infantry support weapon. The Katyusha was six feet long, five inches in diameter and weighed $92\frac{1}{2}$ pounds, of which more than half was payload. The rocket had a range of three miles and was fired from multi-tube batteries, which sprayed a dense barrage on the enemy. The Germans learned to respect the hitting power of the slim Katyusha on their many campaigns on the Eastern Front.

The Japanese effort was less conventional. They used rockets to power their tiny suicide planes in a last ditch effort to halt the advance of the Americans. The most successful of the suicide planes was the Okha, a wooden monoplane 20 feet long and 16 feet in span. The Okha carried a 2,645-pound bomb in its nose and was powered by three 1,200-pound thrust rocket engines, which after a 10 second burn, gave it a speed of 600 miles an hour. In combat the Okha was carried by a parent plane to within 50 miles of the target and, when released, it glided towards its target at a speed of about 235 miles an hour.

On spotting his objective, the pilot then ignited the engine and commenced his rocket-powered dive onto the enemy. A direct hit could sink an aircraft carrier. Though dangerous, there were not enough Okhas to make them a crucial factor in the war.

The Americans had a varied rocket programme during the war, but the best known rocket product was the bazooka, a rocket propelled grenade and the infantryman's friend. The prototype bazooka was seven feet long and 2·36 inches in diameter, although later versions were made more compact to suit combat conditions.

The bazooka was a revolutionary breakthrough in infantry weapons. It made the foot-slogging soldier the equal, under certain conditions, of the heavily armoured tank. It first saw service in North Africa in the autumn of 1942 and soon became standard equipment on all fronts.

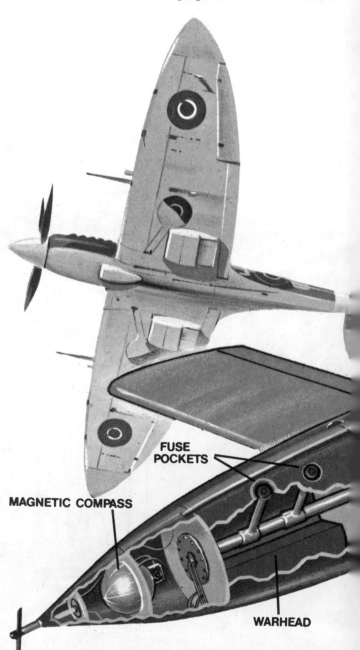

FUSE POCKETS

MAGNETIC COMPASS

WARHEAD

The Guided Missile

After the war the combination of guided missiles, rockets, and nuclear warheads resulted in the most awesome war machine known to man. Experiments with the guided missile had been going on since the early years of this century, but it was not until after the Second World War that guidance systems were joined to ballistic missiles. For years experimenters thought of the guided missiles as a pilotless aircraft.

As early as 1911, American scientists at the Delco and Sperry companies were experimenting with a pilotless biplane called the 'Bug'. The Bug weighed about 600 pounds, half of which was payload, and was powered by a 40 horse-power engine with a gyro-controlled flight direction. When the Bug had flown a predetermined distance a cam was automatically dropped pulling the bolts that attached the wings to the fuselage. The wingless aircraft plummeted, hopefully, on target.

A similar project was undertaken in England. Professor A. M. Low hoped to guide a 'flying bomb' to its target by radio. Development work continued at the Royal Aircraft Establishment at Farnborough, which resulted in monoplanes and biplanes being converted into flying bombs. The two most successful products were the *Queen Bee* and the *Queen Wasp*, both launched by catapult.

But it was the Germans, again, who took the first big step in perfecting a practical guided missile system. In 1942, German scientists began work on a long-range pilotless aircraft, coded Fieseler Fi-103, later redesignated V-1.

The major feature of the V-1 was its pulse-jet engine. The engine fed on gasoline and produced

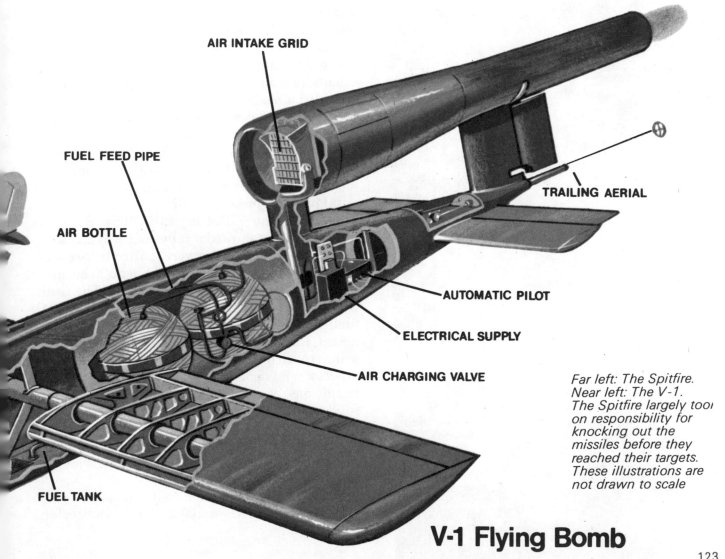

AIR INTAKE GRID

FUEL FEED PIPE

AIR BOTTLE

TRAILING AERIAL

AUTOMATIC PILOT

ELECTRICAL SUPPLY

AIR CHARGING VALVE

FUEL TANK

Far left: The Spitfire. Near left: The V-1. The Spitfire largely took on responsibility for knocking out the missiles before they reached their targets. These illustrations are not drawn to scale

V-1 Flying Bomb

a thrust of 1,000 pounds. The V-1 was 27 feet long with a 17·67-foot wing span and carried about 2,000 pounds of high explosive in its nose. Although the missile was guided by an automatic pilot its trajectory could not be changed once launched. It flew at a speed of 390 miles an hour, a speed which put it at the mercy of enemy fighters and anti-aircraft fire.

Like the V-2, the V-1 was a revolutionary development. Though it made no difference to the outcome of the war it established the trend for future guided missile systems.

From V-2 to Minuteman

The modern military missile is almost completely a product of the United States or the Soviet Union. No other country could possibly afford the great costs that these missile systems entail, although more recently some European countries have begun to develop missile weapons. German scientists captured by the Soviets and the Americans in 1945 established the nucleus of missile development in America and were permitted to take part on the missile development in the Soviet Union. Experiments after the war proceeded directly from where the German scientists had left off, namely the V-2 which provided a basis for further work.

The first successful American intermediate range ballistic missile was the Jupiter. This was simply an improved version of the V-2, but it opened the way for the most fearsome war machines in America's arsenal, the intercontinental ballistic missile (ICBM).

Work on the ICBM began in 1954. Six years later the Atlas showed a range of 9,000 miles. All three stages of the Atlas were ignited before take-off. It was felt that an ICBM would be more efficient if each stage fired separately. The result was the Titan. The Atlas and Titan were both fuelled by liquid oxygen and kerosene, which meant that the fuel could only be loaded just prior to firing. This was a time consuming process and possibly dangerous in wartime conditions. To achieve a faster rate of firing, solid and liquid fuels, that could be stored, had to be developed. An additional advantage of storable fuels was that the ICBMs could be kept in underground, concrete silos, impervious to anything but a direct hit.

Titan 2 was the first missile to use storable fuels. It is more than 100 feet tall and weighs

U.S. Air Force Atlas F ICBM begins a 4,000 mile flight

330,000 pounds. The first stage firing produces a thrust of 430,000 pounds. falling to 100,000 pounds of thrust on the second stage.

The Titan is a heavy, costly machine. The invention of smaller but equally powerful nuclear warheads led to the construction of a solid-propellant missile, the Minuteman – the most successful of the ICBMs.

The Minutemen, as the name implies, are quick-launch missiles, requiring only 32 seconds of pre-launch preparation. The first Minutemen series – LGM-30A – were 53 feet 9 inches long, weighed 60,000 pounds and had a one-megaton nuclear warhead capability with a range of more than 6,000 miles at a maximum speed of Mach 2·2. Guidance was provided by an inertia system.

Improvements led to the development of Minuteman 2 (LGM-30F). This was 59 feet 10 inches long and weighed 70,000 pounds. It had an increased range of approximately 2,000 miles with double the nuclear warhead capacity. Minuteman 2 became operational in 1966 and was destined to replace all previous models.

Multiple Warheads

A major breakthrough in missile systems came with the development of Multiple Independently targetable Re-entry Vehicles (MIRVs). As the name suggests, a MIRV missile possesses several nuclear warheads within one shell, each with its own separate target and guidance system.

The destructive potential of a nuclear warhead in ratio to its size diminishes rapidly beyond a certain point. Thus, a lesser but separate number of atomic blasts is far more effective than one single enormous strike. Since 1969, several Minutemen missiles have been equipped with three 0·2-megaton MIRV warheads.

The Soviet Union has deployed MIRVs in 'Scarp', one of their latest design missiles. This is a two-stage, liquid fuel propelled missile 113 feet 6 inches long with a diameter of 10 feet, which can carry up to three five-megaton MIRVs or a single 25 megaton warhead. It was assumed when Scarp came into operation that 500 of them could effectively destroy the entire United States' ICBM force. Latest research suggests a new factor – the *fratricide effect*. Most of the warheads would destroy one another rather than the target, by radiation from the first warhead, debris, or severe winds which would blow warheads off course.

A Minuteman ICBM on test aims towards a smoke ring

Honest John, a free flight missile, blazes skywards

Safeguard

It was this possibility that led to the development of the 'Safeguard' anti-ballistic missile system (ABM) in the United States.

Safeguard was made possible by recent advances in radar technology, specifically in the development of *phased array radar*. Conventional radar is limited in the amount of traffic it can handle. It uses electromagnetic radiation fed into a single-beam antenna which is mechanically revolved to do its job. In the phased array radar system there is a continuous emission of millions of beams in different directions on a computer-based time phasing. The antenna remains fixed and detection, location and tracking are done electronically, allowing for a greater number of objects to be handled.

In Safeguard, two sets of radar are at work. The *perimeter acquisition radar* (PAR) detects and locates hostile missiles. Once it has fixed position and trajectory of the incoming missile it 'hands over' to *missile site radar* (MSR).

MSR is linked to an intricate computer set-up and not only tracks the hostile missile but also discriminates between warheads and decoys. Once certain of its target it launches the Spartan missile for extra-atmospheric interception, being ready to follow-up with a terminal atmospheric interception by a Sprint missile.

Radar, however, would be practically ineffective in the case of bombardment by *fractional orbital bombs* (FOBS). Under the terms of the 1966 Outer Space Treaty it is illegal to send nuclear warheads into orbit. But anything under one complete orbit does not come within the terms of the treaty. The great advantage of fractional orbit delivery is the element of surprise. An ICBM, with its fixed parabolic trajectory, is a highly visible object. By sending a nuclear warhead into low orbit (approximately 100 miles above the earth) the bomb escapes long range radar detection. The FOB dropped vertically down allows only about three minutes warning. The disadvantages of FOBS are loss in accuracy (no pin-point bombing of missile stations), a reduced payload and a poor ratio of cost-effectiveness.

A Variety of Missiles

The missiles we have mentioned are only a few of those available in the vast and varied collection on the military market today. Rocket and missile technology is an enormous industry quite distinct from general military aviation. Advances are continually being made and the missiles themselves are becoming more and more specialized in their objectives. The range includes surface-to-air, surface-to-surface, surface-to-ship,

American missiles under heavy guard await the orders that will direct their lethal load

ship-to-surface, ship-to-air, ship-to-underwater, air-to-ship, air-to-air, and air-to-surface missiles.

For instance, there is the interesting and unique Quail which possesses no destructive capabilities, for it is an air launched decoy missile. The reinforced plastic body is stuffed full of electronic devices and stored in the bomb bay of the B-52 Stratofortress. Its stubby wings and fins collapse for easy storage. The Quail is powered by a 2,450-pound engine. Guidance is by automatic pilot. The Quail is 12 feet 10 inches long with a wing span of 5 feet 4 inches and weighs 1,230 pounds. It has a maximum speed of 600 miles an hour and a range of 245 miles. As the parent plane approaches enemy territory the

Top: Hughes AIM-54A Phoenix, long range air-to-air missile, range about 200 km. (125 miles), speed about mach 5+ (4000+ mph). Shown here being fired from a U.S. Navy Grumman F-14A Tomcat fighter, whose AWG-9 computer can control six Phoenix missiles fired at six different targets simultaneously. Above: McDonnell-Douglas AGM-84A Harpoon, anti-ship missile which can be fired from surface ships, sea patrol aircraft or submarines. Range about 60–80 km. (37–50 miles). Can be fired over horizon. Lower right: Manpads (Man-Portable Air Defence System). Designed to replace Redeye missile, which gives the smallest army unit or patrol the ability to defend itself against air attack. Missile homes on target using an infra-red seeker to pick out the 'hottest spot in the sky'—the jet exhaust close to the aircraft's tail

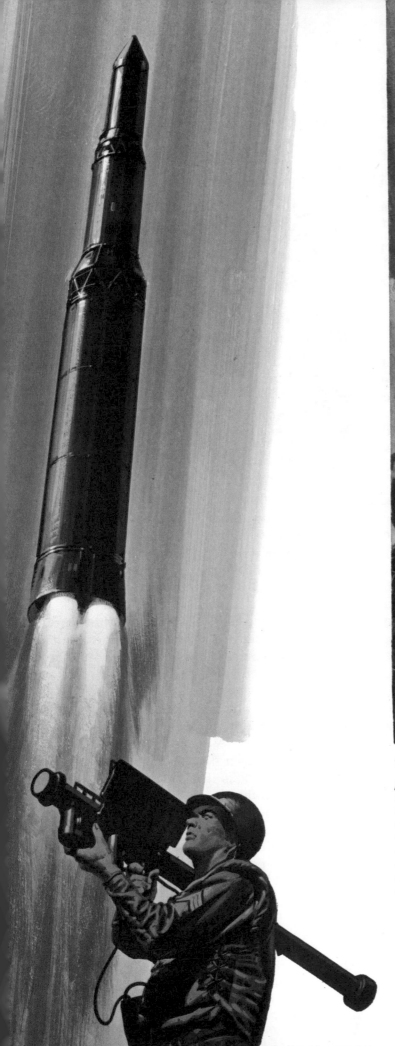

Above left: Soviet SS-13 ICBM (NATO code-name
'Savage') — Intercontinental Ballistic Missile
powered by three-stage solid-fuelled booster
rocket. Length 20 metres (65·5 feet), range
8,000–10,500 km. (about 5,000–7,000 miles).
Carries multiple nuclear warheads. Steered by
inertial guidance system, which corrects its
own course automatically, given point of
departure and point of target.
Above: Lockheed UGM-73A Poseidon C-3 —
submarine-launched ICBM replacing the
famous Polaris missile in three-quarters
of the U.S. Navy's 616-class FBM (Fleet
Ballistic Missile) nuclear submarines. Each
submarine carries 16 missiles, each reported to
carry 10–14 individual warheads. Maximum range
2,500 nautical miles.

Quail is released and acts as a powerful confusing and jamming force. Without it, bombing operations would be almost impossible, for the B-52 could not penetrate the enemy's radar screen.

This particular electronic counter measure (ECM) is just one of many developed in the past few years in a new area of warfare tagged 'the electronic battlefield'.

Senator Barry Goldwater, in United States Senate hearings on the electronic battlefield (Nov. 1970), said: 'I personally think it (i.e. electronic warfare) has the possibility of being one of the greatest steps forward in warfare since the invention of gunpowder.'

The Shape of War to Come

Perhaps we should conclude our review of aerial war machines by taking a brief look at the shape of any future warfare. Like rocketry and guided missiles, electronic warfare is a vast industry which cuts right across army, navy and air force subdivisions. Let us look at a few devices used by the United States Air Force in the war in Vietnam.

In order to fight you must find the enemy, which is not as simple as it sounds given the conditions of guerrilla warfare. Thus, one of the primary functions of electronics is in enemy detection, what is known as *sensor aided combat* (SAC). SAC is a surveillance system which consists of detection devices (sensors) which pick up movements of vehicles or troops; a communications link (usually radio) from the sensor to a 'readout' device. The information is then processed by computer and appropriate instructions relayed to strike aircraft.

The USAF operation of the system, code name IGLOO WHITE, in South East Asia (working out to Laos) was entirely air supported. Sensors were air delivered and the information relayed to aircraft which was then processed in a computer ground station, although some aircraft have processing capabilities. Among some of the sensors used were (a) ACOUSID (acoustic and seismic intrusion detection), (b) COMMIKE (commandable microphone) and (c) ADSID (air delivered seismic intrusion detector).

ADSID, for instance, is dropped and implanted into the ground to the depth of its breastplate, which stops it disappearing completely under the surface, leaving only a camouflaged antenna. Further specifications remain classified.

ACOUSID, 48 inches long with a 3-inch dia-

A detail from Ferranti's laser ranger

meter and weighing 37 pounds, contains only seismic detection logic; that is, it can pick up the tremors of vehicles or personnel. But it can also transmit audio information by means of a small, remotely controlled microphone at the base of the antenna.

According to the testimony of the generals before the United States investigating committee, the sensor devices have been invaluable in detecting and thus leading to the destruction of enemy forces.

Electronics warfare has also affected munitions development, such as in the guided bomb, in which a small TV camera transmits pictures of the terrain to a display unit in the cockpit. The aircrew locks the bomb on the desired target then homes in on the picture onto which it has been locked.

Also in use is a laser guided 2,000-lb. all-purpose bomb. Specifications remain classified but this does point to the future of war machines in the age of limited war.

Progress on remote controlled aerial vehicles and further development in the electronics field point to a state of war where the machines will fight it out while personnel become redundant. Undoubtedly, as in industry, complete automation is the ultimate development.

Above: The QUAIL was a useful decoy missile. Below: The Ferranti laser target marker

An Egyptian papyrus boat used on the River Nile, c.3000 B.C.

WAR AT SEA

THE EARLY SEAFARERS

At Medinet Habu, in the tomb of Egypt's last great pharaoh, Ramses III, there is a carving of a naval engagement fought between the Egyptians and the dreaded 'people from the sea'. The carving is significant for it is the first extant illustration of a naval combat. There must have been many hostile encounters on the sea prior to that battle, for wherever men gather there arise conflicts of interest. Yet no earlier ones are

The earliest surviving illustration of naval combat, from the tomb of Ramses III (c. 1200 B.C.). Shows the use of archers and spearmen.

recorded. Evidently, Ramses III's battle is the first one to impress itself on the minds of the ancients. In effect this is where the history of naval warfare begins. What were the early sea-fights like? What kind of boats were in use and how were they manned? And what were the weapons that gave final victory to Ramses?

More than two thousand years of experience went into the construction of Ramses' warships. Egyptians were river people. They depended almost completely on the Nile for their livelihood and for centuries they had built boats and sailed and paddled on the broad back of the Nile.

The earliest boats were constructed of the most readily available material – papyrus. The papyrus boats were spool-shaped with pointed prows bent upward to enable easy shore handling. They were paddled, though a rectangular mast was situated in the forward part of the craft.

It is not until much later (*c*.3000 B.C.) that we find illustrations of oarsmen. The exchange of paddle for oar was a major innovation, for the oar proved to be a much more flexible and controlled means of propulsion. For the next 4500 years oars were to be the main motive force for all warships until the coming of the cannon made the sail a more practicable alternative.

Egypt under the pharaohs became a richer nation and was able to import wood for its vessels. The wooden boats were built in a peculiar fashion which was to remain the norm for centuries to come. Since the Egyptians had not then come upon the idea of ribs, thick wooden blocks held

Bas-relief of Egyptian ships from the tomb of Sahu-Re, c.3000 B.C. Note the cable stretching from fore to aft, used to prevent the extremities from drooping.

together by wooden pegs were used instead. Water pressure forced the blocks together while at either end ropes were tied round the hull to strengthen the structure.

From the rivers, the Egyptians made ever widening excursions into the Mediterranean. For the longer sea voyages the boats had to be further strengthened as well as prepared to meet the forces of the hostile naval powers of Crete and Phoenicia. Thick blocks were still the basic method of construction but for additional support a strong twisted rope was stretched over several queen posts fore and aft. In addition the bipod mast was collapsible, allowing easier manoeuvrability for the oarsmen in unfavourable weather or when engaged in military action. The oarsmen stood, thus gaining greater impetus and speed. The relief carvings on the pyramids at Abu Sir also show stem and stern posts – the fore post carrying the protective, all-seeing eye of Osiris.

Around 1500 B.C. Queen Hatshepsut sent a convoy of ships to the land of Punt. The temple at Deir el Bahari has detailed relief carvings of her vessels. The general features were the same as the earlier ones but in detail the ships had improved. The hulls were constructed around a high and strong keel-plank which projected up and inward in the aft while projecting forward in the fore. The mast was moved closer to the centre and the square sail became considerably larger. Two great steering oars with tillers replaced the six small steering oars in the bow.

Three hundred years later (1200 B.C.), Ramses III built a fleet that was to defeat the invaders from the north. His ships were basically the same as those of Queen Hatshepsut yet a few important

An Egyptian sea-going vessel of about 2500 B.C. Ships like this were tougher than they may have looked. This one has just left port and is heading for the open sea. The crew are raising the mast from its support amidships, preparing to set sail.

adaptations were made, borrowings from the maritime invaders.

Interesting new features were the high washboards to protect the oarsmen; furling of sails by means of vertical brails, an advancement over the previously existing necessity of lowering the yard; and a crow's nest atop the mast. The ships were about 80 to 90 feet long and usually carried about 30 oarsmen in addition to military personnel.

The invaders, the 'northerners of the isles', were a tough sea-faring people from the Aegean Islands and the Mediterranean coast line. Driven from their own bases they moved southwards to Egypt. The relief at Medinet Habu shows the invaders in full sail, in other words unprepared for combat. For until the coming of the cannon naval combat meant hand-to-hand fighting, ramming or archery. All these manoeuvres depended on skilful oarsmanship. Sails did not allow the necessary flexibility in battle, and the ram had as yet not been invented.

Quite rightly, since it was the Egyptians who had first discovered the oar (c.3000 B.C.), 1800 years later Ramses was able to prove his supreme skill with it in battle. Caught unawares, sails still flying, the invaders suffered a crushing defeat. Egypt was saved. Unfortunately, the death of Ramses III signalled the decline of Egypt and it is to the rude maritime peoples of the north that we must look for further developments in warships.

THE PENTEKONTER AND THE POWER OF THE RAM

For several centuries (about 1100 B.C. to 800 B.C.) the Phoenicians were the undoubted masters of the Mediterranean. Their ships roamed the seas from the shores of Syria to Carthage in northern Africa, to the Atlantic coast of Spain on the outskirts of the then known world, and even beyond in an aggressive search for trade and wealth.

Because they were a trading nation the Phoenicians had to develop a powerful naval fighting force to protect their trade routes. Necessity led to creative experimentation in the shipwright's craft and to the first significant improvements in ship design.

The earliest warships of the northern Mediterranean were large narrow dug-outs. The dug-outs had sharp jutting rams but these were merely extensions of the main body of the vessel and not specialized for military purposes. The dug-outs were fitted with outriggers to handle the oars.

To increase the fighting power of the vessel the Phoenicians developed the *pentekonter* – a type of bireme (i.e. a galley with two banks of oars). The basic design of the dug-out was maintained but the outriggers were planked-in allowing for an extra rank of rowers. The top thwart extended outward from the hull leaving room for the extra rank on a lower level below the raised decks. The inner oars were placed through oar ports cut out of the hull.

The pentekonter was approximately 60 feet long and carried 50 oarsmen. The ram had by now become a powerful weapon and extended from the hull into a sharp point just below water level. The mast was situated amidships and carried a large square sail. The supports of the narrow upper deck tied the thwarts to the bottom of the boat and stiffened the whole structure. At maximum efficiency the pentekonter could race at six knots.

Above: Side section of the pentekonter, showing the ram projecting forward below the water line.
Left: Outriggers provided space for a second bank of oarsmen and left room for soldiers in the centre of the vessel.

Officers and soldiers were stationed on the narrow upper deck while the rowers had their weapons ready. In battle they stayed by their oars.

The advantages of the new design were many. The narrow, easily propelled hull of the dug-out was maintained; a narrow deck for soldiers and archers was added without upsetting the efficiency of the oarsmen or the balance of the vessel; and, finally, with the addition of an extra rank of rowers, the vessel moved at a greater speed enabling a much more powerful ramming force.

The pentekonter, undoubtedly, proved its worth many times in maintaining Phoenician supremacy on the sea for such a long period. And even when Phoenician power was on the decline, challenged by the young, upstart city states of Greece, the pentekonter proved itself a weapon to be feared.

An early bas-relief of a Phoenician pentekonter. These were the ships that established the Phoenician empire.

The Battle of Alalia

The Phocaeans were the first of the Greeks to perform long voyages and to establish colonies in the western Mediterranean, in what was once the sole preserve of the Phoenicians. But not only did they set up colonies, they also began to harrass their neighbours and indulge in piracy. This the Phoenicians would not stand.

Together with their Etruscan allies they gathered 60 men of war and sailed to Alalia in Corsica where the Phocaeans had their head-quarters. Though the Phocaeans had also mustered 60 ships they were no match for the Phoenicians, whose ships, fitted with bronze and wooden rams, demolished the Phocaean fleet in a matter of hours. Two-thirds of their fleet was destroyed and the rest had their rams so badly wrenched as to make them unfit for service. The Battle of Alalia was important in two respects. First, it prevented the Mediterranean from becoming a Greek lake; and second, it determined the nature of naval warfare to come. The role of the ram was thenceforth established. The first move had been taken to distinguish naval tactics from land tactics. No longer was a preponderance of soldiers and archers necessary for victory. Victory depended more on the speed and sturdiness of the vessel and the skill of the oarsmen and captain to manoeuvre the ship properly in battle.

THE TRIREME RULES THE SEA

The Greeks were quick to learn from the Phoenicians and they soon developed their own biremes which further advanced the shipwright's art.

The bireme was more than just an extension of the dug-out; it was a ribbed ship with a proper keel and a carvel-built hull which provided stability and strength in the face of enemy ramming.

The two hundred years from 500 B.C. to 300 B.C. constituted the classical age of Greek shipping, which saw the development of some of the most graceful ships ever known, ships that were light, sturdy and elegant of line. And the prince of the classical ships was the trireme.

No other ship has caused as much difficulty in

interpretation as the trireme. Like the bireme, it was born out of a desire to create a faster ship which would not lose anything in lightness, manoeuvrability or sturdiness. The faster the ship the greater ramming power it possessed and speed depended on the number of oarsmen that could be fitted into a vessel. The problem was, therefore, to add another bank of rowers on to existing vessels without making them cumbersome.

There are a few generally accepted facts about the trireme. We know that its maximum length was 135 feet with a beam of about 20 feet; that it lay low in the water with eight feet of freeboard above the waterline and a draught of approximately three feet. We also know that it had a crew of around 200, including 170 oarsmen known as *thalamites* (27 to a side), *zeugites* (27) and *thranites* (31). The remaining crew were made up of officers and military personnel, which usually included foot-soldiers and archers.

There was little storage room on the trireme, which meant that it had to be close to land bases to restock on supplies. The mast, situated amidships, was, was lowered in time of battle.

The whole ship was considered as a weapon and eventually the ram became a separate, detachable instrument which could be replaced when necessary. The early triremes were incompletely decked and the top row of oarsmen would be protected by the shields of soldiers placed on the outrigger. Difficulties in interpretation arise when we look at the actual seating of the oarsmen. There are two main theories which try to resolve the question, both nautically sound but there is little direct evidence for the first.

This theory holds that the thwarts were placed at an oblique angle running from the centre line of the ship forward and outward. Two oarsmen (the outermost were the thranites, the ones nearest to the centre-line the zeugites) sat side by side on the upper thwart and had their oars running through ports on the outrigger. The third oarsman (the thalamite) would swing his oar between the upper two and have it run through a port in the hull just above the water-line.

The second, and more likely, theory states that the oarsmen were in three rows one above the other, the oarsman above seated a little forward of the one below him.

Far Left: Three ranks of oarsmen gave additional speed to the trireme but created seating problems. Below: A trireme of the 4th Century B.C., with a fearsome ram, two stern rudders and a sail full set. Triremes were responsible for the Greek's stirring victory against the invading Persian fleet at Salamis.

THE FORMIDABLE FIRE–SHIP

Even the victory against the Persians at Salamis, where the trireme triumphed, could not stop the Greek city-states from quarrelling amongst themselves; a quarrel which finally erupted into the thirty years long Peloponnesian War, a war which doomed Greece's fragile independence. To the west, however, a new world power was slowly gathering strength. That power was Rome.

The Romans were quick to learn the art of shipbuilding as they spread across, first the Italian peninsula, and then, further afield, the Mediterranean. Rome came to depend on its ships for its daily bread and for the transport of troops to protect its far-flung empire.

Their first ships were biremes and triremes on the Greek model. But the Roman taste for size soon asserted itself; the triremes became quinqueremes and septiremes – that is, vessels with five or seven banks of oarsmen. The deck became completely covered and a fighting tower was erected in the stern. These ships were formidable indeed yet curiously enough it was not the quinquereme or the septireme but the lowly fire-ship which decided the fate of the Empire.

A fire-ship is an old, unmanned ship filled with combustible materials. In combat it is set alight and directed at the enemy fleet in the hope of setting it on fire. Wooden ships were very vulnerable to that sort of tactic and fire-ships, if used effectively, could be deadly. They had never been used so effectively before as at the Battle of Actium (31 B.C.).

Right: A Roman warship. This trireme has a double steering paddle, one on each side. There is a fighting tower at the front, soldiers on the deck and a small but highly effective ram at the prow. Above: Another example of a Roman warship.

Marc Antony's Defeat at Actium

Actium is the promontory on the south side of the entrance to the Gulf of Ambracia (today Arta) in northwestern Greece. In ancient times Actium was situated in unhealthy marshland that harboured disease-carrying insects. It was at Actium in 32 B.C. that Marc Antony set up a base camp preparatory to an attack on Italy.

Ever since the assassination of Julius Caesar the Roman Republic had been beset by factional strife and civil war. Thirteen years later only two contestants were left in the arena – Octavian, Caesar's grand-nephew and designated heir, and Marc Antony, Caesar's lieutenant. With the aid of Cleopatra and the wealth of Egypt Antony had set up a powerful mini-kingdom in the east. But it was Rome that he wanted.

Antony's main supply lines lay along the Peloponnesian coast stretching from Patras in the north to Methane in the south-west, to Corinth and from there by sea to Egypt and Asia. The supply line was as vital to Antony as, four and a half centuries earlier, it had been to the Persians – Greece was still much too poor a country to support a large invading force.

While Antony gathered troops and material and waited for an auspicious time for the crossing, Agrippa, Octavian's naval commander and a brilliant tactician, massed his fleet of small, light and very fast ships at Brindisium. He quickly crossed the Adriatic, setting up a post north of Antony's. Instead of offering battle immediately Agrippa shrewdly began to erode Antony's supply routes. One by one Antony's garrisons fell – Methane, Patras and finally Corinth. Agrippa occupied the island of Leucas, just south of the Gulf of Ambracia, a base closer to the enemy.

Antony's army, hungry, ill and demoralized, began to fall apart. The number of desertions

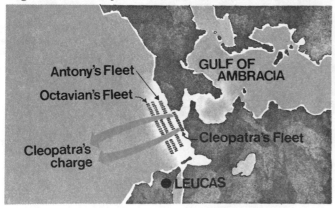

Antony and Cleopatra escaped but lost at Actium

increased daily. Antony had to act soon or he would have had no army left to fight with, much less conquer an empire. It was necessary to put aside his dream of taking Rome in the interests of survival. He had to find some way back to Egypt and comparative safety. Once back he could refurbish his forces and set out anew, wiser and more wary of his cunning foe. But first – how to get back? The overland route was too hazardous and, besides, would take much too long. His only choice was to break Agrippa's sea blockade. On September 2, 31 B.C., Antony readied his fleet for battle and flight, a fleet which was composed of the large and somewhat cumbersome quinqueremes and septiremes, which, to add to their awkwardness, had timber structures fitted to the hulls as anti-ramming devices.

As the morning progressed the fleets drew into position. The forces of Octavian lay in wait at the entrance to the Gulf. Octavian held the honoured right flank, Agrippa the left, where he could expect to face Antony.

Antony's force issued forth slowly, cautiously

Left: Detail of the Battle of Actium, 31 B.C. Note the blazing ship in the foreground. Agrippa, Octavian's general, broke the stalemate at Actium by the unconventional use of fire-ships
Right: Marc Antony. He gambled everything at Actium and lost.
Below: Cleopatra at Actium. She waited for a chance to break through, then made for home.

hugging the shore line. A squadron of 60 Egyptian warships under Cleopatra's command kept to the rear. Antony moved from ship to ship giving orders and encouraging his men. He ordered them to stay put and wait for the enemy to move first. But the enemy refused to act. Agrippa had patience and plenty of time. If the battle was not joined today then it would be tomorrow. Each day would see a further attrition of morale in the camp of Marc Antony.

The day dragged. Marc Antony grew nervous and impatient with the waiting. At last, unable to restrain himself any longer, he gave the signal to attack. The left wing opened by advancing towards the enemy. Agrippa countered by moving northward to entice Antony's ships to move forward and apart from each other. The stratagem worked and Agrippa's faster ships were able to converge in lightning attacks on Antony's solitary vessels. Swiftly moving in and out, Agrippa's ships caused havoc by ramming or, more frequently, by stripping the enemy's oars which were too heavy to be shipped quickly. Even so no rout was to be had. Antony's ships

were cumbersome but they were sturdy and his men fought hard and valiantly.

Meanwhile Cleopatra, seeing her chance, broke through both centre lines and sailed for home, followed close at heel by Antony.

Despite Antony's desertion the battle raged on as fiercely as ever. On both sides the fighting men were Romans, strongly disciplined in their trade and with similar methods of battle.

Agrippa was no usual commander, however. He earned his name by his ingenuity and his ability to apply novel methods of fighting in battle. He fought to win, not as a gentleman's game of honour. So when, at Actium, the usual methods of combat did not produce the desired result he brought out the flame throwers and the fire-ships. Catapults tossed blazing missiles (pots of flaming charcoal and pitch) at the enemy. Rafts laden with combustible materials were set alight and thrown into the ranks of Antony's fleet. By late afternoon the battle was over. Antony's forces could not stand up to this kind of assault. Antony's fate was sealed. Octavian had proved himself master of Rome.

THE DROMON – A COASTAL RUNNER

For 250 years thereafter the Mediterranean remained a Roman sea. The Roman fleet reverted to being a kind of coast guard protecting the shipping lanes and suppressing piracy wherever it arose. As the Roman Empire crumbled under the impact of barbarian invasions all attention was concentrated on beating back the Germanic and Asiatic invaders. These were essentially land affairs and little money or time or energy was left for the development of the navy.

In the east the Byzantine Empire became stabilized and revived the coast guard activities of the old Roman navy. A type of warship was evolved which became known as the *dromon*, literally 'the runner'.

Not much is known of the dromon but, as its name indicates, it was presumably a fast warship with 50 thwarts on two levels making for a total

The Dromon was a fast coastguard runner, developed by the Byzantine Empire. The lethal ram was retained, raised above the water line perhaps to give added speed and to break up the oars of the enemy vessel. With ships like these, the Byzantines defeated the Gothic invaders.

of 100 oarsmen. Later on the ship was equipped with a forecastle which was used as a fighting tower. Another interesting feature was that the ram was elevated well above the water line.

Eventually, the dromon became a general term for warships and several types developed, such as the Pamphylian Chelander – a smaller and lighter version of the earlier dromon; or the galea, which was an armed reconnaissance boat.

The Battle of Sena Gallica

The first important naval battle of the regenerated fleet took place in the reign of Justinian I (482–565). He had established peace with the Persians on his eastern frontier and was eager to reunite the Roman Empire. And over a period of 30 years his aims were achieved by two very remarkable generals – Belisarius and the Armenian eunuch, Narses.

Belisarius had done much to reconquer Italy from the Goths but Byzantine politics and the lack of adequate military back-up support, led him to resign his commission. The Goths rapidly encroached on the conquered territory and were soon at the doors of Ancona, the gateway to the Adriatic.

The Byzantines had to obtain a foothold in the Adriatic in order to ferry troops and supplies to the Italian peninsula. At Salona, on the Greek side of the Adriatic, a combined force of army and navy was being assembled. By the summer of 551 the forces only awaited the arrival of Narses to lead them on to victory.

Narses, however, was delayed in Constantinople on Imperial business and in the meanwhile the situation was growing critical on the Italian side of the peninsula. Ravenna, the last Byzantine stronghold on the peninsula, could not hold out much longer against its besiegers. Valerian, its commander, sent a desperate request to Salona for reinforcements to avert disaster.

Happily, Narses had as a subordinate an able commander who took the initiative at this crucial juncture. With 38 dromons he crossed the Adriatic and joined Valerian's fleet of 12. Together they sailed to Sena Gallica, about 17 miles northwest of Ancona.

The Gothic force of about 47 vessels hurried northwards to offer battle. The fleets faced each other – the Byzantines, with their greater experience of the sea, in an orderly and well spaced line; the novice Gothic seamen huddled together in close formation.

The Goths, pursuing their land tactics, rushed forward in a massive attack in an attempt to grapple with the enemy. But what worked on land did not work at sea. Their ships collided, a lot of time was wasted separating themselves from tangles and meanwhile the Byzantine archers, taking careful aim, picked off the Goths and rammed their ships.

The Goths were helpless. The engagement was a total defeat for them, with a loss of 36 ships.

GREEK FIRE HALTS THE SARACEN

Soon the Byzantine emperors had more pressing concerns than a distant empire in the west. A new and very dangerous enemy had arisen in the east – the Saracens. But at the same time the Byzantines developed what was undoubtedly the single most powerful weapon in the ancient world – Greek fire, and it was with Greek fire that the Saracen onslaught was stayed.

In 622 Muhammed made his famous *hegira* (or pilgrimage) to Medina and established an Islamic brotherhood of the Arabic tribes. In the years to come the Arab tribes, fired by the passion of their new religion, spread across the greater part of the then known world from Persia to the western coasts of Spain. But in their path stood a seemingly weak and degenerate Empire – Byzantium. An easy conquest, the Arabs thought. Yet over and over again the Byzantines exhibited a great resilience and inner strength. And although her territories were slowly eaten away over the years she did not finally succumb until 1453 to the steamrolling power of a rising eastern nation, the Ottoman Turks. Twice the Saracens tried to capture Constantinople, the capital and heart of the Empire, and twice they failed. Byzantine ingenuity defeated the massed attacks of the Arab navies. For when the Saracens arrived at the gates of Constantinople they were greeted by the awesome and overpowering force of Greek fire.

Greek fire was the name given to a series of incendiary compounds consisting of, in various proportions and combinations, naphtha, bitumen, pitch, sulphur, vegetable gums, resins of coniferous trees, turpentine and oil. Often quick lime was added to make 'moist fire' so called because water would greatly increase its volatility. A perfect weapon against the fire-prone wooden vessels of those days.

Greek fire placed in closed earthen pots with an attached wick would be catapulted or thrown by hand at the enemy. On ships, however, the more usual means of fire was through long copper tubes placed in the bow.

The tubes were shaped into gargoyles, horrendous masks of fabulous monsters meant to instil panic in the enemy. A pneumatic device worked the actual firing mechanism, blowing the compound through the tube where it would be lit as it emerged from the other end. A contemporary account describes how the compound would 'burst into flame and fall like a streak of lightning on the faces of the men opposite'.

It is difficult to conceive the great horror caused by the sudden unleashing of that monstrous weapon. Nothing like it had been seen before. More than 500 years after its invention John of Joinville called it 'a dragon flying through the air'.

In 900 the Emperor Leo VI, the Wise, wrote of the 'fire prepared in tubes (issuing forth) with a noise of thunder, a fiery smoke which burns the ship at which it is directed'.

The Siege of Constantinople

When the Caliph Walid died in 715 the Arabian Empire stretched from Asia to Spain. Yet the Byzantine Empire lay like a thorn in its side. The great expedition against Constantinople in 677 had ended in miserable failure with most of the retreating Moslem fleet lost in a storm. For the next 40 years or so internal disputes prevented a renewal of hostilities. Finally peace was

In the simpler form of bellows, the burning mixture was poured down the barrel and then blown quickly out again. The ladles and pot were used for pouring and brewing the fire.

In the more sophisticated bellows, the mixture was kept on the boil in the built-in pot. A valve stopped it from being sucked back into the bellows themselves.

restored in the land and in 715 Suleiman assumed the Caliphate. He was determined to humble the Byzantines.

Constantinople, the object of the Saracen attack, was a virtually impregnable fortress. It was located on a promontory flanked on the north by the Golden Horn and on the south by the Sea of Marmosa. To the west lay a strong double wall – one of the finest military fortifications of antiquity. The Imperial fleet lay in the Golden Horn protected by a chain that lay across the narrow opening to the sea.

The only way to take the city was by starving it out, which was the plan adopted by the Arabs. Suleiman appointed his brother, Moslemah, commander-in-chief of the armed forces, while Suleiman the General was to command the fleet. Victory depended on a complete blockade of Constantinople by land and sea.

On August 15, 717, Moslemah arrived before Constantinople with an army 80,000 strong.

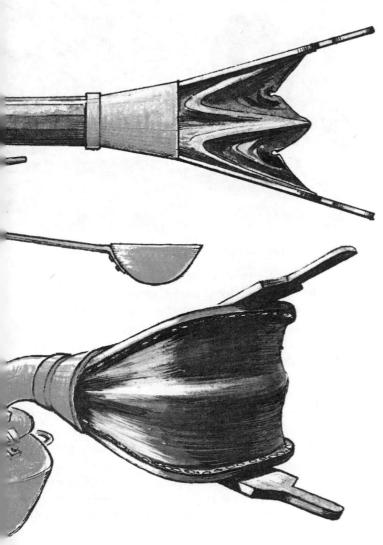

Immediately he set about digging a deep ditch round the city. However, the crucial factor lay at sea. For not only did the Saracen fleet have to supply all the necessities of the besiegers, it also had to cut off Byzantine communications both to the north and south.

Suleiman the General sailed into Byzantine waters with a fleet of 1,800 warships and fast sailers, two weeks after Moslemah had positioned his forces. The fleet was divided into two detachments: one stationed at Eutropicus on the Asiatic coast, to cut off supplies from the Aegean; the other was to move through the Bosphorous above the city and cut off communications with the Black Sea and the rich grain fields of the north.

On September 3, 717, the second squadron set sail for its objective. As it approached the Golden Horn, Leo, the Byzantine Emperor, ordered the great chain to be lowered and in a lightning attack let loose the ship-destroying Greek fire. Twenty enemy vessels were smashed before the rest of the party retreated to the safety of the Horn. The guerrilla raid proved so successful that Leo kept the boom lowered hoping thus to lure the remainder of the squadron into the narrow isthmus where it could be destroyed at leisure. Fearing a trap, the enemy declined the proposal. Constantinople remained open to her vital supplies.

The coming of winter saw the death of the caliph and of Suleiman the General. The Saracen troops were decimated by the cold and disease, yet they persisted in their folly. Further reinforcements were sent in the spring, when a squadron of 400 Egyptian ships managed to sneak into the Bosphorous, succeeding where Suleiman had failed. Constantinople faced the prospect of a slow death by starvation.

Fortunately for Leo most of the enemy crew were impressed Christian slaves and many of these deserted. They were able to provide Leo with precise details on the enemy formation. Acting quickly Leo lowered the boom and caught the Moslem fleet by surprise. The copper mouths spewed their deadly fire, the Christian crew rose up in rebellion against their masters, and soon the enemy vessels were easily subjugated. Leo had won a decisive naval victory. The back of the siege was broken. On August 15, 718, one year to the date of its inception, the siege was lifted and the Arab army retreated south in ignominy. It was a great victory for the Byzantines thanks to the destructive power of Greek fire.

THE VIKING LONGSHIP

For the next major developments in maritime warfare we must turn our attention northward where the Viking longship set new standards of ship construction. At the same time that the elaborate and sophisticated Byzantine court was fighting for its life in the semi-tropical waters of the Mediterranean there appeared in Northern Europe a fearless race of warriors who were making the sea their second home – the Vikings.

The peninsular nature of Scandanavia, her innumerable fjords, and the difficulty of access through the interior made it natural for the Vikings to take to the water. They led a harsh life governed by the strict code of the fighter. The skalds, their national epics, spoke of great contests and mighty deeds in battle. And many of the most famous battles took place on the sea.

As in other parts of the world the Viking warship, the longship, was an adaptation of existing shipping, either fishing or merchant

Gokstad ship, showing fixed rudder (without tiller).

vessels. Their ships, however, differed radically from those in the Levant. Naturally so, for the challenges that the Viking shipwright had to face were of a different sort from those in the Mediterranean. The northern seas were harsher and more turbulent than those in the south. The Viking ship had to withstand greater stress, especially on the long, lone voyages across the Atlantic. Finally, the enemies they faced were fellow Vikings, not some alien power. And in battle honour was to be had by honest fighting, not by the cunning blow of the ram to the rear.

One of the earliest and most finely preserved examples of the Viking ship is the Gokstad vessel dated to the 10th Century. Not quite a longship,

Clinker-built and riveted this Viking ship has a

it provides the prototype of the Viking warship. Seventy-nine feet long and sixteen feet across at its widest point, the Gokstad ship stands as a tribute to the skill of her builders.

The Viking warship was clinker-built with the hull planks overlapping each other and held together by rivets. The Gokstad ship has 16 strakes on either side and her keel, bows and stern are made of one piece. There are 16 oarports on either side with wooden discs attached to them to prevent seepage of water. There are no thwarts and it is likely that the oarsmen sat on removable benches or on their sea-chests. A mast situated slightly forward of amidships stood directly on the keel and carried a large square

fixed rudder to starboard. Note the supports for the sails when lowered and, of course, the protective value of the shields.

sail. A fixed rudder on the starboard side was manipulated by a small tiller. The ends of the vessel curved up and out and in time of battle were festooned with elaborately carved dragons' heads. A replica of the Gokstad ship was built for the Chicago World Fair of 1893 and crossed the Atlantic in 28 days, going as fast as 11 knots under sail.

The actual longships were of similar design, though we find a raised platform in the forepeak – the beginnings of the forecastle. Longships were classified according to the number of rooms they possessed. A room was the space between deck beams, with each room carrying a pair of oars. Thus the great longships of 30 or 40 rooms carried 60 and 80 oarsmen respectively. The Viking warship, unlike her counterparts in the south, was not fitted with a ram and battles were decided by hand-to-hand combat; the arms of the oarsman the same as the soldier – sword, axe, spear, and bow.

The most famous of the longships was the 34-roomed *Ormen Lange* ('Long Serpent') built for Olav Tryggvason in the year 1000. It was not the vessel, however, that counted in combat but the manpower and, in the renowned Battle of Svolde (1000 A.D.), Tryggvason was defeated by the overwhelmingly superior force of Sven Forkbeard who subsequently took possession of Norway.

THE STURDY MEDIEVAL COG

Well into the middle ages the ships of northern Europe were modelled on the Viking longship. Then in the 12th and 13th Centuries significant improvements were made, improvements which transformed the oared longship into the sailing man-of-war.

The first of these innovations was the invention of the stern rudder. Hitherto the rudder had been attached to the starboard side of the vessel. This proved admirable as long as the ship was oared or sailed *leeward* (against the wind). But as soon as merchants, for reasons of economy, wished to take full advantage of wind it became necessary to find an alternate position for the rudder. For if the vessel sailed *windward* (with the wind), with the wind blowing starboard, the side rudder would be swept out of the water. Thus the curved stem gave way to the straight stern post to which a rudder could be hung quite easily.

In the south the low-lying galleys operated a double rudder system, one on either side, but eventually the superiority of the stern rudder (in terms of ease of handling and greater control and manoeuvrability) proved itself and was adapted for their use as well.

The second innovation was the deep-draught hull. The Viking ships had been shallow built for greater speed but it was soon discovered, again by merchants with an eye to cargo space, that a ship with a deep hull, though slower, made a much better sailer.

To take advantage of these improvements better sailing techniques and rigging had to be developed. For instance if a ship was *close-hauled*, in other words brought as near as possible to the wind, it was found that the vertical edge of the sail would flap and curl in the wind, reducing its effectiveness. Thus *bowlines* attached midway down the edge of the sail were invented. In smaller ships it was necessary to extend the bowlines beyond the stem, which led to the invention of the *bowsprit*, a shaft protruding from the stem of the vessel.

So by a slow and often laborious hit-and-miss method progress was made. The Viking longship became the early medieval *nef* and that in turn was transformed into the one-masted *cog*. Over two centuries, from the mid 13th to mid 15th, the cog was the most prominent ship, either for war or peace, in northern waters.

An English cog — the stern rudder is now firmly established. Note the grappling iron hanging from the bow-sprit and the castles fore and aft.

The cog, like the longship, was clinker built. On average the keel length was about 100 feet, with a 23-foot beam. The lone mast situated amidships carried a square sail. In later years the *shrouds* (ropes attached to the mast to relieve it of stress) acquired *ratlines* (cross strips of rope), which served as a ladder for the lookout to the crow's nest.

The raised platform of the longship had by now become full-fledged fore- and aft-castles. The castles were turreted fortifications built high at either end of the vessel. They were specially designed for combat use since they enabled archers to clear the enemy's deck prior to boarding. And if boarded by the enemy the castles, mini-forts, were powerful strongholds which could only be taken with the very greatest of difficulty.

The cog proved a sturdy, sea-worthy vessel, an effective compromise between warship and merchant ship. For no medieval king could afford a fleet of specially constructed warships. In times of crisis he called on a levy of private ships which, when outfitted with fore- and aft-castles, were ready for combat.

Lepanto — one of history's most definitive battles, in which Don John of Austria defeated the Turks.

GUNPOWDER – THE GREAT DIVIDE

In northern Europe the naval powers were experimenting with, and eventually using, sail as the major means of propulsion. In the Mediterranean the classical heritage, the oared fighting ships of Greece and Rome, continued to provide the models for warship construction. Not that there were no developments but those that did occur consistently remained within the sphere of oared warships.

Then, in the mid-14th Century, the invention of gunpowder and the mariner's compass changed forever the nature of naval warfare. In 1260 an English monk, Roger Bacon, had noted a formula for gunpowder – seven parts of saltpetre, five of charcoal, and five of sulphur. It was another 50 years before the first gun appeared, but by 1345 firearms were coming into regular use on the battlefields of Europe.

The introduction of heavy artillery onto warships posed severe technical problems of design. To bear their weight ships had to become much sturdier; to protect themselves from enemy shot they had to become much stronger.

The compass had a similar effect on ship construction. The compass put navigation on a scientific basis. Sailors no longer had to turn their heads anxiously to the sky. The compass gave them their direction and also opened up vast new possibilities of sea exploration. Ships had to be adapted for long journeys and unknown dangers. Again, as with artillery, ship design had to be rethought to meet contemporary needs. In this way, two different approaches merged to produce the next stage in marine development.

The challenge of these two inventions was met in two distinctive ways – the galeass of the Mediterranean and the galleon of northern Europe.

THE GALEASS AND THE GUN

Up to the 16th Century the oared fighting galley retained an honoured place in the Mediterranean world. It had proved its worth in many battles, from the Venetian conquest of Constantinople, in 1204, to engagements in the French revolutionary wars. The invention of gunpowder, however, posed problems which could not be shrugged aside. The time-honoured battle method of ram and grapple had no place in a world where an opponent could keep his distance and still blow the enemy to smithereens. Yet the naval

authorities were reluctant to exchange the clean, fast lines of the galley for the bulky sailers of the north. So the galeass was built – a compromise between the oared fighting ships of the Mediterranean and the now dominant sailing ships of the northern seas.

The galeass was to provide the manoeuvrability of the oared ship with the fighting power of the sailing man-of-war. The ship was about 160 to 170 feet in length and 28 feet across, with a draught of 11 feet. It had a displacement of about 700 tons. The galeass was manned by 52 oars, 26 on either side, rowing on the *al scaloccio* system whereby each oar would be manned by

anywhere from four to seven men. It was also rigged with three lateen masts and at times a fourth mast, possibly a bowsprit carrying a small square sail. A protective deck covered the rowers, providing a fighting platform for the soldiers and room for the sailors to handle the rigging.

The most important feature of the galeass was the guns it carried. The galeass was the first stage in the development of the broadside. Of the 30-odd guns on the vessel about 18 were fitted on the sides, spaced out on the deck above the oarsmen. The remainder were placed on the castles in the stem and stern of the vessel.

The guns were a combination of periers (short guns firing stone missiles), cannon (medium length guns firing heavy shot), and culverins (long guns firing medium weight shot). The weight of shot varied between two to 50 pounds. In addition to the heavy guns there could have been as many as 60 smaller pieces on board.

In the end the galeass proved a stop-gap, neither fish nor fowl. It was soon to be superseded completely by sail. Yet it was a decisive factor in the Battle of Lepanto and deserves credit for its fine performance there. The Battle of Lepanto was one of the most significant fought in the western world, for it was there that the threat of a Turkish Mediterranean was crushed forever.

A galeass as used in the Battle of Lepanto. There are gun ports on either side and in the fore turret. There are also smaller guns on the stern rail.

157

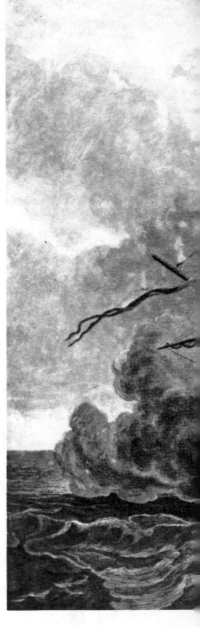

ARTILLERY ADAPTS TO THE SEA

Lepanto was the last major battle of the oared fighting ship. It was a battle fought at close range with ship grappling ship, Spaniard fighting Turk, in close hand-to-hand combat. Seventeen years later the defeat of the Spanish Armada taught the navies of the world that a new method of fighting had superseded all previous ones. The Spanish Armada never came within heavy shot range, much less grappling distance, of the newly developed English galleon. The age of sail in naval warfare had arrived, its inception spurred on by the improved ordnance available for wartime use.

Guns were early introduced into warships but they did not have a central role to play until the beginning of the 16th Century. Until then cannon were too unreliable to be depended on as the sole weapons. The method of construction (shrinking iron rings over longitudinal wrought-iron bars placed over a wooden core) was primitive and the early cannons were only too liable to shatter under stress. Matters were made worse by the unreliability of the gunpowder. The dried powder used, called 'serpentine', would if left too long either explode or completely lose its efficacy. Thus it was inadvisable to mix until just prior to use and even then the gunners were never too sure what would happen.

Firearms were therefore used only as auxiliary weapons placed in the fore- and aft-castles, where they would serve much the same purpose as the archers of previous years – clearing enemy decks prior to boarding.

The steady development of the gun-founder's

craft over the late 14th and 15th Centuries was to change all that. The forged guns gave way to brass initially and subsequently iron cast guns – sturdy weapons capable of withstanding very considerable stress.

The guns were placed on wooden beds known as stocks. Mobility was introduced with the invention of trucks – small wheels placed at the head of the stock. By the mid-17th Century the gun carriage became completely mobile, with the extension of the trucks to the rear of the stock. Recoil, however, always posed a problem and was one of the most serious stresses that a warship was subject to.

At about the same time that cast guns were coming into general use 'corned' powder was invented. Corned powder was wet gunpowder rolled into tiny pellets. Not only was it safer to handle than serpentine powder, it also gave a much better performance. This was very necessary if artillery was to assume the main burden of fighting in the future.

The Blast of the Broadside

The promise of artillery was realized by Henry VIII of England. He was the first European monarch to be aware of the great changes about to take place in naval warfare and did much to promote those changes. His policies set the foundation for England's rise to supremacy on the high seas. He seized upon the gun and broadside (gunports cut in the sides of the hull) as of crucial importance for the new warfare, which indeed they were. He imported guns from the best smiths in Europe and strove to establish gun-founding as a flourishing craft in England. He made sure that his warships were fitted with broadside armament.

THE GALLEON – WARSHIP OF AN ERA

The improvements in ordnance, the introduction of broadside fire, and the subsequent changes in ship construction marked the dividing point between the ancient and modern in naval warfare, between naval warfare as an extension of land combat and naval warfare as an entity in its own right. Henceforth navies began to form a separate and very important arm (in the English case, dominant) of a nation's military forces. And the ship that formed the backbone of the modern navy was the galleon.

The galleon, as one naval historian put it, 'changed the naval art from its medieval to its modern state'. Not until the advent of steam was there to be such a major technological upheaval in the warship. Under the direction of Sir John Hawkins the galleon became the leading warship of Elizabethan England. Variations on the galleon spread across Europe to form the proto-types of the classical European warship (the ship-of-the-line) of the 17th and 18th Centuries.

The galleon was a smaller ship than the older carrack. It displaced a mere 500 tons but more than made up for smallness by speed and immense sea-worthiness. The galleon was built long (length three times the beam) and lay low in the water. As shipwrights still avoided cutting gunports through the wales – timber strips used to strengthen the hull – the decks were not flush but broken into short sections with connecting steps. The bottommost deck, known as the *orlop*, was built just below the water-line and was used as storage room. Above it was the main or gun deck. The gun deck carried the heaviest pieces of artillery – on average 16 culverins, seven on either side and two in the stern. The upper deck carried the medium sized cannons (14 demi-culverins and sakers).

The forecastle at the bow and the half-deck and poop deck at the stern were semi-fortified areas, as in earlier vessels. But even here changes had occurred. In the age of grapple and board, the lofty forecastle, though a hindrance to the sailing quality of a vessel, made sound military

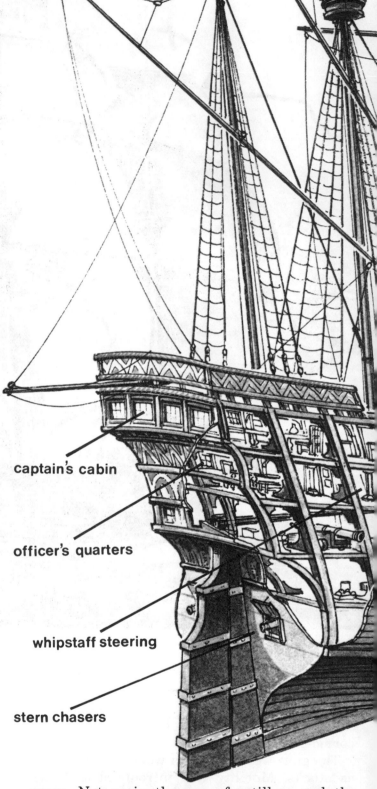

captain's cabin

officer's quarters

whipstaff steering

stern chasers

sense. Not so in the age of artillery and the broadside. So we find the forecastle on the galleon built low and set well back from the stem. The space below the half-deck served as officers' quarters.

The normal complement for the galleon was about 340 sailors, 40 gunners, and 120 soldiers. No quarters were provided for the men and they placed themselves wherever possible on deck.

That the galleon was superior to the Mediter-

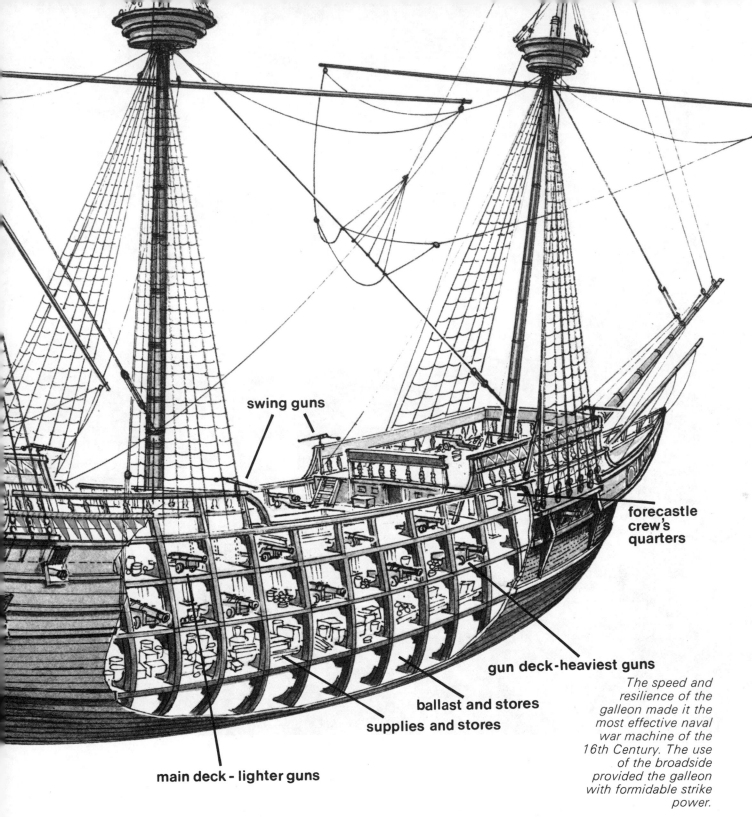

swing guns

forecastle crew's quarters

gun deck-heaviest guns

ballast and stores

supplies and stores

main deck - lighter guns

The speed and resilience of the galleon made it the most effective naval war machine of the 16th Century. The use of the broadside provided the galleon with formidable strike power.

ranean galley was shown by Drake's famous raid on the port of Cadiz in 1587. With four galleons, only two of them royal ships, he challenged 12 of Philip II's (the king of Spain) finest royal galleys to battle. The conditions were perfect for galley warfare – a calm sea in confined waters. The Spaniards unhesitatingly rushed the English marauder. Drake manoeuvred out of range and then gave the order to fire. The battery of guns let loose its deadly charge. Two galleys were sunk, the rest scuttled back to safety. The English devil had the best of them. The reason: Drake's formidable broadside fire (35 battery guns on his flagship) did not allow the galleys to come within ramming range. It was a decisive and important victory. The rising star of the galleon in naval warfare could no longer be denied. It took the defeat of the Spanish Armada, however, to set the cap-stone to Drake's convincing argument at Cadiz.

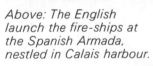
*Above: The English
launch the fire-ships at
the Spanish Armada,
nestled in Calais harbour.*

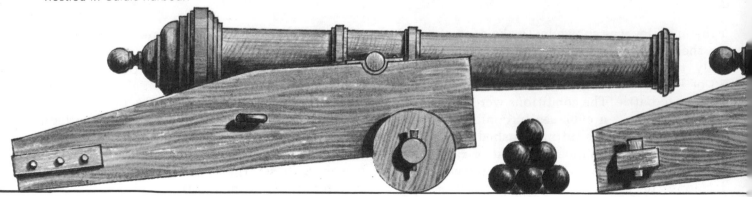

The Spanish Armada

The Spanish Armada was the culmination, but not the termination, of years of hostility. The conflict was a basic one – money. Who was to control the seas and thus the all-important access to the riches of the newly established colonies both in the east and west? Spain and Portugal were the first imperial powers but then Spain annexed Portugal which left Spain as the dean of imperial Europe.

At the same time England, just beginning to flex her naval muscles, was anxious to claim a share of the wealth. So, daring buccaneers, really little more than pirates, of the ilk of Drake, Hawkins and Frobisher, set about plundering Spain's cargo vessels. They, however, aspired to higher things than a mere buccaneering career. They wanted to prove their and England's naval strength in an all out war with the hated rival.

Elizabeth I was somewhat more cautious. Spain, after all, was the most powerful European kingdom, if not the most powerful kingdom in the world. It would not do to tax her too much. Yet, while Elizabeth negotiated, Drake provoked.

In the end there was nothing Philip II could do but go to war. Religion was invoked. The Catholic Philip, zealous for the faith, prepared to conduct a holy crusade against the Protestant jezebel of the north.

Philip was not stupid and he learned the lesson of Cadiz well. The original 1586 Armada proposal was based on a belief in the continued pre-eminence of the galley in combination with those compromise ships – the galeasses. The Armada actually assembled in 1588 was radically different. The galleys were scrapped and in their place stood 73 galleon warships (only 24 were Philip's own, the rest were mainly Portuguese and Castilian), 41 merchant ships adapted for war, four Neapolitan galeasses, and four Portuguese galleys which never reached England.

The English, with 197 ships (which varied greatly in fighting power), matched Spanish strength in ships. The crucial difference lay in armaments. The Spaniards banked their hopes on the short range but heavy-shotted cannon; the English depended on the long range but medium shotted culverin.

Lord Howard of Effingham commanded the English fleet, which lay in wait at Plymouth.

The English routed the Armada with the long range culverin on the left. The Spaniards relied in vain on the heavier shot and shorter range of the cannon on the right.

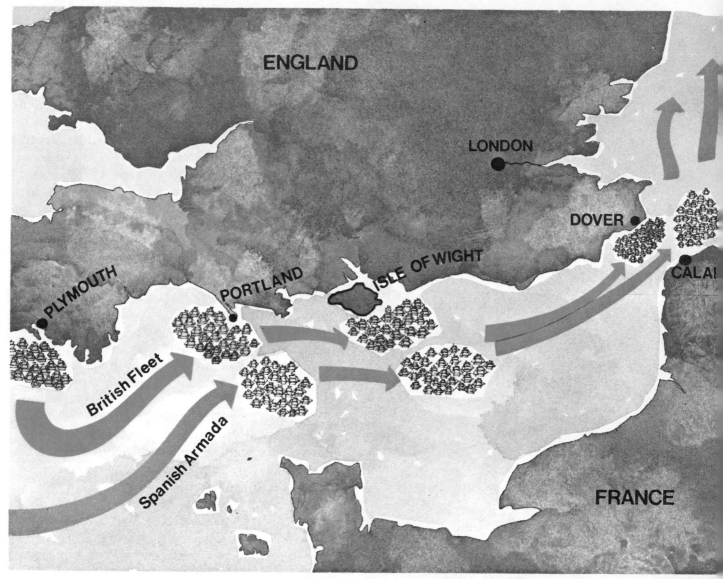

For 11 days the English fleet harassed the Spanish Armada from the rear, as it struggled up the Channel to Calais.

His Vice-Admirals were the fearsome triumvirate, Drake, Frobisher and Hawkins.

The Spaniards rounded the Lizard, off the Cornish coast, on July 19, 1588. The Spanish Commander-in-Chief, the Duke of Medina-Sidonia, held the right centre with the Portuguese men-of-war. On his left, Diego Flores de Valdez led the Castilian force. To the rear and left was the vanguard (an infantry term which had no relevance in the naval battle) under De Leyva. To the left of De Leyva was the rearguard under the command of Recalde. In the centre for protection were placed the hulks and store ships. The overall configuration was of a quarter moon with the horns trailing west.

The first day of contact proved the consummate sailing skill of the English. Tacking hard against the wind they rounded the enemy, unnoticed, gaining the advantageous windward side. With-out firing a shot the English had won a splendid tactical victory.

English tactics were to harass the enemy from the rear, break their tight formation, and then close in for the kill. For 11 days the Spaniards beat up the channel, dogged by the English who remained well out of range of the heavy Spanish guns. Several skirmishes, one off Portland, another off the Isle of Wight, ended in stalemate.

The English guns could damage but not cripple the Spanish fleet; the Spaniards, on the other hand, could not hurt the English but their formation remained solid.

Unable to establish a base on the Isle of Wight Sidonia decided to make towards Calais to await support from the Duke of Parma. This was his fatal move. The English saw their advantage and took it. Eight fire ships, loaded with gunpowder and other combustible matter, were

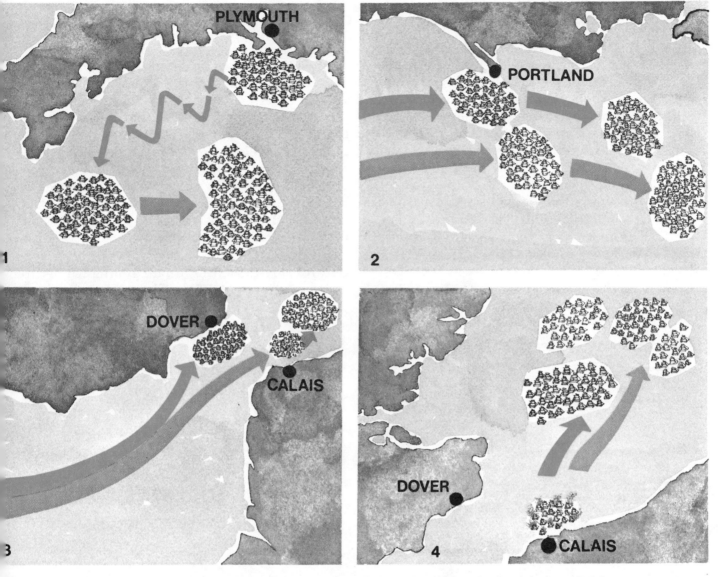

The English make contact off Portland and the Isle of Wight. Fire ships drive the Armada from Calais.

prepared and sent floating into the massed Spanish fleet.

Nothing was more feared in the age of the wooden ship than fire. Not only were the ships very susceptible to destruction by fire but also nothing caused more agony in terms of human suffering. The sight of those horrendous fire ships, possibly set to explode, created an immediate and dangerous panic in the Spanish fleet. There was nothing the Spanish commanders could do to stop the sudden rush to clear the harbour. Cables were cut and anchors jettisoned as ships fought to reach the supposed safety of the open sea.

None of the fire ships reached their targets but the English had achieved their objective. The Spanish formation was broken, leaving them open prey to the English. All hopes of a Spanish victory were dashed. The best Sidonia could

hope for was a safe return home.

That was the beginning of Sidonia's hardest fight. Unable to beat against an adverse wind and a hostile English fleet, he had no choice but to brave the treacherous North Sea. 'The troubles and miseries we have suffered cannot be described to your Majesty,' wrote the unfortunate Duke to Philip. And he was by no means exaggerating. The route home, over the top of Scotland, was a long and arduous one. Many of the ships were wrecked off the Scottish and Irish coasts and the survivors of the wrecks butchered mercilessly by local inhabitants. Of the 130 ships which set sail from Lisbon only 67 returned. The English did not lose a single ship. The Armada proved conclusively that the galleon, properly armed and handled, would dominate the high seas. Henceforth all who aspired to be naval powers equipped their fleets with galleons.

THE DUTCH THREAT

While Philip II was still planning the great Armada his Dutch provinces rose in revolt. The Dutch were a strong-willed and adventurous people who had long depended on trade for their livelihood. Immediately independence was established they were sending ships to the far east. In 1595 four ships set sail for the East Indies, thus setting the foundations for Holland's considerable colonial empire.

A good navy was the necessary corollary and result of trade and colonies. The Dutch were not too proud to learn from their soon-to-be-rivals, the English. It was not long before Holland had assembled a fleet of galleons.

To service the shallow bays and inlets of her country the Dutch galleon was built slightly smaller than the English variety (only two gun decks) and of shallower draught. It made the galleon a better sailer but weaker in war.

In the meantime the English had developed the first full-fledged three-decker galleon – the 100-gun *Sovereign of the Seas*, built for Charles I by the famous shipwright Phineas Pett. The *Sovereign of the Seas*, with a keel of 127 feet, a beam of 48 feet and draught of $23\frac{1}{2}$ feet, was the largest ship ever constructed to that date (1636). In addition to its size, it was also one of the most richly decorated – the work of the master carver, Gerard Christmas. Her ornate gilding led her to be called 'The Golden Devil' by the Dutch, whom

she fought in many battles. An overturned candle sealed her fate and she went up in flames in 1696.

The English were also improving the ordering of their whole fleet. The mid-17th Century saw the introduction of the ratings system. The decision to use in-line-ahead battle formation meant that *ships-of-the-line* (those directly facing the enemy) would have to be of approximately the same strength. The old maxim applied here: clearly, the line would only be as strong as its weakest ship.

A first rate ship had over 90 guns, a second over 80, a third over 50, a fourth over 38, a fifth over 18, and a sixth over six. The first three rates were considered strong enough to fight in line.

Changes were made in the rating system but a classification norm had been established for use over the next three centuries which was invaluable as navies grew increasingly complex and organization became vitally important.

It was almost inevitable that the two small but powerful and very plucky trading nations of the north should come to arms. A Dutch captain wrote after the first Anglo-Dutch War (1652–1654), 'the trade of the world is too small for us two, therefore one must down'. Three times the English and the Dutch fought each other and though in the end the English asserted their superiority it was not always a certainty that they would defeat their dogged enemy.

Left: The splendid vigour of an English three-decker running in full sail before the wind. Note its fearsome broadside capacity. Above: One of England's most famous ships of all time – the Sovereign of the Seas *which combined the design skill of Phineas Pett and the decorative genius of Gerard Christmas.*

167

THE RISING FRENCH NAVY

Among the many achievements of Cardinal Richelieu, the great French statesman, was the creation of the French navy. In 1624 he ordered a fleet of five warships from the Dutch. Those warships formed the nucleus of the French navy and the models for French shipwrights. By the late 1630s France had built up an Atlantic fleet of 38 war vessels, including the great ship *Couronne*. The 72-gun *Couronne* was France's answer to the English *Sovereign of the Seas* and, though smaller than her English counterpart, could fire as many deadly broadsides.

The French galleon proved to be a better sailer than either her Dutch or English equivalents. She was shallower of draught and wider of beam, making her main gun deck a better platform for the artillery. The 70-gun two-decker became the standard first rate French warship and when properly handled was more effective than any rival vessel. Indeed, the French vessel so impressed the English that they were led to make copies, and captains fought for the privilege of commanding captured French ships.

The Purpose-built Bomb Ketch

The improved galleon was not the only French contribution to naval warfare. In 1682 the pirate town of Algiers on the north coast of Africa was devastated by the French naval hero Abraham Duquesne. The ordinary fire power of a warship could damage but not destroy a protected harbour. To accomplish his aims Duquesne adapted a land weapon for naval use – the mortar. Mortars had been considered too heavy and unwieldly for use on the sea. A mortar-carrying ship would lose all mobility and be at the mercy of hostile vessels. Yet, Duquesne reasoned, in a static situation requiring heavy bombardment nothing could be more ideal than the mortar. The result was the bomb ketch.

The bomb ketch was a broad, sturdy vessel with the foremast removed to make room for two heavy mortars. Heavy beams supported the gun deck and distributed the shock of the recoil. The mortars fired the incredibly heavy 200 pound shot (compared to the average of 60-pounders for heavy cannon). The bomb ketch was heavy and difficult to manoeuvre but she was a purpose-built weapon, not an all-round warship, and she served her purpose admirably. It was a long time before the pirates of Algiers recovered from the shock of 1682.

The bomb ketch, above, cleverly adapted the normally land-based mortar. In this French ketch the fore-mast has been removed.

SHIPS-OF-THE-LINE

The 18th Century was the great era of the sailing warship. The ship-of-the-line, with its classical simplicity and neat elegant lines, claimed the sea as its natural home. Writers and artists, as well as lesser beings, fell sway to her charm. Old sea-dogs spoke lovingly of their 'Mary', referring not to their wives or lovers but the sailing ship which was their home and life. The ship-of-the-line represented a limit in human achievement. It was both the peak and end of centuries of development.

Throughout the century-long struggle between France and England, the greater part of which took place on the high seas, no major technological changes were introduced either in warships or artillery. The great developments were in leadership and tactics. Thus it was generally agreed that the French had the finer ships but time and time again the English asserted their naval supremacy. Nelson's flagship at the Battle of Trafalgar, the *Victory*, was not a newly-built wonder ship but a somewhat old-fashioned vessel, 40-odd years old and the veteran of many sea fights. This did not deter Nelson from achieving his greatest feat-of-arms.

There were certainly progress and improvements. Well into the steam age fine sailers were being built. Yet these remained strictly within the confines of the genre established so many years before in Elizabethan England.

Copper-sheathing for Protection

One seemingly minor but vital improvement was the use of copper sheathing to prevent fouling of a vessel's bottom. This fouling was one of the most persistent and annoying difficulties that a ship's captain had to face. Not only would fouling involve lengthy and frequent dockyard repairs but a ship's life could be cut drastically due to the rotting of her timbers by fungi.

Many methods had been devised to deal with the problem; none of them altogether successful. One early way of dealing with the problem was to attach a layer of felt and tar on the ship's bottom covered by elm boards. Unfortunately, it so increased the drag on a ship that it was

little used. Attempts were made to use lead sheathing but the electrolytic action of the salt water on the sheathing corroded the rivets. Initial experiments with copper sheathing proved eminently successful but copper was expensive and it was some time before it came into general use. It was to copper sheathing that Admiral Rodney attributed his victory in the 'Moonlight' Battle of 1780. Two years later at the scene of his greatest triumph (the Battle of the Saints) he wrote, 'None but an English squadron and copper-bottomed could have forced their way to the West Indies as we have done'.

Above: Oil painting of the Battle of Trafalgar.
Ships from left to right are: Royal Sovereign, Santa Anna, Bellisle, Fouqueux, Temeraire, Redoubtable, Victory, Bucentaure, Neptune, *and* Sta. Trinidad.

Right: Nelson cut through the French to win at Trafalgar.

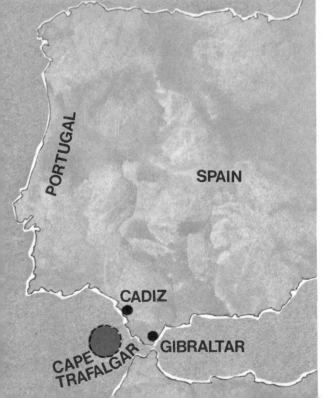

PORTUGAL

SPAIN

CADIZ

CAPE
TRAFALGAR

GIBRALTAR

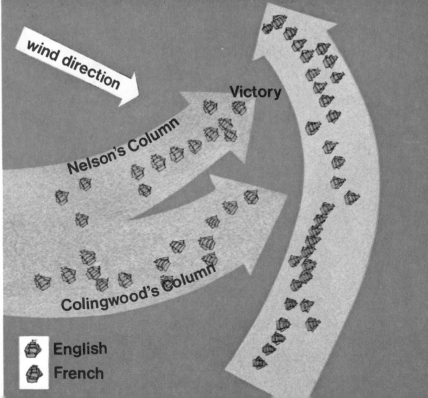

wind direction

Victory

Nelson's Column

Colingwood's Column

English

French

THE CARRONADE 'SMASHER'

The Battle of the Saints in 1782 was important in many respects. Primarily it was a turning point in the history of naval tactics. Nelson called it, 'the greatest victory, if it had been followed up, that our Country ever saw'. Technologically it was important for it introduced the carronade, the first new gun to be developed since the 16th Century.

The ships of the 18th Century had so evolved that existing artillery could do little irreparable damage to them. In battle the rigging was susceptible to damage but the structure of the warship remained inviolable by cannon shot. It was the specific purpose of the carronade to act as a ship-killer.

First manufactured in Scotland in 1778, the carronade was a short, stubby, thin-walled gun with a relatively large calibre. It carried a heavier shot than the cannon but at a reduced range. The carronades were intended to be short range 'smashers', most effective at point blank range, about 400 yards for a 68 pound shot and about 200 yards for a 12 pounder.

The carronade used a smaller amount of powder than the cannon but to greater effect. Unlike the cannon most of the explosive charge was not wasted in *windage* – the space between the shot and the sides of the gun. The small amount of powder used also had the added advantage of ease of recoil. This substantially lessened the stresses upon its mounting and supporting structure.

The first carronades found an eager market in the merchant marine. Especially popular were the smaller carronades of 24, 18, and 12 pounders. But they soon found their way onto the men-of-war and for a time some ships were exclusively fitted with the new weapon.

The great disadvantage of the carronade was, of course, its limited range. Eventually, this consideration led to its being scrapped. Yet in its initial engagements the element of surprise more than made up for the deficiency, as in the Battle of the Saints.

The Battle of the Saints

The French admiral, Comte de Grasse, was jubilant. He had just defeated the British at the crucial battle of Chesapeake Bay. He could now hope to sweep the Caribbean clear of his hated rivals. His next objective was therefore Jamaica, the British stronghold in the West Indies. If Jamaica fell the lesser islands would follow suit. It was imperative to Britain that de Grasse be stopped.

The man chosen to do the job was Admiral George Lord Rodney, capable but capricious and often ailing. With 37 ships-of-the-line he made his way to Gros Islet Bay in St. Lucia where he anchored and awaited news of French movements. He had not long to wait.

De Grasse had stationed himself at Fort Royal, Martinique, conducting lightning raids on the British-owned Leeward Islands. By April, 1782, he had assembled 36 ships-of-the-line and enough troops to conquer Jamaica. On Tuesday, April 8, the French fleet emerged from Fort Royal and headed north to collect more of their trade from Guadeloupe. Rodney was notified of the French move and set off in pursuit. The next day sporadic gunfire was exchanged between the hostile fleets but battle was not engaged. Towards late afternoon a fresh breeze enabled the French to disengage and continue their way northwards.

The winds, however, were uncertain and progress slow. April 12 found the French just south of the Saints islets – their northward path blocked by the islands. A few miles south of the French lay the British, north of Dominica. De Grasse had little choice but to force his way

The Battle of the Saints, 1782. The British close in.

172

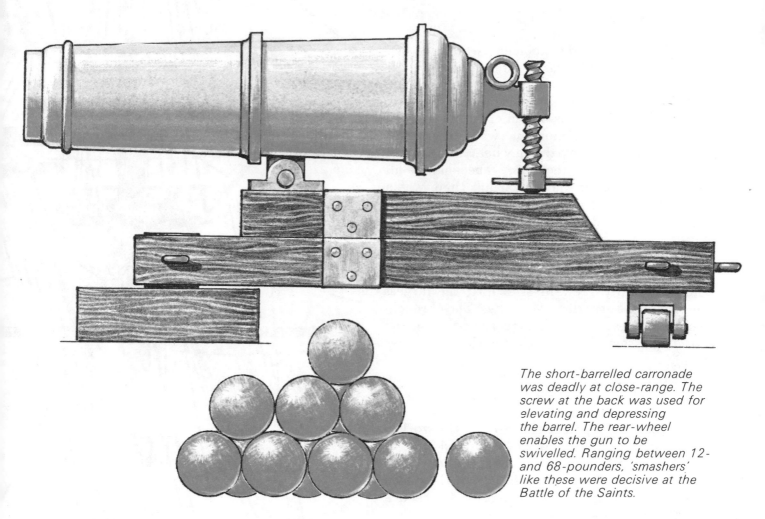

The short-barrelled carronade was deadly at close-range. The screw at the back was used for elevating and depressing the barrel. The rear-wheel enables the gun to be swivelled. Ranging between 12- and 68-pounders, 'smashers' like these were decisive at the Battle of the Saints.

southwards, windward of the British fleet.

Orders were given to form the battle line. The French vanguard of 10 ships was under the command of the intrepid Bougainville; the centre was held by de Grasse and the rear brought up by de Vaudreuil.

Reports of the French manoeuvre soon reached Rodney, who wasted no time in getting his fleet into line. Rear-Admiral Drake led the vanguard, Rodney kept the centre, and Rear-Admiral Hood took the rear.

De Grasse was in a difficult situation. He had not dictated the battle conditions and he would be forced to pass the British at close quarters – ideal for carronade use.

At about 7.30 on the morning of the 12th the van of the two fleets made contact. The French began firing from extreme range. Captain Penny, in the lead of the British van, held fire until he was within 400 yards of the enemy. The signal was then given and the 'smashers' discharged their destructive burden.

Penny bore away to lead along the French line while the rest of his division followed suit. Half an hour later the *Formidable*, Rodney's flagship, was in the thick of the fight. Rodney's main concern at the time was to contract his line even further and to close the range. Carronade fire was most effective at 200 yards or even less.

The French ships received a brutal beating but still had hope of gaining their objective. A shift of wind was to dash those hopes. The 74-gun *Glorieux* was taken aback and forced leeward. A gap opened in the French line. Seizing his opportunity Rodney forced his way through the gap, carronades blazing. Soon a second and a third break was made in the French line. The British had gained the windward side, thus breaking the back of French resistance. With the capture of de Grasse's flagship, the *Ville de Paris*, Rodney called a halt to the bloodshed. So it was that with the help of the carronade Rodney opened a new chapter in naval history.

THE FRIGATE – LIGHT AND FAST

One 18th Century development which we can only mention briefly was of vital importance for the new kind of naval warfare: the introduction into European navies of the frigate and corvette class of warships. Nelson had cried out in 1798, 'Were I to die this moment, want of frigates would be found engraved on my heart!' As tactics, rather than superior technology, became the all important factor in naval warfare there was a greatly increased need for light, fast warships that could be used for convoy and reconnaissance duties.

The early frigates were one-decked warships carrying 24 to 28 guns with a crew of about 160. They gradually grew in size until the largest English ones carried 44 guns. The French-designed frigates were among the finest in the world and served as models for those of other nations.

The frigate was the basis of the early American navy, serving it in good stead in the War of Independence and the War of 1812. In the last decade of the 18th Century three of the world's largest frigates were built in the United States – the *United States* and the *Constitution* (both launched in 1797) and the *President* (launched 1800). These frigates had a keel of 146 feet, a beam of 44 feet and supported 30 long 24-pounders on the gun deck, 20 to 22 12-pounders on the forecastle and half-deck plus another two long 24-pounders on the forecastle.

The corvette (the English sloop) was a class of warship under the frigate serving a similar function. The corvette carried 18 to 20 guns and it was not unusual for them to be propelled by oars as well as sail.

Above: The U.S. frigate Constitution *takes the British frigate* Guerriere *captive in the war of 1812.*

The light, fast frigate was an important tactical machine at the end of the 18th Century, used by all the main warring nations with marked effect.

A NEW FORM OF POWER

The introduction of steam powered engines into ships revolutionized not only construction but the whole nature of naval warfare. Essentially, steam freed a ship to move as it pleased – an obvious advantage for naval commanders. The idea of propelling a ship free from the whims of wind and weather and with greater efficiency than oared power was an old and cherished dream. And for centuries it remained a dream, for the would-be inventors were faced with the seemingly insoluble problem of finding an independent, mechanical source of power. Then came the great scientific and industrial advances of the 18th and 19th Centuries. A means was finally provided to realize the ancient dream; power could be had by harnessing the energy of steam.

The first practical steam engine was patented in 1698 by Thomas Savery. It was a primitive engine utilizing the vacuum created by condensing steam to drive a piston. Though its use was limited to pumping water from mines (the Savery engine was known as the Miner's Friend) it was the first of a series of technological innovations which radically altered the face of human history.

The next step was taken by Thomas Newcomen, a Dartmouth blacksmith. He improved upon Savery's design, creating the atmospheric engine. An overhead beam with arched ends oscillated, by means of a gudgeon, on a fixed support. One end of the beam was connected by a chain to a brass piston which fitted into a large bore, vertical cylinder. Leather flaps were placed round the edge of the piston and water poured on top to form an airtight seal. A heavy pump rod with plunger hung from the other end of the beam.

At rest the piston remained at the top stroke due to the weight of the pump rod. Steam was

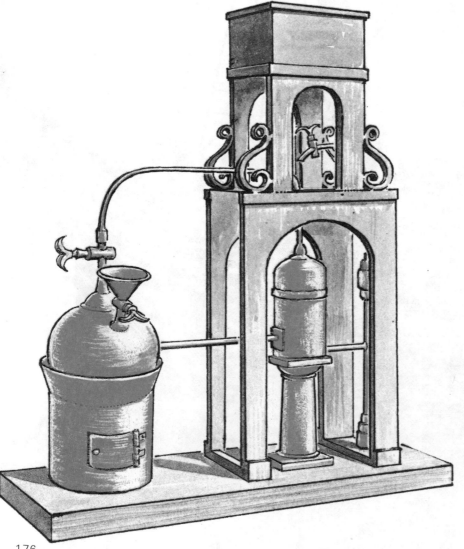

Left: Thomas Savery's steam engine of 1696. It was known as the Miner's Friend, because it was used for pumping water out of the mines. This was the first practical use of steam as a source of power, although it was nearly a century before it was used for motive power.

Near Right: A plan of Newcomen's pumping, or 'atmospheric', engine of 1712. This was also used in mines. The downward stroke of the piston, caused by atmospheric pressure on top of it and the creation of a vacuum beneath it, developed the working stroke.

Far Right: It was in working to repair this model of a Newcomen engine that James Watt discovered how to increase the efficiency of the steam engine. It was not long before the new form of power was driving warships across the oceans of the world.

introduced into the cylinder and condensed to create the vacuum. Atmospheric pressure acted on the piston to force it down, thus raising the rod and plunger. When steam was admitted again into the cylinder the weighted pump rod pulled the piston up and the cycle would start anew.

For decades Newcomen engines proved their usefulness in mines across Europe, but the problem of applying steam power to machinery in general was not solved. Watt's double-impulse engine and Pickard's crank and rod were the crucial elements in actualizing the potential of steam power.

In 1764 James Watt, an instrument maker in the employ of Glasgow College, was asked to repair a Newcomen engine. Not only did he repair it, he had soon increased considerably its efficiency by the invention of a separate condensing chamber. From there he was led into further investigations of the properties of the steam engine. The end result was the double impulse engine, patented in 1769.

The first thing Watt had done was to close off Newcomen's open-ended cylinder, replacing atmospheric pressure with steam. Improved though it was it still remained a primitive, single-acting engine. The motive power of steam was not yet recognized.

Watt's next step was the invention of the slide-valve, by means of which steam was distributed and condensed on both sides of the piston at the appropriate stroke. Steam then provided the piston's driving force on both the upward and downward stroke. Gears were fixed to the arched end of the beam and the chain connecting piston to beam was replaced by an iron rod. James Pickard's invention, the crank and connecting rod, converted the reciprocating motion of the steam engine into a rotary motion. The steam engine was ready to try its hand at anything.

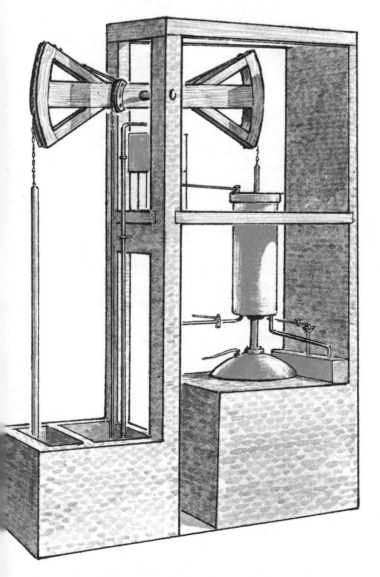

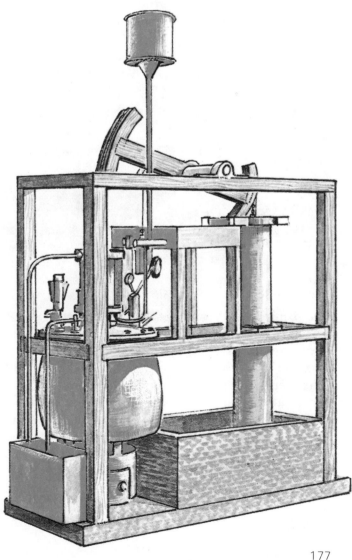

STEAM TAKES TO SEA

As early as 1783 the Marquis de Jouffroy constructed a small steamship, the *Pyroscaphe*, which plied the waters of the River Sâone, near Lyons. The engine turned a paddle wheel set in the stern of the vessel. (Nearly all the early steamships were of the paddle wheel type.)

In 1787 the American John Fitch successfully ran a steam boat on the Delaware River. She was fitted with a horizontal, 12-inch, 3-foot stroke cylinder double-acting engine which drove 12 vertical oars, six on either side of the vessel.

In 1788 a wealthy Scottish banker, Patrick Miller, joined forces with an enterprising engineer, William Symington, to construct Britain's first paddle steamship. The double-hulled boat (one containing the boiler, the other the engine) paddled happily up and down the Firth of Forth at the speed of five miles an hour.

In 1801 Lord Dundas commissioned Symington, Miller's old collaborator, to design an engine for a tug which was to service the Forth and Clyde Canal. The resulting engine was rather unusual for its day: a horizontal direct-acting condensing engine with a 22-inch, 4-foot stroke cylinder.

The *Charlotte Dundas* was launched in 1802, undergoing its first test in March of that year.

Patrick Miller's steamboat, the first paddle boat to be built in Britain. Masts and sails remained.

The diminutive vessel (56 feet in length, 18 feet across) towed two 70-ton boats 19 miles in six hours against strong head winds. The *Charlotte Dundas* was a great technical success but fears that her waves would erode the banks of the canal caused her to be consigned to the dockyards.

The next major developments came from America. In 1807 Robert Fulton built the *Clermont*, a flat-bottomed craft 166 feet in length but only 18 feet in beam. It steamed along the Hudson – the first steamship in active commercial service – at the amazing speed of five knots. The *Comet* (built in 1812) was Europe's first merchant steamship. Rolling along at 6·7 knots she gave regular service on the Glasgow-Greenock run.

The first steam warship was designed by Fulton in 1813. Originally intended to serve in the War of 1812, the *Demologos* was not completed in time to take an active part in the war. She was a double-hulled vessel with a single, stern paddle wheel motivated by a 120-horsepower engine. Her armament consisted of 30 32-pounder guns placed behind 58-inch thick wooden walls. She was also equipped with several submarine guns firing 100-pound projectiles below the waterline. The *Demologos*, renamed the *Fulton*, was never

Henry Bell's Comet *plied the waters of the Clyde for eight years until she ran aground off the West Highlands. Initially, two pairs of paddles were used but it was soon found that performance improved with just one pair.*

tested in action and in 1829 was destroyed by an explosion in the Brooklyn Navy Yard.

Fulton's warship, ingenious though it was, had severe limitations – the limitations of all early steamships – which hindered the acceptance of steam in the navies of the world. Firstly, the large and cumbersome paddle wheel presented too obvious a target for enemy guns. A few rounds of shot could easily disable a steamship, thus removing her main advantage, freedom of movement. Secondly, the heavy machinery of the steam engine displaced the space required for the broadside guns. There would have to be a very good substitute before broadside fire would be sacrificed.

These difficulties, rather than restraining, acted as a spur to further developments. The perfection of screw propulsion and improvements in ordnance heralded the coming changes.

Figure 1.
Scale one quarter of
an inch to a foot.

Demologos.

Transverse section. A her boiler B the steam engine C the water wheel
D. D gun decks. E E her wooden walls 5 feet thick, diminishing to below
the water line as at F F. draught of water 9 feet.

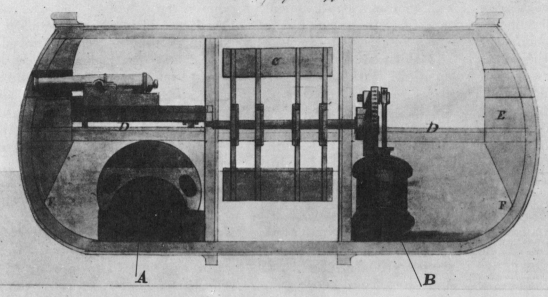

Water line

A   B

Figure 2.
eighth of an inch
a foot. this shews
gun deck 140 feet
42 feet wide
ting 20
s. A the
r wheel.

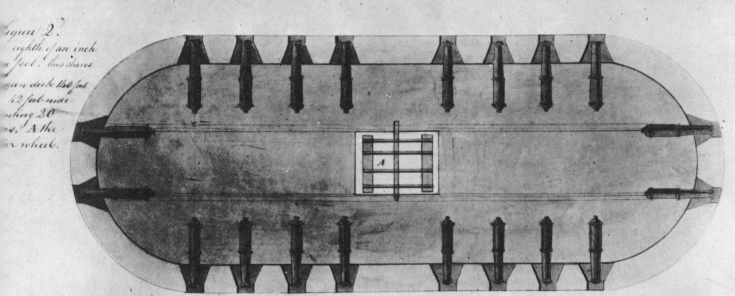

Robert Fulton's design for the Demologos, the first steam warship ever built.
Top: Transverse section. (A) boiler; (B) the steam engine; (C) the water wheel; (D) gun decks;
(E) wooden walls five feet thick diminishing below the water line at (F).
Draught of water is nine feet.
Middle: The Demologos' gun deck, 140 ft long and 42 ft wide, it mounted 20 guns.
(A) is the water wheel.
Bottom: Side view of the warship.

Figure 3.
Side View.
⅛ of an inch to a foot

line

A Tug-of-war for Progress

The changeover from paddle to screw propulsion was the essential innovative factor, making steamships into practical and superior warships.

In 1836 two patents were taken out on screw propellers, one by Francis Pettit Smith, the other by John Ericsson. Smith's screw, a small, helical shaped propeller, was fixed to the recess in the stern *deadwood* (wooden blocks fastened just above the keel). It had its first success on a six-ton barge which was used for working the City and Paddington Canal.

Four years later Brunel's Atlantic liner, the *Great Britain*, was fitted with a Smith screw. The *Great Britain* was the first large ship to be built of iron and the fact that she was supplied with the screw did much to further the cause of screw propulsion.

John Ericsson, a former Swedish army officer, had equal success with his screw, a twin-bladed propeller. Fitted onto the 40-foot launch *Francis B. Ogden* it had a smooth trial run, towing a barge laden with Admiralty officials down the Thames. The officials remained unmoved by her performance but two American witnesses were enthusiastic. They urged Ericsson to emigrate to the United States where his talents, they decided, would not go unrecognized. 'We'll make your name ring on the Delaware,' Captain Stockton told him. Ericsson did not need much convincing and in 1840 he arrived in New York on a small iron steamer fitted with his screw.

Three years later Ericsson equipped the 10-gun sloop, *Princeton,* with a six-bladed screw. An unfortunate accident marred the otherwise smooth running of his invention. An experimental 12-inch wrought-iron gun shattered, killing the Secretary of State and the Secretary of the Navy.

Even with the repeated successes of the screw naval opinion continued to remain divided on the question of paddle versus screw. A practical test was devised in 1845 to see which was the superior of the two. In a series of races the screw-driven *Rattler* proved herself quicker than her paddle-driven rival, the *Alecto*. But, it

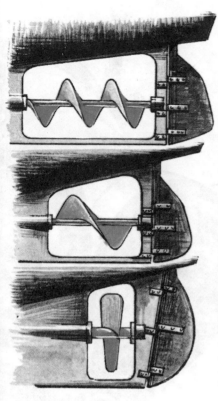

Left: At first it was thought that the longer the screw was the better it would work. At the top, Smith's earliest design of 1836, modified in the centre. At the bottom, Ericsson's improved propeller of 1839.

Below: The famous contest between the paddle (Alecto) and the screw (Rattler) in the North Sea on April 3rd, 1845. Both the 888 ton Rattler and the 800 ton Alecto had 200 horsepower engines. The Rattler, with a Smith screw propeller, proved her superiority by towing the Alecto forward at a rate of 2·8 m.p.h.

was claimed, the paddle had stronger towing powers. That hypothesis, too, was immediately put to the test.

So came about one of the most bizarre tug-of-wars in history. Strong cable lashed the two sloops together stern to stern. The waters churned, the vessels heaved and chugged as the firemen furiously stoked the boilers. Nothing happened. Neither vessel gave way. Then, almost imperceptibly, the *Rattler* inched forward, slowly picking up speed and finally achieving $2\frac{1}{2}$ knots, with the *Alecto* thrashing behind her. The victory was conclusive. There could be no more argument about the superiority of screw propulsion.

One of the principal attractions of the screw for the navy was that the top deck was kept clear for guns and masts. For, until late into the 1860s, steam propulsion was considered simply an auxiliary to sail. 'Down funnel. Up screw,' was a cry familiar to all who served on those curious amalgamations, the steam-sail warship.

HIGH EXPLOSIVE SHELLS

The introduction of the shell gun into the navies of Europe signalled the end of the wooden sailing ship-of-the-line. A wooden ship could not compete with high explosives.

Shells had long been considered too dangerous for use on the ship of the line until, in 1788, Sir Samuel Bentham, working for the Russians, outfitted a fleet of boats with shell-firing brass ordnance mounted on a non-recoil system. At the Battle of Azov the Russian fleet resoundingly defeated a superior force of Turks. The Turkish ships had no defence against the barrage of explosive shells.

In 1822 the French general Paixhans urged the naval authorities to develop the direct-aim shell gun. He prophesied the total eclipse of the sailing ship by armoured battleships propelled by steam and firing explosive shells. The French were hesitant but in 1837 adopted shell guns as auxiliary armament. The British followed suit in 1839 and the Americans in 1841.

RIFLING INCREASES THE RANGE

In 1855 William Armstrong invented a wrought-iron, rifled, breech-loading gun. The Armstrong gun was faster, safer and more accurate than the old smooth-bore muzzle loading rifle. Rifling (cutting grooves into the barrel) gave the lead-coated projectile a spin which greatly increased its range and accuracy. It was not long before the Armstrong process was being applied to heavier guns. However, difficulties with breech-loading retarded progress. Whitworth took up where Armstrong left off and developed a medium weight cannon which, in its trial, proved spectacularly successful. The way was open for the growth of bigger and better guns. As guns grew in size and were more and more protected by armour it became very difficult to maintain the traditional broadside. The advantages of the *central battery* were made quite obvious and it was not long before it was adopted by the great naval powers. At first used in broadside fire the central battery was soon altered to allow for ahead fire. The next major step was the introduction of the armoured turret. The armoured revolving turret gave the big guns full command of the whole sweep of the horizon. John Ericsson in America, Captain Cowper Coles in Britain, and Dupuy de Lôme in France were the men who made the revolving turret a practical proposal.

This massive Armstrong 100-pounder naval gun was of a type that was first tested in 1862. It was made of wrought-iron, had a breechloading mechanism and a rifled bore. Guns such as these introduced a new era of naval warfare. The old, wooden ships could not withstand the power of the high explosive shells.

SHELLS, GUNS AND SHRAPNEL

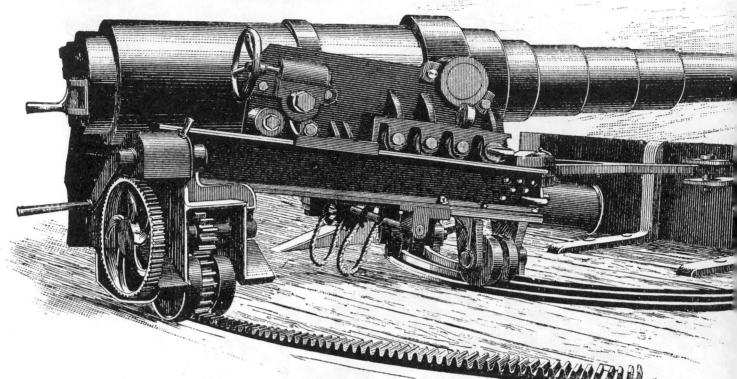

Above: American six-inch steel breech-loading rifle on a swivel mounting.
Right: The French Reffye cannon which was adapted for naval use – see top right.

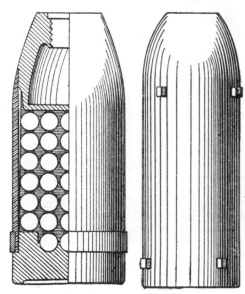

Far left: Shrapnel shell, named after the British general who invented it. The thin shell walls are burst by a fused charge dispersing a quantity of lead or iron balls.
Left: Muzzle-loading studded shell. The studs engaged in the rifling of the barrel thus imparting spin to the projectile.

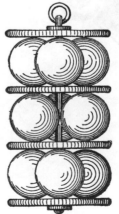

Left: Grape shot. The iron or lead balls placed on discs around a central rod were covered with a canvas bag. The shock of discharge broke the balls loose but they remained within the bag for a short distance before dispersing.

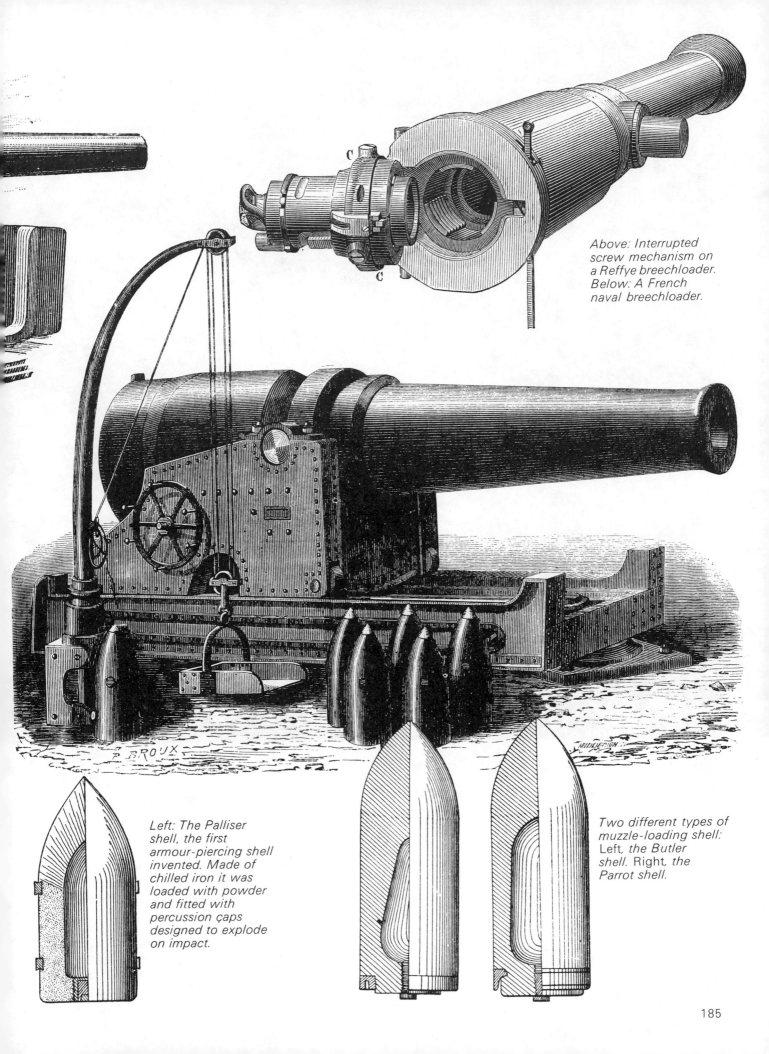

Above: Interrupted
screw mechanism on
a Reffye breechloader.
Below: A French
naval breechloader.

Left: The Palliser
shell, the first
armour-piercing shell
invented. Made of
chilled iron it was
loaded with powder
and fitted with
percussion çaps
designed to explode
on impact.

Two different types of
muzzle-loading shell:
Left, the Butler
shell. Right, the
Parrot shell.

THE MIGHTY IRONCLAD

The ironclad warship was the inevitable corollary to the shell gun. Experiments with iron ships had been going on since the beginning of the century. In 1838 Brunel's transatlantic liner, the *Great Britain*, proved the immense durability of iron. Not only did she operate very well on her run but when she ran aground off Ireland and was recovered a little less than a year later she was found to be barely damaged. The advantages of armour plating in the age of shell fire were obvious. Dramatic proof of its worth was to be had in the Crimean War (1854–1856).

Cross-section of the Great Britain.
1. Boilers.
2. Engines – 4·88 ins cylinders.
3. Promenade and state rooms.
4. Saloon and state rooms.
5. Fore promenade and state rooms.
6. Fore saloon and state rooms.
7. Officers' berths.
8. Seamen's berths.
9. Stores.
10. Water tanks.
11. Cargo.
12. Coalroom and berths for the engineers on the upper part of the room.
13. Stokehole and fire-place.
14. Engine room.
15. Shaft of screw.
16. Screw.
17. Galley.

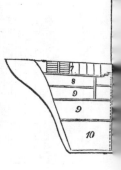

The Great Britain *on her maiden voyage.*

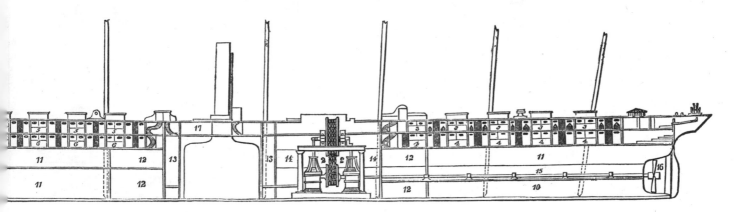

The Crimean War – a Testing Ground

The Crimean War put to the test of war both the theories of shellfire and the ironclad warship. The first test came in a skirmish prior to the war itself. In November, 1853, a Russian squadron replayed the feat of 1788. A Turkish squadron of frigates anchored off Sinope was annihilated by Russian shellfire.

The second test took place two years later. The British and the French had joined forces to defeat the Russian bear. The Kinburn forts were proving an obstinate obstacle in the path of the allied forces. The regular ships-of-the-line could not approach the forts for fear of shellfire.

The French, however, were old masters of bombardment techniques. Three armoured (4½-inch iron plates with a 17-inch thick wooden backing) ships were towed within range of the troublesome forts. The *Dévastation, Tonnante,* and *Lave* remained impervious to the enemy's heavy firing. The Russian shells exploded harmlessly on their iron sides. The hapless forts, however, had no protection against the French bombardment. Barrage upon barrage slammed into the Russians. In a matter of hours the Kinburn forts lay smouldering, an utter ruin. The French had stated the most convincing argument against wooden walls.

The ironclad developed quite rapidly thereafter. In 1859 the French laid down the ironclad *Gloire*. She still carried three masts and appropriate rigging but by then the sailing equipment was the auxiliary means of propulsion. The British, not to be bested, launched the *Warrior* in December, 1860.

The *Warrior* was the first large iron-hulled ironclad warship. She was fitted amidships with a

The British ship Warrior, *the first large iron-hulled, iron-clad warship. Full rigging was maintained despite the introduction of boilers, smoke stacks and steam engine.*

The French ironclad warship, the Gloire.

long and carried a 1,250 horsepower engine giving her a speed of 14 knots. Another unusual feature of the *Warrior* was the iron ram fitted on the bow below the figure-head. The ram was to make a comeback in naval warfare of the late 19th Century. For a while it would prove the only means of sinking enemy ships. The feeling about the renewed importance of the ram received confirmation at the battle of Hampton Roads when the Confederate ship *Merrimac* rammed and scuttled the Union vessel *Cumberland*. That was in 1862. Four years later, at the Battle of Lissa, the Austrian admiral, Tegethoff, rammed and sunk the Italian ship *Re d'Italia*, further impressing naval opinion about the importance of the ram. The ram, however, could not replace the gun. The latter half of the 19th Century saw startling developments in armaments.

belt of iron armour 4·5 inches thick. Her armaments consisted of 48 smooth-bore guns, 26 of them behind the armour, placed in the soon-to-be outdated broadside position. Like the *Gloire* she retained full rigging but again only as an auxiliary to her steam engine. She was 380 feet

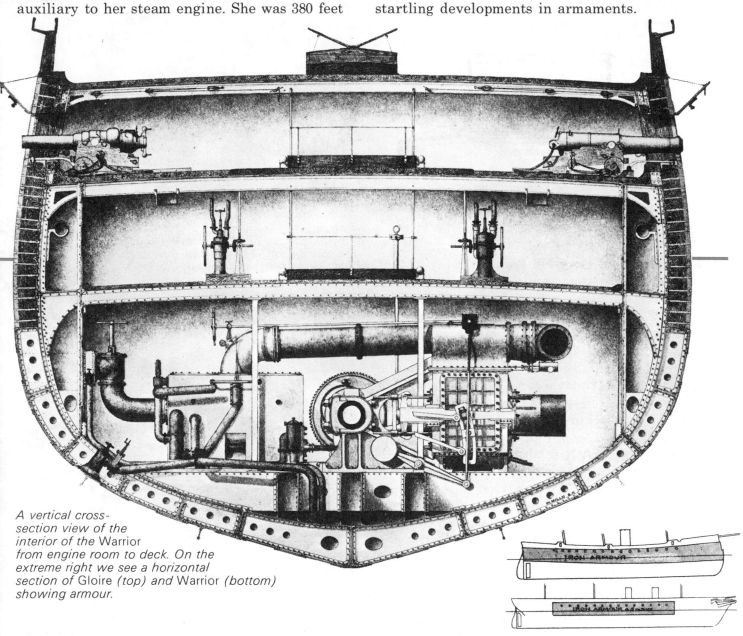

A vertical cross-section view of the interior of the Warrior *from engine room to deck. On the extreme right we see a horizontal section of* Gloire *(top) and* Warrior *(bottom) showing armour.*

THE REVOLVING GUN TURRET

Ericsson, the man who brought the screw to America, in the intervening years had been busily engaged in numerous projects designed to improve warships. A major contribution was his design for the turret ship *Monitor*, built in 1862 under pressure of war. The *Monitor* was powered by a steam engine driving a screw. She lay low in the water and was armoured down to the water-line with five layers of one-inch iron plate. On her deck was mounted a single revolving turret carrying two 11-inch muzzle-loading smooth bore cannon firing solid shot. The turret measured 20 feet in diameter and nine feet in height. The *Monitor* was a strange vessel, hastily built and not very seaworthy. But she incorporated a revolutionary concept which was greatly to influence naval thought in the coming years, especially after the performance of the turret had been tested in battle.

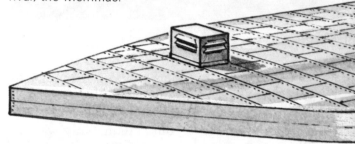

Below: Ericsson's Monitor, *designed and built for the Union forces, was the strangest looking war machine ever to enter battle. But her revolving turret and armoured construction made her more than a mere curiosity. She would have caused immense havoc had she not become locked in a stalemate struggle with her equally well-armoured rival, the* Merrimac.

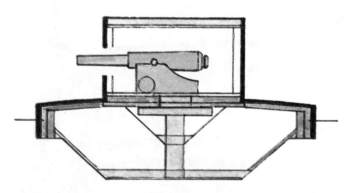

Left: A cross-section of the Monitor *shows her gun in its revolving turret. The compound iron and wooden hull was made additionally strong by the overhang construction.*

Right: The Confederates raised the sunken Merrimac *and converted her to use against her original masters. She became the first ironclad American vessel, dispensing altogether with vulnerable sails and rigging, too easily ripped and cut by broadside fire. More heavily armed than the* Monitor, *she was as impregnable as her adversary. Union and Confederate navies clashed in the first ironclad sea battle in history and neither side could claim a victory.*

Monitor versus Merrimac

When the American Civil War broke out in 1861 neither side had a particularly strong navy. The Union forces in their retreat from the naval base at Norfolk had scuttled a wooden frigate, the *Merrimac*. The Confederate forces raised the ship and upon seeing that she was not badly damaged decided to convert her into an ironclad. The *Merrimac* thus became the first ironclad American ship as well as the first warship to completely discard rigging. Protected by 16 inches of wood and four inches of iron, the *Merrimac* set out on the hunt. She was armed with three nine-inch smooth-bore guns, a six-inch rifled pivot-gun (all firing explosive shells), and two seven-inch rifled guns placed fore and aft. She was also fitted with a cast-iron ram projecting two feet below the waterline.

The Union forces responded to the challenge by commissioning Ericsson to design the *Monitor*. By March 1862 the *Monitor* was heading south to

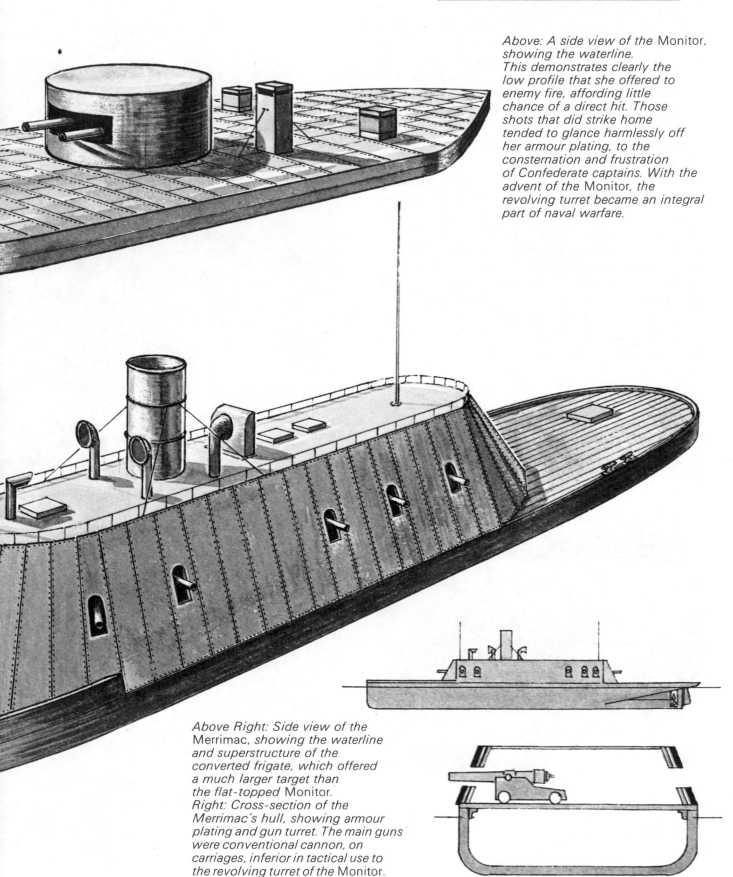

Above: A side view of the Monitor, *showing the waterline. This demonstrates clearly the low profile that she offered to enemy fire, affording little chance of a direct hit. Those shots that did strike home tended to glance harmlessly off her armour plating, to the consternation and frustration of Confederate captains. With the advent of the* Monitor, *the revolving turret became an integral part of naval warfare.*

Above Right: Side view of the Merrimac, *showing the waterline and superstructure of the converted frigate, which offered a much larger target than the flat-topped* Monitor.
Right: Cross-section of the Merrimac's *hull, showing armour plating and gun turret. The main guns were conventional cannon, on carriages, inferior in tactical use to the revolving turret of the* Monitor.

challenge her redoubtable adversary.

The *Merrimac*, meanwhile, had just gone out on its first sortie. Steaming out of the Elizabeth River she attacked the Federal warships on the north shore of Hampton Roads. Within a matter of moments the *Merrimac* had destroyed the helpless wooden ships. Their fire bounced harmlessly off her thick armour while she leisurely picked off the *Congress* and then rammed the *Cumberland*. As night fell the *Merrimac* returned to her mooring in Norfolk.

The next day, March 9, 1862, the *Merrimac* returned to Hampton Roads to finish off the remaining Federal ships only to find herself faced with the ungainly *Monitor*. Immediately the two ships began to pound away at each other. The two-gun *Monitor* gave as much as she got but neither side could make any headway. Shells burst harmlessly off the iron sides of the vessels while shot bounced into the waters. By mid-afternoon the fight died down. The captains of both ships realized they could do nothing against the other and retreated to their respective stations. The great ironclad epic ended in a stalemate.

Although the battle ended in a draw it had important consequences in the naval world. The vulnerability of the wooden ship was once again decisively proved by the *Merrimac's* first day of operation. Secondly, the revolving turret showed itself to be equal to the most devastating broadside fire.

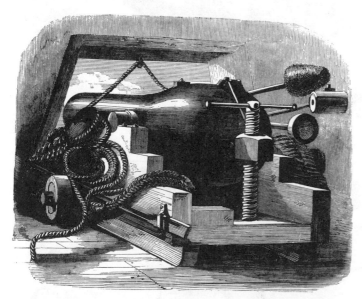

Above: One of the six Dahlgren 9 ins smooth bore guns on the Merrimac. *The gun recoiled on the wooden carriage and was braked by the ropes. The screw mechanism altered the elevation angle of the gun.*
Right: The Merrimac *rams the helpless, wooden sloop, the* Cumberland.

THE BIRTH OF THE BATTLESHIP

The construction of the *Devastation* in 1872 marked the transformation of warships from sailing ironclads into the forerunners of the modern battleship. Prior to 1872 controversy raged between the proponents of the revolving turret and the diehard conservatives who remained faithful to the standard of broadside armament. There were many practical factors which made the turret system appear superior. The use of the naval ram and the increasing size of naval guns were two strong arguments for the switch away from the broadside conception. If the naval ram was to be used in sea warfare then it was essential that a ship fitted with such a device should fire ahead. Likewise, with naval guns becoming increasingly larger to penetrate thicker armour, ships would have to carry fewer guns but these, therefore, had to be able to fire in a great variety of directions.

Sir Hugh Childers, Britain's First Sea Lord, took the plunge and asked Edward Reed to

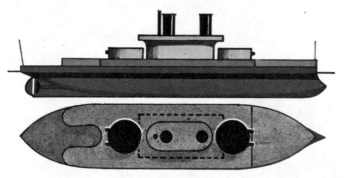

Above: The siting of the Devastation's *gun turrets and, right,* Devastation *under steam.*

design 'a smaller ocean-going turret ship, with a light sailing rig'. Since a contemporary battleship was estimated to require at least 12 inches of armour to halt the penetration of shells, a sailing rig would certainly prove to be a poor second to steam propulsion. For this reason, together with the fact that a sailing rig would hamper the firing of multi-directional armament, the *Devastation* was built solely to be driven by steam.

The design of the *Devastation* was epoch-making. She possessed the rudimentary qualities of the modern battleship, she was iron-hulled, armoured, steam-driven, her guns were mounted in turrets, and of course she was not encumbered by masts, sails, or rigging. She was 285 feet long, 62 feet wide and her twin propellers gave her a top speed of 12½ knots. The *Devastation* was armed with four 12-inch muzzle-loading guns

sited in turrets along the centre-line – one fore, one aft. Each of these guns weighed 35 tons, which, of course, enabled them to fire larger shells, though this raised problems of its own. The increase in gun weight in concentration around the turret meant that the ship had to be more durably constructed throughout to support the gun, and to withstand its recoil.

A further advantage the *Devastation* had over her predecessors or contemporaries was the large volume of bunkering space. Room was made on board for the storage of 1,800 tons of coal. The economical use of her fuel was heightened when a few years later she was refitted with triple expansion engines with cylindrical boilers. In earlier steam-propelled ships the expansion of the steam was done in one or two stages. It was discovered that the economy of the engine would be increased greatly if this operation was done in three stages – hence the triple expansion engine. This engine and boiler enabled steam to be produced at 60 pounds

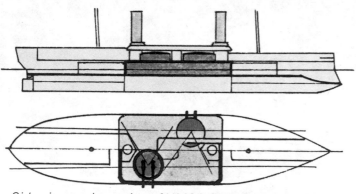

Side view and top plan of HMS Inflexible

pressure instead of the hitherto normal 25 to 30 lbs. For the first time a vessel could cross the Atlantic and return without coaling.

A sister ship to the *Devastation* was launched a little while later. She proved to be even more successful as she was fitted with faster engines and larger guns. The *Thunderer* was also fitted with a hydraulic loading system for her 12·5-inch guns. The guns were depressed until they were over the loading tubes. Hydraulic pressure then forced the rammer, cartridge, and projectile up the loading tube and into the gun via the muzzle. Another novel feature of the *Thunderer* was that these guns could be fired electrically from the bridge.

Although designed as ocean-going battleships, these ships did not take part in any major naval activity apart from minor roles in the Russo-Turkish war of the late 1870s. The *Devastation* was mainly used as a port guard ship, first at

Plymouth and later at Gibraltar, before being broken up in 1908.

Britain's policy at this time was not to take the initiative in naval issues but to counteract the advances made by the other powers. Relying on her efficient ship building and engineering industries, rapid counter measures were employed to produce ships of comparable or greater efficiency. The race for larger armament and thicker armour accelerated at a tremendous rate in the late 19th century. Larger guns were built to penetrate thicker armour, and thicker armour used to combat larger guns and considerably more efficient shells.

The *Inflexible* was built in response to the 15-inch guns of the Italian vessels *Duilio* and

Dandolo. Commissioned in 1876, she was equipped with four 16-inch muzzle-loading guns, mounted centrally in turrets. She had the greatest thickness of armour ever in the history of the battleship. The armour (known as 'compound') was specially constructed for her use and consisted of 24 inches of iron plus 17 inches of teak backing at the waterline, with 20-inch armour plating and 21 inches of teak on the citadel. The *Inflexible* was also one of the first ships to employ an armoured deck. She was fitted with two 60-foot torpedo boats and was equipped with the first underwater torpedo tubes. She was the first ship to be fitted with electric lights, which were run off an 800 volt generator. Her guns were at first worked by pile-type batteries.

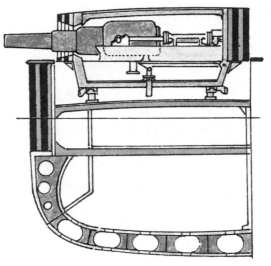

A cross-section of the Inflexible *showing a gun turret and the great thickness of her armour plating. The guns were muzzle loading and could swivel to cover in combination a wide field of fire. It was no longer necessary for the vessel to turn to deliver a broadside.*

Below: The ironclad might of HMS Inflexible.

The torpedo and mine, close relatives, had far reaching effects upon naval design and involved radical changes of strategy during warfare at sea. As early as 1776 an attempt was made to mine Lord Howes flagship, *Eagle*, while anchored in New York Harbour. A man was reputed to have approached the ship in some kind of submersible boat. His attempt failed, however, because the *Eagle's* hull was copper plated.

The first mines to be anchored in sea lanes were made by the Russians during the war of 1854–56. Zinc canisters were filled with gunpowder and set to explode by means of a detonator. The detonator was a glass tube filled with acid which, when broken, would ignite the charge of gunpowder. Luckily for shipping at the time, these mines were too small to cause any real damage.

The torpedo, unlike the mine, does not remain stationary but travels below the surface of the water towards its target, the submerged portion of a ship's hull. One of the more prominent early methods of delivery was that used by the Union officer, Lieutenant Cushing, against the Confederate ironclad, *Albermarle*, in 1864. Known as a 'spar torpedo' it consisted of an explosive charge placed at the seaward extremity of a pole projecting from the ship's bow. The ship would steam towards the adversary and the charge would explode upon impact. Perhaps Lieutenant Cushing should have used a longer pole, because in his case the charge exploded to the disadvantage of both ships.

The British 'Harvey' torpedo also had its drawbacks. The device, towed by means of a long cable was constructed so as to diverge from the course of the towing vessel. But there was no way of ensuring that the towing cable would not foul small boats in the vicinity of the target ship.

The breakthrough in torpedo development came in 1866 with the Whitehead-Luppis torpedo. Invented by Captain Luppis of the Austrian Navy and Robert Whitehead, a Scottish engineer, the torpedo was a long cylindrical case, streamlined for easy movement, with a fairly large explosive charge in the 'nose' driven by a compressed air engine situated at the 'tail'. The early torpedo travelled at a speed of eight knots, which meant that it was only effective at a stationary target at a very short range.

The Whitehead-Luppis torpedo was first used in combat by the British frigate *Shah* in 1877. The *Shah* attacked a Peruvian monitor *Huascar*

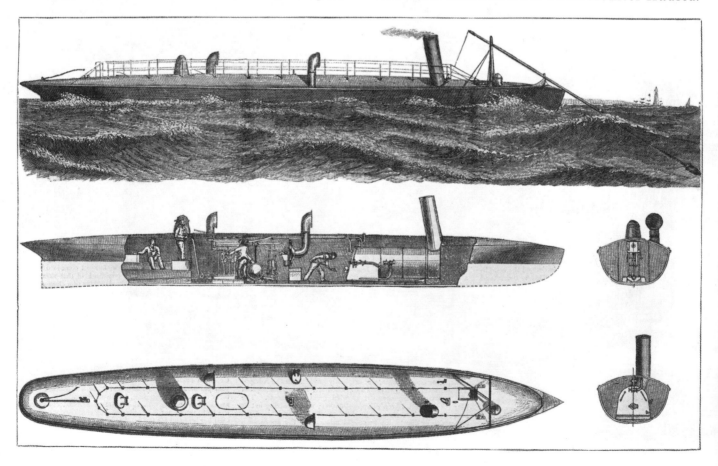

A Russian torpedo boat of 1878. The boat is 75 ft in length and 10 ft across with a draught of 5 ft and a maximum speed of 22 mph. Built on a multicellular design to increase strength and preserve buoyancy in case of enemy fire damaging it, the vessel was armed with three torpedo poles of hollow steel. The torpedoes were either copper or steel cases loaded with between 40 and 50 lbs of dynamite exploded by an electrical charge.

Above: The first true submersible used by the Confederacy, the H. L. Hunley (named after its inventor) was deployed against the Federal sloop Housatonic. It used a spar torpedo to sink the ship but, unfortunately, was itself destroyed in the devastating explosion that followed the impact.

within a range of about 600 yards. The *Huascar* luckily managed to change direction after the launching of the torpedo and escaped.

In succeeding years, Whitehead made changes to the prototype. He further streamlined it and fitted fins which stabilized the movement of the torpedo. He also replaced the gunpowder charge with guncotton which increased the explosive power by three times. Brotherhood's three cylinder air engine was adapted to his later models which gave them a speed of 18 knots. The first successful torpedo attack was launched in 1878 when a Russian ship sank a Turkish vessel in Batum Harbour at a range of 80 yards.

A torpedo attack in the early stages of its history was, to say the least, hazardous. The attacking ship had to steam well within gunnery range to launch its torpedoes. Surprise was of paramount importance during a torpedo attack and a ship making such a move must be fast, elusive and, if possible, invisible.

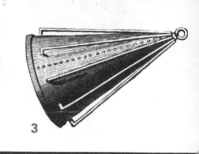

A ship encompassing these qualities was launched by the Admiralty in 1877 – the first torpedo boat. The *Lightning* was 90 feet long and capable of a speed of 19 knots. She carried one Whitehead torpedo which was mounted on davits at the stern. Later the delivery method was changed for a rotating launching tube and shortly afterwards changed again to permanent tubes positioned in the bows. The latter positioning of the tubes meant that she would have to steam towards her target right up until the precise moment of firing.

A point that had been overlooked in the designing of the torpedo boat, and others in her class, was that she was only fit for home waters, thus employing an essentially offensive weapon in a defensive role. The answer was to build larger boats. The slim narrow lines of the first torpedo boats were kept, but the length was increased to 123 feet. The lengthened boats were classed as ocean-going vessels, but not so by the crews who spent uncomfortable days and sleepless nights on manoeuvres with the fleet.

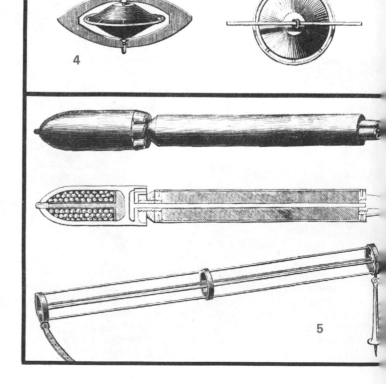

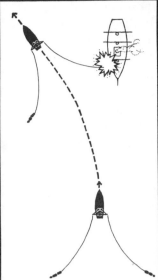

1. *Self-acting electric torpedo. When a vessel hit the guard it touched the plate thus completing a circuit and exploding the mine. (A) the torpedo guard; (B) insulated plate; (C) fuse; (D) battery on shore; (E) wire to earth; (F) wire to torpedo.*

2. *A mine-laying launch.*

3. *Turkish self-acting torpedo.*

4. *Punshon's floating torpedo; left: side view; right: top view.*

5. *Top: Hall Macdonald anti-torpedo-boat rockets. Middle: A cross-section view. Bottom: Rocket carrier.*

6. *Deck of a vessel towing torpedoes towards enemy. The windlasses lower the torpedoes. (Ignore reference letters on this contemporary print.)*

6a. *The torpedo boat approaches the enemy vessel from the south. One such has already veered away allowing towed torpedo to strike target.*

7. *One of the earliest mines. First experimented with in the mid-19th Century and used sparingly in 1917, it came into its own during the Second War. The magnetic field of a steel ship triggers it off.*

8. *An outrigged torpedo-pinnace attacking an ironclad.*

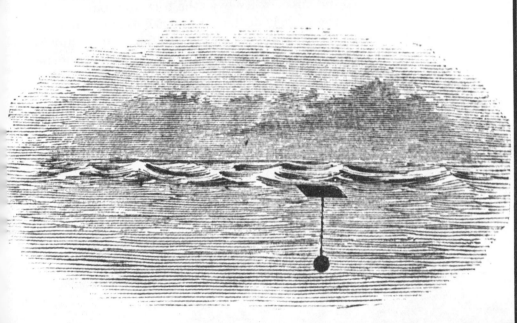

7

8

TORPEDO BOAT DESTROYERS

The torpedo boat was looked upon by the British navy as a serious threat to blockading squadrons. Many other countries were speedily developing these boats, especially the French, who were constructing extremely fast and very effective models. To counteract the threat of this, Yarrows shipyard obtained a contract to design and build ships that would surpass the torpedo boat. These later became known as 'torpedo boat destroyers'. The torpedo boat destroyers (later 'destroyers') were designed to be much larger and faster than the French torpedo boats. H.M.S. *Havock*, which was launched in 1893, was 180 feet long and could approach speeds of 26·7 knots. Her sister ship, the *Hornet*, was fitted with the Yarrow water-tube boiler (as opposed to the *Havock's* locomotive boiler), which enabled her to reach a top speed of 27·3 knots.

The water-tube boiler was a major contribution to the advance of naval engineering. In the ordinary cylindrical boiler water was heated in the boiler by copper tubing carrying hot air. The water-tube boiler reversed the process by having the water carried in the tubing which passed through the furnace. The steam pressure was inside instead of outside the tube, leaving very little danger of boiler collapse. The amount of metal necessary to resist bursting at high pressures in the water-tube boiler was comparatively light, though the bigger the bore of the tube, the thicker the metal had to be.

Apart from the overall economy of weight, the small amount of water required meant that steam pressure could be increased much more rapidly than with the cylindrical boiler. This was a very important consideration, for naval vessels were apt to make sudden departures, or fast increases of speed (at the sighting of an enemy), which was difficult with the old-type boilers.

Both the *Hornet* and the *Havock* were armed with three 18-inch torpedo tubes and one 12-pound and three six-pound guns, giving them all-round superiority over the torpedo boat.

These early destroyers were certainly superior to the torpedo boat on paper but not so during sea-faring trials. Much trouble was reported from the engine room. Apart from signs of hull strain, excessive vibration, extreme discomfort on the part of crew members, the ship was also reported as being too wet and a very bad roller

in heavy weather. These troubles were only temporary. Changes in the design of the superstructure and increases in weight displacement made life easier.

Later models, particularly the *Viper*, were widely praised for their fine sea-faring qualities and it was soon evident that a magnificent new type of warship had materialized. The *Viper* had the fortune to be the first naval vessel to be fitted with a steam turbine engine. It enabled her to reach a top speed of 34 knots and was at the time (1889) the fastest ship afloat.

The Parsons steam turbine made its debut at the naval revue held in honour of Queen Victoria's Jubilee in 1897. Steam heated by means of a water-pipe boiler was passed through a series of nozzles, expanding and gaining velocity, and was then directed onto a selection of blades on the periphery of a rotor. The velocity of the steam would pass along these blades, turning the rotor, to power the propellers.

By the late 1870s the torpedo was standard equipment in ships of all classes. Indeed, towards the end of the century, there was speculation that the submerged launching of torpedoes

would render the battleship obsolete, as by this time torpedoes were carrying 250 pounds of explosive at a speed of 30 knots.

To counteract the effects of the torpedo, great changes had to be made in hull construction. They were more heavily armoured below the water-line, and were further subdivided by way of bulkheads and water-tight compartments.

For total immunity a steel net apron was boomed out around the ship's hull. When not in use it was hoisted aboard and tied to a shelf constructed on the ship's side – a very awkward and frustrating operation. The immunity conferred by the steel apron did not last very long due to further improvements in torpedo design.

WARFARE BENEATH THE WAVES – THE SUBMARINE

One of the greatest developments in naval warfare was the invention of the submarine. The submarine proved to be the most deadly force in naval warfare since the invention of broadside fire in the 16th Century.

Man has always sought to imitate animals. Birds have long inspired him to fly and fish have fired his imagination with the desire to travel underwater. The idea of building an underwater craft was being explored as early as 1578 when an Englishman demonstrated a submersible boat to King James I. A quarter of a century later, Cornelis Drebbel built a wood and greased leather contraption that could submerge and be pulled about by oars.

The first underwater ship that could properly be called a submarine was built in the late 18th Century. This was a one-man ship designed by an American, David Bushnell, and christened the *Turtle*. During the American War of Independence, it attempted to set a mine under *H.M.S. Eagle*, Admiral Lord Howe's flagship. The *Turtle* approached the vessel, driven by a hand-cranked propeller. The attempt to attach the mine to the copper-sheathed bottom failed, however, and the mine blew up harmlessly.

A hand-driven submarine finally made a successful submerged attack when the *Hunley*, a Confederate submarine, sank the Federal warship *Housatonic* during the American Civil War. Built from an iron boiler, the 30-foot *Hunley* proved a death trap for her crew. In February, 1864, she drove a spar torpedo into the *Housatonic* which was anchored in blockade of Charleston harbour. The subsequent explosion sank both of the ships.

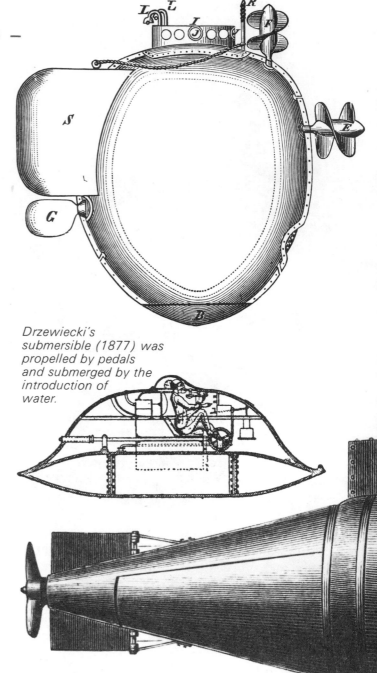

Drzewiecki's submersible (1877) was propelled by pedals and submerged by the introduction of water.

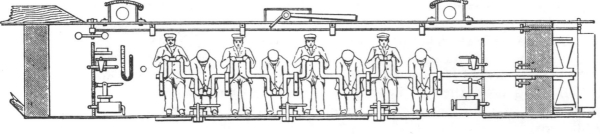

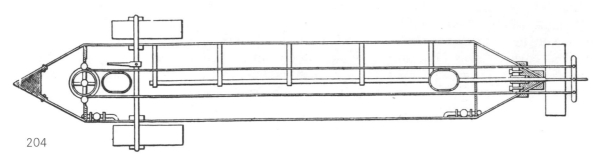

Hunley's David, *one of a number of hand propelled semi-submersibles used by the South during the American Civil War.*

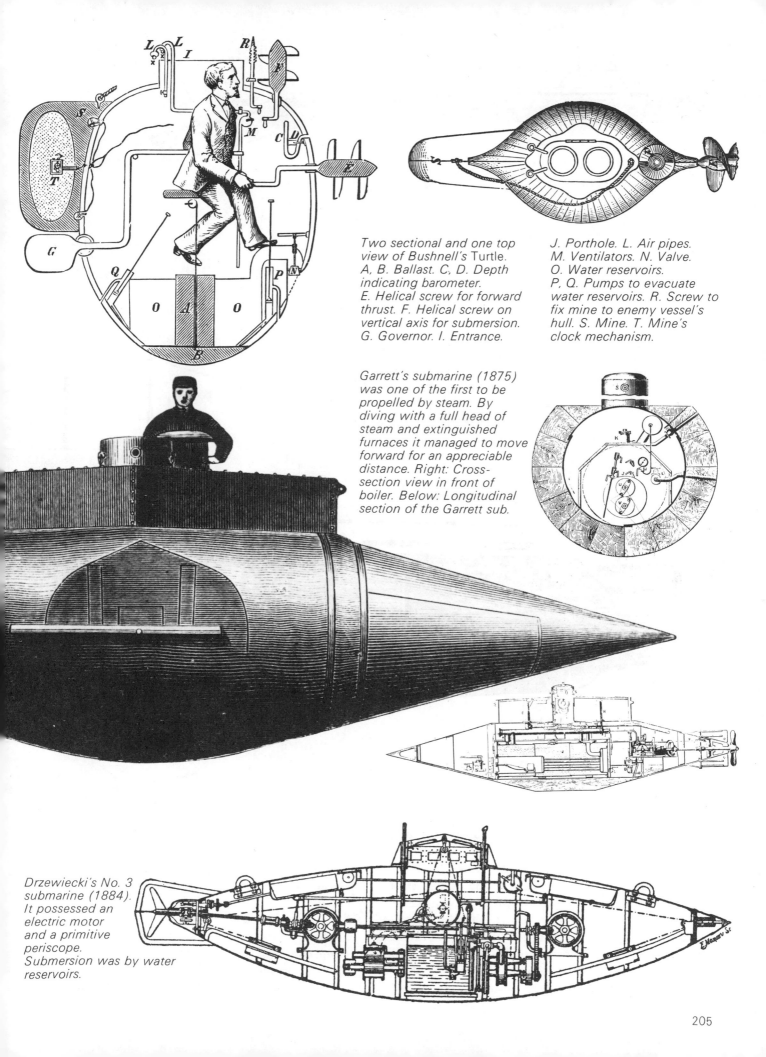

Two sectional and one top view of Bushnell's Turtle. A, B. Ballast. C, D. Depth indicating barometer. E. Helical screw for forward thrust. F. Helical screw on vertical axis for submersion. G. Governor. I. Entrance.

J. Porthole. L. Air pipes. M. Ventilators. N. Valve. O. Water reservoirs. P, Q. Pumps to evacuate water reservoirs. R. Screw to fix mine to enemy vessel's hull. S. Mine. T. Mine's clock mechanism.

Garrett's submarine (1875) was one of the first to be propelled by steam. By diving with a full head of steam and extinguished furnaces it managed to move forward for an appreciable distance. Right: Cross-section view in front of boiler. Below: Longitudinal section of the Garrett sub.

Drzewiecki's No. 3 submarine (1884). It possessed an electric motor and a primitive periscope. Submersion was by water reservoirs.

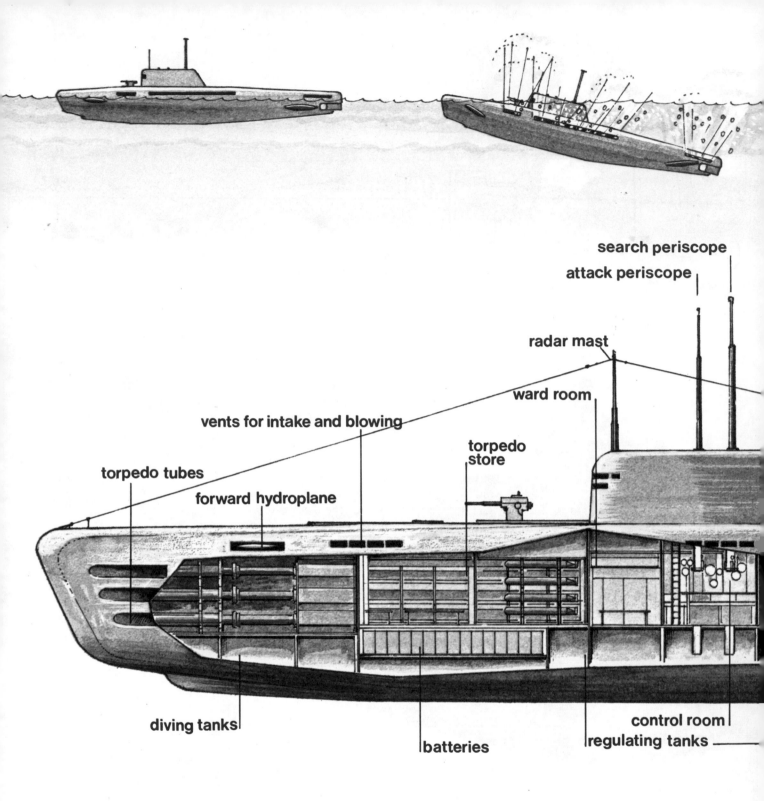

search periscope

attack periscope

radar mast

ward room

vents for intake and blowing

torpedo store

torpedo tubes

forward hydroplane

diving tanks

batteries

control room

regulating tanks

How Submarines Operate

Submarines, like all ships, depend on buoyancy to stay afloat. A series of tanks are fitted to all submarines. When flooded with water they give the ship a negative buoyancy and it begins to sink. At a desired depth, pumps or compressed air clear the water out of the tanks until a neutral buoyancy is achieved. The submarines will then float at the desired depth. To surface, the tanks are blown empty to give the ship a positive buoyancy.

All submarines depend for their ability to dive upon changing their buoyancy. They are equipped with thick inner pressure hulls and lighter outer hulls. The space between the hulls is divided into several diving and trim tanks. The diving tanks control the depth at which a submarine will ride and the trim tanks are used to keep the ship steady on an even level and at a neutral buoyancy.

But diving tanks alone are insufficient to

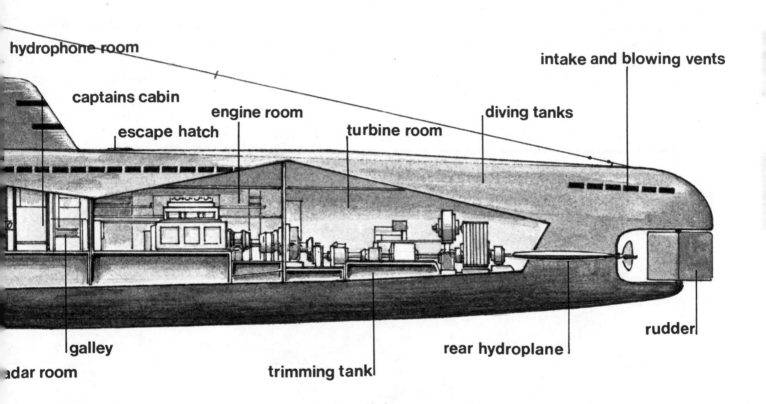

snorkel

hydrophone room

captains cabin

escape hatch

engine room

turbine room

intake and blowing vents

diving tanks

galley

adar room

trimming tank

rear hydroplane

rudder

manoeuvre a submarine. Some form of propeller is essential to drive it forward. Rudders are also necessary to steer the ship to the left or right and diving planes are usually attached to help control the angle of a dive. The planes are short, stubby wings which can be tilted to force the submarine up or down. The interaction of the tanks, propeller and diving planes are used to achieve a perfect balance in every variety of submarine vessel.

Top: The submarine dives (on the right) by flooding its tanks with water (arrowed). This increases its weight. To surface, the submarine blows the water out of its tanks and increases its buoyancy once more. By taking in more or less water and by achieving a balance of air and water in its tanks, the submarine can hold itself at any depth under the surface. The stubby hydroplanes give added control over the angle of dive, by being tilted so as to force the submarine up or down more rapidly. Above: A cut-away section of a typical submarine, showing the main working parts. These war machines posed a threat from a new angle — an unseen enemy.

The Birth of the Modern Submarine

The late 19th Century saw the predominance of sail gave way to the steam, and later the diesel, engine. These advances in mechanical propulsion soon led to efforts to install engines in submarines as well as other warships. At first, these attempts met with little success since the heat of a steam engine's furnace and its ponderous bulk made it totally impractical in an underwater ship. However, with the invention of electric engines powered by a system of batteries, a practical power plant was found.

In 1886, two Englishmen, Andrew Campbell and James Ash, designed the first electrically driven submarine, the *Nautilus*. It had a speed of six to eight knots and a range of 80 miles. But electric engines of this type had a severe drawback. Unless their batteries could be readily recharged, a submarine of this kind would be marooned without alternative power once it had cruised its maximum range.

The first submarine to overcome the limitations of the electric engine was designed and built by J. P. Holland in the late 1890s. Holland, working in America, took one of the newly developed automobile petrol engines, combined it with an electric motor and produced a power plant suitable for both underwater and long-distance surface cruising. Running on the surface with its hatches open, the ship was driven by the petrol engine. At the same time, the engine ran a generator that recharged the batteries. Once submerged, the electric engine took over the propulsion of the ship until the batteries were exhausted. The first *Holland* submarine to be produced was accepted by the U.S. Navy in 1900. It displaced close to 75 tons and had a length of 54 feet. Its cruising range was 1,500 miles, travelling at seven knots on the surface and six knots submerged.

At the same time that Holland was perfecting his invention another American, named Simon Lake, was working on the problem of a submarine's manoeuvrability. Through trial and error he finally came up with a periscope which

The Nautilus *was the first electrically driven sub. The Admiralty took a poor view of it when Sir William White, Director o*

could be used when submerged. Instead of running blind when underwater, a submarine could have a wide-angle view of the surface as well as a magnified image of it. Although a periscope had a very limited horizon, its slender silhouette poking above the surface was difficult to spot from a ship's bridge. The submarine became an effective, nearly invisible hunter.

By the nature of their design, the early petrol engines were dirty and dangerous to run. The volatile engine fumes could never be vented entirely from the submarine. In the cramped enclosure of the ship's hull, the danger of a shattering explosion was ever present. The solution was found in an engine built in the 1890s and named after its German inventor, Rudolph Diesel. Diesel engines burned a fuel oil that was far less volatile then gasoline. They were cheaper to run and more efficient in their fuel consump-had successfully launched the first diesel-electric powered submarine.

Although research and development had pro-duced an underwater boat capable of long distance travelling and submerged manoeuvring, without any armament it was little more than a transport and reconnaissance vessel. Even fitted with a deck gun a surfaced submarine could never hold its own against a conventional warship. It was the invention of the Whitehead torpedo, in 1868, that introduced a weapon whose potential was well suited to the submarine. Early torpedoes ran just below the surface on compressed air and had a limited range of only several hundred yards. A Swede, Torsten Nordenfelt, was the first to fit torpedo tubes inside the hull of a submarine. The tubes could be loaded from inside and the torpedoes launched while the submarine was totally submerged. By the First World War, torpedoes had been fitted with electric motors and stubby vanes to control their running depths, and could travel seven to eight thousand yards at speeds of 36 knots and deliver a 500 pound charge of TNT. The *Holland* submarine was the first to make use of torpedoes.

Naval Construction, was stuck in it at the bottom of the Thames on its test run.

Fitted with a periscope, a diesel-electric power plant, and armed with torpedoes and four- to five-inch deck guns, the submarine became a fearsome weapon. Travelling 17·5 knots on the surface and seven knots submerged, the long-range 'Unterseeboote', or U-boat, that Germany put to sea in the First World War, was a weapon fit to challenge the mightiest of conventional warships. In September, 1914, the German *U-9* sank three British cruisers steaming off the Dutch coast in slightly over 90 minutes. In the following four years more than 11,000,000 tons of Allied shipping, about 2,500 vessels in all, were sent to the bottom.

The only flaw which kept submarines from being used as fully submersible ships was the need to surface when running the generators that recharged the batteries. This limitation meant that submarines could only function as diving torpedo ships. None could operate beneath the waves for longer than 48 hours. Running the diesel engine and generators was a surface operation which revealed a submarine's course to reconnaissance aeroplanes and made it a vulnerable target to warships. The *schnorkel* was Germany's answer to the problem. Copying a Dutch design of 1938, they attached a pair of airpipes to the conning tower. One pipe sucked in air for the engine and crew, while the second operated as an engine exhaust. Valves in the pipes kept seawater from entering. In the course of the Second World War, German submarines were fitted with schnorkels, enabling them to breathe while at depths of up to 30 feet.

U35 *surfaces in the Mediterranean in 1917.*
The U35 was the record breaking submarine of the
First World War. In a two
month period in 1916, July and August,
it sank 54 ships in the Mediterranean, almost
all by gunfire. The major
casualties were French and Italian but the
British suffered heavy losses
as well. Unrestricted submarine warfare
in the North Atlantic and the
use of torpedoes eventually led the United States
to declare war on Germany.

The propulsion system which finally made submarines into truly underwater ships was developed by Hellmuth Walther, a German scientist. Using concentrated hydrogen peroxide as a fuel, he offered the German Navy plans for a totally self-contained turbine engine in 1937. The Walther engine operated independently of fresh air. Hydrogen peroxide was broken down chemically into water and oxygen. The oxygen was mixed with diesel oil in a combustion chamber and burned at a very high temperature. Water injected into the combustion chamber turned to high pressure steam and was drawn off with the hot gases to power a turbine unit which drove the propellers. This high-powered engine carried its own oxygen in its fuel and thus never required a source of fresh air.

Fortunately for the Allies, construction of Walther U-boats was only authorized in May, 1944. The first ships only appeared a year later; far too late to affect the course of events. They were small boats of only 850 tons but they were able to reach an underwater speed of 25 knots. None of the existing Allied anti-submarine devices would have been able to cope with a U-boat of this sort if it had appeared earlier in the war. In the last days of the war a Walther engine submarine was able to stage a dummy run on a group of British warships, coming within 500 yards – completely unnoticed.

'Happy Time' for U-Boats: the Summer of 1940

During the summer of 1940, the German 'blitzkreig' steamrollered through Western Europe. In July, the U-boat command established its first Atlantic base at Lorient on the coast of the Bay of Biscay. This cut the length of the U-boats' old routes to the open sea by more than 400 miles, and the number of boats that could be kept in action at any one time sharply increased. At the same time, the U-boat shipyards were moving into high gear and were easily able to replace combat losses.

The lessons of the First World War had been well learned by such commanders as Karl Dönitz, admiral of the U-boat fleet. He remembered the constant frustrations of foiled daytime attacks. Time and again, his boats were spotted on the surface and obliged to submerge and run. He devised new tactics of shadowing convoys during the day and attacking only at night. This way his U-boats could approach with impunity, their low silhouettes virtually invisible against the inky night waters. In turn, they were presented with the near perfect target of ships sharply etched against the light night sky. An additional advantage to this kind of attack was the speed at which a surfaced submarine could travel. Underwater, it was barely possible to attain five knots compared to 18 knots on the surface. This was faster even than some of the smaller escort ships that were herding the convoys. It permitted the submarines to creep right into the heart of a convoy and deliver repeated attacks before disappearing at high speed to a safe distance.

The use of tactics learned during the First World War and the enormous increases in manoeuvrability and endurance permitted U-boats to range far into the Atlantic, delivering attacks in all but the roughest weather. Against this well-armed foe, the out-numbered, harried Allied escorts were almost defenceless.

These were the conditions which led the German submarine captains to name the summer of 1940, 'The Happy Time'. From June to early fall, a total of 270 ships were sunk, nearly 1,400,000 tons. On the other side of the tally sheet only six U-boats were destroyed.

Under these foreboding conditions, the slow convoy SC7 prepared to sail in October, 1940. For the crossing 34 battered merchantmen gathered in Sydney, Nova Scotia. These underpowered, overladen ships could barely manage seven knots in the best of conditions. The lightly armed sloop, Scarborough, was the only escort protection the convoy had until a Western Approaches force could rendezvous with them.

The fourth day from Sydney, a gale sprang up which separated four unwieldy Great Lakes steamers from the main body of ships. Three of them were sunk by U-boats prowling for stragglers. On the eleventh day, two more escorts joined convoy SC7. They were the Fowey, a sister sloop of the Scarborough, and the Bluebell, one of the newly commissioned Flower class corvettes. With the escorts positioned ahead, astern and to the starboard, the convoy proceeded on its way.

A distance of at least five miles separated each of the three escorts, forming a defensive screen so widely spaced that any surfaced U-boat could easily penetrate the convoy's centre. The first U-boat to spot the convoy, U-48, radioed its course and speed and brought six other submarines hurrying to intercept. Then moving in to attack it fired a round of torpedoes, scoring two hits. The attack brought the three escorts hurrying to the sinking ships. While one picked up survivors, the other two crisscrossed the area hunting with their asdic units. Although this tactic left the convoy defenceless, U-48 had been forced to submerge and break off all contact. The escorts' response revealed a fatal lack of planning. Not having worked out a cohesive defence and being over-eager to counter-attack the U-boats, they often left the convoy without any protection whatsoever. Under a sustained wolfpack attack, the convoy's protection would be a shambles.

The convoy managed to shake off U-48 but

Death of a merchantman as a U-boat claims another victim.

the following evening a solitary submarine, *U-38*, penetrated the escort screen and torpedoed a freighter. At the same time, the U-boat pinpointed the convoy's position and was able to call in the approaching wolfpack. That evening two additional escorts, the sloop *Leith* and the corvette *Heartsease*, joined convoy SC7. The *Scarborough*, meanwhile, had fallen so far behind in a vain search to hunt down a sighted submarine that it failed to rejoin the convoy for the crucial battle that was approaching.

The following evening the convoy sailed into the ambush of the waiting submarine pack. A Swedish ship was the first to be hit. The *Leith* and *Fowey* rushed to pick up the survivors and to conduct a search sweep. Once again, the convoy was left with virtually no effective escort. The attacking submarines swept in, roaming through the columns of ships at will. Torpedo after torpedo rammed into the merchantmen, crippling or sinking them. In the confusion, the risk of collision drove the remaining ships to break formation entirely.

The escorts were desperately overworked, picking up crews from the water, hunting for the attacking U-boats and herding the remaining ships into some form of order. The lack of a systematic plan of defence made their task impossible. Ship after ship was hit and yet the escorts were unable to strike back and halt the continuous attack.

Dawn found the convoy totally scattered. The *Fowey* was able to round up eight ships that day but driving rain the following night scattered them again. By now, the surviving ships were well within the channel between Ireland and Britain. Here, aircover made the U-boats reluctant to follow and few, in any case, had sufficient torpedoes left to continue the attack. The remaining ships finally made their way to port. Of the 34 ships that had sailed from Sydney, 20 were sunk and two damaged. During the final battle only one submarine had been sighted and even that had been able to escape. The U-boats held the initiative throughout the entire engagement. Had their success continued, the British war effort would have come to a halt.

After the war, Britain experimented with two Walther-engine submarines. Although they performed excellently, the launching of the first atomic-powered submarine in 1955, the U.S.S. *Nautilus*, made them obsolete. The United States began to build a fleet of nuclear submarines that revolutionized naval warfare.

Above: The SS Kemmendine, *sunk in June, 1941.*

Bottom left: A U-boat captain in his conning tower. Below: A U-boat gun crew in action.

BREAKTHROUGH ON THE POWDER FRONT

We must now turn back and follow the major breakthroughs in other areas of maritime warfare. Although speculation towards the end of the 19th Century suggested that the major role in sea warfare would be usurped by the torpedo, armaments and battleships underwent further development, thus reasserting their prime importance.

The first breakthrough came with the manufacture of slow-burning large grain powder (called prismatic powder) which gave guns a much greater muzzle velocity. The aim of the new powder was to prolong the charge on the missile for as long as possible. It was later discovered that if the gun was *chambered* (that is, making the powder chamber larger than the charge) a greater amount of slow burning powder could be used without increasing the maximum pressure on the gun casing. It was soon found, however, that the shell left the barrel before the charge was completely consumed. Longer muzzles proved the solution to that particular problem but the lengthened muzzle made muzzle-loading a problem. The alternative was to switch to breech-loading mechanisms.

Breech-loaders had been overlooked in the British navy because of the fact that the guns could possibly be fired without the breech being properly closed, a dangerous hazard to both gunners and ship. The French and Germans had perfected breech-loading mechanisms, using automatic safety devices to ensure against

The Mercury *was one of the first all-steel-hulled cruisers in the Royal Navy.*

accidents. The French adapted an American design for an interrupted-screw breech block which was introduced into the French navy in 1858. The breech block was divided into four sections of interrupted screw threads. The operating lever swung the block into the breech, rotating it so that the screw threads engaged, thus locking the mechanism in place. The Germans used an improved Armstrong wedge system to achieve the same effect.

The universal adoption of breech-loading mechanisms left guns free to develop as large as they could within the confines of existing warships. Slower-burning powders were invented to take full advantage of increased barrel length. Prismatic powder became 'cocoa' powder which in turn was replaced by cordite. Cordite was a smokeless powder made up of guncotton and nitroglycerine. It was a much more powerful explosive agent than ordinary gun powder and made possible the development of larger guns capable of quicker fire.

The introduction of more efficient ordnance led, as usual, to changes in armour. But the usual response of thicker armour could no longer apply. There was a limit to the weight of armour a ship could carry. A new kind of armour was needed, not just more of the same. The eventual solution was the use of steel. In the late 1870s steel was introduced in the cruisers *Iris* and *Mercury*, making them the first all-steel hulled ships in the Royal Navy.

HMS Majestic *showing the interior of the barbette or gun turret.*

The Crucial Factors at Tsushima

For well over a generation a seemingly endless flow of technological innovations gave promise of stronger and more destructive navies. The transformation of the sailing man-of-war to the iron (later steel) hulled modern battleship was completed by the 1870s. The broadside had given way to the revolving turret, the small smooth bore cannon to the big guns with their greater speed, accuracy and hitting power. But no matter what the theoreticians said or what the reports of naval manoeuvres indicated the real test remained battle on the high seas. It was with great interest, therefore, that the naval powers of the world studied the Battle of Tsushima during the Russo-Japanese war of 1904–5. This battle, as one historian put it, 'was the first (and also last) occasion when opposing lines of ironclads joined battle and fought to a finish in the way naval theory prescribed'.

From being a backward, feudal nation, subservient to the gunboat diplomacy of European and American powers, Japan had in the short space of 50 years become the most powerful Asian country and was well on her way to being one of the world's great powers. She had shown

Russian ship breaks Japanese blockade at Port Arthur.

herself a willing and able student of the Westerners whom she had loathed so much. By 1904 she was ready to show the results of her studies.

The Russo-Japanese war was a contest between two imperialist countries squabbling over shares of the dismembered China. In February, 1904, without a formal declaration of war, Japan swooped down on the Russian ships anchored in Port Arthur, using the much-touted torpedo

boats. The torpedo, due to its small range and great inaccuracy, proved to be a much less formidable weapon than had been claimed by the protagonists. Further action around Port Arthur showed that the great and medium range quick-firing gun shooting from some distance was to be the decisive element in combat.

By the spring of 1904 the Russian Eastern fleet had been destroyed by the Japanese. In a

A Russian battleship is towed into captivity. Speed and accurate gunnery shattered the Russian navy at Tsushima.

desperate attempt to curtail his Far Eastern losses the Russian Czar, Nicholas II, ordered his Baltic fleet to the Sea of Japan. 'The Japanese must be put in their place,' Rozhdestvensky was told. The 56-year-old Rozhdestvensky was a brave man but he had last seen action years before in the Turkish campaigns. The Baltic fleet was a disparate collection of five modern and three old battleships, three coastal defence ships and an old armoured cruiser. It would take an experienced admiral to weld that motley collection into an effective fighting forcé. Alas, Admiral Rozhdestvensky had neither the necessary experience nor had he the capabilities of a really good commander.

Admiral Togo on the other hand already had the destruction of the Russian Eastern fleet to his credit. He also had ample time to prepare for the next and final stage of the war while Rozhdestven-sky continued on his laborious way round the Cape of Good Hope.

Sixteen months after the opening of hostilities the Baltic fleet arrived in the Sea of Japan. Rozhestvensky formed his fleet into two columns hoping to force a passage through the straits of Tsushima to Vladivostock. Rozhdestvensky led the stronger, starboard line in his flagship, the *Suvaroff*. Nebogatoff commanded the port line of eight ships. Three fast cruisers formed a vanguard while two cruisers and four destroyers held the rear. These were followed by the supply and hospital ships.

Togo's tactics were simple. The Russians had the superiority in heavy guns but he had the advantage in speed. Therefore his big battleships would cut off the Russian advance while the cruisers would circle around the Russian line and take it from the rear. The battle began just after 2 p.m. on May 27. Everything seemed to follow the book. Togo chose his range at about 9,500 yards and opened fire on Rozhdestvensky's column. Within an hour the *Suvaroff* was disabled, her flag-captain killed and the Admiral himself wounded twice. The speed of the Japanese boats and the accuracy of their fire left no doubt as to the outcome of the battle. The Russian were ill-prepared, a high proportion of their shells failed to explode and their gunnery collapsed after the initial Japanese onslaught.

As night fell the surviving Russian ships hoped to escape to Vladivostock but even this was not allowed them. Togo wanted a complete victory. The torpedo boats were sent in and completed the devastation wrought by the battleships and cruisers. The Russian fleet was completely annihilated. Fourteen battleships and five armoured cruisers were lost. Only one small cruiser and two destroyers reached Vladivostock. From a potentially great naval power, Russia was reduced overnight to a third class naval force.

Tsushima taught the navies of the world that guns and speed were the crucial factors in a naval engagement. Superior gunnery, the use of high explosive shells, and the speed of the armoured cruisers were the important factors in the Japanese victory. The much-vaunted torpedo boat was seen in its true perspective – an important auxiliary weapon, not the dominant factor in naval warfare. Henceforth the naval powers of the world concentrated on the development of the big gun battleship.

220

The Russians had the superiority in heavy firepower but the Japanese navy had a distinct edge when it came to speed. The Japanese also displayed considerably greater firing accuracy.

Below: The Russian Baltic fleet. On the left is Rozhdestvensky's flagship, the Suvaroff.

DREADNOUGHT OR DINOSAUR?

The Dreadnought ship was the greatest development of the battleship but, unfortunately, in many ways it resembled the dinosaur – too big for its own good.

As early as 1903 an Italian engineer, Cuniberti, wrote an article arguing for a big gun warship which would be armed with 12 12-inch guns and which would have a speed superior to any contemporary battleship. At the time Cuniberti's proposals were quite revolutionary and raised a great deal of resistance in naval quarters. It was felt, and quite rightly too, that the development of such a ship would render obsolete all preceding classes of warships.

Yet three years later King Edward VII launched the *Dreadnought*. The outstanding features of the *Dreadnought* were the 10 12-inch guns mounted in five turrets: one facing fore, two aft, and one on each side just forward of amidships. The positioning of the turrets enabled six guns to be fired forward and a possible eight guns fired in broadside.

Of the 27 12-pound guns, 12 were mounted on the superstructure, 2 on each turret top, and 2 on the quarter-deck. These guns were to be used as a counter-offensive against torpedo boats and destroyers. The *Dreadnought* was plated with an armour of 11-inch toughened mild steel below

HMS Dreadnought.

the waterline with a belt of eight-inch plating just above it. The bow and the stem were protected by six-inch and four-inch armour respectively.

The *Dreadnought* was the first large battleship to be fitted with a turbine engine, giving her a maximum speed of 21 knots. She was the most efficient ship in the world in her time, for the turbine engines dispensed with the time-consuming and laborious process of overhauling the engines, so necessary with the old steam engines even after a single day's steaming at high speed. She also made use of wireless.

This revolutionary battleship gave her name to a new world-wide class of warships. Not only was she bigger than anything that had been built previously, she was stronger and was capable of engaging two and a half of the older warships on an equal basis. Indeed the Germans soon referred to the pre-dreadnoughts as 'funf-minuten' ships – able to survive for only five minutes under the terrible firepower of the all-powerful dreadnought.

It can be seen, therefore, why it was that the British launched the dreadnought programme with some trepidation. Her undoubted naval superiority was put in jeopardy, for the Germans could commence to build their own dreadnoughts and maintain an even pace with the British.

BATTLECRUISERS AT SPEED

Speed and firepower were the two important factors in naval warfare. The dreadnoughts accounted for firepower and the battlecruisers were developed at about the same time for speed.

In aim the battlecruiser was the descendant of the sailing frigate: that is, the eye of the fleet. The design was directed towards producing a ship of superior speed, enabling her to reconnoitre in the face of the enemy. The British launched the first battlecruisers in 1907 – the *Indomitable*, *Inflexible* and *Invincible*. Of necessity speed meant a sacrifice in heavy-weight armour and armament. The battlecruisers were constructed with a medium armour seven inches thick but their firing power was kept nearly equal to ships of the dreadnought class. For, by lightening the ship in other respects, eight 12-inch guns could be retained. These 12-inch guns were mounted two to a turret with two turrets along the centre-line, fore and aft, and one each side. She also carried 16 four-inch guns able to fire 12 times a minute, and five submerged torpedo tubes placed in the bow and stern. The cruiser was also fitted with two anti-aircraft guns (A.A. guns), which were introduced owing to the success of early experiments with 'heavier than air' flying machines. The battlecruiser had an indicated horsepower of 41,000 (18,000 for the *Dreadnought*) and attained a maximum speed of 26 knots.

Speed and Firepower Decide Battle of Coronel and Falkland Islands

As with the dreadnoughts the Germans were quick to follow the British lead. They swiftly built up a fleet of battlecruisers which proved cruelly effective in the early years of the First World War. The battlecruiser was ideal for the tasks the Germans gave them – quick hit-and-run raids on merchant shipping and unprotected ports and harbours. As Vice-Admiral Graf Maximilian von Spee wrote, 'A single light cruiser can coal from captured vessels and maintain herself for longer . . . as there are great prizes to be won there, I despatched the fastest light cruiser.' Spee had just given permission for the *Emden* to operate raids in the Indian Ocean. For two months, through September and October of 1914, the *Emden* conducted devastating raids on allied shipping. Nine ships were sunk in September, a Russian cruiser and a French destroyer were sunk in Penang harbour in October. But then her luck ran out. In an attempted raid on the Cocos Islands she ran into

Top: HMS Inflexible. *Above:* HMS Indomitable *at full speed Right:* HMS Invincible. *These three were the first British battlecruisers (1907), descendants of the frigate and used as the eyes of the fleet.*

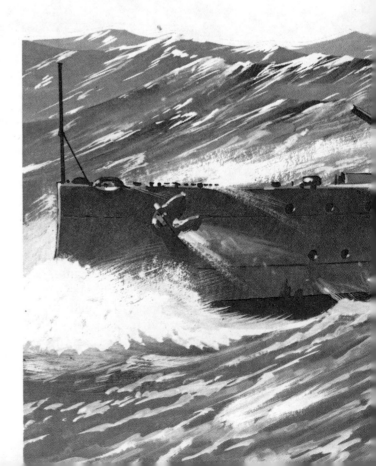

a heavily escorted Anzac convoy. Captain Glossop of H.M.A.S. *Sydney* was despatched to pursue the bold raider. After a long running battle he managed to run her to ground on the coral reefs off the islands.

Meanwhile the rest of von Spee's squadron had been operating in the Pacific, off the Chilean coast. The British High Command feared he would begin raiding operations on the trade routes in the Atlantic. The Admiralty ordered Rear-Admiral Craddock to the Falkland Islands with the command to 'get Spee.' At Craddock's disposal were the old armoured cruiser *Monmouth*, the modern light cruiser *Glasgow*, and the armed merchantman *Otranto*. Craddock's flagship was the armoured cruiser *Good Hope*. Also present was the old battleship *Canopus*. The search for the German raider began.

Spee commanded two heavy cruisers, the *Scharnhorst* and *Gneisenau* and three light cruisers, the *Nürnberg*, the *Leipzig* and the *Dresden*. The German ships were faster and more powerful than the punitive British force.

Upon learning the nature of his opponents, Spee set off immediately to seek a confrontation. On Sunday November 1, 1914, the Germans espied the British ships off Coronel. By six in the evening the battle lines were formed and at 7.04 the Germans opened fire at a range of 12,000 yards. The *Scharnhorst* and *Gneisenau* concentrated their fire on the *Good Hope* and the *Monmouth*. The German shells found their mark and the *Good Hope* was disastrously hit; her foredeck exploded, burning brilliantly in the dark night. The brightly lit *Good Hope* provided an excellent target for the German gunners who were themselves sheathed in darkness.

The only hope for the British now lay in closing the range. Craddock led his ships towards the German line but Spee was too fast and kept the

Above: The German armoured cruiser Gneisenau. Weight: 11,600 tons; speed: 22·5 knots; armament: eight 8·2 in guns.

Above: The Gneisenau's *sister ship, the* Scharnhorst.

range to his own advantage. In a last desperate attempt to gain satisfaction from the enemy, Craddock charged the *Scharnhorst*. The heavy German ships turned their broadsides on the ill-fated cruiser, subjecting her to a ferocious barrage from which there was no escape. The *Good Hope* exploded and sank with all hands on board. A similar fate awaited the *Monmouth* at the hands of the *Nürnberg*. Only the *Otranto* and the *Glasgow* managed to escape.

News of the defeat at Coronel shocked the Admiralty into action. The *Invincible* and *Inflexible*, as superior to the German vessels as they had been to the *Good Hope* and the *Monmouth*, were sent to accomplish what Craddock with his inferior ships could not, the complete destruction of Spee's squadron.

On December 7, 1914, Vice-Admiral Sir Frederick Doveton Sturdee arrived at Port Stanley in the Falkland Islands. In addition to the two battlecruisers he had with him six cruisers and an armed merchantman. There was no doubt that with his superior force Sturdee

Left:
Von Spee,
dreaded raider
of the Pacific. Right: Sir Doveton Sturdee.
He finally put paid to Von Spee's activities.

The Inflexible *and* Invincible *chase Von Spee's squadron at the Battle of the Falkland Isles.*

would defeat the Germans. The problem was to find them. Luck was with the British, for the day after their arrival at Port Stanley Sturdee received the news that *Gneisenau* and *Nürnberg* were steaming towards the port followed by the rest of Spee's ships.

In choosing to attack the Falkland Islands Spee made the critical error of his career. Why he chose to do so is not known but it is certain that if he had ordered an immediate attack he could have inflicted serious damage on the unprepared British fleet, although at the cost of his own ships. As it was, when informed of the presence of the British warships Spee gave the order: 'Do not accept action. Concentrate on course east by south. Proceed at full speed.'

Sturdee gave chase and the first shots of the Battle of the Falkland Islands were fired just before one in the afternoon. Seeing that he was outnumbered, Spee ordered his light cruisers to slip away, hoping to hold the British with his armoured cruisers. The British cruisers gave chase while the *Invincible* and the *Inflexible*

concentrated their fire on the *Gneisenau* and the *Scharnhorst*. Just as the German ships had pounded the *Good Hope* and the *Monmouth* into the sea so now the *Invincible* and *Inflexible* savagely mauled the *Scharnhorst* and the *Gneisenau*. Twist and turn as they might, the German vessels could not escape the inexorable fire power of the British. By five in the afternoon the battle was over. The two German cruisers had been sunk; of the light cruisers the *Nürnberg* and *Leipzig* suffered the same fate that night and the *Dresden* was captured four days later.

The lesson of Coronel and the Falkland Islands battles was clear: no matter how brilliant the commander, it was not possible to send an inferior fleet to face a more powerful enemy and hope to win. The *Scharnhorst* and the *Gneisenau* outclassed Craddock's vessels and were easily able to destroy them; the *Invincible* and *Inflexible* greatly outclassed the German armoured cruisers and annihilated them in face-to-face combat. In each case speed and firepower were the important elements leading to victory.

Jutland: The Clash of the Leviathan

Coronel and the Falkland Islands were diversionary engagements. The main British and German forces of dreadnoughts and battle-cruisers lay waiting apprehensively to the north in the North Sea. Both sides were eager to test the might of their naval arms but, wary of head-on conflict, sought to engage the enemy by means of various traps.

The German fleet, commanded by Vice Admiral Scheer, could not attack the whole British fleet owing to its numerical inferiority. The alternative was to trap part of it, probably the battle-cruiser force, and engage before the larger battleship complement could intervene.

With this end in mind Scheer settled upon two plans. The first was to mount an attack on one of Britain's east coast ports, Sunderland, using Vice-Admiral Hipper's battlecruiser fleet. Submarines and the main battle force under Scheer's personal command would cover for Hipper.

The second and similar plan was to have Hipper raid British shipping steaming off the nearby Danish coasts. Again the submarines and Scheer's battleships would stay hidden, to emerge at the crucial moment of battle.

Scheer hoped to put the first plan into operation but bad weather made it inadvisable and on May 30, 1916, he ordered Hipper's cruiser force to make an appearance off the Norwegian coast. Scheer thus thought to lure an investigating enemy fleet into his trap.

The British Admiralty were well aware, however, that the Germans were up to something. The British had decoded the German's secret message and were kept well-informed of impending moves. Admiral Sir John Jellicoe, stationed at Scapa Flow in the Orkney Islands, was ordered south. Vice-Admiral Beatty led a vanguard force of six battlecruisers escorted by cruisers and destroyers.

The first phase of the Battle of Jutland, the South Run, saw Beatty dash towards Hipper's fleet, guns blazing. Hipper, meanwhile, drew back leading Beatty towards Scheer. The battlecruiser duel went badly for the British. Three of Beatty's ships were badly hit before he scored a return hit against the Germans. Fortunately a fast battleship force under Evan-Thomas appeared within

The Indefatigable *steaming into battle at Jutland.*

range. The heavy 15-inch guns bombarded the enemy fleet, forcing Hipper to retreat. At about the same time (4.30 in the afternoon) Scheer's main battleship force hove into sight. Hipper was saved but the delighted British could now hope to bring the full weight of their naval might on the Germans and finally, irrevocably crush them into defeat.

The second phase of the battle saw a complete turnabout on the first. Beatty drew the enemy after him, leading them towards the main British fleet in the north.

Unaware of the trap awaiting him, Scheer was jubilant at the thought of victory over such a redoubtable adversary. He congratulated himself on his clever plans and looked forward to the accolades of the Kaiser. Great was his surprise when out of the smoke and haze he saw looming ahead of him the massed might of the British fleet. The horizon from the north to east was a sea of fire; destruction seemed certain. His only possible move was a complete about face which he immediately ordered. He still, however, had to make his way back to base. Several times

Above: A rare photograph of the Battle of Jutland taken from a British destroyer engaged in the action. Below: The König Albert, *one of Scheer's battleships.*

Artist Norman Howard's impression of the Battle of Jutland. To the left are the British, on the right the Germans.

during the late afternoon Scheer changed course, always managing to avoid Jellicoe's fleet. To gain valuable time he ordered Hipper's cruisers back into the fray. The battleships must be saved at all costs, reasoned Scheer, even if it meant the sacrifice of the cruisers.

Night fell and Scheer knew that either he must get past the British fleet or else face utter ruin on the morrow. Three choices of route lay before him. He could head south-west towards the River Ems, south-east towards the Horn Reef and the River Elbe, or south to Heligoland and Wilhelmshaven.

Jellicoe decided that the Germans would choose the southerly route despite advice that the Horn Reef route was more likely. He did, however, despatch a minelayer to block the Horn Reef channel. Jellicoe's plan was to cut off Scheer's route into the German Bight. And even if Scheer took the Horn Reef route he would have to pass astern of Jellicoe's battle squadrons and Jellicoe could count on the flotilla to keep him informed of Scheer's position. As it turned out the flotilla did nothing of the sort. Scheer slipped past the British fleet and by daylight was safe. Thus ended in anticlimax what was to be

the greatest naval engagement of the war.

Years of controversy, massive armaments build-up, and anxious expectation led up to the Battle of Jutland. At last, it was felt, the dreadnought would be put to the test. The results were inconclusive, to say the least. The British lost three capital ships, three cruisers, and a few destroyers; the Germans lost one battlecruiser, four cruisers, a pre-dreadnought battleship, and some destroyers, though many of the other German ships were severely mauled. Both sides claimed victory and even 60 years later debate rages as to who in fact won. One outcome of the battle was the Kaiser's decision not to risk his fleet again in dangerous ventures. Once again he ordered the submarines to take the offensive, thus bringing the United States into the war.

The big gun battleship never had a chance to display its combat virtuosity and it was not long before the days of the dreadnought were numbered. 'Never again,' wrote one historian, 'would long lines of the steel clad leviathans move ponderously into action and prepare to fight it out in an exchange of shell fire.' The whole nature of naval warfare was changed by the submarine and the availability of aircraft.

THE WASHINGTON TREATY: A LIMIT TO POWER

After the end of the First World War there was a virtual halt in ship construction. Naval power shifted from Europe to America and Japan. After the war the Japanese announced that they were about to build a fleet of eight battleships and eight cruisers, none of which was to undergo more than eight years of service. The Americans took this as a challenge and commenced a building programme of ten battleships and six cruisers. Due to the Washington Treaty of 1921 the Americans only completed two of their battleships – the *Colorado* and the *West Virginia*. Displacing 32,000 tons and armed with eight 16-inch guns, the two ships were also fitted with the new turbo-electric engines. The turbo-electric engine differed from the conventional steam turbine by having the propeller shaft driven by an electric motor. The turbo-electric engine added to the efficiency and speed of the newly constructed battleships.

The trend towards bigger gun battleships was cut short in late 1921 by a conference called by the United States government to discuss a limitation on naval armaments. The United States, Britain, Japan, Italy, and France signed a treaty limiting their capital ship tonnage to a proportion of 5:5:3:1·75:1·75 respectively. They also agreed not to build or acquire any new ships except in replacement of those lost or upon reaching 20 years of age. In addition any new ships built would not exceed 35,000 tons displacement.

The first ships to be built to these standards were the British battleships *Nelson* and *Rodney*. Their main armament consisted of nine 16-inch guns mounted in three turrets, two fore and one aft, with a secondary armament of 12 6-inch guns mounted in two power-worked turrets. Apart from abandonment of all-round armour protection, these ships saved valuable weight by the introduction of super-heated steam, reducing the number of boilers to eight.

The design of the armoured cruiser was also constricted by the terms of the Washington Treaty. The cruiser was limited to a maximum displacement of 10,000 tons and to armament not exceeding eight inches calibre.

The effect on cruiser construction was the attempt to squeeze as many eight-inch guns as possible on the reduced cruiser with all thoughts of armour protection thrown out the window.

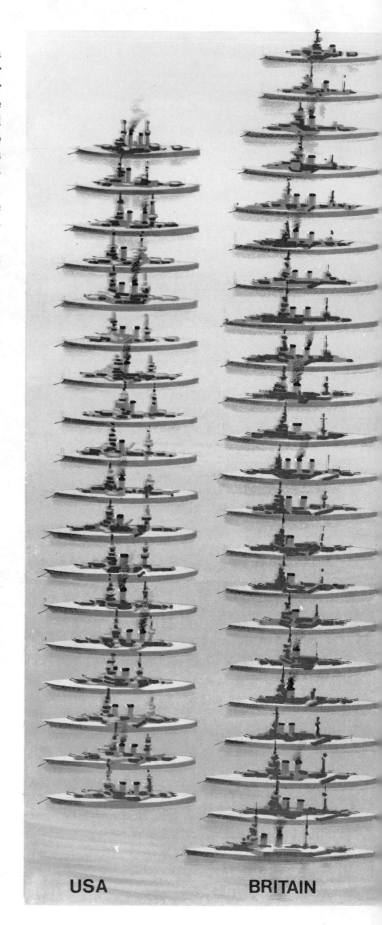

USA　　　**BRITAIN**

In 1924: relative naval strengths of the five signatories, 2½ years after signing the Washington Treaty.

USA	BRITAIN	FRANCE	ITALY	JAPAN
	Thunderer			
	King George V			
	Ajax			
	Centurion			
Utah	Iron Duke			
Florida	Marlborough			
Wyoming	Emperor of India			
Arkansas	Benbow			
New York	Barham			
Texas	Warspite			
Nevada	Queen Elizabeth			
Oklahoma	Tiger			
Arizona	Malaya			Kongo
Pennsylvania	Royal Sovereign	Voltaire		Hiyei
Mississipi	Resolution	Diderot		Haruna
New Mexico	Revenge	Condorcet	Napoli	Hirishima
Idaho	Royal Oak	Courbet	Roma	Fuso
Tennessee	Ramillies	Jean Bart	Dante Alighieri	Yamashiro
California	Valliant	Paris	Guilio Cesare	Ise
Maryland	Repulse	Provence	Conte di Cavour	Hiuga
Colorado	Renown	Bretagne	Caio Duilio	Nagato
West Virginia	Hood	Lorraine	Andrea Doria	Mutsu

FRANCE ITALY JAPAN

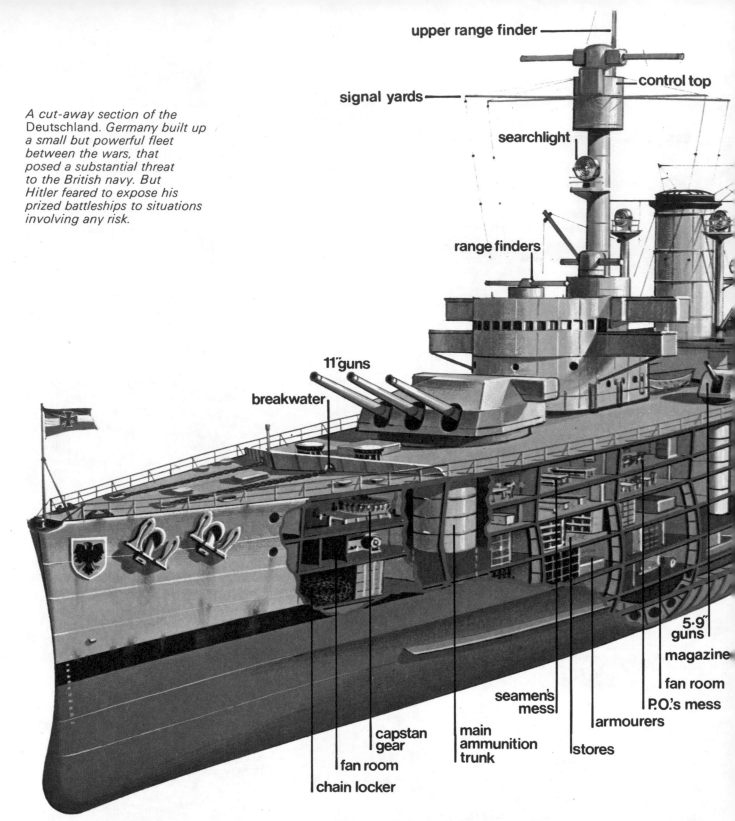

A cut-away section of the Deutschland. *Germany built up a small but powerful fleet between the wars, that posed a substantial threat to the British navy. But Hitler feared to expose his prized battleships to situations involving any risk.*

upper range finder

signal yards

control top

searchlight

range finders

11″guns

breakwater

5·9″ guns

magazine

fan room

P.O.'s mess

seamen's mess

armourers

capstan gear

main ammunition trunk

stores

fan room

chain locker

The most interesting and revolutionary designs were those of the Germans, whose ships came to be know as pocket battleships. Building ships of 12,000 tons displacement, the Germans armed them with six 11-inch guns and a mixed secondary armament of 5·9- and 4·1-inch guns as well as eight torpedo tubes. Diesel engines developing 56,000 horsepower gave these ships a speed of up to 26 knots, making them formidable commerce-raiders.

Later the Germans created the first all-welded ship. It replaced the standard riveting process of making the ships stronger and lighter.

The Washington Treaty expired in 1930 but was renewed as the London Naval Treaty. The latter treaty was due to expire at the end of 1936 and desperate efforts were made to renew it. However, by that time international relations had become very strained. Hitler publicly denounced the Treaty of Versailles and managed to negotiate

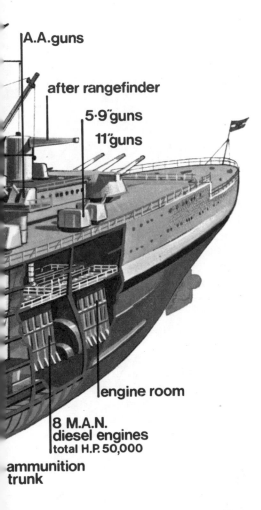

A.A.guns

after rangefinder

5·9" guns

11" guns

engine room

8 M.A.N.
diesel engines
total H.P. 50,000

ammunition
trunk

Top: The Yamato *carried the largest guns (18·1 ins) of any battleship in the world. Above: The* Deutschland, *one of the revolutionary German pocket battleships built in the inter-war period. An innovation in the use of welded (as opposed to riveted) hulls.*

an agreement whereby Germany could build up her naval strength to 35 per cent of that of Britain. Both Italy and Japan adopted aggressive attitudes and it was not long before the armaments race was on again.

Capital ships of great size, armour, speed, and striking power were being built, the most powerful of these by the Japanese. The *Yamato* and *Murachi*, displacing 64,170 tons, mounted nine 18·1-inch guns and maintained a top speed

of 27·5 knots. However, during the Second World War the usefulness of the capital ship diminished, her role being usurped by submarines and aircraft. Battleships and cruisers alike were hurriedly equipped with greater anti-torpedo protection and high angle guns for use against aeroplanes.

The aeroplane was of paramount importance during the Second World War and its advent saw the rapid development of the aircraft carrier.

The English Atlantic Fleet in line of battle led by HMS Rodney.

THE AIRCRAFT CARRIER: A NEW DIMENSION

By the Second World War the aeroplane was without a doubt the single most powerful weapon available. The development of the aircraft carrier extended that power to the sea. Primitive aircraft carriers had been·built and tested in the early years of the 20th Century. The Curtiss seaplane had aroused the interest of the United States Navy in the possibilities of aircraft. In 1910 the newly constructed *Birmingham* was made available for flight experiments. A wooden platform 83 feet long and 24 feet wide was built over the ship's bow. On November 14, a Curtiss pusher biplane was hoisted aboard and its pilot,

Eugene B. Ely, made ready for take-off. Racing the engine at full power he rolled it down the ramp. The plane dipped slightly into the water but the wooden prop held and he was airborne. It was the first successful flight of an aeroplane from a ship.

In January, 1911, Ely added another first to his collection by landing a biplane on the armoured cruiser *Pennsylvania*. Twenty-two pairs of 50-pound sandbags placed at three-foot intervals were used as arresting gear. Each pair of sandbags was connected by a line 12 inches above the deck. Three pairs of hooks were

Eugene Ely's famous landing on the U.S. cruiser Pennsylvania. *Flying at 35 mph, he was stopped within 60 ft by means of hooks on the plane which caught on to ropes on the vessel.*

attached to the aeroplane so that on landing they would catch the taut line, thus bringing the plane to a halt. Ely's hooks took hold on the 12th arresting line, stopping the biplane with a deck run of only 30 feet. Ely was greeted by the cheers of the gathered sailors and the Captain exclaimed, 'This is the most important landing of a bird since the dove flew back to the Ark.'

Developments on the other side of the Atlantic saw the birth of the first carriers. In 1912 a biplane took off from the forecastle of the British battleship *Hibernia*. A year later the French outfitted a cruiser to carry aircraft on her

Another American, Glenn Curtiss, takes off from the
Birmingham in his hydroplane — a pusher biplane with
clumsy fore-and-aft structures.

Mediterranean manoeuvres. In the same year the British adapted an old cruiser to carry two seaplanes which were launched from a short deck built forward of her bows. In 1914 an oil tanker still under construction was taken over by the Admiralty and converted to carry ten seaplanes. The *Ark Royal* had hangar space below decks and like the earlier models used cranes to hoist the planes into and out of the water.

The first true aircraft carriers were built in 1917. In that year wheeled fighter aircraft were used for the first time on a carrier. Commander F. J. Rutland flew a Sopwith Pup biplane off the deck of the *Manxman*. He proved the point that a fighter could take off on a flight deck of less than 45 feet. After Rutland's experiments orders were given for all cruisers capable of having them to be fitted with 20-foot flight decks. In March of the same year the cruiser *Furious* was completed as a partial carrier. She had a flight deck 228 feet long and 50 feet wide and supported four seaplanes and six wheeled aircraft. In November the *Furious* was overhauled and fitted with a rear landing deck 287 feet long and 70 feet wide. She now could carry 12 Sopwith Pups and eight seaplanes. In 1918 seven of her Sopwiths made history by successfully bombing the Zeppelin base at Tondern.

In 1916 the British bought the unfinished Italian liner *Conte Rosso*, rechristened her the *Argus*, and converted her into the first full-length aircraft carrier. Unencumbered by masts or funnels, she was the first flush-decked carrier, with a flight deck 550 feet long and 68 feet wide. Two elevators brought the planes up to the flight deck. The *Argus* was also the first carrier to carry torpedo aircraft but the First World War ended before their usefulness could be gauged. In 1920 the carrier *Eagle* was launched. She introduced the 'island' structure by having her mast, bridge and funnel set on the starboard side of the vessel. This allowed a great deal more landing space on the deck.

By 1925 the British navy was clearly in the lead in the development of aircraft carriers but the transfer of aviation responsibility from the Admiralty to the newly formed Royal Air Force meant that less money was spent on developing the carrier. The Americans and Japanese quickly caught up the British lead and by the Second World War were among the dominant naval powers in the world.

Early in the century Japan had sent naval officers to France and the United States to learn

Right: Official U.S. Navy photograph of Battle of Midway (June 1942) shows a Japanese heavy cruiser of the Mogami class after heavy bombardment by carrier based naval aircraft.

Below: The do's and don'ts of landing on a carrier. Many problems faced the pioneer pilots.

(a) Incorrect landing on a rolling carrier.

(b) Correct landing between rolls.

(c) Correct landing on pitching carrier – well up the deck.

(d) Landing between the smoke and ship's turbulence causes 'bumps'.

(e) Flying from the bows into a headwind.

(f) Too low an approach.

(g) The approach is too high.

(h) This is the correct approach angle.

Above: Squadron-Commander Dunning's fatal landing on the Furious.

the techniques of flying. The first Japanese Navy aeroplanes were British-bought Farman float biplanes. In 1913 the naval transport vessel *Wakamiya Maru* was refitted to carry two seaplanes. In 1919 the Japanese began construction on the second purpose-built aircraft carrier, the *Hosho* (the first was the British *Hermes*). Displacing 7,470 tons, the *Hosho* had a maximum speed of 25 knots and carried seven fighter aircraft, ten attack planes and four reconnaissance aeroplanes.

The terms of the Washington Treaty limited the United States, Britain, and Japan to two aircraft carriers. Both the United States and Japan chose to convert two of their projected capital ships. The Americans selected the semi-completed *Lexington* and *Saratoga* for conver-

sion. The completed carriers had a displacement of 36,000 tons and an armament of eight eight-inch guns and twelve five-inch anti-aircraft guns. They were 888 feet long with a huge island superstructure, and were the first carriers to incorporate flight decks and hangars as part of the main hull structure and not simply as above-hull appendages. Despite their size the *Lexington* and *Saratoga* were capable of a maximum speed of 33 knots. They were designed to carry and operate 72 aircraft.

The Japanese converted the *Akagi* and *Kaga* into carriers. The *Akagi* carried 60 aircraft, displaced 26,900 tons and could attain a speed of 32·5 knots. Her armaments consisted of ten eight-inch and 12 4·7-inch guns. The *Kaga* carried the same number of aircraft as her sister ship but

Far left: The Kaga, with its sister ship the Akagi, was one of the largest aircraft carriers in the world in 1941.

Left: A seaplane hoisted on to the Ark Royal.
Below left: The makeshift launching platform on the British battleship Hibernia (1912).
Below right: A Sopwith pup lands on HMS Furious, a cruiser converted to carrier.

was slightly smaller (783 feet as opposed to 856 feet for the *Akagi*) and slower (maximum speed 27·5 knots).

The expiration of the London Naval Treaty in 1936 enabled the Japanese to build two of her finest carriers, the *Shokaku* and the *Zuikaku*. Displacing nearly 26,000 tons, these sister ships were 846 feet long and carried 84 aircraft. They were armed with 16 five-inch guns and a great number of 25-millimetre guns. They could reach a speed of 34 knots. They were also the first carriers to carry sonar equipment.

The United States established a major class of aircraft carriers with the construction of the *Yorktown* and the *Enterprise*. Displacing just under 20,000 tons, both ships were 809 feet long. carried 80 aircraft and could move at a top speed of 34 knots. The aircraft could be catapulted from the hangar deck as well as from the flight deck, which meant that a greater number of planes could be put into action at short notice. The main armaments of these vessels consisted of eight five-inch guns.

The Second World War saw the emerging dominance of the aircraft carrier. Each of the warring states deployed their naval vessels in task forces, the hearts of which were the carriers. The aircraft carrier was also accepted as a must for freight convoys, for they gave the necessary air cover against U-boat attacks.

Perhaps nowhere did they play a more important role than in the Pacific where a life and death struggle was raging between the powerful Japanese and American forces.

Dive-bombers at Midway

The initial Japanese onslaught saw her spreading rapidly to the south and west. Disregarding the risks of an over-extended supply line, Admiral Yamamoto wished to establish an outer defensive perimeter which would encompass the Aleutian Islands, Midway, Fiji, Samoa, New California, and Port Moresby. Stiff resistance from the United States and Australia at the Battle of the Coral Sea prevented the Japanese from taking Port Moresby. The turning point in the Pacific War came a month later at the Battle of Midway. An American aircraft carrier force halted a fearful Japanese onslaught on Midway and thus began the process of beating back the Japanese.

By May 1942 the Americans had broken the Japanese code and were aware that a major action was planned around Midway. The two carriers *Enterprise* and *Hornet* were immediately ordered to Pearl Harbour to join Admiral Fletcher's carrier, the *Yorktown*, undergoing extensive repairs. On May 30, 1942, the three carriers set out for Midway covered by eight cruisers and 14 destroyers. Rear-Admiral Spruance was placed in command of the *Enterprise* and *Hornet* while Fletcher retained command of the *Yorktown* as well as being put in charge of the overall operation.

To ensure success Yamamoto committed the full strength of the Japanese navy to the Midway assault. Eight of Japan's ten aircraft carriers, 11 battleships, 13 heavy cruisers, seven light cruisers, 68 destroyers and numerous small craft including minesweepers and supply ships formed the Japanese flotilla. The combined fleet was divided into four, with Yamamoto leading a main force of one carrier and seven battleships, Vice-Admiral Nagumo in charge of the carrier striking force, Vice-Admiral Kondo in charge of the Midway invasion force and Vice-Admiral Hosogaya leading a northern force.

Yamamoto hoped to distract American attention from Midway by bombing raids on the northern Aleutian Islands. With that accomplished, carrier bombers would devastate Midway's defences, preparing the way for the landing of the invasion force. He allowed for the U.S. Pacific Fleet by stationing submarines between the Hawaiian Islands and Midway. If necessary the carrier force would bring its strength to bear against the Americans.

Thanks to American intelligence the American warships evaded the Japanese submarine cordon and by June 1 were stationed 325 miles north-east of Midway.

Two days later the enemy was sighted by reconnaissance aircraft. A force of unescorted B-17 bombers were sent to attack the Japanese but without much success. The Japanese continued their approach towards the island. When 200 miles north of the island the bombers and fighter planes were sent in to destroy the local island force. The Americans spotted the strike and 15 Flying Fortresses were sent to attack the carriers while fighter planes rose to intercept the Japanese bombers. The inferior U.S. fighters were outnumbered and outclassed by the Japanese Zeros. Fifteen fighters were shot down and seven badly mauled. The Japanese bombers got

Yorktown *receives direct hit from Japanese assault plane.*

through and wreaked havoc on the completely defenceless island.

Later the same morning Admiral Nagumo gave orders for a second attack on Midway. But then he learnt of the presence of the American carrier force 200 miles to the east. Countermanding his previous order he gave directions for an assault on the American ships. Meanwhile American dive-bombers from Midway maintained a steady harassment of the Japanese.

By 9.00 a.m. all the Japanese carrier planes which had gone out on the Midway strike were recovered and Nagumo turned his ships north, preparing to do battle with the American carriers.

At 9.20, with his flight deck still clogged with planes, Nagumo was informed of the approach of enemy aircraft. The American carrier force was about to strike.

Sixty-eight dive-bombers, 29 torpedo planes and 24 Wildcat fighters from the *Enterprise* and *Hornet* rushed to engage the enemy. A little while later Fletcher, on the *Yorktown*, ordered

17 dive bombers, 12 torpedo planes and six fighters to join in the attack. The *Hornet* strike force arrived at the reported enemy position only to find nothing there. Nagumo had evaded the attack group by moving north. The initial carrier attack proved a disastrous failure. Of 41 torpedo planes only four survived and none of the torpedoes found their mark. Yet the suicidal torpedo attack paved the way for an American victory. Arriving late on the scene of battle, 33 dive-bombers from the *Enterprise* had an unopposed run on the four Japanese aircraft carriers. Bomb after bomb hit into the *Akagi* and *Kaga*. The *Enterprise* force was soon joined by the *Yorktown* bombers, who immediately took on the *Soryu*. The American bombs did their deadly work, leaving only the *Hiryu* undamaged. The Japanese immediately launched a counter attack, badly damaging the *Yorktown* but losing three fighters and thirteen dive bombers. A second attack was ordered in the early afternoon which led to the abandonment of the *Yorktown*. But by late afternoon the *Hiryu* had been spotted by the Americans, who launched a strike force of fourteen dive-bombers against the Japanese carrier, which was finally knocked out. The Americans won the battle, a victory almost solely due to the power of her aircraft carriers.

As the war progressed the carrier played an ever more vital role in defeating the Japanese.

A water-colour painted from memory by Lt. D. C. Chepler of a kamikaze attack on the USS Hornet.

The Super-carriers: a self-contained Island

The end of the Second World War left the Americans as the strongest naval power in the world. Post-war developments saw a continued emphasis on aircraft carriers. Three new battle carriers were completed between 1945 and 1947.

Known as the Midway carriers, they included for the first time an armoured flight deck in the design. They were enormous ships measuring 968 feet in length and 113 feet across. Armed with 16 five-inch guns, 84 40-mm and 28 20-mm anti-aircraft guns. the new carriers could support 123 aircraft and maintain a steady, impressive speed of 33 knots.

The introduction of jet-propelled aircraft forced further rethinking of carrier design. The faster, heavier planes required more powerful launching systems and longer landing runs. In 1951 the British operated the first steam-driven catapult. This was infinitely more powerful than previous ones.

Previously the flight deck was divided into two parts; the forward third was used as an aircraft park while the remaining two-thirds, separated by a crash barrier, formed the landing and launching area. It was suggested that by angling the landing area the crash barrier could be dispensed with and planes failing to pick up the landing wire could fly on and circle to make another attempt. Initial trials on H.M.S. *Triumph* and U.S.S. *Midway* were so successful that an elongated landing deck was immediately built into the U.S.S. *Antietnam*, jutting out over the port side.

The canted flight deck and the steam catapult were employed in succeeding carriers of all navies, including the American 'super-carrier', the *Enterprise*, completed in 1961.

Displacing 74,700 tons, she is 1,123 feet long. She has an angled flight deck, four steam catapults, four elevators, and a large starboard island structure.

From the front the island structure resembles a large billboard, being completely square except for a large central dome-shaped structure covered with fixed-array radar antennae and other electronic equipment.

The *Enterprise* is driven by eight nuclear reactors supplying to eight turbines which turn four screws. The ship's original nuclear 'core' enabled her to steam for three years, covering 200,000 miles before refuelling. The replacement core enabled the mileage, impressive as it was, to be increased by 25 per cent.

The development of nuclear weapons fore-shadows the eventual decline of the aircraft carrier. The aircraft carrier is not as powerful a deterrent as the nuclear submarine and is more vulnerable to attack. It seems that it will more and more drift into an auxiliary role, its functions being taken over by the guided missile. In the Vietnam War the carrier was used mainly as a support vessel for land engagements.

Far left: HMS Ark Royal *modernised in 1970 to operate the Phantom II fighter. Left: The nuclear powered* USS Enterprise. *An enormously versatile ship, she can carry up to a hundred aircraft, including fighter aircraft for defence, strike aircraft, bombers and helicopters. The photo shows a view of the 'island' on the flight deck with its mass of antennae and radar equipment. Right: The flight deck of the* Enterprise — *1040 ft long and 257 ft wide.*

An unusual characteristic of the United States Navy's acoustic-homing torpedo, MK 32 — it does not have to be fired from a torpedo tube but can be tossed over the side of the ship from an open launcher. Below: Long Beach, the United States' first nuclear powered surface ship, a guided missile cruiser. Opposite top: The U.S. guided missile cruiser Albany fires three surface-to-air missiles simultaneously.

Opposite below: One of Britain's latest nuclear-powered submarines armed with atomic missiles — the Navy's deadliest weapon.

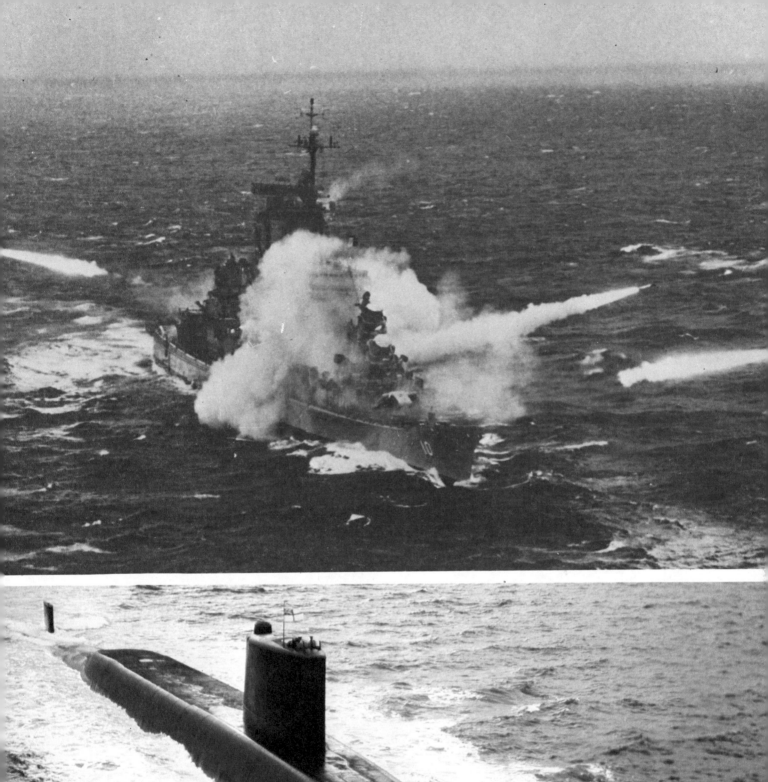

NUCLEAR POWER – WEAPONS FOR THE FUTURE

After the Second World War the only major development in battleships was the introduction of the nuclear-powered turbine, the rocket and the nuclear-guided missiles.

The flying bomb was first successfully exploited by the Germans in their V1 and V2 rockets and later by the Japanese with their rocket-propelled Baka bomb. In response to the Baka bomb the United States worked on an interceptor missile. For this they employed the ram-jet to give it supersonic speed.

The ram-jet dispenses with the bulk and weight of the turbine and air compressor of the turbo jet. It uses compressed air pushed into the front end by the forward motion of the missile. The air is then mixed with kerosene to burn and expand. The hot air is pushed out through the nozzle by the inflowing air, thus providing the jet power. Its major drawback is that an initial forward thrust is needed. That problem was solved by using a booster-jet to launch the missile. A radar guidance system was fitted to the ram-jet missile (called the Terrier) and made its first fully-guided flight in 1948. The Terrier had a range of just over ten miles, which at twice the speed of sound and operating at a maximum altitude of 50,000 feet can intercept planes moving at 600 miles per hour.

The cruisers U.S.S. *Canberra* and U.S.S. *Boston* were fitted with the new missiles in the early fifties. They retained some of their eight-inch guns and 40-mm anti-aircraft guns but most of the armament was removed to make room for the two missile launchers.

The launchers were loaded by being turned to a vertical position with the missile rising through the open deck hatches and engaging lugs fitted onto the launcher. The cruisers held 144 missiles

The world's first atomic-powered submarine, the Nautilus, *on her first test run (1955).*

stored below deck on a circular rotating wheel. This arrangement allowed a rate of fire of two missiles every thirty seconds.

The Talos nuclear warhead missiles driven by ram-jet were introduced soon after into the cruisers *Galverston*, *Little Rock* and *Oklahoma City*. Later the *Albany*, *Columbus* and *Chicago* were converted to complete nuclear armament without any standard ordnance.

The most advanced American missile cruiser built was the *Long Beach*. She was the first surface ship to be powered by nuclear-driven turbines. She also has the distinction of being the only American cruiser built after the Second World War. Completed in 1961, she is 721·5 feet long with a displacement of 14,200 tons. She is armed with two twin Terrier launchers forward and one twin Talos launcher aft. She also carries two eight-inch guns installed amidships (an

afterthought). Though she was designed to carry eight Polaris missiles they were never installed.

The anti-submarine rocket (ASROC) was developed soon after the Terrier and Talos missiles. Signals of nearby submarines are fed into the ship's computer, which plots the exact position of the submarine and the course the torpedoes will take.

When fired from the deck of a ship the ASROC follows a ballistic trajectory and, upon hitting the water, the torpedo separates from the rocket. The torpedo's entry is slowed down by a parachute and on contact with salt water the torpedo's batteries are activated. It then begins a systematic sonic search for the submarine.

Another method of torpedo delivery was code named DASH. A radio-controlled, unmanned helicopter carries the torpedo to the area in which a submarine has been detected.

Polaris missile launched from the nuclear sub, George Washington *(1960).*

First officially released photo of SUBROC, a submarine launched anti-sub missile.

WAR ON THE LAND

THE FIRST DEVICES OF WAR
Sticks and Stones

The earliest devices used by man for hunting and fighting were primitive extensions of his own physical strength. In one form or another, sometimes in a simple device, sometimes in a more sophisticated one, man has continued to try to extend his power through an increasingly complex range of contraptions.

In the beginning man stood naked, with only his fists with which to grip, strike, tear and strangle his enemy. When he held a stone in his hand, he discovered that he could strike with greater force and inflict a deeper wound. When he wielded a stick, the length of his arm was doubled and the weight of his blow vastly increased. When he learnt to throw both stick and stone, the range of his firepower was extended far beyond the threatening reach of club or knife or axe. Bullets and rockets are the sticks and stones of today.

In ten thousand years of inventive destruction, between the hurled stone and the guided missile, man has produced an astonishing array of war devices. Not all of these have been wholly offensive. In defence, man has had to strengthen his own skin, first with the skin of other animals, later with metal, sometimes with massive walls, fortifications and extensive barriers. More often than not, the ideal war machine has incorporated the functions both of defence and attack. The armed footsoldier with his shield was as much a machine of war as the armoured horse, the elephant or the tank. To think only of mechanical devices as the true war machines would be to pass over those devices which, though primitive by comparison and less complicated in structure, nonetheless dominated the battlefields of many parts of the world for thousands of years.

From Stone to Bronze

The wooden stick became a spear with a sharpened point; the tip of the spear was sometimes shaped in the fire, which gave it a greater capacity for penetration. Then the stone and the stick were combined to form the axe and a still sharper spear.

Flint was first used almost 10,000 years before Christ. Its excellent cutting properties and its ease of access, on or near the surface of the earth, made it the ideal material for man's most elementary weapons. It is probable that flint came into use quite independently both in Africa and China.

Flint was, however, impractical for daggers and swords because it broke easily. Early axes and daggers were sometimes made of copper, which the Egyptians also used for spears at least 3,000 years before Christ. Copper alone proved far too soft and required constant sharpening, so tin was added as an alloy to form bronze.

Bronze was used by the Shang Dynasty in China in 1800 B.C. for spears, swords, axes and daggers. One particularly effective device called a 'ko', consisted of a dagger fixed to an axe handle. A great many bronze-age weapons have also been found in graves and barrows in Scandinavia, dating from 1,000 years before Christ. The Scandinavian axe was called a 'palgrave'.

Another metal used effectively in similar weapons was iron, which was probably first smelted in Asia Minor in about 3000 B.C. The Assyrians made good use of iron-tipped weapons when they ousted the Sumerians from the area between the Tigris and the Euphrates rivers. The Hittites, who swept through Asia Minor in the middle of the Second Millenium B.C., also used iron weapons with marked success.

Slings and Bows

It is one step forward to grasp a weapon in the hand, another to throw it, but the effect becomes greater when further impetus is provided by such devices as the sling and the bow.

The sling has been used since earliest times. In

Above: Assyrian archers and slingers advance behind a heavy shield. Right: Bronze dagger and arrowheads, once used by Greek warriors. Below: Acheulean hand axes from prehistory.

its simplest form it was a strip of leather folded over so that the thrower held the two ends and the stone was contained in the loop. The sling was then swung round in the hand several times to gain momentum until at the right moment one end of the leather strip was released and the stone hurled out. It was effective as a lethal weapon up to a distance of about 25 yards.

Once again, it was the Assyrians who recognized the value of the sling; although normally it was considered a weapon for individual combat, they used it effectively in their organized armies. The best sling-stones were usually to be found in river beds. The Assyrians occasionally exacted a supply of these stones as tribute from subjugated tribes in Asia Minor.

One of the most famous incidents in which the sling proved its worth was in the single-handed combat between the Israelite David and the Philistine Goliath, set against each other to decide the outcome of the general battle in front of their respective armies. The giant Goliath, protected by armour and wielding a sword, and possibly a spear as well, proved no match for the sling-stone of young David, which struck him between the eyes and knocked him down.

A sophisticated type of sling held the stone in a special patch that was attached to a couple of thongs. A more effective development, although difficult to use accurately, was a sling attached to the end of a long pole. The momentum attained by the sweeping arc of the pole gave the stone great additional power and range.

The combination of bow and arrow was the next most important war device to develop. As with swords and spears, the earliest arrows were tipped with stone; later they were fitted with iron and bronze. Examples of the first bows can be seen in Neolithic cave paintings in Spain.

The Sumerians did not use the bow, but the Assyrians came with archers not only on foot but also mounted on horses and in chariots. The Assyrians generally used a long arced bow, whereas the Egyptians, who had dominated the Nile delta ever since the Sumerian Empire had begun, used as well as the single arced bow a double curved bow, consisting of two pieces of wood bound together or joined by a handgrip made of horn.

Blow-pipes and Spear-sticks

Both the sling and the bow were part of the equipment of civilized nations and organized armies. The sling developed into a more elaborate device, the ballista or missile-throwing machine of the Assyrians and Romans, and the bow made its most effective re-appearance as the longbow of the English army in the 14th Century. Two other devices, as primitive as the sling, failed to survive in organized war. These were the blow-pipe and the spear-stick.

The blow-pipe is still used in certain parts of Africa and by primitive tribes in the Amazon jungle and New Guinea. With or without a poison

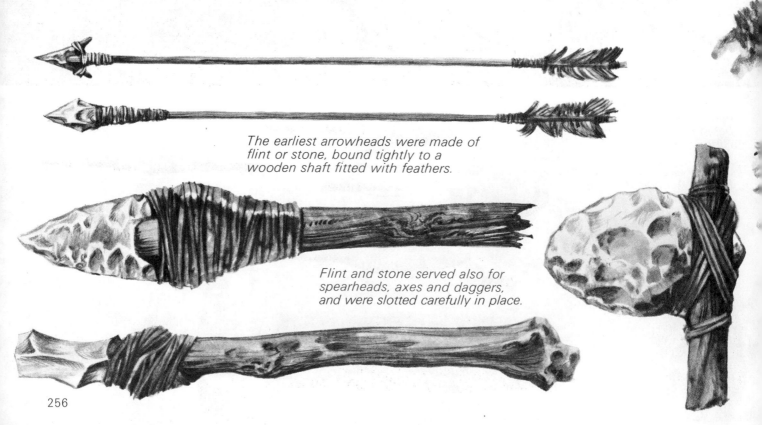

The earliest arrowheads were made of flint or stone, bound tightly to a wooden shaft fitted with feathers.

Flint and stone served also for spearheads, axes and daggers, and were slotted carefully in place.

dart, it is a simple and effective weapon with a range that enables it to be used against an unsuspecting enemy.

The spear-stick had the same advantage as the sling attached to a pole. The base of the spear fitted into a notch in the stick along which the spear lay. The thrower held the stick and used it as a lever to give added impetus to the spear itself.

Protection for the Soldier

There was little point in arming a soldier with an offensive device unless he survived to use it and was therefore given some protection. Armour gradually became an increasingly important part of the foot-soldier's equipment. The oldest surviving illustration of armed warriors – the Standard of Ur, which dates from 3500 B.C. – shows soldiers with clubs and spears wearing leather protection. We know that the Sumerians used a metal-studded leather cape and a leather and metal helmet.

The Egyptians at first used only a shield for protection. This was made of animal skins fitted over a wooden frame; later the shields were completed with a metal rim. By 1250 B.C., the Egyptians wore breastplates made from pieces of leather or crocodile skin, or small metal plates.

The Assyrians were particularly careful to use armour. Even their horses – highly valued assets, well worth protection – were covered in cloths made probably of wool overlaid with flaps of leather and, occasionally, pieces of metal.

Stone Age man was well equipped with bows and arrows, knives, spears and axes, sharpened by laboriously rubbing stones together until a point was achieved.

Armed with such weapons, man became first a hunter then a warrior.

257

THE WAR CHARIOT
Solid and Cumbersome

It would seem a simple step to fit the horse with some kind of platform on which the soldier could stand and from which he could more easily use his weapon. But a certain amount of mystery surrounds the origin of the chariot. We do know, however, that chariots were an important war machine in Mesopotamia as long ago as 3000 B.C. and we can guess that they probably date from even earlier.

These first recorded chariots were primitive affairs by comparison with the later models known to the Romans. The wheels were solid and cumbersome. The bodywork had a stout wooden frame over which skins were stretched to give protection to the driver and his companion, usually a spearman or javelin thrower.

Even in these very early days there seem to have been two distinct types of chariots – two-wheeled and four-wheeled varieties. Chariots found in Egyptian royal tombs have high protective shields guarding the riders. From this we can deduce that the chariot was used as a first-strike weapon, designed to smash an enemy line by the thrust and terror of the initial attack. A line of several thousand war chariots must have presented a formidable spectacle. Once a line or an enemy position had been broken up, the charioteers leaped down into the fray to fight as foot-soldiers.

Speed and the Spoked Wheel

By about 2500 B.C. considerable refinements had taken place in chariot design. Greater speed was achieved through the introduction of spoked wheels, which considerably lightened the chariot. The effectiveness of the pulling pole was also improved by arching the pole over the backs of the horses. This enabled greater manoeuvrability. But in one curious respect the chariot remained unchanged for thousands of years: the harnessing of the horses was never efficient. The wide leather collars of the yoke attached to the pole were slipped round the horse's neck and not its chest. In consequence the true pulling potential of the horse was never fully exploited and the war chariot never reached its maximum speed capacity.

The early Egyptians adopted the chariot from a rival tribe called the Hyksos and were responsible for many of the refinements in its development.

The first recorded battle in which the clever use of chariots won the day was Ramses II's

victory over the Hittites about 1290 B.C., at Kadesh, in Syria. The light Egyptian vehicles – so light that it is difficult to see how they could have survived tough usage over rough ground – armed with long-range bows, proved decisive against the heavier Hittite chariots, which were only armed with short-range spears.

The Spread of the Chariot

By the end of the Second Millenium B.C. the four-

Heavy wooden chariots and the first recorded army from the Sumerian Standard of Ur, 2750 B.C.

wheeled war chariot in its more sophisticated Egyptian form was in use throughout the eastern Mediterranean countries. By that time, also, the chariot had been introduced to the powerful and highly developed Minoan culture centred in Crete and was a favoured war machine throughout the southern European mainland. By the 14th Century B.C. the Chinese were using chariots not unlike the Celtic chariots of the two-wheeled variety that were constructed in Western Europe.

Chariots were in common military (and civilian) use in central and northern Europe by about 1000 B.C. and the Celtic tribes introduced them into Britain in about 500 B.C. These Celtic chariots were heavier in design than the late Egyptian and Greek chariots. Metal was used for the axles and pole and the wheels themselves were often fashioned in solid metal. The Celtic people frequently adorned their chariots with finely worked enamel inlays.

THE EARLIEST SIEGE MACHINES
The Assyrian Assault Tower

With the appearance of fortified cities and organized armies in Asia Minor, siege machines became increasingly important. Just as they had led the way in so many other military fields, it was the Assyrians who first laid proper emphasis on cohesive army organization and an effective siege train well equipped.

The land between the Tigris and the Euphrates was largely without natural defences – a flat, open and vulnerable area. For self-protection, the Assyrians had to build substantial forts. Their understanding of the techniques involved naturally helped them to appreciate what was needed to attack forts as well as to defend them.

The most formidable siege machine that they developed was the mobile battering ram, which was often combined, within the same machine, with a double assault tower. The tower was built of wood and wickerwork. It was drawn up on wheels to the walls of the besieged fort and, while the heavy-ended ram, looking remarkably like a modern tank gun, thudded against gate or wall, archers and spearmen fired a withering volley at the defenders along the parapet. The tower could also be used as an assault platform once it had been brought close up against the fortification.

Other hand-propelled armoured vehicles, made of similar materials, were used to protect troops attempting to get close to the walls in order to scale them with ladders or to follow up any breach that had been prepared by the battering ram. The Assyrians were also pioneers in the art of undermining the walls of fortifications: armoured vehicles could be used for protecting the 'sappers', as they were called.

The Torsion Catapult of the Macedonians

It was the tyrant Dionysus I of Syracuse who may well first have discovered and employed catapult artillery. This was in about 400 B.C. Though used to excellent purpose throughout his campaigns, the catapult was not fully developed until Philip of Macedon recognized its potential as a military machine more than 60 years later.

Philip's engineers invented the torsion catapult. The base end of a long arm was fixed to a spring consisting of tightly twisted rope. The extended end of the arm was winched down against the force of the spring and a hollowed out bowl or a sling at the end of the arm was fitted with the missile. When the arm was released it

shot upright and was brought to an abrupt vertical stop against a solid cross-bar. The missile – stone or burning material – continued through the air to land, causing havoc among the defenders. By angling the whole machine or changing the angle of the cross-bar, the trajectory of the missile could be altered.

Philip used these machines at the sieges of Perinthes and Byzantium. It is not hard to imagine the consternation that such a barrage of firepower would have had on a civilian population and also on the morale of the besieged warriors, quite apart from the physical effect of large boulders crashing against the walls, through the roofs of houses, or ploughing into groups of defenders.

Philip's son, Alexander the Great, continued the siege tactics of his father and gave further impetus to siegecraft by instituting a corps of engineers whose special responsibility it was to develop effective siege machines. In his long, penetrating campaigns east toward India and the River Sutlej, Alexander used this corps of engineers to construct siege weapons when and where they were needed out of materials available on the site. This was a good deal easier than dragging the ungainly machines across the thousands of miles of unknown country that his armies had to traverse.

Above: A bust of Alexander from the Ottoman Museum.
Right: An Assyrian army attacking a well-defended fort with archers and a moving siege tower and battering ram, from a bas-relief found at Nimrod.

Above: Alexander the Great, riding on the left, was a master of land warfare.

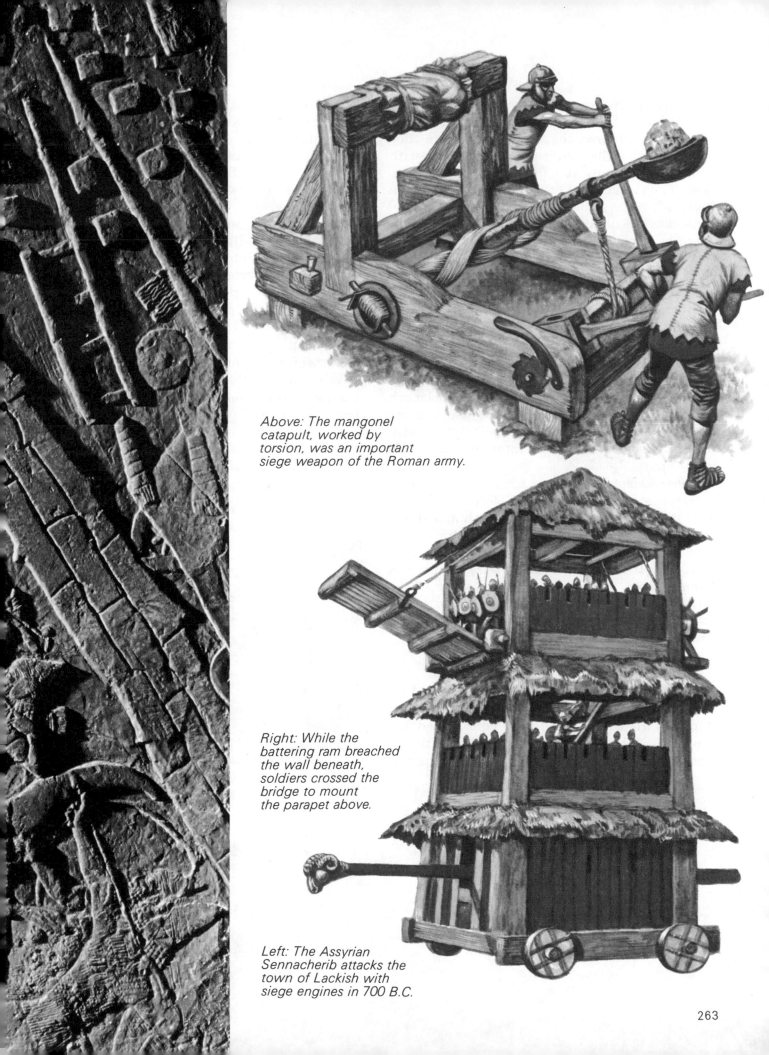

Above: The mangonel catapult, worked by torsion, was an important siege weapon of the Roman army.

Right: While the battering ram breached the wall beneath, soldiers crossed the bridge to mount the parapet above.

Left: The Assyrian Sennacherib attacks the town of Lackish with siege engines in 700 B.C.

FRONTIERS AGAINST INVASION
The Great Wall of China

The natural development of the walled city was a system of defence that halted the enemy even before they entered the homeland, before they could attack either with massed troops or with artillery the cities and forts within the homeland. The Great Wall of China was just such a device. It dates from 300 B.C. and has been described as the greatest feat of military engineering in history.

Before the emperor Shih Huang Ti established China along the lines of the country we know today, it consisted of a number of walled-in territories. Shih, the first Emperor of a united China, knocked the walls down and constructed the Great Wall as a formidable obstacle to his enemies, the nomads to the north.

The wall stretched for about 1,600 miles, from the Yellow Sea to Central Asia. The entire length of this enormous barrier against the warlike Huns to the north was heavily fortified, with towers placed at strategic intervals about 200 yards apart.

These 40-feet-high towers topped a wall that in its steepest place was at least 30 feet high. The wall itself was built mainly of earth and stone, faced with bricks. Great modifications took place over the centuries and in the 15th and 16th Centuries the central sections were rebuilt and strengthened. A roadway along the top of the wall was designed to take a column of marching soldiers, and chariots could also run along its length, covering the wall from end to end.

On the Edge of the Roman Empire

A smaller and later version of the Great Wall was built in Britain by the Roman Emperor Hadrian. Hadrian's Wall was constructed between 117 and 138 A.D. and marked the northernmost limit of the Roman Empire. It also helped to keep at bay the warlike tribes of Picts that raided the north of England and terrorized the populations of the cities and the countryside.

The wall stretched for 73 miles across the narrowest part of Britain, from Wallsend, on the river Tyne, to Bowness, on the river Solway. It was defended by a system of forts, mile-castles and fortified turrets. In all, Hadrian's Wall boasted more than 80 mile-castles, between which the turrets were built for added protection. The main wall was an average of 15 feet high with a six feet parapet on top. The Roman forts were quite sophisticated affairs with central heating and hot bath facilities laid on.

Hadrian's Wall was permanently manned by cohorts of conscripted soldiers, both infantry and cavalry, and a Roman legion at nearby York was always on hand in case of any serious trouble from the north.

In comparison with China's vast creation, Britain's wall was very small, but it was nonetheless an impressive piece of war machinery.

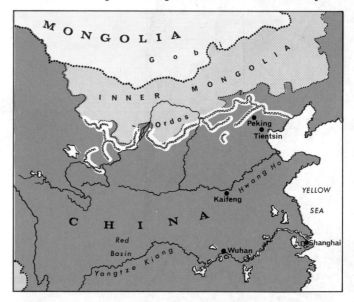

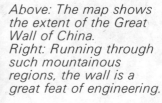

Above: The map shows the extent of the Great Wall of China.
Right: Running through such mountainous regions, the wall is a great feat of engineering.

Left: Hadrian's Wall made use of natural defences as well. This photograph is looking east.

THE GREEK PHALANX
The Hoplites – an Elite Force

Once some sort of organization had been introduced into the warring armies of Asia Minor, the foot-soldier became of greater importance, not as an individual but as an integral part of a military formation. In the earliest days of the Assyrian empire dense concentrations of foot-soldiers had been employed but had been displaced in favour of the greater manoeuvrability of light cavalry. It was therefore in Greece, where the mountainous and broken terrain did not suit cavalry nearly so well as the plains of the Euphrates, that the foot-soldier in formation – the phalanx – was first established with any marked success.

Whereas military power in Greece had been with the nobility in their chariots, internal reasons in about 600 B.C. hastened the transference of this power to the middle class citizens. Organized into infantry, they were called the hoplites. Above all else, these were the people, led by the Spartans, who established the dominance of the Greek city states in the eastern Mediterranean.

The hoplites were the élite among the Greek warriors and since their equipment was not by any means cheap it was something of a privilege to belong to the class from which they were picked. They were very conscious of this honour.

Armour consisted of the famous round shield, held in the left arm by an arm loop and a hand grip. In the use of the shield lay the essence of the formation. Each soldier held his shield so that it overlapped his neighbour, thus protecting half of himself and half of the man on his left. This resulted in a serried wall of shields interrupted by the eight-feet-long spears that each hoplite held in his right hand in the initial stages of the battle. Sometimes this spear was pointed at both ends so that if one point broke the spear could be reversed. For closer fighting the hoplite had a short stabbing sword held from a strap under his left arm.

Apart from his shield, which was usually decorated with the owner's motif and often embossed with some kind of animal's head (this provided a means of crushing his opponent in close combat), the hoplite was protected by shin guards, called greaves, and back and breast plates. The more elaborate and best known of these were close-fitted and fashioned with simulated muscles raised from the surface. Helmets varied in style, with emphasis laid on cheek guards and nose guards, The early Corinthian

helmet, hammered out of a single piece of bronze, was all-enveloping. The Doric helmet was more elaborate and had a large horsehair crest.

Marathon and Thermopylae

Initially the hoplite formations were used in the internal wars between the Greek states themselves. Victory in these conflicts depended largely on numbers. It was not until the phalanx came up against enemies from outside Greece that it was able to prove itself to be an irresistible machine of war.

The Persians invaded Europe in 490 B.C. with a highly efficient élite army, whose pride were the lightly armed archers. They landed in the Bay of Marathon, north-east of Athens. 11,000 Athenians faced 15,000 Persians and employed the regular tactics of the phalanx to put them to

Hoplites advancing in line, part of a frieze from the monument of the Nereids. When fighting, each shield would overlap the hoplite to the left.

rout. One of the most important factors in the success of the phalanx was that, though well-armoured, the hoplites were not too encumbered to advance quickly. They formed a highly mobile force that could be adapted to conditions.

This agility was used to close with the enemy before the Persian archery took its full toll. Then, holding the centre just long enough to envelop the Persian flanks, the Athenians attacked the enemy where they lacked protection and drove them back to the sea. Over 6,000 Persians fell and barely 200 hoplites.

Ten years later, at Thermopylae, 300 Spartan hoplites held off an overwhelming superior force of Persians for three days. The battle at the narrow pass has become one of history's most renowned encounters. Persian cavalry, reputed to be the best in the world, and Persian open infantry were no match for the Greek phalanx.

It was only when Philip of Macedon combined the use of the phalanx in the centre with heavy cavalry on the wings and a force of light pursuit cavalry that the Greeks were defeated. This was at the Battle of Chaeronea, in 338 B.C.

Philip subsequently developed the phalanx, increasing its breadth and depth to 16 ranks of 96 men each, and lengthening the spear (*sarissa*), to as much as 12–15 feet, or more. Lengths varied so that the phalanx presented a formidable and fearful wall of spear-points. With this machine Philip and his son, Alexander, went on to many further victories.

THE LEGIONS OF ROME
A Formidable Fighting Machine

The Greeks were not the only ones to organize an effective fighting machine out of their infantry. The organization of the Roman army was partly learned from its former enemies, the Etruscans. On the whole, new ideas are evolved by a process of adaptation; complete innovation is rare. As a result of a series of defeats and setbacks at the very close of the 2nd Century B.C., the Roman army was reorganized with such success that it became the most formidable military force the world had ever seen.

The Roman legion in the 1st Century B.C. consisted of 4,000–5,000 men. These were divided into 10 *cohorts* of approximately 400–500 men each, and each cohort was subdivided into six *centuries*. It is clear that each century did not necessarily contain 100 men; its full complement would rarely be realized, but it served as a useful basic unit whose numbers varied depending on the situation, recruitment, illness, depletion by death, and so on. Nor was the Roman legion a standard formation throughout the hundreds of years of its existence. By A.D. 400 its organization and equipment had changed greatly – the usual strength of an effective legion unit was then 1,000 men though it was often less.

The centurion was the lynch-pin of the entire organization, invaluable to his commanders as much as to his soldiers because of the depth of his combat experience. It was often the centurion who was responsible for turning a crisis into victory, despite the orders of his superiors.

Within the cohort, the centuries were organized into two ranks of three centuries each, the second rank to support the first. Within the legion, the cohorts were drawn up in three rows. Formation on this basic plan differed. The simplest was to have four cohorts in the front, with three behind to follow through in the gaps between the first four. The third row of three cohorts was then used as a reserve in case the engagement was prolonged and the first cohorts needed relief; in retreat, the third line acted as cover for its companions.

An alternative formation set three cohorts in the front line, three in the second and four to the rear. But the tactics employed were much the same. Flexibility, support, leap-frogging one line of cohorts through another, acting as cover, formations in columns, in squares, in line abreast – all these manoeuvres were easily undertaken once the basic units had been established. This mobility was only attained by extreme discipline and organization, for which the Romans were justly famous.

Even before the army's reorganization, when the legion had been larger – about 6,000 men – and considerably less flexible, it had been sufficiently mobile to defeat the Macedonian phalanx. With its increased mobility it was far too powerful a machine for the barbarian tribes of Europe to handle, however numerous they were. By the time of the Emperor Augustus, the Roman army consisted of almost 30 legions, with very nearly as many auxiliaries in reserve.

The legionaries, as the individual soldiers were called, were all equipped with a large rectangular shield (*scutum*). This was slightly convex in order to provide protection round the body. Instead of being used to overlap each other, as the Greek hoplite shields had been used, the Roman shields were held edge to edge, as the legionaries advanced, presenting an impenetrable barrier. The famous Roman short sword (*gladius*) was usually held on the right side, so as not to get in the way of the shield. Each legionary also carried a javelin (*pilum*) with a long iron point, a sharp addition to his effectiveness.

The helmet was lighter than that of the hoplites; it did not have the nose-guard, though it retained the cheek pieces. Sometimes only a breastplate was worn, with strips of leather hanging like a skirt to give lower protection; sometimes body armour of mail (*lorica*) stretched down to waist or thigh. Greaves were generally worn only by those in the front of the battle line. Those behind, requiring to be more mobile, preferred to do without them.

The Tough Test of Civil War

At the height of their power the Roman legions were put to the test not so much by the barbarian enemies of the Roman people but by internal war. Roman legions strove against each other with sophisticated tactics in which both sides were well experienced but against which neither side had come as yet in battle. The war machine confronted itself on the battlefield. It was a novel experience.

Hitherto the Gallic and Germanic tribes had put up fierce but ineffectual resistance. The advance of the Roman machine had been steady determined and inevitable, and Roman losses had been slight in comparison. It was not until

A Roman centurion looks over his legionnaires, who are armed with a rectangular shield, short sword and javelin. Helmet, breastplate and shoulder armour complete their equipment.

the civil wars that the machine began to suffer real damage.

Julius Caesar's confrontation with Pompey at Pharsalus, in Thessaly, in 48 B.C. was an important battle in the history of Rome. Despite vastly superior cavalry and an army double the size, Pompey was defeated and Caesar's authority re-established. It was a tactical victory in which Caesar used his forces most effectively by holding back his reserve cohorts until the last moment. By that time Pompey's cavalry had expended their effort against Caesar's first lines and had been thrown back in confusion by a previously prepared flanking movement. As the flanking cohorts struck Pompey's army, Caesar's main reserves attacked through his first line.

The ensuing rout resulted in surrender by the larger part of Pompey's army.

The Fortified Roman Camp
The Roman legion was able to march about 15–16 miles a day. On campaign, fortified camps were constructed at frequent intervals along the route. These acted as protection for the night, to cover the rear of an advancing army and, when fortified more strongly, as outposts of the Empire. They were fortified according to the permanence of their position. But their layout and organization were rigidly established and, since the Roman legion spent a great deal of its time in encampment, these camps became an integral part of the Roman military machine.

Remains of camps can still be seen in Europe and Britain today. Sometimes these merely take the form of earthworks but occasionally the remains of solid fortifications have been found, as at Richborough, England, in the picture.

The Human Tortoise
The legionary himself had one very useful and interesting function in any attack on an enemy fortification well-guarded by walls of any height. The human 'tortoise', or clambering device, was a machine of war as important and effective as the scaling ladder and the grappling hook. By bending down and holding their shields hori-

zontally above them, several legionaries could provide a platform on which their companions could stand in order to scale the wall.

Marching in tight formation and crouched under their shields, the legionaries were also well protected from the javelins, arrows and stones that rained down on them from above as they advanced toward the fortification.

The Lost Legions

Adaptability was the key to the legion's success, as it must be to the continued success of any machine. So when, slowly, the Germanic tribes began to learn from their successful adversaries and the Romans themselves failed to adapt to frontier conditions while simultaneously finding those frontiers overstretched and themselves torn apart by further internal wars, the Roman machine faltered, began to break up and gradually collapsed.

This collapse took place steadily over two to three hundred years. But it began when German auxiliary soldiers, tribesmen under Roman jurisdiction, rose up under their leader Arminius against the Roman commander Varus in A.D. 9. Varus could not adapt to the guerilla-style warfare of the German tribesmen. He lost three legions to the Germans in the Teutoberger Forest: from that moment the legion ceased to be an invincible machine.

A THOUSAND YEARS OF SIEGE DEVICES
The Forts Become Stronger

The legion was not the only Roman contribution to the art of war; the Romans also developed siege artillery of powerful and varied ability. Before the invention of gunpowder, the motive forces available to propel large missiles into an enemy stronghold, or to gain access to that stronghold, gave rise to an odd-looking assortment of machines. As we have already seen, the Assyrians used covered battering rams and assault towers almost 2,000 years before Christ. The Macedonians used catapult artillery 300–400 years before Christ. And similar machines were still being used, alongside some of the earliest cannon, when the Turks besieged Constantinople in A.D. 1453.

Siege machines developed side-by-side with the development of fortifications. Earthworks gave way to constructions of stone, with thicker and thicker walls, deeper and wider ditches and an increasing number of towers and turrets, in order to combat machines aimed at scaling the walls, crossing the ditches and bombarding within the fortress.

There were three main types of machine that evolved for propelling missiles. Each used a different source of power. The catapult of the Macedonians used torque provided by twisted ropes. The trebuchet, used by the Romans and late into the Middle Ages, worked on counter-balancing weights. And the spring engine employed the flexibility of wood.

Catapult and Spring-engine

The Romans developed a comprehensive siege train in which the catapult played a major part. This was the conventional catapult that used a single arm on which the missile was placed. The arm was held between thick, twisted ropes. Torque, or twisted tension, increased as the arm was pulled down. This was virtually the same as the Macedonian torsion catapult, although the Romans often called it an *onager*, which was another word for wild ass.

There was another form of Roman catapult that was lighter than the onager and used more often in the field against enemy soldiers than against fortifications. This catapult had two smaller arms, each slotted into twisted ox-sinew and fitted on either side of the shaft up which the missile ran. Rope, or sinew, joined the outstretched ends of the arms like a bow; the missile was fitted into the arc of the sinew. Power was

derived from the torque of the twisted sinews and from the flexibility of the arms when the missile was drawn back in preparation for firing. In this machine the missile was likely to be an arrow, javelin or large spear. The machine could be adjusted to provide a certain angle of accuracy.

A third variation dispensed with the twisted rope in favour of a large metal bow. This type of 'ballista' grew in complexity during the Middle Ages until sometimes two or three bows were used on the same machine. The principle of the device was like a giant crossbow and the power was derived from the tension in the metal. Like the onager, the ballista could hurl large stones with great force a distance of 300–400 yards.

The spring-engine also used the tension of wood or metal and was primarily used to fire arrows. The arrow rested on one piece of wood, with the flight end of the arrow projecting slightly behind the wood. Another piece of flexible wood, lying upright against the first piece, was bound tightly to the first piece at its base. The top of the second piece of wood was then drawn back under great tension by a rope and winch. It was then released sharply so that it sprang back against the base of the arrow, which shot from its resting place with armour-penetrating force.

It may not seem that this would be a very accurate device but some degree of accuracy was attained either by resting the arrow in a groove or, more often, by shooting it through a hole in the support. Various ingenious ways of altering its angle of inclination included a hinged rest for the arrow that could be raised or lowered on a series of stepped sockets.

One of the most telling modifications of the spring-engine was a multiple battery of arrows fired simultaneously. The system was the same as on the single shot machine, using holes in the support for the arrows. A large piece of wood was drawn back and struck against a board on which were set several rows of arrows. The consequent rain of arrows on the enemy could, as might be imagined, tear a gap in their ranks with fearful and dispiriting effect.

The Powerful Trebuchet

The *trebuchet* was used in wars all over Europe and Asia Minor for over 1,500 years. One of the most powerful of the ancient siege machines, it could hurl stones weighing anything up to two to three hundredweight over several hundred

Above: The lighter form of Roman catapult, using two arms fixed in twisted sinews.

yards and over the highest walls and ditches.

The principle of the trebuchet was very simple. A long arm was set on a pivot so that it had a longer and a shorter end. The pivot was supported by a solid frame. At its shorter end the arm was weighted by a large box full of earth or stones. The box was hinged to the end of the arm so that, as the arm moved up and down, the contents of the box would not fall out. The longer end of the arm held the missile – usually in a sling – and was drawn down against the weight of the box at the other end by a winch or capstan. When the long end was released, the weight at the short end swung the long end up and the missile was flung through the air.

Missiles varied from rocks and barrels of burning tar to the putrescent corpses of friend and foe. These not only demoralized the opposition but were likely to spread disease. Such drastic action was generally a last resort, even before the days of supposed chivalry, but nonetheless was a recognized and effective method of shortening a siege.

Both besieged and besiegers used trebuchets. The missiles of the besieged could create considerable disruption in the camp of the enemy, on grouped soldiers, on mobile wickerwork shields, on assault towers and on covered battering rams, as well as on the opposing missile machines. Just as important, the trebuchet could be used to disrupt the construction of these devices, which were generally put together on the spot.

THE MOUNTED KNIGHT
Saddle and Stirrup

The heavily armoured mounted knight threatened to dominate the medieval battlefields of Europe. He was a moving fortress that sprouted offensive weapons – lance, sword and mace – with which to smash down the forces of opposition. In a dense charge, the ordinary foot-soldier could not withstand him; as a roving, individual combatant, he could do what he liked. He was a fully-armed, fully-armoured, fully-mobile fighting machine.

Mounted horsemen had been used in preference to chariots 1,000 years before Christ. A mounted soldier could manoeuvre far more easily than one on foot. The Assyrians used mounted archers and spearmen; so did the Phrygians and Scythians of Asia Minor, in about 500 B.C. The Macedonians and the Romans both used cavalry. But in all cases the horsemen were lightly protected and used neither saddle nor stirrup.

Without these essential pieces of equipment, the early cavalryman was easily dismounted, and could not deliver a blow with the full force of his body behind it. Both saddle and stirrup seem to have originated in China but it is difficult to conclude when precisely they came to Europe and Asia Minor. It is generally accepted that some of the tribes in Gaul possessed saddles of a kind in about A.D. 100–200. Stirrups appeared later. They were certainly in use in the 8th Century but they may have come into use in a simpler form in the Byzantine Empire even earlier. There is evidence of their use at the end of the 6th Century in the 'Art of War' of the Byzantine Emperor Maurice Tiberius.

The Byzantine Cataphracts

It was the Byzantine army, committed to a vigorous and aggressive foreign policy under the Emperor Justinian and led by the brilliant commander Belisarius during the middle of the 6th Century, that first made good use of fully armoured cavalry. Belisarius's élite horsemen, the Cataphracts, were well-equipped, well-trained and superior to almost any troops they encountered.

The Cataphracts were clothed entirely in scale armour or mail, which was also used to protect their horses. They were armed usually with a bow, a sword and a spear. Similar cavalry used by the Persians sometimes had the added protection of a beautifully worked visor that covered

Above: A horseman from the decorated palace of Guzana, with helmet and shield but no stirrups. Right: Cataphract with carefully moulded face mask and a complete covering of scale armour for himself and his horse.

the whole face and followed its contours to form a remarkable face mask.

Scale armour consisted of many rows of overlapping scales secured on the undersurface to a tough lining. Until plate armour came into general use in the 14th Century, scale armour was the only alternative to chain mail, although during the 11th and 12th Centuries mail and scale armour were often combined to give additional protection. The advantage of mail was its flexibility, although it was a tedious job to produce since every ring had to be woven individually into the coat. Each ring interlocked with four surrounding rings and was secured by having its ends flattened, drilled and rivetted together. One of the disadvantages of mail was that a powerful blow by an adversary could sever the links and drive the sharp-ended pieces of metal wire into the body of the wearer. His own armour therefore, at times, became more dangerous to him than the sword of his enemy. In order to protect himself, the knight often wore a well-padded garment beneath his mail.

The Knights of Charles Martel

Under the Carolingians of the 8th Century A.D. the knight became not only an important part of the army but an integral part of the feudal structure of society as well, as the definition of 'feudal' suggests: 'the holding of land for military service'. Charles Martel increased his power in France by distributing land (seized from the Church) to his vassals, in return for which they guaranteed to turn up – fully equipped – on demand, together with an agreed number of followers, ready to join any proposed campaign. It was with an army shaped of this material that Charles Martel managed to stem the advance of the Arabs through Europe at the Battle of Poitiers, in AD 732 – and so avert a major disaster.

Poitiers was an important turning point in European history. The Arab threat was diminished and Carolingian power established. Charles Martel's heavy cavalry, equipped with stirrups and high saddles played a large part in the victory and the subsequent expansion of the Empire that Charlemagne took to even greater heights and established with authority.

With the aid of his stirrups, the knight could virtually stand up, leaning his whole weight forward, and thrusting with his legs. By this means the full force of his horse's impetus could be brought behind the knight's lance, which became a personal battering ram, lethally tipped, and capable of great penetration. Meanwhile, the high saddle, with pommel to the front and cantle behind, kept the knight firmly on his horse, despite the shock of his own charge and the blows of his adversaries. There was a danger that the lance would stick in the target, either breaking or twisting the knight from his saddle. This was averted by a small cross-bar or pennant just behind the point of the lance, that stopped the lance from penetrating too deeply.

Helmets and Plate Armour

Norman knights of the 11th Century and Italian knights of the 12th Century all wore scale armour, sometimes as coats that stretched down to their knees. Loose-fitting surcoats often covered the armour and served the double purpose of a distinguishing mark and an additional protection against sword cuts; the folds of the material greatly reduced the direct force of the blow.

From the simple conical helmet with a *nasal* (a protection for the nose), there developed more elaborate face-plates that eventually formed a helmet that covered the face totally, as well as protecting both the front and the back of the neck. It was provided with eyeslits and ventilation holes. It is difficult to imagine that either of these were very efficient. Range of vision was greatly limited, rather as if blinkers were being worn not only to the sides but above and below the eyes as well. Anyone who has ever taken fencing lessons and knows how hot a mesh fencing mask can become after only a few moments exercise may be able to imagine what it must have been like inside a solid metal cannister after several *hours* of battle!

Another protective device was a breastplate or waistcoat of *cuir bouilli*, which was made of leather boiled and pressed and made additionally stiff with wax. But the classic 'knight in armour' wore plate mail, which began to become popular at the end of the 13th Century and developed into increasingly heavy and complex styles over the next three centuries.

Plate armour began with plates of metal inserted into a leather or cloth garment. Plate covers for knees (*poleyn*), shins (*chausse*) and elbows (*couter*) followed. By the end of the 13th Century, gauntlets were made of plate metal and gorgets, to protect the neck, were in general use.

During this century horses were also covered in curtains of mail. With both rider and horse virtually unrecognizable within their armour,

Left: This stone-carving of Roland represents one of the most famous of all the Carolingian knights, whose death in the pass of Roncevalles in 778 began a legend. Charlemagne's army was defeated by an ambush, but his knights subsequently helped him to establish a powerful empire.
Right: This richly ornamented helmet is from the Anglo-Saxon ship burial at Sutton Hoo in Britain's East Anglia. The date of the burial — a king's treasure in a Viking longboat—has been estimated between 650 and 670. Other weapons found at the site included a sword with a gold and garnet pommel, a shield, a mail coat, an iron-handled axe, some javelins, spears and a knife.

ⵔODO EPS·BACVLV·TEN

An incident from the Bayeux Tapestry, showing Norman knights advancing into Battle.
The Tapestry was created to commemorate the Norman invasion of Britain in 1066.

there was an increased necessity to wear some kind of distinguishing marks. 'Heraldry' goes back to the Greeks and Romans, and even earlier. The elaborate system of medieval heraldry began properly in the 12th Century and spread widely in the 13th Century. Family marks appeared on shields, surcoats and helmets and added a touch of gaiety to the austere clank of metal.

Gradually plate armour covered the entire body, elaborately hinged and designed to make the blows of the enemy glance off. The names of the various pieces of armour conjure up a romantic picture far removed from the agonies of the battlefield. *Solerets* were broad, plated shoes; the *cuisse* were the thigh guards; *tassets*, a kind of plated skirt, overlapped the cuisse; and *taces*, bands of plate linked to allow flexibility, protected waist and stomach. Underneath the tassets and behind the joints of the limbs, there was often an additional protection of chain mail. A *vambrace* protected the forearm and a *rerebrace* the upper arm; the shoulders were guarded by heavy *pauldrons* with a *haute-piece* projecting up to give extra protection to the neck. The helmet usually had a visor that could be raised either by hinges at the side of the head or by a single hinge at the top.

There was never any one style of armour that was at any time universally worn. Styles came and went according to need as much as fashion and different countries had very different designs. For instance, the more rounded shape of 15th-Century Italian design, with a lance rest fixed to the right side of the breastplate, was a good deal plainer than German design of the later part of that century. In German Gothic armour there were many flutings, which gave the armour extra strength and helped to deflect the assailant's weapon. A later German style was known as 'Maximilian' and was characterized by a series of ridges over the entire armour, with the exception of the greaves.

The Obsolete Knight

During the 16th Century heavy cavalry still wore armour; indeed some of the heaviest armour, weighing up to 90 pounds, was worn at this time. But firearms had already rendered the armoured knight an outdated machine. Driven to protecting himself more and more fully from the threat of crossbow and longbow, he could not resist the force of shot backed by gunpowder, however much armour he adopted. And although armour was still used in the English Civil War of the

Above: Armoured knights clash at the Battle of Auray, between John de Montford (left) and Charles de Blois (on the ground). The battle was in 1364, during the Anglo-French 100 Years War Right: The 15th-Century Italian knight has a rest for his lance attached to his breast-plate, and is carrying a mace.

mid-17th Century and the European 30 Years War of the first half of that century it became much lighter; by the middle of the next century, protection was reduced to half-armour.

For a time the charge of the armoured knight had been an irresistible force. Foot-soldiers could only hope to cut the horse from under him; they had no hope of standing up against him. He could roam where he liked, killing where he felt inclined. The clash of two bodies of knights was probably the most awe-inspiring sight the battlefields of Europe had ever seen. In every way the armoured knight dominated his surroundings. The disappearance of this formidable machine, through the force of progress, brought to an end a style of warfare and an attitude of life.

THE DEADLY QUARREL OF THE CROSSBOW
The Little Ballista

The knight was countered at first by the cross-bow, which probably originated in the East and was known, in a modified form, to the Romans. Its other name, 'arbalest', comes from the Latin 'arcu', a bow, and 'ballista', an engine of war. The Romans made good use of the full-size ballista but do not seem to have exploited the full potential of its smaller relation.

This potential was not realized until the 11th and 12th Centuries, when armoured knights became increasingly dominant in European war-fare. The crossbow enabled an unarmoured man to knock down a mounted knight from a safe distance. The realization that the knight was no longer invulnerable – worse still, that the inferior infantryman now possessed a machine that could penetrate the knight's armour – shocked the Orders of Chivalry. What frightened them even more was the realization that they them-selves could not use the machine in retaliation from horseback. Their disadvantage was ir-remediable and their demise assured.

The Crossbow is Banned

In a last ditch attempt to stem the spread of this insidious threat, the Pope spoke out against the crossbow. In 1139, the Second Lateran Council banned the use of the new machine in civilized warfare; they called it an atrocity. There was, however, a proviso – a proviso that was to be echoed when the first machine gun was intro-duced: although it was forbidden to use the cross-bow against fellow Christians, it could freely be used against the infidel Moslem.

The Crusaders used the crossbow to good enough effect against the Saracens, particularly during the Third Crusade. Richard Cœur de Lion's victory at Arsuf, in 1191, was greatly assisted by the chaos caused amongst the enemy by his crossbowmen. But the papal interdict against the crossbow did not restrict it to the Middle East for long; it was far too useful a machine. By the late 13th Century the crossbow-men of France and Spain were an important branch of the army and were recognized as such. Genoese crossbowmen, often hired as mercen-aries, made their mark on the battlefields of the early 14th Century, until tested against the English longbow at the Battle of Crecy, in 1346.

One great advantage of the crossbow was that its use did not require much training on the part of the bowman, nor did it require the

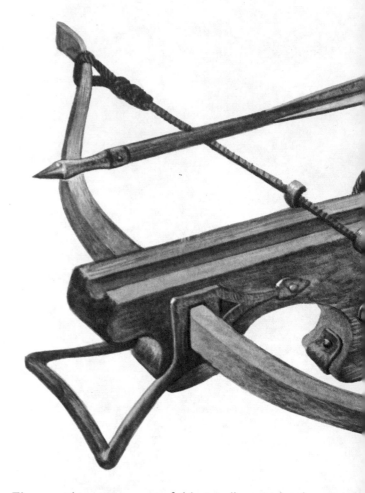

The crossbow was powerful but tedious to load

strength necessary to the longbowman. The early wooden crossbow was drawn back by hand but the later and more effective steel bow required a winch to 'span' or draw it. The bow consisted of a short cross-arm mounted on a stock, with a groove cut along the stock to guide the missile and a trigger by which to release it. While the bowman used both hands on the winch, he held the bow steady by placing his foot in the stirrup at the front.

Rewinding the bow was a slow and vulnerable job. The bowman had to stand upright and was therefore fully exposed to enemy fire during the operation. In consequence, Genoese bowmen were well protected with body armour and some-times had a companion to hold a large shield before them while they reloaded.

The slow rate of fire was perhaps the cross-bow's greatest disadvantage. It could fire little more than one shot a minute. Also, it was not

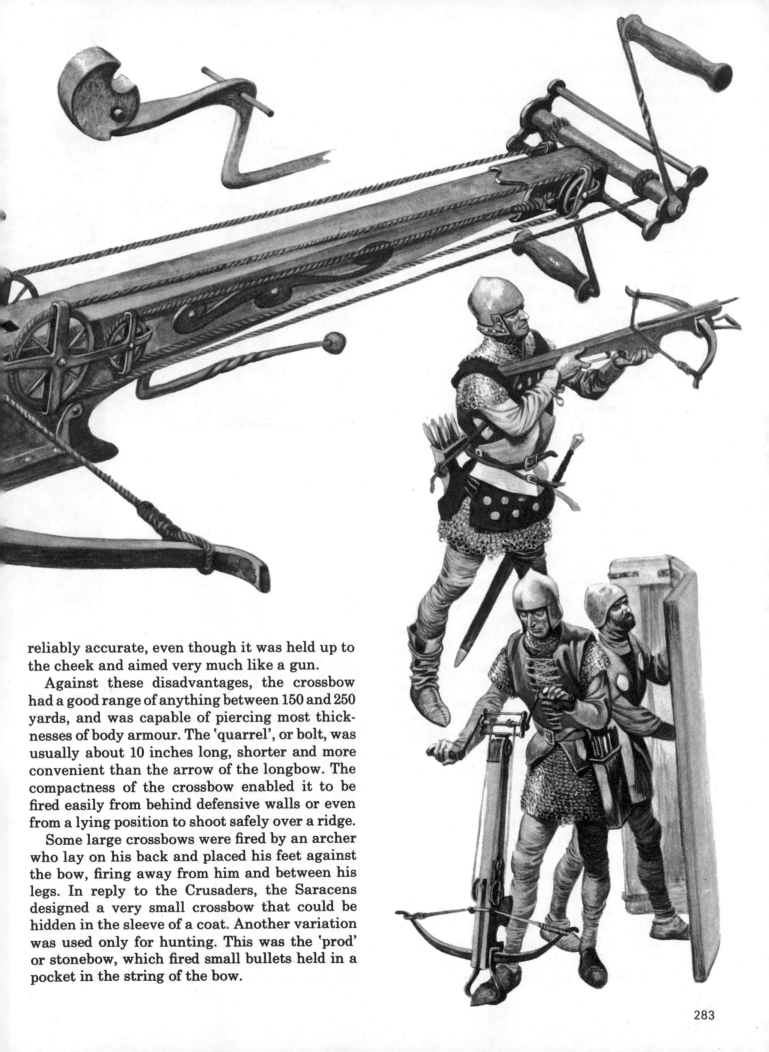

reliably accurate, even though it was held up to the cheek and aimed very much like a gun.

Against these disadvantages, the crossbow had a good range of anything between 150 and 250 yards, and was capable of piercing most thicknesses of body armour. The 'quarrel', or bolt, was usually about 10 inches long, shorter and more convenient than the arrow of the longbow. The compactness of the crossbow enabled it to be fired easily from behind defensive walls or even from a lying position to shoot safely over a ridge.

Some large crossbows were fired by an archer who lay on his back and placed his feet against the bow, firing away from him and between his legs. In reply to the Crusaders, the Saracens designed a very small crossbow that could be hidden in the sleeve of a coat. Another variation was used only for hunting. This was the 'prod' or stonebow, which fired small bullets held in a pocket in the string of the bow.

THE CLOTHYARD SHAFT OF THE LONGBOW
From Cavemen to Hastings

The crossbow and the longbow fought out many conflicts during the 13th and 14th Centuries. The longbow had a far greater rate of fire and, in the hands of an expert, greater range and accuracy as well.

Bows of one shape or another had, of course, been used for thousands of years, first by the Egyptians, Assyrians and in China, then by the Persians, Greeks and Macedonians, later by the Moslems and even the Vikings. It is perhaps surprising that the Romans never made more use of the bow. There are arrowheads surviving from Paleolithic and Neolithic times. And, in more recent American history, the American Indians made highly effective use of bows and arrows against the early settlers.

Self bows were made of one material only – a stave of wood, for example. If more than one piece of the same material was used in the bow, it was called a built bow. A composite bow consisted of several different materials glued together, such as wood, horn and animal sinew. These were the common variations of bow in early times. The first English bows were quite short, but the Normans arrived in 1066 with a medium length bow, which in combination with their cavalry gave them victory at the Battle of Hastings and the conquest of Britain.

At first King Harold of the Saxons held back the Norman infantry attacks against the hill-top on which he set up his defence. His formidable wall of shields and the threatening sweep of his long axes proved impenetrable, until Duke William broke the line by luring the Saxons down the slope and into the open by a feigned retreat. Caught beneath a rain of high-angled arrows, the Saxons were cut apart by the Norman cavalry charge, as the famous Bayeux Tapestry so vividly shows. It is clear from that picture what an important part the bowmen played in the battle. And it was an arrow – so for a long time the story was told, though now it is questioned – that decided the outcome by piercing King Harold fatally in the eye.

The Welsh Longbow

The so-called 'English' longbow should be called the Welsh longbow, since the true origin of the bow that dominated the 100 Years' War in Europe, and has become an integral part of the emotional saga of English history, was Wales. In 1120, Welsh archers ambushed the English under

Above: A statuette of an early Etruscan warrior drawing his bow, possibly from Sardinia.

Right: The English longbowmen on the right face the Genoese crossbowmen on the left at the decisive Battle of Crécy in 1346. The crossbowman was virtually defenceless during the slow process of reloading. It was the longbow that won the day.

Henry II, near Powys. A hundred years later the longbow was in common use in England. By 1250, Edward I had wisely ensured that the longbow was part of the standard equipment of his army.

Unlike the crossbow, the longbow took years of practice and great strength to use effectively. The bow was about six feet long, as tall as a man or taller, with a linen or hemp bowstring. The clothyard shaft, or arrow, was about three feet long, fledged, or feathered, with goose feathers and pointed with a small, sharp head that would deliver the greatest possible impact on the smallest possible area. Peacock feathers were sometimes used for special peacetime occasions.

The longbow could fire about six times faster than the crossbow – that is, about six aimed shots a minute – with an effective range of 200 yards, although an experienced archer may have been

able to fire almost twice that distance. The bow had a pull of about 100 pounds and, to string it, the bowman usually bent the bow between his legs. To fire the bow, the string was drawn back to the ear; because of the great pull, the knack was to put the weight of the body *into* the bow with the left arm.

The bow itself was made of yew and the growth of these trees was encouraged, although hickory, ash and elm were also used. The manufacture and sale of bows was carefully controlled from about the middle of the 13th Century and, from the age of 15, all able-bodied Englishmen were compelled to train with the bow regularly. Archery practice was at one time made compulsory on Sundays.

Victory over the Crossbow

The relative merits of longbow and crossbow were tested at Crécy, where the English proved that a force of infantry and archers in an extended position could stand against an advancing force of mounted knights. Preceded by a ragged line of Genoese crossbowmen, the French cavalry approached the waiting English line. Strictly disciplined, the English held their fire until the enemy were well within range. Their rain of arrows sent the Genoese tottering back to be cut down by their own lines. The cavalry had no better effect on the solid English line of archers and footsoldiers. At the end of the day nearly 10,000 French were lost; on the English side barely 200 went down.

The French did not learn their lesson. At Poitiers, in 1356, and at Agincourt, in 1415, the English longbowman twice proved his worth against the armoured knight.

SWISS PIKES AND MERCENARIES
Keeping the Knights at a Distance

The knight became the butt of every new device and tactic on the battlefield simply because of the threat he himself posed. The Swiss infantry, brought together in an uneasy alliance between the various cantons against the threat of external forces, were the first soldiers in Europe to introduce the use of long-shafted weapons against mounted knights. While the armies of other countries adopted, instead of the crossbow and longbow, the pistol and handgun, the Swiss continued to achieve such astonishing successes with their long pikes that they became in great demand as mercenaries on all sides of the religious wars that savaged Europe for almost 200 years.

The Swiss pike was 18–21 feet long, with a sturdy shaft of ash and a long steel head. Its full effect was not achieved as an individual weapon but in a massed formation. Forced against their will during the second half of the 15th Century to confront the invading armies of France and Austria in decisive battles on the plains, the Swiss pikemen adopted a phalanx formation similar to the Greek pattern. As a military machine, the formation proved equally effective.

The ranks of the formation were staggered so that an impenetrable barrier of points was presented against a cavalry charge; the extreme length of the pikes enabled the pikemen to keep the horsemen beyond the effective range of their pistols. The length of a pike may seem to be an absurdly short range at which to miss with a pistol but early guns were not reliable and considerable skill was required to fire with any degree of accuracy from astride a galloping horse anxious to avoid becoming embedded on a steel bank of points.

Like a Roman legion, the Swiss phalanx was highly disciplined and could manoeuvre rapidly. Drill had to be precise in order to manipulate with any success a company of men 30–40 across and almost 100 deep. When standing against an enemy charge, they held the end of their pike against their foot and leant into the length of the pike in order to withstand the shock of impact without being pushed over.

After resounding successes against the French, first at Morat, in 1476, and a year later at Nancy, where the French King Charles the Bold was himself killed, other armies adapted the pike to their own use. In slightly modified forms it remained an integral part of many armies until the

17th Century and proved a useful weapon.

Maurice of Orange equipped the Dutch army with pikemen in about 1600, when he was trying to push the Spanish out of his country. After careful study of the Roman legions, Maurice interspersed his pikemen with musketeers, so that the former acted primarily as cover for the latter, particularly as the musketeers reloaded.

In the English Civil War of the 1640s, pikemen were used in a similar capacity to protect valuable musketeers, and during the 30 Years War that came to an end in Europe in 1648, the French used pikemen extensively.

The Gaudy Landsknechts
Meanwhile the Swiss had been hiring them-

Ucello was renowned for the decorative quality of his paintings which found an appropriate subject in the gaudy trappings depicted in The Battle of San Romano, *painted about 1456.*

selves out to whomever could pay them well enough. In the paintings of the period, dense with the rich pattern of infantry and cavalry marching seemingly in every direction or struggling in combat, there are always to be seen, like tall ears of wheat or barley, the multiple fences of the pikes rising above the heads of the contestants or lowering rank upon rank to receive and repel a new assault.

Among the most outrageous and colourful of those who wielded the pike for one nation or another during these years were the so-called *Landsknechts*. These were the real mercenaries, usually German, sometimes Swiss – the Emperor Maximilian I of Austria recruited a body of German Landsknechts against the Swiss them-

selves in about 1500 – who enjoyed their independence and flaunted gaudy trappings to their armour. Besides pike and short fighting sword they wielded, with terrible effect, a great two-handed sword that often stood over five and a half feet high.

Swiss discipline and ferocity – for which they were equally famous – made a tremendous impact on the battlefields of Europe until the advent of more refined artillery pronounced their doom. In close ranks, relying on close combat, they were completely vulnerable to accurate and powerful fire from greater range. Like the English bowmen, brilliant in their time, they were a machine that had to give way to the more efficient devices of progress.

THE MEDIEVAL CASTLE
Roman Origins

The knight and his castle go together in popular imagination, but they are not inseparable. As war machines they performed very different functions.

The Romans had been the great exponents of fortifications, though the Assyrians, a thousand years earlier, had built sturdy city forts with walls sometimes 75 feet thick. Ancient Babylon was supposed to have had walls 85 feet thick. But the Romans built fortifications whose remains still stand in North Africa and whose concept and design were barely equalled in one and a half thousand years.

As with the Assyrians, it was largely the efficiency of their own siege trains that provoked the Romans into developing forts strong enough to withstand their own sophisticated methods of attack. This necessity for castles and forts to keep one step ahead of contemporary siege machines was one of the causes for the steady evolution of their design. The process of action and reaction runs through the development of almost all war machines.

Forts were essential to the Romans because of the extent of their conquests, as a result of which they found themselves trying to hold down alien and often aggressive peoples with minimal troops. The forts acted as outposts of the Empire. This continued to be their function in later centuries and for other nations: the fort acted either as an outpost or a last method of defence.

The Byzantines under Belisarius built walled towns as well as isolated forts throughout North Africa during the 6th Century A.D. One good example of a fort constructed in a commanding position is Aïn Tounga, which guards a pass in Tunisia and once controlled the area.

The motte and bailey castle was common in France during the 11th Century. The motte was a high mound in the centre of the walled area and the bailey was the area of ground between the outer walls. There would often be several lines of walls surrounding the central fort; this resulted in Inner and Outer Baileys.

Norman castles of the 11th Century still stand. Most of these were built of stone. In England, the outer shell of the Windsor Tower dates from 1075 and the rectangular White Tower, at the Tower of London dates from 1080.

Below: Windsor Castle and the Round Tower (right).
Right: The Tower of London, centre of much of England's history.

The Castles of the Crusaders

The greatest boost to European castle design came from the Holy Land. The First Crusade marched against the Saracens in the last decade of the 11th Century and found them firmly entrenched and well-defended in captured Byzantine castles. Having battered their heads against Antioch and Nicaea and captured Jerusalem in 1099, the Crusaders quickly learnt their lesson and started to build their own castles in order to hold what ground they had gained in a strange and distant land where they were surrounded by the constant fear of attack by the infidel.

The Crusades lasted for over 300 years and the castles that the Crusaders built were con-structed to last for ever. Over that period, although Crusading armies came and went, many generations were born and died in the Holy Land and knew no other home. The finest of the Crusader castles is undoubtedly Krak des Chevaliers, although there are plenty of others – at Saone, Margat and elsewhere.

The influence of the Byzantine-style castle, with its circular towers to give a better all-round view of the attacker and its retention of the *keep* or *donjon* as a last line of defence, returned to Europe with the Third Crusade. Richard I built Chateau Gaillard along these lines on a natural eminence 300 feet above the River Seine.

This extra height gave the castle added protection against siege machines, an important precaution after the lessons of the Holy Land. The main defences were constructed against the approach, with three baileys as three separate lines of defence. Château Gaillard fell to Philip II of France not long after it was built, but it stretched the French king to a long and expensive siege that weakened his army.

In the Holy Land the Byzantine traditions continued until the middle of the 15th Century. One of the most impressive fortifications still standing was built by the Saracens at Rumeli Hisari, commanding the northern shore of the Bosporus.

Left: Château Gaillard, built by Richard I on the lines of the Byzantine castles. It holds a commanding position on the cliff-top.
Top: The 15th-Century German Tower in the Castle of St Peter at Bodrum, in Turkey.
Above: The tower and walls of Rumeli Hisari, built by Mahomet II, the conqueror of Constantinople.

This was constructed in 1452. It has walls 24 feet thick and is said to have been built by 10,000 men in four and a half months. A year later Mahomet achieved his great ambition to capture nearby Constantinople and add it to his empire.

Castles and Cannon

Meanwhile, in England, some of the most remarkably durable castles since Roman times had been constructed under Edward I to stand guard along the border between England and Wales and to assist his conquest of the vigorously insurgent Welsh. In most cases, the central castle, square or round, was surrounded by two or more lines of walls with well-fortified circular towers at the corners and highly defensible gateways. The siting of the castles was carefully thought out to use natural defences such as water and rock to the best advantage.

Caernarvon is a good example of a late 13th-Century castle built by Edward I. Its walls are up to 15 feet thick and remain virtually intact. There are other surviving examples of the same period at Caerphilly, Harlech and Conway.

Features of the Medieval castle were the *enceinte*, or outer wall, the moats or ditches surrounding the wall, often filled with water for additional defence (though this undoubtedly added to the dampness of life within the castle), the retractable drawbridge for crossing the moat, the barbican which was a double-fortified construction for protecting the gateway, and the portcullis made of oak plated with iron for lowering across the gateway. The walls were usually crenellated, or topped by battlements,

and the round towers and faces of the walls were punctuated by narrow loopholes from which the defenders could fire while offering the smallest possible target to the attacker.

Russia had 14th-Century fortified citadels, called kremlins, characterized by numerous towers. In India, emphasis was laid on outworks and heavily fortified gateways. Spikes often protruded from the great teak doors as additional defence against elephants used to act as living battering rams.

The appearance of cannon in the siege trains of the 15th Century gradually brought about the collapse of the Medieval castle, whose uprearing, vertical walls offered a prime and vulnerable target to the massive battering of the guns. Castles throughout Europe were rapidly reduced. Charles VII of France swept the English out of his country with a commanding siege train and his son pushed south through Italy with similar success. In the first half of the next century the Turks, under Suleiman I, battered fort after fort into submission throughout eastern Europe as they advanced threateningly toward Vienna, where eventually they were stopped.

For centuries fortifications had adapted themselves to the prevailing means of attack; it was time for them to do so again.

Above: From a painting of the Vodozvodnaya Tower of the Kremlin, in Moscow, as it used to appear.
Left: The imposing walls of Caernarvon Castle, one of the best preserved of Edward I's 13th-Century Welsh castles.
Right: The map shows the strategic positions of Edward I's castles in Wales.
Below: A ground plan of Conway Castle, another of Edward's fortifications, showing the typical round corner towers.

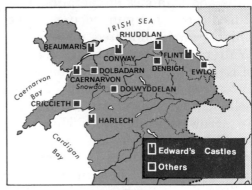

IRISH SEA
RHUDDLAN
BEAUMARIS
CONWAY
FLINT
DOLBADARN
DENBIGH
EWLOE
CAERNARVON
Snowdon
Caernarvon Bay
DOLWYDDELAN
CRICCIETH
HARLECH
Cardigan Bay

Edward's Castles
Others

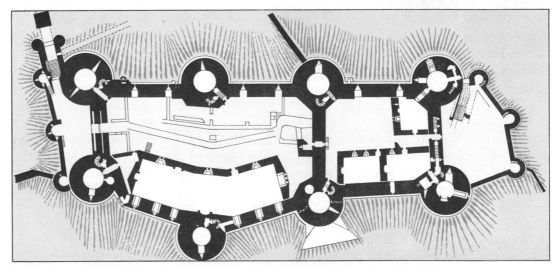

GUNPOWDER BREAKTHROUGH
Friar Bacon and Black Berthold

The use of gunpowder as an explosive charge to provide the power to fire missiles was the most influential innovation in the history of warfare. To this day the gun remains one of the most effective machines of war in a variety of shapes and sizes. But it is still not known who invented gunpowder nor who built the first gun.

The invention of gunpowder has been credited to the Chinese. There is no certainty of this. Experiments were made at an early date with oil, pitch and sulphur, but results were variable and often unstable. The Arabs may also have known about gunpowder in the early 13th Century A.D. But the first convincing report of its manufacture was by the Franciscan Friar, Roger Bacon, in the middle of the 13th Century. In a cyphered report, Bacon gave the formula for the correct mixture of saltpetre, charcoal and sulphur.

Bacon's claim to fame is certainly stronger than that of his rival, the German monk, Berthold Schwartz. Despite 'portraits' of him and a statue to his memory, as well as reports of his supposed invention of gunpowder, it is possible that Berthold was only a legend.

The first positive record of a gun is not until at least 50 years after Bacon's gunpowder formula. In 1326, permission was granted by the city council of Florence for a delivery of cannon balls and 'canones de metallo'. The first known illustration of a gun occurs in the same year. This is an illuminated manuscript written by Walter de Milemete in honour of King Edward III of England. In the illustration, a knight has just put a red hot iron to the touch-hole of a pot-bellied, vase-shaped cannon from whose mouth an arrow is being fired. This kind of cannon, because of its shape, was called a 'pot-de-fer'.

A year later there is evidence that Edward used guns in his first Scottish campaign; the Scots were using them in sieges soon afterwards. In 1346, we know that Edward used a small number of cannon in his victory over the French at the Battle of Crécy. The terrible noise of the cannon was feared as much as the destructive power of the cannon balls.

Stone Shot and Breeches

Early cannon, or bombards as they were often called – petarara and culverin were names for other types of cannon – were not necessarily cast. Staves of wood were laid lengthwise in a circular formation to form the barrel and were forced

Roger Bacon an Englishman

Above: Roger Bacon knew the formula for gunpowder. Right: A scene from the Battle of Rosebecque, from the Chronicles of the French Historian, Froissart. There are examples of early cannon in the scene itself and two shown in action below the battle.

together by rings of brass or iron. Sometimes the staves were made of iron as well. It was not a satisfactory method on the whole, as the gases from the explosion of the gunpowder tended to escape through the cracks.

Stone shot was used as an economy and convenience. It required less charge than iron; this also meant that there was a correspondingly reduced chance of the whole cannon blowing up, as frequently happened. But iron and lead shot came into use very quickly. Small shot was used against troops in the open.

Breech-loaders were introduced early in the history of guns. A trough was left at the rear of the gun into which was wedged a mug-shaped cylinder with a handle, complete with powder and shot. When the gun had been fired the cylinder was taken out and replaced by another that had already been prepared with powder and shot. By this means a fairly rapid rate of fire could be maintained; if enough cylinders, or chambers, were available, from 12–15 rounds could be fired in an hour.

Early carriages for the guns consisted merely of a great beam of timber, hollowed out so that the gun could lie snugly along its length. More elaborate carriages soon evolved to enable elevation and depression of the gun. This was particularly important for siege warfare, which was one of the immediate uses to which the new machines were put.

Bataille de Rosebecque.

Perrodin pinx[t].   Imp. Fraillery   Daumont, chromolith.

THE GREAT CANNON
Characters from a Mighty Past

The use of cannon against castles and fortified city walls led very quickly to the construction of monster cannon, some of which are still intact today. Their dimensions and the statistics of their firepower and capabilities make formidable reading but can surely never recreate in the mind the terrifying effect on defenders to whom cannon of any kind were still a novelty.

Mad Margaret, or *Dulle Griet*, was one of the earliest, built about 1410 and still to be seen in the Belgian town of Ghent. Mad Margaret is over 16 feet long, weighs about 15 tons and has a bore of about 30 inches.

An even earlier cannon was Krimhild, which stood inside Nuremberg in 1388. It is reported that Krimhild's cannon balls had a range of 1,000 paces and could penetrate a wall that was six feet thick. Though not as large as Mad Margaret, something of Krimhild's size can be imagined when we know that 12 horses were needed to pull it and another 22 to draw up its ammunition and equipment.

Mons Meg is another famous cannon, built in Flanders in about 1470 and now at Edinburgh, in Scotland. Mons Meg is 13 feet long and weighs five tons. The cannon has a bore of almost 20 inches and could fire a stone shot of more than 300 pounds. With the right charge – and set at the right angle – the cannon could fire an iron ball over 1,400 yards and a stone ball nearly twice as far.

Mahomet's Dardanelles Monsters

Mahomet used several huge cannon at the siege of Constantinople in 1453, alongside his old-fashioned trebuchets. The strength of the fortification and the determination of the defence can be guessed at when it is remembered that, despite the battering of these cannon, the siege lasted for nearly two months. The 'Dardanelles Gun' now at the Tower of London, was built for Mahomet in the 1460s and is probably very like those used at the siege.

This gun was cast in bronze and weighs over 18 tons. It is 17 feet long, has a bore of 25 inches and fired a shot of approximately 800 pounds. An

unusual feature of the gun is that it was made in two pieces, which were screwed together. This was probably done for ease of transport.

It was fired experimentally almost 200 years after it was first built and the fragments of shot flew almost a mile to cross the Dardanelles. Even 350 years after their construction, Mahomet's siege guns were still in action: a British squadron was fired on in the Dardanelles and one ship received a hit from a 700-pound shot.

From an account of the construction of the guns we know that one was made in about 18 days and that it took 140 oxen and 200 men to haul each of the monsters into position against the walls of Constantinople. From that moment, Mahomet's 12 great cannon – a thirteenth burst early on – were each able to hurl about seven shots a day at the city defences for the duration of the siege.

The King of Cannon

One of the biggest cannon ever produced was in Russia, at the beginning of the 16th Century.

This was the massive 'King of Cannon', which had a bore of about 35 inches and a barrel of 17 feet. It could fire a stone ball weighing up to one ton.

At last the stubborn walls of cities that had been able to withstand sieges of months and intermittent attacks for years came crumbling down in only a few days. Some idea of the importance and charismatic value of these dominating monsters might be gained by reading C. S. Forester's *The Gun*, a story which was also made into a film. The story is set in more recent history and the gun itself is not as vast as some of the monsters in this chapter, but *The Gun* is a vivid account of the 'presence' which this outstanding and vital piece of artillery exerted over the soldiers who made use of it and among those against whom it was used.

Far left, top: Mons Meg, restored and remounted, stands at Edinburgh Castle. Far left, bottom: The Dardanelles Gun, built by the Turks in the 15th Century, now at the Tower of London. Below: The 17th-Century Tsar Pushka, or Emperor Cannon.

CANNON FOR EVERY PURPOSE
Making Good Use of the New Machine

As soon as the first guns appeared, inventive minds turned their attention to the novelty of the new machine and produced a proliferation of shapes and sizes, all with different purposes. Some of these never got further than the drawing board; illustrations and reports still exist even of these. It was one thing for an army to possess artillery but when both armies were in possession of the same advantage what was important was the manner in which the new machine was put to use and how its merits were exploited.

The first move was to combine several guns in one piece of artillery on the same gun-carriage.

These were usually fixed around a central block and each had its own touch-hole. One gun could be fired at a time or several together for added effect – and the effect could be startling. But the danger was as great for the artilleryman as it was for the enemy. While intending to fire only one of the guns, the gunner might explode the whole contraption in a self-destructive conflagration, much to the delight of the opposition.

Organ-guns, which were a variation of this multiple principle, had their barrels laid in a row, sometimes as many as ten side by side. Another form of organ-gun had three rows of

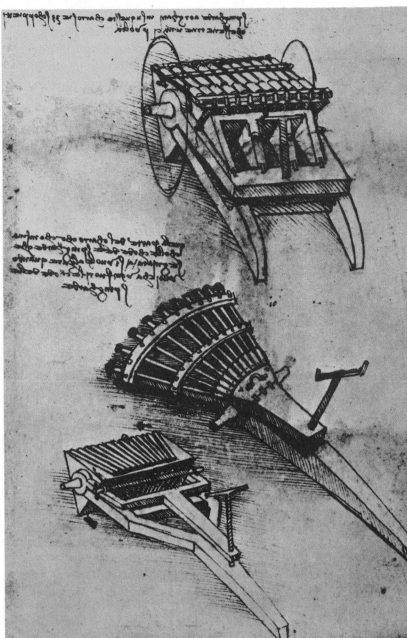

*Above: Leonardo da Vinci's imaginative
designs for organ-guns, with multiple fire-power.
Left: An eight-barrelled gun carriage using a
sledge base. Wheels would probably have stuck fast.*

gun barrels laid side by side on the three sides of a triangular block that revolved in a frame so that each row aimed forward in turn and could be fired in rapid succession. Leonardo da Vinci made several drawings of organ-guns into which he incorporated a worm-screw system for elevating the contraption.

Ribaudequins and Shrimps

War chariots had been used before guns were invented but they took a new turn with the new circumstances. Immediately prior to the introduction of guns, the war chariot had consisted of a two-wheeled shield, pushed forward by soldiers, with pikes protruding through its face and loopholes provided for crossbow fire.

In the *ribaudequin*, the crossbows were replaced by small cannon, little more than tubes. We know that Edward III ordered a hundred of these ribaudequins to be prepared for his invasion of France, which led to the battle of Crecy. 150 years later, these basic war chariots were still in use in Germany.

Gun carts were a more sophisticated form of ribaudequins. Henry VIII of England tried to make use of them at the siege of Boulogne, in

1544. In this case the guns were given better cover. A conical nose to the gun cart culminated in one or more spikes. The guns themselves appeared through openings in the side of the cone. This type of gun cart was sometimes known as a 'shrimp'. Its bite was more than shrimp-like.

One illustration of a gun cart or ribaudequin from the 15th Century shows a horse in harness behind the gun pulling against the back of the frame in order to propel the whole machine forward. A shield protects the gunner and a vicious looking arrow projects forward of the gun barrel. Since the horse could hardly have been expected to attain much speed with the weight of the whole contraption, the arrow probably served the purpose of defence against charging cavalry rather than attack.

Zizka's Snakes

Another type of early gun cart or waggon was that used by the Protestant Hussites, led by John Zizka, against the Catholic Monarchists of Bohemia at the beginning of the 15th Century. Zizka organized wooden waggons, mounted with cannon, into circular formations. The waggons were covered and protected by thick boards, presenting a formidable defence, bristling with armament, against which the Bohemian cavalry, protected only by conventional armour, flung itself with self-destructive futility. Zizka's can-non were called 'snakes' and their bite was appropriately lethal.

The waggon barricade also served as a sanctuary for Zizka's infantry, who could make sudden sorties against the enemy and retreat as quickly behind the waggon train. The mobility of this train of artillery was one of its greatest assets. It amounted to a moveable fortress that could be set up on any prominent position ready for action at very short notice.

Three major innovations in early artillery warfare occurred during this century. Wheels were introduced on gun carriages, *trunnions* were developed and, in the middle of the century, bronze casting began to take the place of iron. Bronze could be cast more evenly and the cannon made with this metal were therefore less likely to explode under the shock of firing.

Trunnions were the pivots on either side of the cannon, cast at the same time as the cannon, and set slightly forward of the point of balance so that, when unsupported, the breech of the cannon came down and the muzzle was raised. The use of trunnions made it a great deal easier to elevate and depress the cannon in order to adjust the range and achieve maximum accuracy.

The Names of the Guns

The great siege cannon and giant bombards often had their own characterized names, such as

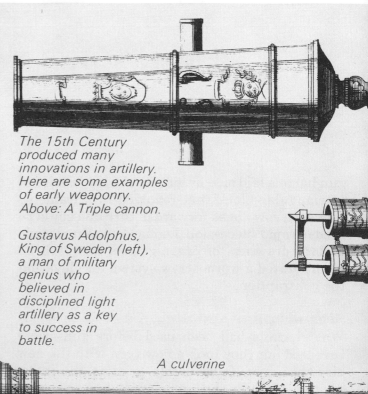

The 15th Century produced many innovations in artillery. Here are some examples of early weaponry. Above: A Triple cannon.

Gustavus Adolphus, King of Sweden (left), a man of military genius who believed in disciplined light artillery as a key to success in battle.

A culverine

Mons Meg, which has already been described, and the Katherine, a Tyrolean cannon cast in 1487, 12 feet long and inscribed with the verse, in German:

'My name is Katherine.
'Beware of my strength.
'I punish injustice.'

But apart from these special cases, the ordinary names for the various types of gun varied according to country, time and use, as did their shapes and sizes. Used initially as individual pieces of artillery, it was some time before any kind of standardization was applied to the guns that were being produced. And until that happened no rational organization of ammunition and equipment could be put into practice.

One of the enlightened commanders who contributed to this organization was the Emperor Maximilian, in about 1500. But still the proliferation of names and the variations in size and shot between countries and periods make for plenty of confusion. All the same, it gives an idea of the range of guns in use to name some of them and their capabilities.

The siege artillery of Maximilian consisted of demi or double cannon that fired shot of between 36 and 50 pounds, quarter cannon that fired 24–40-pound shot and basilisks or long culverins (from the French couleuvre, a snake) that fired shot from 12–24 pounds. The long basilisk had the accuracy needed for siege work. Basilisks bore names such as 'ibex', 'lizard' and 'crocodile', as well as 'wall-breaker' and 'beater'. Other guns were called 'nightingales' and, in the same refrain, 'singers'.

English cannon, later in the century, were divided into cannon royal or double cannon (in this case the double cannon seems to have been differentiated from the demi-cannon) that may have weighed up to 8,000 pounds and fired a ball of 60–70 pounds, whole cannon weighing 7,000 pounds and firing a ball of 40 pounds, and demi-cannon of 6,000 pounds, firing a 30-pound ball.

Culverins fired balls varying between 15 and 20 pounds and demi-culverins fired 10-to-12-pound balls. For field artillery there were sakers (from the French sacre, a sparrow hawk) that fired balls from six to seven pounds, minyons that fired three-to-four-pound balls, and falcons and falconets that fired respectively just over two-pound shots and one-pound shot.

But another inventory of artillery given a little earlier in Europe makes reference to falconets using four-to-five-pound shot and falcons using six-pound shot. A serpentine also fired a variable four-pound shot.

Among the less common pieces of artillery were quarter-culverins (half the fire-power of a demi-culverin), the small one-pounder serpentinelles, flankers, bastard cannons, perriers and

Section of the breach of a triple cannon

A twin cannon

NOTE: Scale – approximately one inch to three feet

The Emperor Maximilian, a pioneer in the development of organized artillery

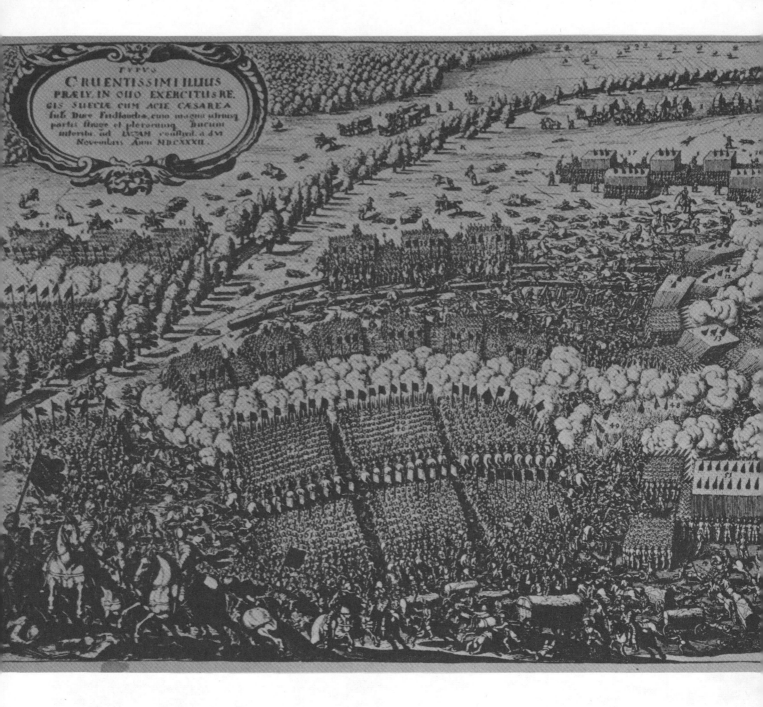

giant perriers (short-barrelled cannon), and the colourfully named 'murderers'. Mortars were also used in siege warfare but those machines are dealt with in the next chapter.

Field Artillery at Ravenna

By the 17th Century light field guns were in widespread use. Chief among the commanders who understood and put into practice the use of manoeuvrable field guns was the Swedish King Gustavus Adolphus, whose light three-pounder could be drawn by one horse or three men and saw action with great success during the 30 Years

War. In many ways, Gustavus's integration of field artillery with infantry and cavalry was the example for many later systems of integrated attack – systems that proved most effective.

But it was Maximilian who had really shown the value of concentrated artillery fire in the field as well as in siegework. The first large gatherings of artillery in the field took place during the Italian War of 1508–1516, in which Maximilian took part, together with English, French, Spanish, Venetian and Papal forces.

Massed ranks of infantry and the massed fire of the artillery played the major roles in these

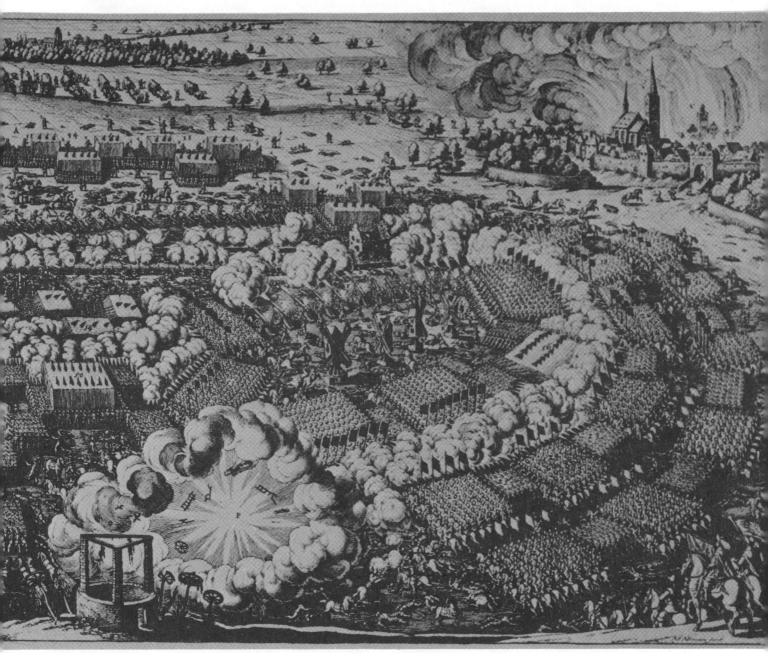

Lützen — The last battle fought by Gustavus Adolphus in the Thirty Years War. The great commander was killed while personally leading his troops into a battle which destroyed the Catholic army of Count Wallenstein.

campaigns. Artillery fire could tear apart the ranks of pikemen and halberdiers. But if the first volley failed to halt or turn the enemy's advance, time was against the guns. In the time that it took to reload the guns, the infantry could easily approach and overrun their positions.

An artillery duel opened the encounter between the French and Spanish at the Battle of Ravenna, in 1512. One report states that one Spanish cannon-ball knocked down almost 40 men. But a year later, at Novara, the cannon proved less effective. Possessing no artillery of their own and after sustaining a barrage of fire

from the French artillery, Swiss mercenaries managed to capture all the French cannon in one daring attack. Good cause for celebration.

The French had their revenge two years later at the Battle of Marignano, when their substantial artillery decimated the Swiss troops. The combination of artillery and arquebus fire proved itself conclusively. 'The sky burst forth as if all the forces of the earth and heavens were preparing to swoop down', wrote one diarist. The hitherto invincible Swiss were routed, leaving 7,000 dead on the battlefield, mute evidence to the effectiveness of the new machine.

MORTARS: THE BARRAGE FROM ABOVE
Specialized Cannon

The mortar was a form of cannon specialized to lob shot over the wall of a besieged fortification or to deliver a plunging shot or spray of shots on an enemy from above. Mahomet used these machines to excellent effect in bombarding the Byzantine fleet in 1453.

The distinction between mortars and cannon was based on their angle of fire and the length of their barrels. Mortars, or short howitzers as they were sometimes known, fired in what was termed the upper register; that is, over 45 degrees. Cannon and guns fired in the lower register, below 45 degrees. The shorter barrel of the mortar, which was a variation on the early bombard, enabled a charge of shot to be spread over a wider area.

Leonardo's Bombard

In 1482, Leonardo da Vinci wrote that he had, 'a type of bombard that is extremely easy and convenient to transport and with which it is intended to shower a veritable hailstorm of small stones and whose smoke will strike the enemy with terror, causing great danger and confusion'. Very soon there were mortars in every train of artillery, although most armies seem to have restricted themselves at first to three or four of these high-angled machines.

Types and calibres of mortar differed as greatly as those of cannon. They continued to be used increasingly until, by the end of the 18th Century, it was generally accepted that the length of a mortar should be approximately one and a half to a maximum of two times its calibre. Mortars were loaded from the muzzle and their trunnions were usually at the extreme base, behind the touch-hole, in order to facilitate a steep angle of fire. Instead of wheeled carriages, flat-based beds were used for supporting the mortar, which was transported on a specially designed waggon, whereas the howitzer, apart from being longer, was generally transported on a conventional gun carriage and its trunnions were usually placed just off-centre.

One of the more popular mortars was the powerful 10-inch mortar that could fire a shot up to 1,500 yards. Once again, distances and size varied greatly. An eight-inch mortar was also commonly used. And as well as single shot and multiple shot, bombs filled with gunpowder were fused to explode after a set time. The accuracy of this timing could not be counted on, nor could

the gunner's estimation of the range. Illustrations of the strategic deployment of troops, showing mortars firing over their heads at the enemy toward whom they are advancing, look dangerous. Many shots must have landed accidentally among friends as well as enemies.

Shrapnel and Exploding Shells

The danger to troops was increased when bombs were timed to burst over the heads of the enemy, adding an increased element of fear to the physical threat. To achieve this effect successfully against the intended target made considerable demands on the accuracy of the gunners.

It was Lieutenant Shrapnel of the British army who invented the famous shell case that bears his name. The case was hollow, fitted with small shot and a fuse light enough to break up the case without dispersing the shot, which continued in the direction in which it had been aimed. Although Shrapnel introduced his idea in the 1780s, it was not used by the British until the Napoleonic wars.

Top right: A sketch by Leonardo, showing a design for elevating a mortar on a toothed arc.
Bottom right: Another Leonardo sketch showing the trajectories of mortar bombs used against a fortress and giving blanket coverage.
Below: Two types of bombard, or mortar, set on flat-based beds, from an engraving published in 1575. The one on the left has its trunnions at the base of the barrel, that on the right has central trunnions. The T-shape and angle lying by the mortar bomb are used for aiming the mortar.

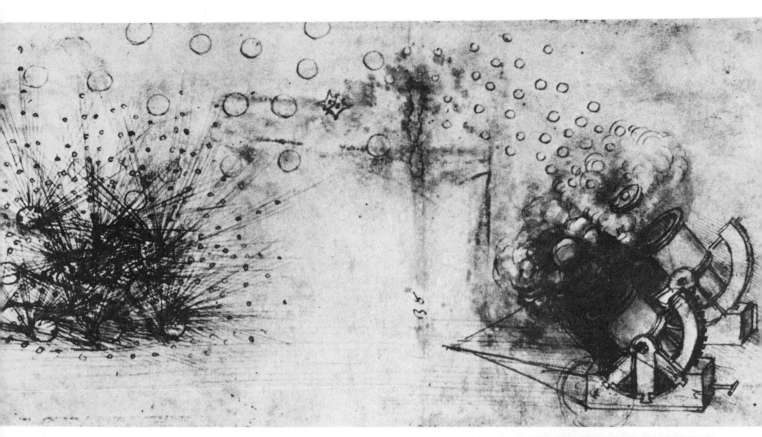

FROM BOMBARDELLI TO FLINTLOCK
Miniature Cannon

Once the cannon had been recognized and established as the most destructive machine so far encountered in the history of warfare, the next step clearly was to arm the foot-soldier with a smaller version of this device – a cannon that could be carried easily and used in a flexible situation.

The first handguns developed directly from early cannon. They consisted of a simple iron tube, or breech, with a touch-hole. After early attempts proved that the tube became too hot to hold once a round or two had been fired, the breech was fitted with a wooden handle, called a tiller, fixed by iron straps or slotted into the end of the breech.

One of the earliest references to handguns is in the town records of Perugia, in Italy. We know that in 1364 five hundred 'bombardelli', to be fired by the hand, were ordered; each was to be about nine inches long. This sounds more like pistol size, but many handguns were clumsy and heavy contraptions, sometimes needing to be supported on the ground and often requiring two people to operate them. One man held the weapon either against his chest or under his arm – occasionally against his shoulder – and aimed at the foe, while the other applied the slow match to the touch-hole.

The slow match consisted of a string of woven hemp that was soaked in saltpetre in order to make it burn more slowly. This was, in fact, a sophisticated method of firing the priming powder that only developed at the end of the 14th Century and replaced the awkward method of heating a piece of wire over a convenient fire (if there was such a thing) and then applying the wire, while still red-hot, to the pan.

The first handguns were a strange and varied collection of machines, motley cross-breeds intended for use not merely as guns, which were far too novel to be considered in any way reliable, but as battle axes, maces, daggers, clubs and other more traditionally effective devices in case of emergency and in the heat of battle when the soldier's mechanical expertise failed him.

This combination within the same machine of the gun and a traditional striking weapon continued long after the gun itself had developed into an efficient and thoroughly dependable contraption; the bayonet was of course a similar, if more rational, form of this combination.

Despite its clumsiness, the handgun proved its worth immediately. The knight's armour, as we have seen, until then only vulnerable to the powerful bolt of the crossbow and the searching aim of the longbow, was no proof against bullets from handguns with calibres varying from half an inch to almost two inches; no proof, that was, so long as the soldier who operated the gun could achieve a hit, which was never certain.

The Problems of Taking Aim

The single gunner, quite apart from knowing little or nothing about ballistics, had both hands full merely trying to fire his contraption without the added but somewhat necessary complication of trying to aim at his target. Holding the gun with one hand, the gunner had to blow on the slow match until it glowed and then apply it carefully to the touch-hole, by which time the

Left: From a painting by Glockenthon of the Emperor Maximilian I's guns. The men are firing a hand cannon of about 1505.
Right: Two early and unusual multi-barrel guns from Maximilian's Arsenal of Tyrol: a four-cornered gun and a triple-barrel matchlock.

March with your rest in your hand.	*March, and with your Musket carry your rest.*	*Unshoulder your Musket.*
Poize your Musket	*Join your rest to your Musket.*	*Take forth your Match.*
Blow off your Coal.	*Cock your Match.*	*Try your Match.*

Guard, blow and open your pan.

Dismount your musket. — *Uncock*

Clear your pan. — *Prime*

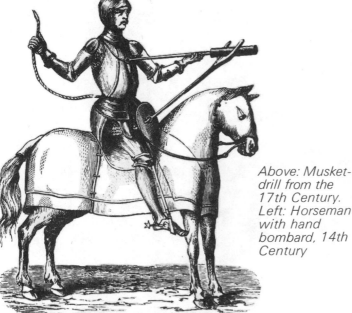

Above: Musket-drill from the 17th Century.
Left: Horseman with hand bombard, 14th Century

priming powder had probably blown away. Sometimes a strap was provided on the end of the tiller, which went round the gunner's neck to steady his aim; later, a regular support was part of his equipment.

What was needed was a method of igniting the powder that would leave the gunner with a hand free to steady his weapon and take more telling aim. This was provided, in about 1480, by the introduction of the serpentine, an S-shaped piece of metal fixed to the side of the gun. The slow match was held in one end of the serpentine and brought down on to the touch-hole when the lower end of the 'S' – the trigger – was pulled.

This invention, simple at first, more complex and more efficient as further sophistications were

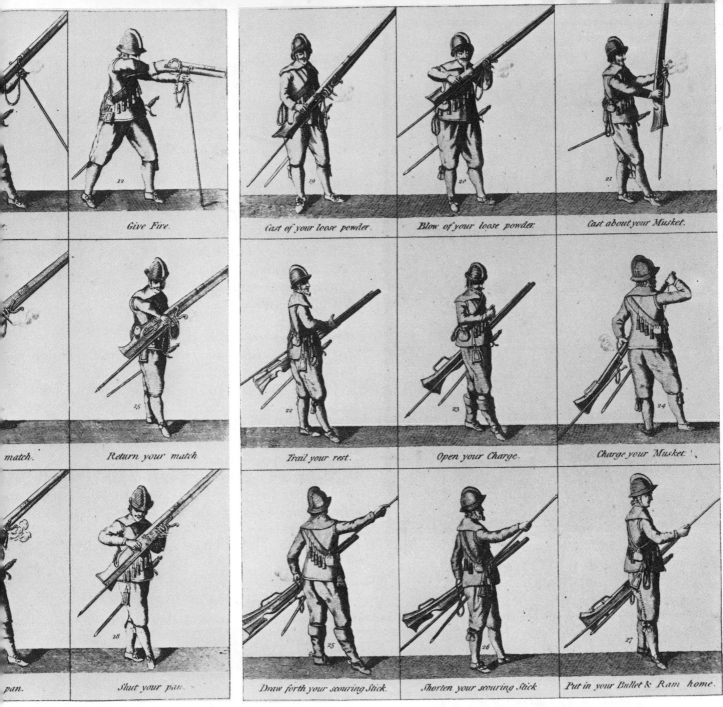

Give Fire.	*Cast of your loose powder.*	*Blow of your loose powder.*	*Cast about your Musket.*
...match. *Return your match*	*Trail your rest.*	*Open your Charge.*	*Charge your Musket.*
...pan. *Shut your pan.*	*Draw forth your scouring Stick.*	*Shorten your scouring Stick.*	*Put in your Bullet & Ram home.*

added, transformed the infantry gunner from a fringe benefit to a lethal and increasingly vital facet of the battle scene.

Early handguns, or arquebus, were first used in an integrated system of infantry at the beginning of the 16th Century, when they began to replace bowmen interspersed between ranks of pikemen and swordsmen. Hopefully, what the arquebus failed to stop the pikes would hold off while the arquebus reloaded.

The variety of early handguns closely paralleled the variety of early cannon. There was even a hand mortar. And in the same way that experiments were made to produce multiple guns, so multiple handguns appeared. Similarly, as spears had sometimes been reversible, so there were reversible handguns, though this style did not survive long. Every innovation had to be experimented with from every possible angle in order fully to explore its potential.

The Arquebus

There were several stages in the development of the gun, each clearly discernible as the machine became increasingly efficient. Over a period of 300 years various mechanisms were invented for firing the handgun, each of which added to the gunner's reliability, accuracy and effectiveness, and each of which in turn produced a new machine with new capabilities.

The matchlock, or serpentine fitting, was, as we have seen, the first to enable the gunner to

take any reasonable kind of aim. This type of gun had a variety of names, the best known of which was probably 'arquebus'. It is possible that the word came from the Italian *arca bousa*, which means the 'bow with a mouth', for the stock of the crossbow was the nearest parallel to this new device that most soldiers had seen. The 'hackbutt' was a heavier form of arquebus, with a hook on its underside which was used to balance the gun against a stone wall or similar support.

The arquebus weighed anything up to 25 pounds and probably fired a one ounce ball about 100 yards. At close range, the ball could penetrate conventional armour of the early 16th Century with little difficulty.

The Wheel-lock and Pistol

Although modifications were made to the matchlock, there was still a tendency for the slow match to blow out in the wind and a likelihood that if it did not then its burning would give away the whereabouts of the gunner. The wheellock, which was invented about 1500, solved both these problems.

The wheel-lock worked by friction, rather like a cigarette lighter. A spark was produced to fire the priming powder when a piece of iron pyrites, a common mineral, struck down against a steel wheel with a milled edge. The pyrites was held

Above: An arquebusier of 1608 charges his weapon. He will then ram home the powder and shot before taking up his stance for firing.
Below: A beautifully decorated German wheel-lock petronel of about 1590, now in the Tower of London, England.

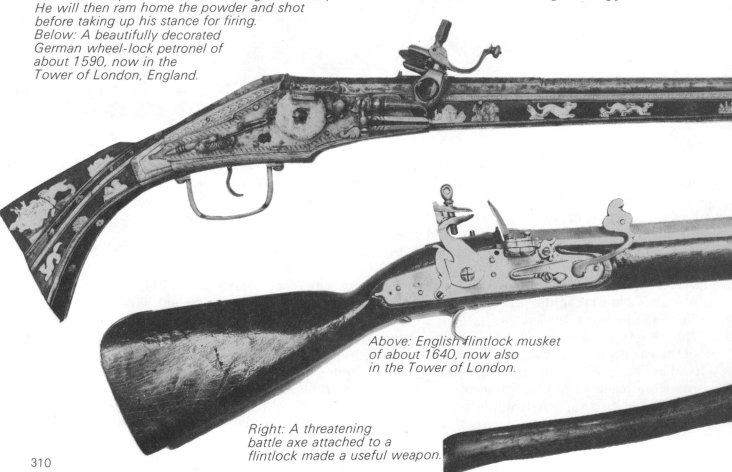

Above: English flintlock musket of about 1640, now also in the Tower of London.

Right: A threatening battle axe attached to a flintlock made a useful weapon.

in the 'dogshead' or 'cock' and the wheel was made to revolve by means of a spring wound up by a handle at the side of the gun. The trigger actuated the spring. You can see from the illustration that the cock was similar in concept to the serpentine that had held the slow match of the arquebus.

One of the earliest forms of friction lock, a great deal earlier than the wheel-lock, was the so-called Monk's gun, which was made in Germany, possibly in the second half of the 15th Century. In this device, the gunner drew out a lever which rubbed a serrated edge along a piece of iron pyrites, similar to the system in the wheel-lock.

The great advantage of the wheel-lock was that it could be fitted to a compact gun. Thus the pistol first appeared at the beginning of the 15th Century. Soldiers on horseback, unable to use the arquebus because it required two hands to fire, carried guns for the first time. Primed before battle, these pistols were often multi-barrelled, enabling the cavalryman to exert a considerable barrage of fire power as he passed close to the enemy before retiring to reload or before charging into the midst of the enemy with sword or mace.

Organized cavalry, armed with pistols, were used in 1544 by Germans attacking the French in Champagne. A hundred years later short firearms with wheel-locks were being used in the English Civil War along with old matchlocks, although by that time the flintlock had been invented. The change-over from one type of gun to another always occurred over a long period of time. A sudden switch was too expensive.

The Snapping Hen

The flintlock appeared in about 1630, possibly in France, and survived for 200 years. But an earlier form of flintlock, called the snaphaunce, dates from about 1530. The word 'snaphaunce' possibly comes from 'snap haan', which meant 'snapping' or 'pecking' hen in Flemish.

In these two guns the cock, holding a piece of flint, struck down against a steel above the pan, where the powder was. As the steel was struck, it moved up and away from the pan, exposing the powder to the spark. In the snaphaunce there was a separate pan cover, which also moved back as the steel was struck. The flintlock was simplified by combining steel and pancover.

The matchlock was not generally abolished until the 18th Century. William II re-armed the British army with flintlocks in about 1700. The famous Brown Bess flintlock musket appeared at the beginning of the 18th Century. Flintlocks were used by almost all soldiers fighting in the Napoleonic wars.

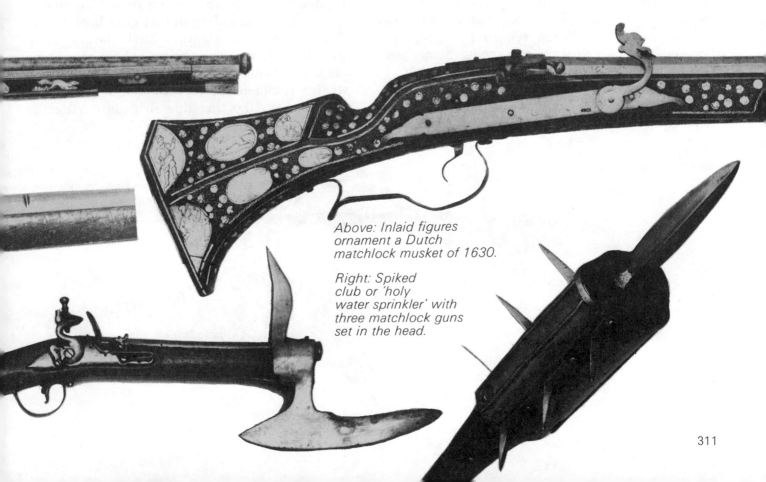

Above: Inlaid figures ornament a Dutch matchlock musket of 1630.

Right: Spiked club or 'holy water sprinkler' with three matchlock guns set in the head.

THE MODERN RIFLE TAKES SHAPE
Bayonets and Skilful Tactics

The word 'bayonet' comes from Bayonne in France, a place that had a reputation for its knives. The first bayonet appeared in about 1640, when a group of infantrymen stuck their knives into the muzzles of their guns and charged the enemy. The usefulness of this innovation was seen at once. Until then only the long and somewhat unwieldy pike had protected the infantryman as he reloaded his gun; with the bayonet he had his own simple defence. In 1647, a French Infantry Commander (also from Bayonne) ordered a quantity of short, round-handled swords from the town, and issued them to his musketeers. These were the first real bayonets.

Subsequent early bayonets were called 'plug' bayonets. A short, pointed, broad-based blade with a cross-guard and a wooden handle was shoved into the mouth of the musket when it was no longer needed. This meant, of course, that the gun itself could not be used simultaneously, a problem that was overcome by Sebastian Vauban, famous for his fortresses, who introduced the 'ring' bayonet, a tube attachment fitted with a triangular tapering blade – the tube slipped over the end of the gun and was help in place by a catch or spring clip.

Quicker to produce in an emergency was the 'spring' bayonet, introduced in the second half of the 18th Century. In this case the bayonet was permanently fixed to the gun but folded back along the barrel. When required it could be released to swing forward on a spring. Sometimes even pistols were fitted with these bayonets.

Marlborough made good use of the ring bayonet in his campaign against the French in the early years of the 18th Century. By this method he could raise the number of his musketeers at the expense of his pikemen and so bring more firepower to bear on the enemy. His victories at Blenheim, Oudenarde and Malplaquet, among others, bear witness to his skilful use of the efficient military machine at his disposal—victories that Britain was thankful for.

Pennsylvania Accuracy

The technique of rifling was known from an early stage in the making of guns but it was difficult to put into practice. In theory, if the ball was made to spin as it left the barrel, its accuracy would be greatly increased. The same theory had even been applied to arrows.

To make the ball spin, delicate spiralling grooves had to be cut on the inside surface of the barrel. This was a long job to be done by hand. But it was successfully achieved by many North American settlers in the middle of the 18th Century, who produced the lethal and renownedly accurate Pennsylvania or Kentucky rifle.

The skill that went into the construction of this rifle was brought over from Europe by German immigrants. At first used for hunting game, it was soon found to be equally effective against Indians. During the American War of Independence its long-barrelled accuracy accounted for the death of many British soldiers.

The history of rifling in fact goes back to the 15th or early 16th Century and soldiers began using them in the 17th Century. A rifled carbine was the armament of at least some of the French cavalry regiments before 1680, and the Baker rifle was used by the Rifle Brigade during the Napoleonic Wars.

Right: Half stock of the long-barrelled and lethally accurate Kentucky rifle.

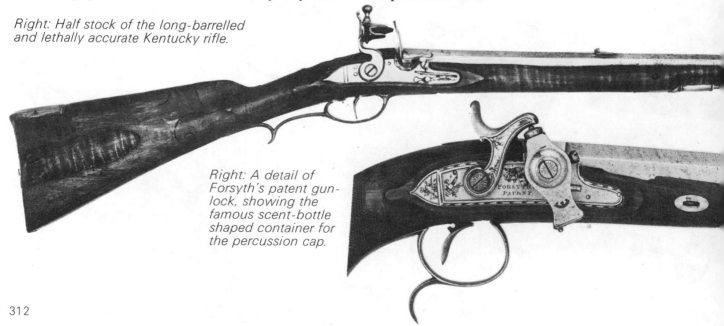

Right: A detail of Forsyth's patent gun-lock, showing the famous scent-bottle shaped container for the percussion cap.

From Scent Bottle to Needle Gun

The Pennsylvania rifle still made use of the flint-lock. A new device for firing a gun was introduced by the Reverend Alexander Forsyth, in 1805 and put into use about 10 years later. The percussion cap was a big step forward.

The drawback to the flintlock lay chiefly in the delay between pulling the trigger and firing the shot. This was called the 'hangfire' and was caused by the necessity, before the powder itself was ignited, to ignite the priming. Something of a chemist, Forsyth applied his knowledge to the firing mechanism of the rifle. He knew that a group of chemicals called fulminates would explode on impact. A few crystals placed in his famous 'scent bottle' shaped container exploded immediately on being struck by the hammer. This explosion ignited the main charge. The result was quicker than the flintlock and more reliable; it was later improved by the introduction of a copper percussion cap.

Captain Patrick Ferguson of the British army invented a breech-loading rifle in 1776. Attempts of a similar nature had even been made early in the 16th Century. But Ferguson's idea was not taken up. Only 100 of his rifles were supplied to the British army. It was left to the Prussians, in 1841, first to adopt a reliable breech-loader. In 1866, the French adopted the Chassepôt and in 1871, the British adopted the Martini-Henry rifle.

The Prussian breech-loader was the Von Dreyse needle gun, designed in 1827. A self-contained cartridge – including ball, powder and percussion compound – was fitted into the bore through a bolt-action breech. The percussion fulminate exploded the powder when the fulminate itself was struck by a long, thin, spring-operated needle. This needle was pulled back when the rifle was cocked and released when the trigger was pulled, so that it shot forward to pierce the cartridge cover. There was only one disadvantage: the delicate needle had an unsatisfactory tendency to snap off.

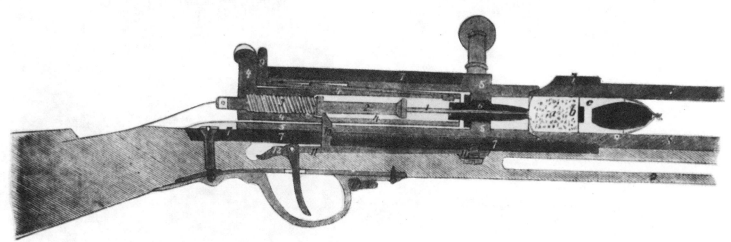

Above: Mechanism of the Dreyse needle-gun. Below: The French Chassepôt.

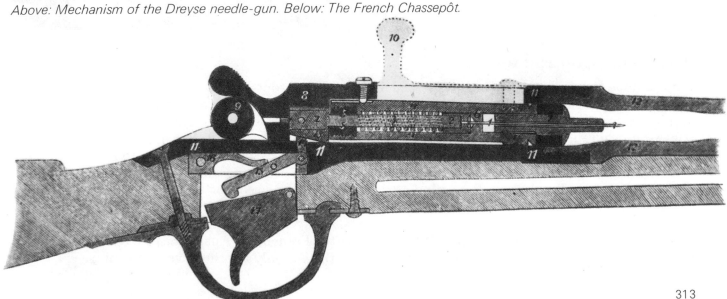

Above: Texas rangers armed with Winchester repeating rifles and revolvers, and equipped with ammunition belts.

Right: Indians as well as Rangers coveted the Winchester. Geronimo, on the right, with three warriors in 1886; the two on the left have Winchesters. Chappo, second from left, is Geronimo's son.

The Winchester and the West

This famous American rifle aptly deserved its title, 'The gun that won the West'. Its repeater action was operated by a lever connected to the trigger guard, in much the same way as the 'Henry' – another famous repeater operated. The Winchester with a brass frame was introduced in 1866 by the Winchester Repeating Arms Corporation, formed, strangely, by a shirt manufacturer, Oliver Winchester.

The magazine contained a spring. When the trigger guard was pulled down, the cartridge was pushed out of the magazine and fed into the breech as the guard was brought up again. Empty cases were ejected as the guard was moved. The rapid fire made possible by the repeater assured its success: to match the opposition, everyone wanted a Winchester.

It was used not only in the West but by the Turks as well. In 1884, the Germans introduced a magazine rifle for their army, to be followed by the French and Austrians in 1886 and then by the British only another two years later.

A Rifle for Two World Wars

Although the Prussian army had been quick to adopt the Von Dreyse needle gun, the modern British army dithered over adopting any specific rifle for general use. If the infantry were to be issued with a universal machine (if the army, that meant, was to go to the expense of equipping the infantry with a specific machine) then the army wanted to make sure that the machine was reliable. No one intended to waste money.

By the end of the 1880s the army settled on the bolt-action, magazine loaded Lee Metford, which held five rounds of ·303 inch ammunition. This had been designed by James Lee. Some modifications were made at the Royal Small Arms Factory at Enfield, which resulted in the Lee-Enfield. Further modifications included shortening the gun and extending the magazine to hold 10 rounds.

This Lee-Enfield ·303 was introduced in 1895 and used by the British infantry in both World Wars, a record of durability and reliability that must rank it as a very successful war machine.

RAPID FIRE FROM THE REVOLVER
The Pepperbox Machine

The pistol was a convenient machine to fire with one hand. At first its mechanical development largely followed the lines of the handgun. Wheel-lock mechanisms were succeeded by flint-locks and double-barrelled and multi-barrelled weapons were also popular. However, the flint-lock still took time – and two hands – to reload. It was the introduction of the percussion cap that gave the pistol the chance to show its true worth and operate with efficiency.

The revolver differed from the early pistol in that it had a 'revolving' chamber into which several bullets could be fitted and fired in succession. Although an American, Elisha Collier, had produced a flintlock revolver of a kind in 1820, and there had been attempts at revolver construction as early as the 16th Century. it was the metallic percussion mechanism that first enabled efficient revolvers to be produced.

By the middle of the 19th Century, the pepperbox revolver had appeared. This had a solid metal barrel with five or six bores which were either revolved by hand or, in the more sophisticated versions, revolved by the action of pulling back the trigger. The pepperbox was barrel-heavy and not very accurate; it was best used in self-

Above: The original wooden model for Colt's first revolver. Right: Samuel Colt, whose revolvers were used all over the world

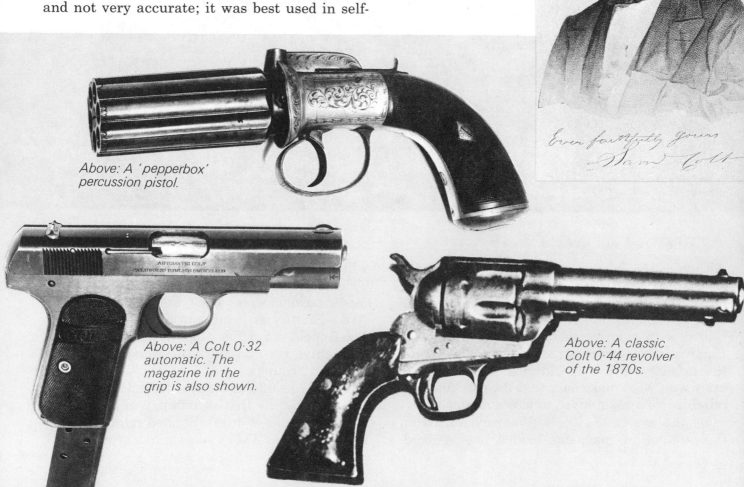

Above: A 'pepperbox' percussion pistol.

Above: A Colt 0·32 automatic. The magazine in the grip is also shown.

Above: A classic Colt 0·44 revolver of the 1870s.

defence. Even so, there were dangers: one barrel might well ignite the others, with alarming results similar to those with early firearms.

The Legend of Samuel Colt

The most famous revolver and the first that was really simple and efficient was made by Samuel Colt, born in Connecticut in 1814. Colt was fascinated by guns from an early age. During a voyage as midshipman in the brig *Corlo*, when he was 16, he carved out of wood a model of a six-chambered, single-barrelled revolver. When his father helped him to get a working model of the revolver made, the prototype blew up on the first shot.

The setback did not last long. Colt soon had a patent out and was in production. His revolvers were 'single action': as the hammer was pulled back, or cocked, with the thumb, the cylinder automatically rotated and was locked into position. Pressure on the trigger released the hammer. Two of Colt's most famous models were the Navy Colt, bought in large quantities by the British for use in the Crimean War, and the Frontier Colt, which went into production after his death.

Colt's revolvers were used in the Mexican War and the American Civil War; they became part of the legend of the great gold rushes; they endured in a modified form into the 20th Century. The name of Colt became a symbol for the age of American mid-west expansion.

Rivals to the Colt

When Colt came to England in 1851 to manufacture his revolvers, he met a rival in the form of Robert Adams, who had produced a double-action revolver. This was self-cocking: when a certain pressure was applied to the trigger, the cylinder automatically rotated and the hammer cocked; with additional pressure, the hammer fell forward and the revolver fired.

The Tranter revolver improved on the Adams by incorporating a double trigger. Pressure on the lower trigger cocked the gun and revolved the cylinder; pressure on the upper trigger, within the guard, fired the gun.

Another famous name in revolvers was Webley. The short, stocky, 'British Bulldog' saw service with the British army all over the world, during the First World War and even into the Second. It was a convenient machine that won the respect of all who used it, as well as the respect of those against whom it was used.

Above and right: A revolver from the Crimean War, with cleaning and cap-making equipment.

Above: A Colt 0·38 revolver.

Above: Smith and Wesson 0·38 revolver.

MACHINE GUNS FOR MASSACRE

Above: Gatling 0·65 inch calibre machine gun made by Armstrong. Below: Gardner single-barrelled 0·45 inch calibre machine gun.

Left: Puckle machine gun with square shot magazine, and spare magazine on the ground.

MACHINE GUNS FOR MASSACRE
Square Shot for Heathens

Since the invention of the gun, everyone's idea had been to make it fire faster, but the modern automatic machine gun took a long time to evolve. The mid-14th-Century organ guns were among the first quick-firers, but one of the first recognisable machine guns – a long way ahead of parallel designs – was that invented in 1718 by James Puckle. It was said to have fired 63 shots in seven minutes – in a rainstorm!

Puckle's patent was for a 'portable gun or machine called a defence'. There was a single barrel and a chamber of six or more cylinders, ignited by flintlock. A handle at the rear turned the cylinders and moved forward on a thread to lock each firmly into position. Two magazines were provided, one for round shot against 'Christians' and one for square shot against 'Heathens' or Turks. In his advertisement; Puckle stated that:

'Defending King George, your Country and Lawes

Is Defending Yourselves and Protestant Cause.'

Although Puckle formed a company to promote his gun, it never became popular; in fact it saw virtually no action. But manually operated machine guns reappeared over 140 years later, during the American Civil War, where they caused tremendous slaughter.

Civil War Suicide

Several types of machine gun appeared, the first of which, designed by an American called Williams, was initiated at the Battle of Fair Oaks, in 1862. The most famous was the Gatling, which came into use toward the end of the war. Richard Gatling was a planter, who lived in North Carolina. He patented his first quick-firing gun in 1862 and three years later obtained another patent. The following year his machine was officially adopted by the army.

A crank, or handle, was still used to turn the cylinders, which contained from six to ten barrels. The magazine with the cartridges was a hopper fixed above the gun so that the force of gravity dropped the cartridges into the magazine as the empty chambers came round. Each chamber fired in succession at a certain point, after which the case was automatically ejected as the crank continued to turn.

Early Gatlings could fire about 300 rounds per minute, although some of the ten-barrel models

The Puckle Gun and some of its equipment. The Magazine for round bullets is shown immediately below the front of the barrel, the one for square shot is shown below that. The tongs on the right are a mould for bullets.

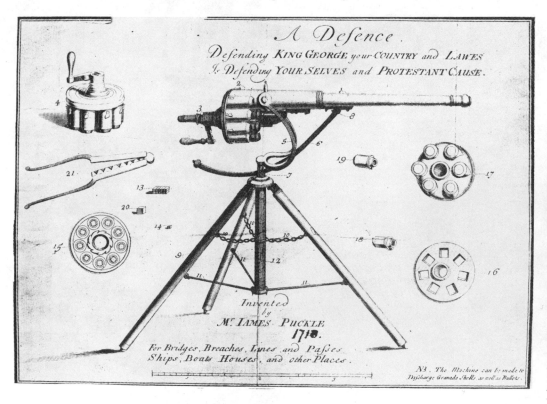

TH

could fire up to 600 rounds. The effect of this kind of barrage on massed troops accustomed only to the rate of fire of the ordinary rifle may be imagined in both physical and psychological terms. Men fell and their courage faltered.

Grant's bloody victories in the latter part of the Civil War must have seemed suicidal to those involved on both sides. During the summer of 1864, over 80,000 men were killed in the two armies during six weeks fighting – slaughter on a scale that had never been encountered before. The Gatling was bought by the British for trials in 1870 and used with devastating effect in the Zulu wars in South Africa.

From the Mitrailleuse to the Maxim

It was in the Franco-Prussian war of 1870 that another, and earlier, machine gun proved itself. This was the French mitrailleuse. In French, *mitraille* meant 'grapeshot' and the Montigny mitrailleuse, invented in 1851, delivered a rate of fire of approximately 175 rounds per minute, though some said that this could go as high as 444 rpm – more destructive and a good deal more accurate than old-style grapeshot.

The Montigny had several barrels, which were mounted on a field gun carriage. The magazine consisted of a metal plate, perforated to contain a number of cartridges, that slotted into the breech block. When this was closed, the cartridges fitted into the barrels, which were fired in succession by the usual method of rotating a handle. Well over 100 shots per minute could be fired, with an effective range of nearly 1,000 yards.

Despite their mitrailleuse, the French had not mastered the techniques of tactical machine gun warfare. The Prussians were able to use their needle gun to much greater advantage.

Various other machine guns were tried out at this time, all with cranking handles. Among these was the Gardner, which was used for a while by the British navy to replace the Gatling. But the Gardner was inferior to the Nordenfelt, which appeared during the 1870s. The Gardner fired just over 100 shots per minute; the Nordenfelt ranged from 200 to nearly 600 per minute.

Nordenfelt produced three to six barrel machine guns. The mechanism was more or less the same for each variation. The barrels lay side by side and loading and firing was operated by a lever that worked backwards and forwards. The hopper was above the gun. When the lever was

Mitrailleuse mounted with shields at the Siege of Paris, 1871. The multiple barrels show clearly at the muzzle.

2nd Lieutenant V. A. Browning firing a Browning machine gun invented by his father.

321

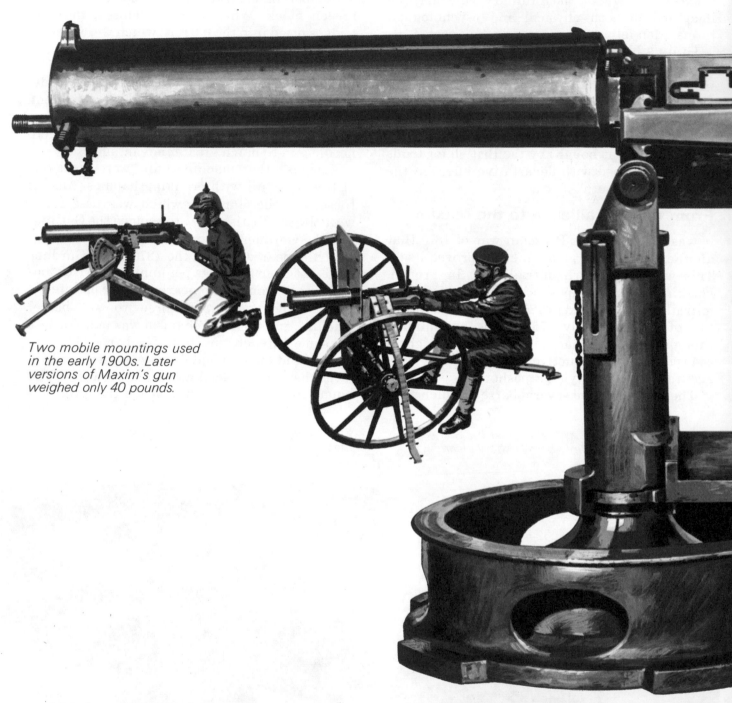

Two mobile mountings used in the early 1900s. Later versions of Maxim's gun weighed only 40 pounds.

pushed forward, a feed from the hopper was brought down and loaded all the barrels simultaneously. The gun was cocked and fired all in the same forward action of the lever. When the lever was pulled back, the spent cartridges were ejected, the bolts withdrawn and the breech made ready for the next feed of live ammunition.

The Nordenfelt became particularly popular with the British navy against the increasing threat of torpedo boats, although it was also used on land. Later, Nordenfelt made several guns with larger calibres and heavier shots.

The first fully automatic machine gun was produced by an American. Hiram S. Maxim patented his design in 1883. For as long as the trigger was pulled the gun would go on firing continuously, with cartridges fed into it from a flexible belt. Loading, firing and ejection of the spent car-

The Maxim machine gun had a rate of fire of up to 650 rounds a minute. Here we show an early model on its heavy, fixed, mounting.

Sir Hiram Maxim proudly displays his original machine gun, patented in 1883.

tridges were all set in motion by the recoil of each shot. On firing, the barrel and recoil frame were driven back about an inch, setting into action the mechanism for reloading the gun.

With a rate of fire up to 650 rounds per minute, the barrel tended to get very hot. Maxim settled this problem by encasing it in a water-cooled jacket. In 1891, a model weighing only 40 pounds was introduced into the British army. This was

used in the Boer War, while the Boers themselves made use of a heavier Maxim machine gun called a 'Pom-pom'. A well-designed war machine could always find a use on either side of any conflict.

The American, gas-operated Lewis gun appeared in 1911 and was used extensively in the First World War. It weighed only 25 pounds and could be handled by one man.

PORTABLE FIREPOWER
The Tommy Gun

Guns have been produced in great diversity and with a wide variety of uses. Although they make use of the same basic principles, each type is a war machine in its own right with a specific task in battle. The siege gun, the anti-tank gun, the anti-aircraft gun, field artillery, the machine gun, the mortar and the infantryman with his rifle – each developed along reciprocal lines of attack and counter-attack, and each development played a new part in new combat situations. So, the infantryman of the 20th Century, armed with new weapons, was a different kind of fighting machine to the arquebusier of the 17th Century.

It was sufficient for the sniper to be armed with a conventional rifle, provided that it was of proven accuracy and range, but it became increasingly desirable for the infantryman to be armed with a lightweight, portable version of the machine gun – a weapon that could produce a high rate of fire, yet be small and compact enough to become the regular equipment of almost every soldier.

The sub-machine gun was developed by the Italians during the First World War and further improved by the Germans, whose MP-18 had a circular magazine with 32 rounds of shot. The explosion of each shot automatically activated the bolt to reject the spent cartridge and insert a new shot.

The renowned Tommy gun was also a sub-machine gun. Its real name was the Thompson machine gun, after the name of its designer, an American general. Equipped with several different magazines, this could fire up to 100 rounds a minute. For convenience, it could also be fitted with a folding butt.

The Tommy gun was first produced in 1920 and was widely used in the Second World War. It was replaced by the M-3 sub-machine gun, with a calibre of ·45 inches and a magazine of 30 rounds. The M-3 had one surprise: there was an extra barrel that could be used with captured German ammunition. Nothing, if at all possible, was ever wasted in time of war.

Guns for Resistance

A different style of war demanded a different machine. For the French Resistance against German occupation there was the sten-gun, light, collapsible and easy to produce. Armed with this, the Maquisards worked undercover to undermine the German hold on their country. The sten

FBI agent firing a Thompson sub-machine gun.

had a magazine with 32 rounds of 9-mm ammunition and could fire at a rate of over 500 rounds per minute, with a killing range of 200 yards. It could be broken down for concealment into four parts: magazine, barrel unit, body and stock.

The sten was not only a resistance weapon. It was used extensively as the standard British sub-machine gun.

A modern type of the sub-machine gun is the Uzi, used by the Israelis in the 1973 Middle East war, and named after its designer, Major Uziel Gal. Short and handy to use, the Uzi has a rate of 650 rounds per minute and made a great reputation for itself during that war.

Even before then, there was a leaning toward a rifle that could double, on automatic fire, as a sub-machine gun. The Soviet AK-47, used by the Arabs, is one of the best of these guns. It is also called the Kalashnikov assault rifle and has a magazine of 30 rounds with a rate of fire of 600 rounds per minute.

On the Israeli side, the Galil has a rate of over 600 rounds per minute and 30- or 50-round magazines. It has an additional device, incorporated into the design – not essential to the machine itself, you might think at first, but encouraging to the efficiency of its handler, and so to the machine as a whole. This is a bottle opener, which the designer added when he noticed soldiers using the lip of their magazine for that purpose.

Bren-gunner in action from the ruins of a house in Douet, Normandy, 1944.

Several types of sten-gun were made, not only for the Resistance. Here are Mark I, II, III and V.

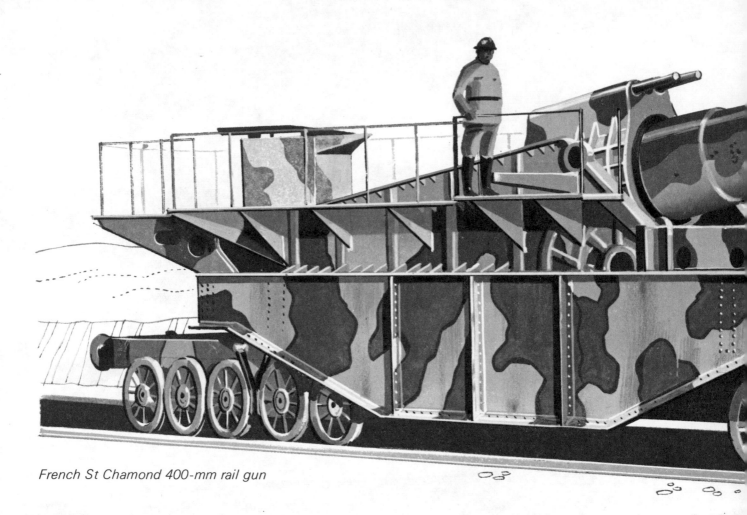

French St Chamond 400-mm rail gun

THE BIG GUNS
Giants of War

The great siege machines of the 15th Century made their reappearance in a more sophisticated and even more destructive form during the end of the 19th Century and particularly during the First World War, as the opposing armies attempted to batter each other into submission. Instead, their massive guns served mainly to tear up into an impassable morass the countryside of France and Belgium. The terrible stark landscapes of First World War Europe characterized that war, and the big guns played an awesome part in the creation of that character.

The German guns dominated the list of the mammoths and, against the Krupp-built monsters, even the French giants were inadequate. Two of the biggest French guns were the St Chamond 400-mm rail gun and the Babignolles 320-mm rail gun. The second had a range of a little under two miles and fired shells between 800 and 1,000 pounds, but the first had a range of nearly 10 miles and fired shells between one-and-a-half and two thousand pounds each.

In between these came the French 370-mm mortar, with a shell of 250 pounds but a range of five miles. It had the advantage of a quick rate of fire – approximately one round every two minutes. But it required a crew of 16 men to operate it at maximum efficiency. The 370-mm was used effectively by the French at Verdun.

Against the French at the opening of war in 1914, the Germans brought the thunder of their 420-mm howitzers, which appeared on the battlefield as soon as hostilities began. Their shells weighed nearly a ton and they slammed into the defences of Liège with marked results and to the considerable surprise of the French, for the Germans had kept their new weapon a great secret from their enemies.

Special tractors and carriages were made to carry the considerable weight of the gun, which had to be broken down into its component parts before transportation. Rail was often used as an alternative means of transport. The barrel alone weighed over 20 tons, the cradle weighed about 15 tons and the mount for the gun another 20 tons. There was also a base of 12 tons as well as ammunition and ancillary equipment – and the crew. 'Big Bertha', as the gun was sometimes

called, totalled over 70 tons and could fire a round every six or seven minutes.

The Germans had announced that the 420-mm was a naval gun, which accounted for the Allied surprise when they found themselves facing it on dry land. Another supposedly 'naval' gun was the 380-mm long range gun that the Germans used later at Verdun. This had a range of nearly 30 miles and could be used to fire well over the front lines of both armies onto communication and transport links to the rear of the enemy.

The Bombardment of Paris

The greatest First World War gun of all was the extraordinary Paris gun that had a range of 75 miles and was created especially for the bombardment of Paris. The idea was first put forward in the spring of 1916 but the first shell did not fall on Paris until Saturday, March 23, 1918. Between those two dates, the Krupp factories were in a fever of calculations and designs.

In order to achieve the range it was necessary greatly to increase the initial velocity of the shell and make it perform a trajectory that would make use of the thinner atmosphere high above the earth. The barrel consisted of one 15-inch barrel, over 55 feet long, into which was put another barrel, or 'inner tube', with a calibre of 8·26 inches, and which, with a small tube or chase added on to the base of the barrel, extended the overall length of the gun barrel to about 112 feet. In order to keep all this straight, a series of struts along the barrel held it braced.

The gun was aimed at an angle of 50 degrees, in order for the shot to enter the lighter atmosphere at an angle of 45 degrees, the angle of maximum efficiency. Allowance had to be made for the rotation of the earth and it was vital that the shell left the barrel at one mile per second. All these considerations had to be taken into account in preparing the gun.

The shell itself weighed 228 pounds and had a triple cartridge which contained about 500 pounds of powder. Since the elevation of the gun remained unaltered, the amount of powder had to be varied with each shot to lessen or increase the range and to compensate for cold or hot weather as well – and this was very important –

for the wear on the inside of the barrel after every shot. It was estimated that the gun would be useless after about 60–65 shots, for each of which the shell would have to weigh a little more. To solve this problem, each shell was numbered. So precise were the calculations involved and the attention to detail was so perfect that it was possible to tell exactly where the shell landed merely by reading off the pressure gauges attached to the barrel and ascertaining the pressure in the barrel at each shot.

Bombs from a Clear Sky

Three of the Paris guns were set up in great secret, carefully camouflaged, in the forests near Laon, 70 miles from the heart of Paris. Their aim was to demoralize the Parisians while a massive German offensive got under way. At a little after 7.16 on the morning of March 23, the first of the guns fired from behind a thick smoke screen, additionally camouflaged by a stepped-up barrage from nearby artillery. The shell reached an altitude of 12 miles in 25 seconds, travelling at a speed of 3,000 feet per second. It left the barrel at just under the required speed of a mile per second, or 5,280 feet per second. A maximum height of 24 miles was reached in 90 seconds, at which point the shell was travelling at 2,250 feet per second. On its downward curve its speed increased to over 3,000 feet per second again, 12 miles above Paris and its unaware citizens.

The shell struck the paving stones outside No. 6 Quai de Seine in the 19th Arrondissement just before 7.20, after a flight of 92 miles in 176 seconds. The Quai de Seine was 67·6 miles round the curvature of the earth from the forest hideout in Laon. No one was injured and the explosion was barely noticed; to those who did notice, it sounded like a single bomb from a plane too high to be seen, for the sky was clear.

A second shell landed within 15 minutes; further shells followed, spattered around the city, at approximately 15-minute intervals. People were injured and killed. Still assuming that it was an air-raid, though mystified by the lack of sound or sight of aeroplanes, the people of Paris took shelter when the sirens went, about an hour after the first shell.

At 10 o'clock the War Ministry announced that 'a few enemy aircraft, flying at very high altitudes, succeeded in crossing the lines and attacking Paris. They were immediately engaged by our fighter aircraft, both those from the entrenched camp and those from the front.

Bombs are reported to have been dropped at several points and there are some casualties'. If fighter aircraft had gone up to investigate, it was unlikely that they had found anything.

In view of the remarkable novelty of a gun of such extreme range – a range of 23 miles had previously been the longest experienced in the war – the experts were, in fact, commendably quick in tracking down the source of the explosions. By plotting the positions of the explosions and by alerting the sound-ranging units at the front line (they located enemy batteries through highly sensitive listening devices), they knew approximately what they were up against by early afternoon of that first day. By early evening, batteries of 12-inch railway guns were on their way to the nearest available point at the front to counteract the threat.

Over 20 shells fell on Paris each of the first two days of the bombardment, although on the second day, Sunday, a second gun joined in. This gun blew up the next day and killed most of its crew. There was a lull for three days after that, until firing resumed on Good Friday and produced the greatest slaughter so far.

At 4.30 p.m. a shell struck the old Church of Saint-Gervais in the Rue Miron, opposite the Hotel de Ville, where several hundred people were praying. The explosion destroyed a pillar and a great chunk of the vaulting so that a large area of the roof came down on top of the congregation. Nearly 90 people were killed and another 70 more injured.

It is possible that this dramatic hit was achieved by a third gun, for by this time the first gun was worn out. The experts had been right: one gun wore out after 50 shots, another after about 60. In all, after four intermittent bombardments, 367 shells were fired on Paris and landed on or nearby the city, being directly responsible for about 250 deaths and a further 620 wounded. But these figures barely reflect the corrosive effect that this long range barrage must have had on the morale of those Parisians who experienced the terror of being struck in the heart of their city from behind an enemy line supposed to be a safe 70 miles away.

The last shell fell on August 9, 1918. But the advancing Allied troops found no significant trace of the guns, which had been demolished as carefully as they had been assembled months before in preparation for the bombardment.

Germany followed up its First World War successes with a 280-mm gun with a range of

24 miles altitude after 90 seconds
Velocity: 2,250 feet per second

12 miles altitude in
25 seconds
Velocity:
3,000 feet per
second

Range following line of earth's curvature: 67·6 miles
In straight line: 67·1 miles

nearly 40 miles and a giant 800-mm cannon 'Dora' with a shell 25-feet-long, a range of nearly 30 miles and a crew of about 250 men. America developed the Long Tom. But the shells from these guns did not have the psychological impact of those first bombardments in March 1918. Even less did they cause the consternation of complete novelty that had characterized the use of Mahomet's great siege cannon outside Constantinople, 460 years before.

Top: German 420-mm siege gun, nicknamed Big Bertha, of the type used against Liège.
Above left: Artist's impression of the German Paris Gun, with a range of over 70 miles.
Above right: Diagram showing the trajectory and range of shells fired by the Paris Gun.

ARMOURED FIGHTING VEHICLES
The Balance of Efficiency

Since mobile war machines of any kind had been first devised, military thinkers and engineers had been trying to strike a happy balance between the amount of firepower that could be exerted by a particular machine, the amount of protection it had from the firepower of another machine, and its mobility.

This balance was rarely achieved. Early cavalry were lightly armed and highly mobile, but unprotected; early siege machines were well-protected, sometimes well-armed, but virtually immobile; elephants had some protection, could be heavily armed with spearmen and bowmen, and were mobile but erratic. For a hundred years or so the medieval knight seemed to provide the ideal answer until, in response to the penetrative power of the arrow, his body armour became absurdly heavy and, with the introduction of firearms, totally useless. He was compelled to disencumber himself of his overweight equipment.

His means of mobility – the horse – was always vulnerable. Early concepts for well-protected, horse-powered machines were imaginative but generally impractical. Among the most ingenious inventors was Leonardo da Vinci, who made several drawings for armoured fighting vehicles. What was needed toward the end of the 19th Century was a machine driven by mechanical power strong enough to carry sufficient armour to stop a bullet from a rifle or machine gun, while

Rolls Royce cars were quickly turned to wartime use. A Rolls Royce light armoured car at Abbéville, in 1916.

at the same time able to move at reasonable speeds and pack its own effective punch.

From Steam Carriage to Traction Wheel

The invention of the steam engine opened possibilities toward the design of such a machine. The first person to realize the potential of steam as mechanical power for military purposes was Nicholas Cugnot, who put his steam carriage at the disposal of the French army in 1770. Because of the machine's unreliability, Cugnot was not taken up on his offer.

Meanwhile ideas for traction wheels were developed, though largely on paper only. The theory of the traction wheel was that a wheel should be surrounded by a linked series of small tracks that would, as they revolved with the wheel, serve as a self-contained roadway along which the vehicle could travel, regardless of the rough surface of the ground.

George Kale recorded a double-wheeled concept in 1825 and a man called Gomper planned a single tracked wheel six years later. Two other single tracked wheels were designed, by Dunlop in 1861 and by Clark, almost 30 years later. They were strange looking contraptions that never went into production.

One or two steam tractors made their appearance at the end of the 19th Century but it was the introduction of the petrol engine that gave a real

An armoured steam-roller from the 1870s.

boost to the armoured fighting vehicle. It was a motley collection of machines that appeared between 1890 and the development of the first real tank during the First World War but some of them are worth a closer look.

The Motor War Car

One of the first was Fowler's armoured road loco-motive, with a train of armour-plated waggons (inspired by armoured railway trains) used during the Boer War of 1899–1902.

In 1902, F. R. Simms, an Englishman, produced his Motor War Car – a grand-sounding name for an odd-looking machine, shaped like an upturned boat hull, with two Maxim machine guns at one end and a large Maxim 'pom-pom' at the other. A crew of four was normal but, if required, the guns could be taken out and the vehicle used as a troop carrier for 12 men.

The Motor War Car was first demonstrated at a Press Conference at the Crystal Palace, London, where its capabilities were acknowledged as being impressive, although the War Office showed no further interest. The die for a new military button or a 'dustman's cap' for the Guards,

claimed one journal of the day, were of much more interest to the officers of the War Office than Simms' Motor War Car.

This was not Simm's first armoured vehicle, however. In 1899, he had produced the de Dion-Bouton powered quadri-cycle, with a Maxim machine gun. In fact, credit for the Motor War Car did not properly belong to Simms – its layout followed drawings produced six years earlier by E. J. Pennington.

Another strange machine that did not get beyond the preliminary stages of a military career was the Armoured Ivel Tractor. This three-wheeled tractor had been the first success-ful, petrol-operated tractor on the market. It was designed by Dan Albone of Biggleswade, Bedford-shire, in 1903; the armoured version appeared three years later. In this version the whole contraption was completely enclosed but, since no weapons seem to have been attached to it, it was probably intended – had it ever been put to use – for towing purposes only. Perhaps it was as well that it was not used: three-wheeled and light in front, it had a nasty tendency to overturn if the load was too heavy.

Top left: A Killen Strait tractor precariously poised to rise over an obstacle.
Left: A Davidson Cadillac of 1916.
Above: Lanchester Armoured Car, of the Royal Naval Air Service, with machine gun.
Top right: Russian Garfords, heavily armoured and bristling with armament, look more like a column of mechanical science fiction monsters.
Right: Another famous name transformed into a military machine—a 1915 Lancia.

Many of the early armoured cars and fighting vehicles appeared with the names of the great car designers and manufacturers. This was because most armoured vehicles were converted civilian cars, or used the same engines. One example is the Daimler Panzerwagen of 1904, mounted with Maxim machine guns and capable of nearly 30 miles an hour. The Armoured Rolls Royce of 1914 is another example, though the armour on this was only light and it was mounted with one light machine gun. Better armoured Rolls Royces followed the first experiments and Wolseleys joined the ranks.

In France, converted Renaults were commissioned as the First World War opened. American Packards appeared. Fiats, Lanchesters, Lancias and even Cadillacs followed. Some were only lightly armed; others were virtually unrecognizable. Every country brought whatever machines it had to hand and improvised what it did not have.

It was the energy of Winston Churchill that encouraged armoured car production in England during the war. He demanded armoured vehicles to support the Royal Naval Air Service aircraft force in France. The Seabrook armoured lorry, mounted with a three-pounder Vickers semi-automatic gun, was one of the heavier armaments of the period. Despite the weight of the vehicle, the gun was successful in this capacity and Sir John French, Commander of the British Expeditionary Force, requested that more should be sent to France.

The Russian Garford Armoured Car was a massive vehicle, built in Petrograd in 1915 on an imported American Garford chassis. The Garford mounted a 75-mm gun as well as three Maxim machine guns, one beside the 75-mm in the rear turret, the other two behind and to the side of the cab. The whole machine weighed about 11 tons – and probably became bogged down very quickly in bad conditions.

The bigger the vehicle and the more powerful it became, the more likely it was to get stuck in the mud of Russia or Flanders. Barbed wire, trenches, obstacles of every kind, and always the mud – they did not suit these basically conventional wheeled machines, however outrageously redesigned. The answer lay in earlier experiments: a machine with tracks.

Below: The first British tank in action, 1916, armed with directional machine guns.

THE TANK TAKES TO THE FIELD
Little Willie

The idea of the tank, with all-round tracks to provide the vital need for a vehicle that could traverse small trenches, crush barbed-wire-type defences, withstand machine gun fire and exert its own firepower was put forward by Levavasseur of the French Artillery in 1903 and by Donahue of the Army Service Corps in 1908. In both cases they conceived of an armoured, self-propelled, tracked field gun. In 1911, Burstyn of the Austrian Army and in 1912, de Mole, an Australian, also put forward the idea of a tracked armoured vehicle. In 1914 Lieutenant-Colonel Swinton, a British Engineer, furthered the idea.

The first tracked vehicle was made up of the body of a Delaunay-Belleville armoured car on the chassis of a Killen Strait tractor. This was in Britain, in 1915.

A rhomboidal shape was first suggested by Lieutenant W. G. Wilson of the Royal Naval Air Service, who had been ordered, together with William Tritton of William Foster and Company, of Lincoln, to design an appropriate vehicle to help the Allied push forward in Europe.

Wilson and Tritton's first machine did not, in fact, use a rhomboidal shape. The Tritton Machine, or Little Willie, as it became known, had a rectangular hull set on tracks that were fractionally shorter than the body, with a turret on top. It was powered by a 105 horsepower Daimler six-cylinder engine and was the first

vehicle to be exclusively designed and built as a landship.

The word 'tank' was purposively deceptive, since it was important to maintain the utmost secrecy and to hide the existence of the new machine from the enemy. It was therefore referred to as a 'large water tank for Russia', from which the name 'tank' naturally evolved.

Mother is Rhomboidal

When Little Willie failed to come up to the War Office requirements for obstacle crossing, Wilson began working on his new rhomboidal design, or lozenge shape, with tracks that ran round the top of the hull. This model carried two naval six-pounders as armament, set in turrets at the side of the body; it was powered by a unit similar to that in Little Willie.

Big Willie, or Mother, as it was called – it was also called Wilson's Machine and H.M. Landship Centipede – had its first trials on January 16, 1916 and easily met War Office requirements to cross a ditch eight feet wide and mount a parapet four and a half feet high.

Tanks at Cambrai

Although Field Marshal Sir Douglas Haig ordered the use of tanks in an attack on the Somme in September, 1916, they were not then reliable enough to have anything more than a

Below: French Renault FT17 light tank. These illustrations are not to scale.

Above: German A7V, Sturmpanzerwagen, of 1918, less efficient than Allied tanks.

psychological effect. Individual actions by tanks took the enemy completely by surprise in the first stages of their use, until the Germans grew accustomed to the preparatory stages of a tank attack. Neither individual nor group applications seemed to promise a resounding breakthrough until the tanks were first used in a major role on November 20, 1917, at Cambrai.

In this action, the tanks appeared unheralded by the usual preliminary artillery barrage. Tactics were conceived by Colonel J. F. C. Fuller, the 'Unconventional Soldier', who had a reputation as a military thinker. 474 Mark IV tanks advanced along a broad front about 10 miles wide; they managed to break through the German lines and to penetrate four miles beyond within a few hours. Since an advance of a few hundred *yards* had previously been considered very successful, it is not difficult to imagine the jubilation at such sudden progress. Moreover, infantry losses on the British side were considerably lower than was usual in an attack of this degree, and well below half those of the Germans, who also lost a considerable amount of artillery.

Developed almost simultaneously with the first British invention was the French Schneider, which mounted a 75-mm gun as well as two Hotchkiss machine guns. The first production order was placed in February, 1916, though the tanks did not go into action until April, 1917. It

had a speed of over three-and-a-half miles an hour, weighed over $13\frac{1}{2}$ tons and had a range of 30 miles. One of its characteristics was a metal bar that projected at the front for the purpose of crushing barbed wire. The St Chamond was another successful French tank; it weighed a further 10 tons more than the Schneider. Much lighter than both these was the Renault Mosquito.

The German A7V was equivalent in weight to the St Chamond but not so effective. The Germans suffered badly from a lack of armour throughout the last years of the war.

The Panzer Tanks

By 1939, however, having learnt their lesson, the Germans were far better equipped and their tanks formed the nucleus of the combined mobile striking force, the Panzer division. One German tank was the 'light-medium' Pzkw (*Panzerkampfwagen*) Mark III, with a 37-mm or 50-mm long-barrelled Kwk (*Kampfwagenkanon*).

The Pzkw IV was armed with a 75-mm gun but had armour no stronger than the Mark III. Light armour, in comparison to that of the Allies' tanks, was usually a feature of the German machines. Until they invaded Russia, the Germans thought their tanks were invincible. But the Soviet T-34 stopped them, literally, in their tracks. They had no foreknowledge of the Soviet development, which was simple to produce and to operate and so could be turned out in large numbers and be manned by fairly raw crews. The T-34 had wide tracks for good cross-country performance, a range of 250 miles on the road, armour that was sloped to repel enemy fire, and a 76·2-mm gun.

The Panther was the German answer to the T-34, and the most successful German tank of the war (about 5,000 were produced). But the most famous German tank was probably the Tiger, which for once was well-protected as well as well-armed. This also was designed for the Russian front, although it was used effectively in the West and in North Africa. Weighing 55 tons, it had a speed of 25 miles an hour and mounted a powerful 88-mm gun.

The Tanks of the Allies

On the side of the Allies, the Char B was probably the toughest French tank. It had nearly double the armour of the equivalent German tank and mounted a 75-mm gun. But it had a small turret in which the single operator was overworked. It was also slow.

The British Valentine was used in the desert war but was not fast enough for the German tanks nor heavily enough armed. The Churchill Mark I also suffered from light armament, although its firepower was increased during the war. The chassis of the Churchill was used for a great many special purpose vehicles, as can be seen in the next chapter. Another British tank used in the desert was the Crusader. The Centurion arrived only at the end of the war.

The greatest American contribution in the heavy tank range was the 75-mm Sherman, mechanically reliable and toughly armoured, with a speed just over 20 miles an hour. The Japanese concentrated on light, fast, and small tanks suitable for Pacific warfare on small islands, where foreign tanks found the going almost impossible. The Type-61 medium tank was one of their most useful designs.

Since the war the British Chieftain established a good reputation. One of the standard American medium tanks has been the M-60. The German Leopard, supplied to several armies, is similar in design to the French AMX-30, although more powerful. One of the most modern designs is the Swedish S-tank, with a low profile, hydro-pneumatic suspension and a 105-mm gun – far removed from some of the drawings made by Leonardo da Vinci in anticipation of the first armoured fighting vehicles.

Above: A war-worn German Panther, Model A.
Below: Column of Crusader tanks in Western Desert.

Above: The highly effective Russian T-34-85 medium tank.

Right: Sherman Crab II, fitted with flail as a mine-destroying device. There were various adaptations of this system.

Above: 88mm gun mounted on Tiger P. chassis.
Below: British Matilda tank.

Above: 'Carpet Roller' attached to tank chassis.

SPECIAL DUTY TANKS
The Trench Annihilator

The tank proved its usefulness as a machine in assault over rough terrain against armed resistance; the revolving turret, mounted with varying sizes of guns and placed on a tracked chassis, became, by the Second World War, one of the most important assets of every army. But the concept of a tracked vehicle could be adapted in many ways to other duties and a variety of machines appeared during the war that took the tank a long way from what was originally conceived in the name the Germans gave to it during the First World War: *Schutzengrabenvernichtungspanzerkraftwagen*, or 'protected trench annihilation armoured vehicle'.

Nearest in purpose to the tank was the Self Propelled Gun, or SPG. This was simpler in design than the tank and had no turret mechanism It mounted a heavy gun but had no secondary armament. Its purpose was to act as fast moving artillery support for infantry.

After their confrontation with the Soviet T-34s, the Germans stepped up their production of SPGs, which began to take precedence over ordinary tank production. SPGs became increasingly powerful but less manoeuvrable.

One of the heaviest of the German SPGs was an adaptation of the Tiger, sometimes called an Elephant. It was a powerful tank-hunter itself, built in 1943 on a Porsche Tiger chassis and mounting an 88-mm gun. Another adaptation was that of the French Char B chassis, which the Germans mounted with a 105-mm gun. On their side, the Soviets mounted a 122-mm gun on their SU-122, which used their T-34 chassis, and a 152-mm gun on their JSU-152.

The Mine-destroyers

Encased in metal, tanks were highly vulnerable to mines. Many adaptations of the tank applied to mine-clearance. A minefield was as much of an obstacle as a trench system or a surface barrier, and pathways for the infantry had to be made before an advance could begin.

One of the strangest-looking of these machines was the British Scorpion, which was built on the chassis of the Matilda tank. Stretching out before it, two long arms supported a revolving drum on which were fitted several sets of chain flails that beat the ground in front of the tank. The flailing chains hopefully made contact with the mines

Over: Pzkw IVs pass Bren gun-carrier in the desert

337

and exploded them at a safe distance from the vehicle.

The Crab was another landmine sweeper. This was based on the Sherman chassis and could clear a pathway about 10 feet wide with a set of chains similar to the Scorpion attached to a drum and held in front of the tank. But an alternative attachment to the Matilda was the mine-roller, which consisted of sets of rollers pushed forward in front of the tank on long arms. The advantage of these over the flails was that they more precisely simulated the *weight* of the tank – and it was weight, more than contact, that was essential in order to detonate the mines.

Carpets and Crocodiles

To help wheeled vehicles over soft patches of ground, and particularly sand, there was the Bobbin, an attachment to the Churchill chassis that was capable of laying a carpet over the ground. The carpet was almost 10 feet wide and made of canvas.

Another obstacle clearer, and another adaptation of the Churchill chassis – the Churchill was the ideal tank for these adaptations – was the bridge-layer. The SBG bridge, carried in front

of the chassis and held up by a wire to the back of the chassis, could be laid over a gap 30 feet wide in about 30 seconds; it could also support up to 40 tons when laid against a parapet 15 feet high. The Valentine was another bridge-layer.

Yet another Churchill adaptation, the Churchill Crocodile, mounted a lethal flame thrower with a range of 120 yards. Fuel was carried in a special trailer towed behind and pumped through to the gun. When the fuel was used up, the trailer could be jettisoned and the tank's gun used as normal.

Towing of a different kind was the special duty of the Churchill ARV, or Armoured Recovery Vehicle; the Sherman was similarly equipped with towing gear and tools for the recovery of valuable tanks from the battlefield. Breakdowns could as easily occur as battle scars: the ARVs were kept busy all the time.

Remote Control

In a more offensive capacity, the remote controlled tank was developed during the Second World War. It had a similar function and effect, you might suppose, as the fire-ship of the early days of sail, or the kamikaze plane of the

Above: One of the many Churchill adaptations was the Crocodile flame thrower.

Right: Tanks made useful mobile platforms for rocket launchers. Shermans are being used here.

Left: Back view of a Sherman Duplex Drive with screens half way up.

Japanese. It was the Japanese who tried out one model before the war – the Nagayama. But during the war it was the Germans who laid greatest emphasis on this type of machine. Remote controlled tanks had small chassis, without turrets, and were filled with high explosive. They were used best against enemy fortifications, although they could also be used against tanks themselves. One German model was the Goliath; a later model was the NSU Springer.

The B-IV was also radio-controlled, although it could, if required, be driven by one man. In this case no suicidal tactics were necessary. The machine held a block in front of it, filled with explosive. The block could be detached and left against a fortification or barricade while the tank made a judicious retreat and watched the explosion from a safe distance.

The Amphibious Machine

Most important for beach landings and river crossings were amphibious tanks. One of the oddest convertible devices, contrived for the D-Day offensive, was the Duplex Drive, that could be fitted to the Sherman tank. When fitted, it gave the tank the shape of something between a perambulator and a playpen. But the collapsible canvas screen – the parallel with the pram grows stronger – kept the water out and buoyed up the tank, which had the additional drive of two propellers and could 'sail' at over four knots.

The Japanese in particular required to adapt their tanks to the amphibious warfare of the Pacific. One Japanese machine was fitted with wooden floats shaped to a bow. Once on land the floats could be blown out of the way.

The Soviet Union also paid considerable attention to amphibious warfare as, more recently, have the Swedes. The Soviet T-37 was fitted with balsa wood floats; the modern PT-76 has a boat-shaped hull and is powered by hydra-jets. Other amphibious armed vehicles are often conversions from armoured cars, with boat hulls and wheels. The American Commando is one of these.

Some tanks are now equipped with rockets. A conversion of the French AMX-13 used rockets mounted forward as well as its usual armament of guns. The rockets were guided on to the target by means of a thin 'fishing line', which unwound as the missile shot toward its target. Other machines use radio-controlled rockets and are essentially rocket-launchers only.

Right: German 88-mm painted in desert colours. Centre: British 17-pounder anti-tank gun. Far right: German 28-mm 'Squeeze-gun'.

THE TANK DESTROYERS
Adapted for Destruction

By now it has become evident that one machine requires a reciprocal machine to counteract it. The tank presented formidable defensive armour for any conventional gun to penetrate. Machine guns and rifle fire were inadequate – the tank, after all, had been especially designed to render them inadequate. So it became necessary to create a new type of gun with a shell that could smash tank armour.

The British army began the Second World War with a 2-pounder gun, which was then replaced by a 6-pounder and finally a 17-pounder; the Germans had a variety of successful anti-tank guns, among which was an adaptation of their highly efficient anti-aircraft 88-mm. The British

17-pounder was bulky, a severe handicap for a gun that it was vital to conceal while lying in wait for its target, but it could knock out a German Tiger tank at a range of 1,000 yards and it had a maximum range of about 3,000 yards. It was probably the most useful of the Allies' anti-tank guns and was mounted, at a later stage, on a variety of tanks, including the Sherman Firefly.

The German 88-mm was one of the most lethal and feared guns in the war. Rommel used it to great effect in his campaign in the desert, in particular when he found himself over-reached and under heavy attack by the Allies. As well as being used as a stationary piece of artillery against tanks, it was also fitted to the Tiger I and

II and could penetrate three inches of armour at 1,000 yards. No Allied tank could withstand the 88-mm, which acquired a reputation amounting almost to a myth among those against whom it was used.

Armour-piercing Shells

The most important part of any anti-tank gun is clearly its shell; if guns and armour were not to vie continually in ever-increasing weight until both became unmanageable, then shells had to be made that, without increasing in size, could penetrate armour of almost any thickness.

Armour-piercing shot was commonly used in 1939 – solid shot that broke through the armour of a tank by sheer force. The stronger the armour, the greater the force with which the shot needed to be fired: the stalemate situation. Armour-piercing shells, on the other hand, also penetrated by force but subsequently blew up inside the tank to cause considerably more damage.

Squeeze Guns and Sabots

Aids to penetration included a soft-capped shell that spread the impact over a wider surface of the target. Another advance was a tungsten carbide tipped shell – harder than steel – fired from a tapered barrel. The Germans used this technique in their 28-mm Panzerbusche 41, or 'Squeeze gun'. The tungsten core was contained in a light alloy casing that was squeezed, as it was fired through the barrel of the gun, from a calibre of 28-mm at the breech to 21-mm at the muzzle. This squeezing increased the velocity of the shot with a subsequent increase in its capacity to penetrate armour.

Another strange shot was the AP (armour-piercing) Discarding Sabot, used by the 6-pounder and 17-pounder. The light alloy sabot, or outer case of the shot, broke away from the steel shot itself as soon as it left the barrel, leaving the shot to continue at increased velocity toward the target. The large outer core helped the shot to attain a high velocity within the barrel, while the small core could more easily maintain that velocity in flight.

The hollow-charge shell, an even more effective anti-tank projectile, was one which the Germans in particular adopted with enthusiasm. In the 18th Century, a Norwegian engineer had discovered that when he slightly hollowed out the face of an explosive charge it would cut deeper than usual into a rockface. He used this technique for blasting purposes. In 1880, an American, called Monroe, discovered that a similar phenomenon could be achieved against armour plate. He called this the 'Monroe Effect', but it wasn't until some Swiss gave a demonstration of the impact of the Monroe Effect against tank armour, in 1938, that its full military significance became apparent.

The hollow-charge shell consists of a hemispherical forward surface lined with a thin piece of metal and protected by a nose cone. On impact, the cone detonates the explosive charge behind the projectile, which is concentrated by the effect of the hemisphere into a jet of explosive gas and metal that accelerates to tremendous velocity within the hollow space between hemisphere and nose cone. It is this concentrated velocity that gives the shell its penetrative capability. In that it gains this velocity from the nature of the shell rather than, necessarily, the power of the gun that fires it, the hollow-charge shell can be used in a variety of weapons – as, for instance, the 68 Grenade, which could be fired from an infantry rifle and was in production at the beginning of the war to great advantage.

The 'Bazooka'

The recoilless gun was widely used in heavy artillery as well as in order to provide the infantry with their own anti-tank machine. An infantry soldier, easily manoeuvrable, easy to hide, was the ideal launching pad for the covert attack on a tank. Until the recoilless gun appeared, most anti-tank weapons had been far too heavy to carry. Of necessity, they carried with them – in the gun carriage – the full paraphenalia of springs and shock absorbers required by the need to cope with the recoil of the gun.

The principle of the recoilless gun had been realized during the First World War by Commander Davis of the U.S. Navy. His invention was used by the British in aircraft against Zeppelins, an area of combat to which it was particularly well suited because of its lightness.

The recoil was avoided in a primitive but effective way. The gun had two barrels, one pointing in either direction. As the shot was fired forward from one barrel, a similar weight of buckshot and grease was fired backward from the other barrel. The two shots cancelled out each other's recoil. By increasing the speed of the reaction shot, its weight could be lessened until it became merely a fast stream of gas, which would still balance the recoil from the forward shot.

The American 2·36-inch recoilless rocket-launcher, or 'bazooka', was one weapon that provided the advantages of the recoilless gun for the infantryman and gave him the ability to

Below: U.S. TOW missile uses recoilless launcher and is guided by two nearly invisible wires.

knock out a tank. It fired a hollow-charge projectile with great effect almost 400 yards. The Germans later adopted an 88-mm recoilless rocket-launcher, the Panzerschreck, that fired a projectile of seven pounds, about twice the weight of the bazooka.

In the 1973 Arab-Israeli war, hollow-charge shells were still being used and will, no doubt, be used again. Recoilless weapons were also in use in that conflict. One of the more effective of these was the Israeli 105-mm anti-tank rifle, which was mounted on a jeep.

Above: Recoilless rocket launchers mounted on trucks in action in forest land.

AIMED AT THE SKY
The Threat from the Air

The growth of airpower during the First World War and the rapid acceleration of that growth between the wars was a great deal more menacing than the development of the tank. The guns turned on the sky above them and adapted themselves once more to a whole range of specialized needs in order to face the new threat.

The anti-aircraft guns of the First World War were largely of one type; they had an approximately equal ceiling and an approximately equal rate of fire. The aircraft against which they were matched were only of limited capability. The British 13-pounder had an elevation of 80 degrees; that is, it could be aimed up to 10 degrees off the vertical (the potential 'elevation' of a gun is always the angle between the horizontal and its maximum elevation). The German 77-mm, that fired a 15-pound shell, had an elevation of only 70 degrees, as did the French 75-mm and the powerful German 88-mm of the First World War, although the British 3-inch had an elevation of 90 degrees. All could be traversed around a full 360 degrees.

The 13-pounder fired 6–10 rounds per minute, at a muzzle velocity (the speed at which the shell left the muzzle of the gun) of 1,700 feet per second, with a vertical range of 13,000 feet. This might be compared with the 3-inch, that fired 15 rounds per minute at a muzzle velocity of 2,500 feet per second, with a vertical range of 18,000 feet.

These figures point to the specialized needs of the anti-aircraft, or AA gun: a high ceiling, or vertical range; a high rate of fire to throw around a fast moving attacker; a relatively high muzzle velocity in order that the projectile should arrive at its target in the shortest possible time, thus lessening the chance of error in aiming ahead of the target; and the maximum possible elevation. (Naturally, this last made loading difficult, if the gun was not to be brought down to a lower elevation between each shot.)

Light and Heavy Fire

During the Second World War, two types of AA gun were developed; lighter guns to counteract fast, low-flying aircraft; heavier guns to reach up to the high-flying bombers. The successful German heavy 88-mm reverted, as we have already seen, to use as an anti-tank gun, with equal, if not greater, success. But the equivalent British 3·7-inch AA gun remained in use almost exclusively as an anti-aircraft weapon; its poten-

British 13-pounder in action during First World War

tial effect against German tanks was never realized. Another heavy gun was the German 105-mm, with a rate of fire of three rounds per minute and a ceiling of about 40,000 feet, slightly less than the 88-mm. The largest American AA gun during that war was the 120-mm, which could, if necessary, be fired by remote control.

In contrast to these, the Germans had a light 37-mm Flak gun, with a rate of 150 rounds per minute, and the Allies had a 40-mm Bofors with a rate of 120 rounds per minute and an effective altitude of 12,000 feet. Flak, incidentally, is an abbreviation for German 'anti-aircraft gun', or *Fliegerabwehrkanone*. The Bofors could also be used to fire tracer bullets. The 20-mm Oerlikon cannon, with a rate of 650 rounds per minute, was used by the Allies on tanks and ships in every field of the war and was also adopted by the Americans. The Germans had an equivalent 20-mm AA gun with a higher rate of fire. The 20-mm Flakvierling (quadruple gun) had a rate of over 700 rounds per minute.

Although anti-aircraft guns are still used against low-flying, fast planes (during the 1973 Arab-Israeli war, the Arabs made use of the successful Soviet twin 57-mm, with a rate of 120 rounds per minute per barrel), the missile has largely taken over the duties of air defence.

The SAM Missile

The SAM missile is probably one of the best known and most effective of this new type of war machine. Variations of this guided missile were used by the Arabs against Israeli air attacks and had ranges between 15 and 25 miles. They would appear to be the complete answer to air attack: planes can be brought down before they reach their target. But new developments in attack will inevitably follow, and the SAM missile will have to adapt to a new counter-machine.

Allied 40-mm Bofors anti-aircraft gun.

German 88-mm Grille 10, anti-tank and AA gun, mounted on Pzkw-IV chassis.

British 3·7-inch anti-aircraft gun matched the German 88-mm.

WAR ON RAILS
Piling up at the Front

The steam railway was not invented for military use but its military possibilities were very soon realized and it made possible the rapid transportation of huge numbers of troops and massive equipment. During the 1840s, railway communication links were busily constructed in almost every country that could afford to do so. Once the track was laid, there was at last at their disposal a method of transport that would not become bogged down in the mud, however heavy its load.

Construction programmes were largely intended for civilian passengers and trade, but at the back of every government's mind was the consideration that the railway would also be used in time of war. It was the Prussians who immediately seized on the implications of the new machine and first put it to general military use, when, in 1846, they moved 12,000 men, with horses and guns, to Cracow. Two years later, when the European revolutions of 1848 broke out, Austria, France and Russia also turned with varying degrees of enthusiasm to the railways.

By making possible large troop movements quickly to the front line, the railways were also directly responsible for the increased slaughter that ensued. Tactical manoeuvring was made difficult not only by the sheer number of troops

Left: Federal railway battery from the American Civil War: a war machine with a new impact.
Centre: British troops arriving at Victoria Station, London, on leave during the 1914–18 War.
Right: Heavily armoured train. Armour and armament make it look more like a tank on rails.

arriving but by the inevitable accumulation of soldiers at set points at the end of established lines of transportation. The troops piled up at predetermined destinations from which they were rushed into battle, often without further deployment.

Troop movements of this nature were made at the bloody battle of Solferino, in 1859, during the Franco-Austrian war. In a headlong, almost suicidal, clash between the two armies, there were altogether about 40,000 casualties – almost a quarter of the total number of troops in the field – an appalling proportion.

Similar slaughter occurred during the American Civil War – the machine guns and artillery combined to add to the slaughter – and, in part at least was caused by similar massed troop

movements to limited disembarkation points. The important part to be played by the railways in future wars was shown from the start. At Bull Run, the arrival of Confederate reserves by rail at a crucial moment of setback turned the tide of the battle against the Federals and produced a rout that continued all the way to Washington. But the Confederates failed subsequently to utilize their railway system to the full, a failure that significantly affected their ultimate defeat.

Again, during the Prussian war with France, in 1870, Prussian victories were made possible by extensive use of railways, which enabled great numbers of soldiers to be brought to the Front at short notice. Since France failed to use such a comprehensive rail system, Prussia's advantage was unchallenged. The First World War saw similar massed troop movements by rail, once again increasing the slaughter to gigantic proportions, as both sides put into use the systems they had been preparing ostensibly for civilian use in the preceding years.

The Railway Guns

The Germans, with a wide railway gauge able to take heavy loads, also put the railways to use to transport their giant artillery. Some of these guns were permanently fixed to a bed set on railway wheels. Others were brought to the Front by rail. The lethal 420-mm and the Paris Gun both used rail transport, though the first could as well be transported by road. The French St Chamond and Batignolle also used a rail bed, as did the German giants of the Second World War, being too heavy for anything else.

Russia laid down extensive railway links to cover the vast distances necessary for communications over her enormous territories. One problem of an invading army was whether or not the same gauge or width of rail was used by both countries. The Russians used a narrower gauge than the Germans, partly on purpose to stop German stock using Russian railways in case of invasion.

Inevitably, as railways became increasingly important for troops, guns, food and equipment, they also became major targets for enemy attack. To blow up a railway link was the aim of every guerilla movement, since to do so was to cut off the lifeblood of an army. To appropriate and make use of the enemy's own system was equally the aim of every attacking force. The railways were fought over as prized possessions, a machine of great value to whomever controlled it.

Below: The circular German Tellermine 42 and the long, thin German Riegel 43, anti-tank mines; and rectangular Italian anti-personnel mine.

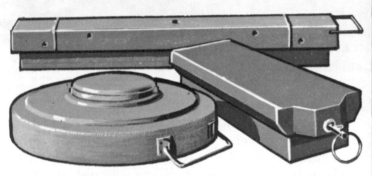

MINES AND BOOBY TRAPS
The Advance of Technology

Before the invention of gunpowder the main conflict between armed forces was the clash of steel on steel, preceded occasionally by a barrage of missiles – arrows, spears, stones, whatever was available. Hand-to-hand fighting still remains an essential part of any conventional war but firearms have replaced the spear and the sword. For centuries battles have been decided by artillery and small arms, the confrontation of the big guns and the infantryman's rifle and, more recently, his machine gun and its variations. Tanks are fundamentally just one other way of sending a gun into action and clearing the way for other guns. But every confrontation makes use of ancillary devices, some primitive, others more sophisticated, but all of increasing importance and ingenuity with the advance of technology and its application to the battlefield.

The simple booby traps of guerilla warfare – the sharpened stake concealed in a pit and

Canadian sappers searching for mines as they enter captured Falaise, 1944.

covered with poison – lie at the bottom of the scale, though they are by no means the least effective, as the Viet Cong have shown.

The hand-grenade provided the infantryman with his own transportable bomb. With a delayed action fuse it could be made to explode at head height, if judged correctly by the thrower, and use the force of its explosion to maximum effect. Although grenades were in use in the 17th Century, probably the best known was the Mills

"I have expressed my deep appreciation of the well-planned and well executed work performed in so few months.

The main defence zone on the coast is strongly fortified and well manned; there are large tactical and operational reserves in the rear areas. Thousands of pieces of artillery, anti-tank guns, rocket projectiles, and flame-throwers, await the enemy; millions of mines under water and on the land lie in wait for him. In spite of the enemy's great air superiority, we can face coming events with the greatest confidence."

(signed) ROMMEL, Field Marshal   22. May 1944

These sketches of German-held beaches and defences against Allied attack were made by Field Marshall Rommel in 1944.

Above: The detonator trips caused the German 'S' mine to explode and spread at head height. Below: Left, Br. Shrapnel Mine Mk II; Top, Fr. light anti-tank mine, Bottom, Br. No. 75 Hawkins grenade Mk I.

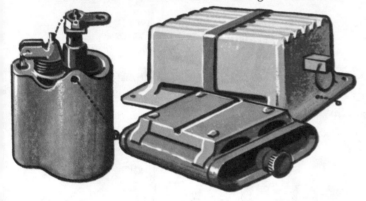

bomb of the Second World War, heavily relied on by the Allied infantry. Rocket-assisted grenades have been used as recently as the 1973 Middle East war.

The Minefield

Mines have proved one of the most effective devices of war. Long before the tank appeared, mines sensitive to pressure were in use, in the Crimean War and in the American Civil War. The advent of the tank established the minefield as one of the most efficient anti-tank contraptions. Mines at first designed only to disable tanks by breaking their tracks became sophisticated enough to blow up beneath their bellies and shatter the inside of the machine.

But the minefield was not restricted to tank warfare. Anti-personnel mines took a heavy toll of casualties in the Second World War and have continued to do so in subsequent conflicts.

Largely a defensive measure, mines could do the duty of a large number of soldiers in guarding a particular area and, if not preventing, then at least greatly slowing down an advance by the enemy. More sensitive than the anti-tank mine, the anti-personnel mine explodes at the contact of a foot or, like the German 'S' mine, will be thrown up into the air and explode at head height, casting a multiple charge over a wide area. More recent variations of this kind of mine are timed to explode at groin level.

Contact is no longer essential for a mine to explode. Devices sensitive to smell, sound, light and heat can be attached to mines to make them explode anywhere in the presence of humans and moving objects. In order to avoid detection by mine-sweeping devices and metal-detectors, mines can be made of plastic or wood. The mine, always insidious, has become increasingly deceptive and subtle.

BRIDGING THE GAP
Air-filled Skins

As much as the weapon itself, a war machine might be considered to be the device that assists soldiers to get to the point at which the weapon is applied – like the railway. Obstacles to the path of an armed force can be natural as well as human. Hannibal had to cross the Alps. Rivers, too, have presented serious obstacles that have had to be tackled with engineering skills and imaginative enterprise.

There are illustrations of Assyrians using air-filled bags as supports in order to help them cross rivers. These bags probably consisted of the skins of animals, sewn up and blown full of air so that they floated on the surface and provided adequate buoyancy to support a man. Many of these skins tied together could support a raft in cases where the wood itself was insufficient to sustain a heavy load – a troop of soldiers, an assault tower or battering ram, a missile-throwing machine. Hannibal himself had rivers to cross as well as mountains and used blown-up skins attached to rafts to support the weight of his elephants across the Rhône, in his advance on Rome.

A Bridge of Boats

Earlier, King Darius I of Persia had invaded Europe by means of a bridge of boats across the Bosporus. The boats were secured side by side and covered with a platform across which he brought his entire army and baggage-train. This saved him from a long and difficult journey around by land or the alternative rigours of a sea journey. He was able to overrun Thrace and Macedonia and advance north as far as the Danube. It was

Assyrian soldiers swimming to attack a city. One is using an inflated pig skin for underwater breathing.

Roman soldiers with standards shown crossing a bridge of boats, from Trajan's column.

the same Darius whose army was subsequently defeated by the Greeks at the battle of Marathon, in 490 B.C.

River crossing was generally achieved by similar, though more sophisticated, methods for the next 2,000 years. Where no adequate bridge existed, to build one of boats seemed the obvious and easiest solution. The manner in which the boats were cross-tied to each other and to the bank, the assessment and counter-action of the stresses and strains caused by the flow of the stream, these had to be taken into account; engineering such emergency bridges became a considerable science. At first constructed on the spot, when required, this was soon realized to be wasteful of time and energy when advancing troops could anticipate the need for a new crossing. Ready-prepared segments of floating bridges were engineered in advance and transported with wheels attached to their sides.

The Bailey Bridge

Floating bridges may still be used, although now the Bailey bridge, made of steel and able to span a river, is the usual equipment of engineers. This is the most famous type of bridge in use with the armed services. It was designed in 1940 by Donald Bailey and made in small sections that could easily be put together on the required site. Initially it could bear weights up to 70 tons, when several sections were joined together to traverse a river. It was used extensively by the Allies during the Second World War and still remains, in modified designs, in use today.

Right: Experiments in military bridge-building. Below right: Bailey Bridge being positioned.

THE TERROR OF FIRE
Greek Fire

Fire has probably been used, ever since it was discovered, as a means of inflicting harm to an enemy or destruction to his possessions, to burn down his dwelling or chase him out of hiding. Wooden forts and towers burned easily. Early catapults and missile-throwing devices hurled burning rags and smouldering faggots into besieged castles, whose defenders replied in like manner against the attacker's wooden engines of war with equal damage.

Ships, being also made of wood, were equally vulnerable to attack by fire, and one of the most dangerous of the early fire weapons was the famous Greek fire, which was not put out by contact with water. Greek fire would seem to have consisted, among other ingredients, of a mixture of pitch and sulphur; it created havoc and spread fear among the vessels of any enemy upon whom it was used. A burning ship at sea is one of the things most feared by any sailor. There is no way of escape, except by committing himself to the sea itself and all its dangers.

Red Hot Cannon Balls

The invention of gunpowder and the use of its explosive properties rapidly furthered the use of fire as a weapon of total destruction. Gunpowder was often used as an explosive device in its own right. Cannon balls were sometimes made red-hot before firing in the hope that they would set fire to enemy fortifications or ships or, if possible, explode the enemy's gunpowder store. It was a tricky operation to fire a red-hot cannon ball, in case it set fire to the gunpowder prematurely. Wadding was placed between the ball and the powder, and the ball had to be fired almost immediately it was put – by tongs – into the barrel.

Fire-carrying Animals

The Chinese used flaming arrows and so did many Western countries. The Mongols used live missiles: they strapped firebrands to the backs of cats and let them run among the enemy. They also used dogs and pigeons. This worked very well sometimes but more often than not, crazed by fear, the animals were as likely to run back into their own ranks as into those of the enemy. In its cruelty, this epitomized the use of fire in warfare.

Flame-throwers and Napalm

Flame-throwers came into use in the First World War. They served several purposes. At close range they were an effective way of clearing out an enemy trench or pill box, where the contents of the entrenchment could not be clearly seen and it was necessary to make certain of maximum coverage and destruction. The knowledge of their use might also intimidate an enemy into early surrender. Or they could be used to clear away covering foliage so that a clear field of fire could be obtained for the guns and rifles that followed. In street fighting, they were particularly useful for clearing out houses.

The French used petrol spray in 1914 and the Germans designed a gun that produced a jet of flaming oil. But the range of this was limited to 20–30 yards and the machine was too heavy to carry with any ease.

In the Second World War, flame was used more extensively, by tanks as well as infantry. The most lethal device was gelled petroleum. The Americans called it napalm and it was widely used in Korea and Vietnam with horrifying results, particularly when dropped in blanket coverage from the air. The vision of people, whether civilian or in uniform, being burned alive has an emotive impact that goes back a long way before the Spanish Inquisition and the *auto-da-fé*. The flame-thrower may have proved an ideal machine for the jungles of Burma and the foxholes of the Japanese islands but was certainly one of the most distasteful.

Right: Germans attack Russian fort with flame-thrower

An arrow with flaming cloths being fired from a 17th-Century gun.

BIOLOGICAL AND CHEMICAL WARFARE
Sulphur Fumes at Constantinople

Gas is clearly not a machine as such but as an adjunct to a military force it can make that force itself more effective. Biological and chemical warfare has been used for longer than might be imagined. Sulphur fumes were used by Mahomet at the siege of Constantinople, in 1453, and their use was contemplated – but rejected as inhuman – in the Crimean War in the middle of the 19th Century, a particularly wasteful war.

Earlier than the use of gas was the far more effective use of putrescent bodies and excretia as missiles for the ballista. Hurled into besieged fortifications, these could quickly spread disease among the confined defenders; often, they might be the bodies of their own comrades, killed outside the wall or fallen from the top of the parapets. As ever, the defenders replied in like kind, firing back similar missiles into the midst of the attacker's encampment, where disease – and famine if, in a strange country, their supplies were inadequate – often prevailed to as great a degree as in the city itself.

This was not only a medieval ploy. The cruel religious wars of the 15th Century – wars backed by religious idealism always seem to be the most cruel – among which John Zizka shone out like a guiding demon, reverted to a similar tactic at a time when death by plague was greatly feared. Such warfare was never a common resort but occurred often enough to arouse the indignation of those who knew about it and instigated a variety of codes of war that deplored such conduct. As was quickly discovered in the First World War, they deplored it to little effect.

Gas in the Trenches

Images of lines of soldiers, blindfolded, dragging their feet, with a hand resting forward on the shoulder of the man in front are easily conjured from the First World War. But although at first the use of gas incapacitated a relatively large number of soldiers, few of that number died – though many might have wished to – and there were a great deal fewer casualties once counter-measures had been learnt.

In the winter of 1914–15 the Germans attempted

French troops prepared for gas attack in First World War

to use irritant tear gas but with poor results. Then they produced the far more lethal poisonous chlorine gas and, in 1917, liquid mustard gas. It was the initial surprise of these gases that produced the high number of early casualties and instilled emotional fear of them into the troops. But when gas masks became regulation issue and the soldiers learnt how to protect themselves against the new danger, the force of the new weapon subsided considerably.

It had, of course, its own disadvantages and dangers. More than once, like the war elephant and the firebrand animal, it turned on its own users. The wind could change suddenly or be misjudged; the gas might not clear from an enemy position before an attack was launched; canisters of gas, like unexploded grenades, might be thrown back – there were many hazards. But the potential of this style of warfare was well realized and it was the knowledge of the very real tragedies it could bring about that prevented its use during the Second World War. Like the nuclear bomb today, the use of chemical warfare carried with it the reciprocal threat of heavy retaliation.

Nerve gases were the killers whose use everyone feared and still fears today, though they have never yet been used. The Germans stockpiled enough nerve gas during the Second World War to wipe out the population of nearly 30 main European cities.

Isolated incidents of the use of liquid gas, however, still occur in local wars, though only rarely. Tear gas of a mild kind – although victims might not agree with the adjective – is frequently used in civil disturbances.

It is a common fear that mind-affecting drugs may be infiltrated by one nation among the civilian and military population of an enemy, with damaging effects on the morale and mental stamina of that enemy. Indeed, it is supposed that such methods have, in specialized cases, already been attempted. No ban will stop such warfare so long as it proves effective and gives the warring nation yet another device with which to press its attack.

Under gas attack in First World War

Improvised gas alarm in the trenches

MISSILES ON TARGET
The Psychological Effect

The essence of a rocket, in contrast to a projectile fired from a conventional gun, is that it contains its own propellant. The advantage of this is that the rocket therefore requires a relatively simple launching platform and is, in comparison to the gun, a cheaper and more convenient method of laying down a fairly heavy barrage of fire. Its disadvantage initially – until efficient methods of guiding it to its target were discovered – lay in its inaccuracy.

It is said that the Chinese used rockets long before the Arabs are supposed to have used them in the 13th Century. But that argument is part of the larger argument about the discovery of gunpowder. Rockets were certainly used in India at the end of the 18th Century and by an Englishman, William Congreve, at the beginning of the 19th Century, after which they were used occasionally but never with any great effect beyond that of causing fear among the enemy.

The German V-weapons

The Germans became interested in rockets between the World Wars. Their experiments reached their peak with the development of the V-1 and V-2 rockets, which they turned with devastating effect on London and other British cities. These rockets seem to fall more readily into the field of aerial warfare. Closer to land, the Germans used rockets as alternatives to heavy artillery, although the rockets were never as accurate. The German *Nebelwerfer* had a range of over four miles. The Soviet multiple Katyusha rockets – usually in sets of 16, carried on the back of a lorry – had a range of about three and a half miles. The British also used rockets as extensions of mortar fire, with increased range.

Atomic Warheads

With the arrival of atomic warfare – a type of warfare that has taken its place on land, at sea and in the air and, in doing so, has dominated, with the threat it poses if not with actual use, all present and future war – the rocket has been turned to effective use as the carrier of atomic warheads. The U.S. Honest John, which originally had a range of just over 22 miles, is probably the best known of this type of rocket.

Other types followed when accurate guidance methods were discovered, such as the thin communication wire that unravelled as the rocket proceeded on its flight, or infra-red tracking devices and photographic tracking techniques. The small atomic warhead that these rockets carry, while providing a lethal and not-to-be-underestimated punch, will inflict only limited damage, the effects of which can be estimated in a way that the megaton explosion of a full-size atomic device never can be. The ostensible limitations of the field of effect of such rocket missiles is dangerous if it encourages nations to think that they can get away with using them without reprisals; although total war might be side-stepped, nervous tension would greatly increase to the detriment of balanced judgment. The increasing ability to pack atomic warheads into yet smaller and smaller containers, so that they can easily be transported across national borders, must be viewed with considerable alarm.

Left: Rocket practice on the marshes, 1845, by the Royal Artillery.

Right: Russian-made SAM missiles on the way back to Israel to be examined by their captors.

Above: Releasing carrier pigeon from tank, 1918.
Below: Carrier pigeon cages on donkey cart.

COMMUNICATIONS AND COMPUTERS

Good communications are important on the battlefield. Without them, coordination of movement is virtually impossible, messages become garbled, confusion is inevitable and the movement of troops greatly hindered. Communication between the battlefield and the source of command, which may well be many miles away, is equally important.

The Romans built a thorough system of roads to enable good communications between the capital and the distant frontiers of the Empire. Cyrus of Persia established a messenger service throughout his empire; it consisted of a carefully planned system of post houses and horses that enabled a messenger to travel 1,600 miles in a week. The vast Mongol Empire also used fast horseback links between its outlying districts and its centre.

Written words ensured greater accuracy than the spoken message, though the former could often be intercepted by the enemy. Bonfires set on hilltops and established in a series over a great distance could transmit pre-arranged signals. The use of modern semaphore, invented by John Edgeworth, a racehorse owner, in 1767, was taken up by France in the Napoleonic Wars in a

Bottom left: Signal post for battery.
Below: Tandem bicycle frame
used by Germans to generate
electricity for wireless in the trenches.
Far right: Signal station
using daylight lamps
at the Battle of Arras, 1917.

chain of relay-stations to keep Paris informed of the activities of her armies at the frontiers.

Each technological advance in communications during the 19th Century was used to great advantage on the battlefield. The electric telegraph, first set up in 1838, the first use of Morse code in 1844, Alexander Graham Bell's telephone of 1876, the invention of the radio at the turn of the century – these were all adopted by the military as machines to use in war. Immediate communication between headquarters and the front line, telephonic range-guidance from forward posts to heavy artillery, co-ordination of advance between troops miles apart, these were only some of the diverse applications of the new technology.

The watch, made accurate and compact toward the end of the 17th Century, was one of the most important devices that contributed toward more precise co-ordination of movement. Combined assaults could be timed exactly without resort to the give-away visual communication, carried message or pre-arranged signal, all of which were either vulnerable to interception or liable to fatal inaccuracy.

Satellite communication systems now allow long-range telephone conversations that have, for instance, enabled the President of the United States to communicate orders directly to his generals in Vietnam or to keep in constant touch with his Secretary of State in the Middle East. Satellites are also used by the superpowers to keep a watchful eye on each other's military installations.

Computers with Memories

Information gained from satellites, information fed in from observation posts in the field, information pre-gathered on enemy statistics – all this can be fed into computers to provide an instant analysis of strategic and tactical situations, minimizing the time-lag necessary for a decision on the right course of action. The memory-stored computer is the latest brain at the head of the communications network that forms the nervous system of the modern army. Automation in this field, as in every other, continues to proceed at an astonishing rate. Only a century or so divides the smoke-signal from the satellite. What might follow in this line constitutes one of the most fascinating fields of military study.

Index

Italicized references are to
illustration captions.

ACOUSID (Acoustic and seismic
    intrusion detection), 132
Adams, Robert, 317
Ader, Clement, 44
ADSID (Air delivered seismic
    intrusion detector), 132
Aerial photography, 10
Aerial steam carriage, 43, *43*
Aerial warfare, 54, 56–7, 60–2,
    64–5, 72, 75, 76, 77
    forecasts of, 13, 17
Aerodynamics, 40, 42, 46, 47, 66,
    68–9, 70, 88–9
    of airships, 26–7
of kites, 6, 8, 10
Aero-engines,
    Bristol, 84
    Clerget, 57
    Cyclone, 71
    Fiat, 62
    General Electric, 115
    Jumo, 73, 114
    Kestrel, 73
    Mercedes, 55, 57
    Mitsubishi, 80
    Oberursel, 54
    Packard, 80
    Pratt and Whitney, 116
    Rolls Royce, 64, 76, 84, 115
    Wright, 89
Aeroplane,
    armament for, 51, 52, 54, 55,
        65, 74, 76, 80, 81, 82, 89, 114
    armour for, 53
    bomber, 62, 64–5, 66, 82–9
    carrier-borne, 238–45, 246–7
    development of, 6, 37, 42–4, 47,
        49, 66–71, 80
    dive-bomber, *74*, 82, 84
    fighter, 54–60, 65, 70, 72–81,
        246, 247
    fighter-bomber, 72
    jet, 72, 111–6, 228
    long-range fighter, 80–1
    in naval warfare, 231, 235, 238,
        246–7
    power for, 47, 49, 54, 68, 80, 89
    role in war, 50, 51, 72, 81, 82,
        83, 89
    torpedo, 241, 246, 247
    types,
        Albatross (Ger.), 54, 56, *56*, 57
        B17 'Flying Fortress' (Am.) 66,
            83, *87*, 246
        B24 'Liberator' (Am.), 66, 83, *83*
        B29 'Superfortress' (Am.), 66,
            83, 88–9, *89*, 90
        B247 (Am.), *68*, 69
        B52 'Stratofortress' (Am.), 114,
            130, 132
        Blenheim (Br.), 66, 82, 84, *85*
        Bristol (Br.), *50*, 51
        Caproni (It.), *61*, 62
        Claude (Jap.), 80
        Curtiss (Am.), 84
        De Havilland (Br.), *53*, 54, 56,
            57, *57*
        Dornier (Ger.), 82, *83*
        Douglas, 71, *71*
        F-86 'Sabre' (Am.), 115
        F-105 'Thunderchief' (Am.),
            115, 116
        FW 190 (Ger,), 72, *79*, 80

        Fokker (Ger.), 52, 53–4, 57, *57*,
            66, 67
        Giant (Ger.) 64
        Gloster (Br.), *111*, 114
        Gotha (Ger.), 62, 63
        Halifax (Br.), 84
        Hampden (Br.), 82
        Handley Page (Br.), 63, 64, *64*,
            69, 84
        Hawker Siddeley Harrier (Br.),
            116
        Heinkel (Ger.), *112*, 114, 198
        Hurricane (Br.), 72, *75*, 76, 77
        I-15, I-16 (Russ.), 75, 81
        Junkers (Ger.), 67, 74, 82, 84
        Lancaster (Br.), 82, 84, *87*, 88,
            92, 94, *97*
        Manchester (Br.), 84
        Maurice Farman, 51
        McDonnell-Douglas 'Phantom'
            (Am.), 115
        Me 109 (Ger,), 72, 73, *73*, 74,
            75, 76, 77, 80, 81
        Me 262 (Ger.), *113*, 114
        Mitsubishi Zero (Jap.), 80, 81,
            81, 246
        Morane-Saulnier (Fr.), 51, *51*
        Nieuport (Fr.), *52*, 54
        P47 'Thunderbolt' (Am.), 72, *79*
        P51 'Mustang' (Am.), 72, *78*,
            80, 81
        S.E.5 (Br.), 58
        Sikorsky (Russ.), 61, 62
        Sopwith (Br.), 54, 57, *57*
        Spad (Fr.), 57
        Spitfire (Br.), 72, 74, 76, *76*,
            77, 81
        Stirling (Br.), 84
        Taube (Ger.), *50*, 51
        TU-22 (Russ.), 114
        Vickers Gun Bus (Br.), 54
        Victor (Br.), *115*
        Vulcan (Br.), *115*
        Wellington (Br.), 66, 82, 84, *85*
        Wildcat (Am.), 246, 247
Aft-castle, 153, 158
Agrippa (Roman commander),
    144–5, *145*
Aïn Tounga, Tunisia, 288
Aircraft carriers, 235, 238–45, *242*,
    243, *244*, 246–7
    Akagi (Jap.), 244, 245, *245*,
        247
    Argus, 241
    Ark Royal (earlier), 241, *245*
    Ark Royal (later), *248*
    Eagle, 241
    Enterprise (Am.) (earlier), 245,
        246, 247
    Enterprise (Am.) (later), 248,
        248
    Hermes, 244
    Hornet (Am.), 246, 247, *247*
    Hosho (Jap.), 244
    Kaga (Jap.), 244, *245*, 247
    Lexington (Am.), 244
    Manxman, 241
    Midway (Am.), 248
    Saratoga (Am.), 244
    Shokaku (Jap.), 245
    Triumph, 248
    Wakamiya Maru (Jap.), 244
    Yorktown (Am.), 245, *246*, 247
    Zuikaku (Jap.), 245
Airships, 25, 26–39
    battery-driven, 28–9
    clockwork-driven, 28
    Deutschland, 29
    first petrol engine driven, 28–9
    Hindenburg, *33*, 37

        La France, 28, 29, 33
        Lebaudy's, 31, *31*, *32*
        non-rigid, 38
        rigid, development of, 32, 33
        role of in war, 35, 36, 37, 38
        Santos-Dumont's, *28*, 29, 31, 32
        steam-powered, *26*, 28
Albone, Dan, 332
Alecto, paddle-driven steamer,
    180–1, *181*
Alexander, the Great, 260, *260*, 261,
    267
Aluminium, 32
Anglo-Saxons, *276*
Anti-aircraft defences, 37, 38
Anti-missile systems, 128–9
Anti-personnel shot, 294
Arabs, 294
Arbalest (crossbow), 282
Archers, 260, 267, 274, 284, *284*
    seaborne, 135, *137*, 141, 147,
        153
Archery, *255*, 256, 285
Armies,
    American, in Mexican War, 119,
        317
        in Civil War, 20, 21, 317, 320,
            349
        in World War II, 354
    Assyrian, 260, *260*, 274
    Austrian (19th Cent.), 314
    British (18th Cent.), 311; (19th
        Cent.), 24, 25, 314–5; (20th
        Cent.), 315, 317
    Byzantine, 274
    Dutch (15/16th Cent.), 286
    English (13/14th Cent.), 256,
        284, 285
    French (mediaeval), 285, 291,
        292, 294, 303; (17/18th
        Cent.), 18, 286, 312, 331;
        (19th Cent.), 313, 321; (20th
        Cent.), 326, 328, 333, 335
    German (19th Cent.), 314; in
        WWI, 35–7, *335*, 346; in
        WWII, 335, 336
    Greek, 268
    Italian (13th Cent.), 282
    Prussian (19th Cent.), 313, 315
    Roman, 268–70, *269*
    Sumerian, *259*
    Swiss (15th Cent.), 286
Arminius, German tribal leader, 271
Armour, 257
    Byzantine, 274, *274*
    Greek, 266
    mediaeval, 274, 276, *279*, *280*,
        282, 284, 285, 286, 288, 306,
        330
    Roman, 268, *269*
Armour and armour plating, for
    ships, 186, 188, 190, *191*, 192,
    196, 197, 203, 217, 222, 223,
    224, 232
Armoured vehicles, 330–2, *331*
    amphibious, 341
    Daimler Panzerwagen, 333
    Davidson Cadillac, 333, *333*
    de Dion-Bouton quadri-cycle,
        332
    Fiat, 333
    Ivel tractor, 332
    Killen Strait tractor, *333*, 334
    Lanchester armoured car, 333,
        333
    Lancia armoured car, 333, *333*
    Packard, 333
    Renault, 333
    Rolls Royce, *331*, 333
    Russian Garford, 333, *333*

Seabrook armoured lorry, 333
Simms' Motor War Car, 332
Steam roller, 331, *332*
Wolseley, 333
Armstrong, William, 182
Army, British, units,
Balloon Corps, 24, 25
Rifle Brigade, 312
Army organisation 260, 266, 268,
284, 302
Arquebus, 303, 309–10, *310*, 311
Arrowheads, 255, *256*, 284
Arrows, 272
Artillery, *301*
catapult, 145, 260, *263*, 272,
273
early types, 298–305
field, 301, 302, 303
light, 300
sailborne, 326, 349
seaborne, 156
siege, 272–3, 296–7, 301, 326
Ash, James, 208
Assault towers, 260, *263*, 272
Assyrians, 254, *255*, 256, 257, 260,
260, *263*, 266, 272, 274, 284,
288, 352, *352*
Atomic warfare, 90, *90*, 91, 125, 358
Augustus, Roman Emperor, 268
Autogiro, *104*, 106, 108
Axes, 254, *255*, *256*

Babylon, 288
Bacon, Roger, 13, 156, 294, *294*
Baden-Powell, Capt B. F. S., 9
Bader, Gp Capt Douglas, 77
Bailey bridge, 353, *353*
Bailey, Donald, 353
Ballista, 256, 272
Ballistic Missile Early Warning
system, 39
Ballonnet, 26, 27
Balloons, 13–26, 50
Crusader, 24
Enterprise, 20
first manned ascent in, 16
in Boer War, 25
L'Entreprenant, 17, 18
Montgolfier's, 14, *14*, 16, 21
observation, 17, 18, *19*, 20, 21
Paris siege (1871), 23–4
Union, 249
Bastard cannons, 301
Battering ram, 260, *260*, *263*, 272
Battlecruisers, 224
German in World War I, 224,
226
in battle, 226–7, 228, 231
Indomitable, 224, *224*
Inflexible, 224, 226, 227, *227*
Invincible, 224, 226, 227, *227*
Battles,
Actium (31 BC), 142, 144–5,
145
Agincourt (1415), 285
Alalia, 140
Arsuf (1191), 282
Auray (1364), *280*
Azov (18th Cent.), 182
Blenheim (1704), 312
Brunette (1937), 75
Cadiz (1587), 161
Cambrai (1917), 335
Chaeronaea (338 BC), 267
Coronel (1914), 226, 228
Crécy (1346), 282, *284*, 285,
294, 299
Fair Oaks (1862), 21, 320
Falkland Islands (1914), 227,
227, 228

Fleurus (1796), 18
Gaine's Mill (1862), 21
Hampton Roads (1862), 189,
192
Hastings, (1066), 284
Jutland (1916), 228–31, *228*,
229, *230*
Kadesh (circa 1290 BC), 258
Lepanto (1571), *155*, 157, *157*,
158
Lützen (17th Cent.), *303*
Malplaquet (1709), 312
Marathon (490 BC), 266, 353
Marignano (1515), 303
Midway (1942), 8, 242
Morat (1476), 286
Nancy (1477), 286
Novara (1513), 303
of Britain (1940), 76–7, 80, 84
Oudenarde (1708), 312
Pharsalus (48 BC), 269
Poitiers (732), 276
Poitiers (1356), 285
Powys (1120). 284
Ravenna (1512), 303
Roncevalles (778), 276
Rosebecque, *294*
Salamis (480 BC), 142
San Romano (15th Cent.), *287*
Sena Gallica (551), 147
Seringapatam (1799), 117
Somme (1916), 334
Svolde (1000), 151
Tannenberg (1914), 52
The Saints (1782), 171, 172–3,
173
Thermopylae (480 BC), 266
Trafalgar (1805), 170, *170*
Tsushima (1905), 218, 220
Battleships, 194, 216, 218, 222–3,
224, 252
Bismarck (Germ.), 93
Colorado (Am.), 232
Dandolo (Ital.), 197
Devastation (Fr.), 188
Devastation, (Br.), 194, *194*,
196
Dreadnought (Br.), 222, 223,
223, 224
Duilio (Ital.), 196
Hibernia (Br.), 239, *245*
in battle, 220, 228–31, 246–7
Inflexible (Br.), 196, 197, *197*
Murachi (Jap.), 235
Nelson (Br.), 232
Rodney (Br.), 212, *237*
Thunderer (Br.), 196
West Virginia (Am.), 232
Yamato (Jap.), 235, *235*
Bayeux Tapestry, *279*, 284
Bayonet, 306, 312
Bazooka, 122, 344
Belisarius, Byzantine commander,
147, 274, 288,
Bell, Alexander Graham, 6
Bell, Henry, *178*
Biological warfare, 356
Bireme, 138, 140, 141, 142
Bismarck, German battleship, 93
Blériot, Louis, 47, 49
Blimp, non-rigid airship, 38
Blois, Charles de, 280
Blowpipes, 256
Boelcke, Oswald, 56
Bolt action rifle breech, 313, 315
Bomb-aiming,
Oboe device, 100
Bombard, early cannon, 294, 300,
304, *304*
Bombardelli, hand gun, 306

Bombing system, electronic, 116
Bomb ketch, 168, *169*
Bombs, aerial, 61; 64, 65, 84, 93–9,
96, *99*
2000 lb, 93
12000 lb, *98*
anti-personnel, 93, 96
atom bomb, 90, *91*
Dam Buster, 94, *95*
FOB, 129
Grand Slam, 92, 93, *99*
high explosive, 93, 96
incendiary, 93, 98, *98*
laser guided, 132
smoke, 93
Tallboy, 93, *98*
Booby traps, 350
Boulogne, siege of (1544), 299–300
Bow, 254, 256, 258, 274, 284;
see also Arrows, Crossbow,
Longbow, Stonebow
Brass, for guns, 159
Braun, Werner von, 120, 121
Breastplate, 268, *269*, 276
Breech-loading, 182, 216, 217, 294,
313, 314
Breguet, Louis, 106, 108
Bridge-building, 352
Broadside, 157, 159, 160, 161, 194,
218
Bronze,
for cannon, 300
for early weapons, 254, *255*,
256
Brunel, Isambard K., 180, 186
Bullets, 306
Burstyn (Austrian engineer), 334
Bushnell, David, 204
Byzantines, Byzantium, 146–9,
260, 288, 304

Campbell, Andrew, 208
Cannon, 157, *301*, 306
basilisk, 301
Bastignolles 320 mm, 326, 349
culverin, 157, 160, 163, *163*,
294, 301
Dardanelles Gun, 296, 297
demi-culverin, 160
English 16th Century, 301
German 800 mm 'Dora', 329
introduction of, 292, 294, *294*
Katherine, 301
King of Cannon, 297
Krimhild, 296
Mons Meg, 296, *297*, 301
Mad Margaret *(Dulle Griet)*.
296
organ guns, 298–9
petarara, 294
pot de feu, 294
St Chamond 400 mm, 326, *326*,
349
Saker, 160
siege, 300, 326
Tsar Pushka (Emperor Cannon),
297
Cannon, aircraft armament, 76, 83
Carbine, 312
Carrack, *158*, 160
Carronade, 172, 173, *173*
Cartridges, rifle, 313
Castles,
Caernarvon, 292, *293*
Caerphilly, 292
Conway, 292, 293
Crusader castles, 290
Gaillard, 290
Harlech, 292
Krak des Chevaliers, 290

medieval, 288, 292
Margat, 290
Rumeli Hisari, Turkey, 291, *291*
St Peter, Bodrum, Turkey, 291
Saone, 290
Cataphracts, 272, *274*
Catapult, 145, 260, *263*, 272, *273*,
Cavalry, 264, 269, 274, 300, 311,
312
heavy, 267, 276, 280
light, 266, 267, 330
mounted Assyrian archers, 256,
274
Cavendish, Henry, 13, *13*
Cayley, Sir George, 40, 42, 43, *43*,
44, 49
Centurion, 268, 269
Century, Roman military unit, 268
Chadwick, Roy, 84
Chain mail, 280
Chariots, 258, 259, *259*, 274, 299
Assyrian, 256
Celtic, 259
Chinese, 259
Egyptian, 258, 259
Greek, 259, 266
Roman, 258
Charlemagne, 276, *276*
Charles Martel, 276
Charles, the Bold, 286
Charles VII, of France, 292
Charles, Alexander, 16, *16*, 17
Château Gaillard, 290, 291, *291*
Charlotte Dundas, S.S., 178
Chelander, 147
Chemical warfare, 356, 357
Childers, Sir Hugh, 194
China, Chinese, 116, 254, 259, 264,
274, 284, 294, 354, 358
Great Wall of, 264, *264*
Churchill, Winston S., 77, 333
Cierva, Juan de la, 106, 108
Clark, traction inventor, 331
Cleopatra, 144–5, *145*
Clermont, S.S., 178
Cody, F. S., 10, *10*, 11
Cog, mediaeval ship, 152, *152*, 153
Cohort, Roman military unit, 268
Coley, Capt Cowper, 182
Collier, Elisha, 316
Colt, Samuel, *316*, 317
Comet, S.S., 178, *178*
COMMIKE (commandable micro-
phone), 132
Communications, 360
Compass, mariners', 156
Computers, 361
Congreve, William, 118, 119, 358
Constantinople, sieges of,
(717–18), 148–9
(1453), 272, 291, 296, 297,
356
Convoys, 212
blimps as escorts, 38, 39
Copper, 254
sheathing for ships, 170
Cordite, 217
Cornu, Paul, *104*, 106
Corvette, 174, 212, 214
Crete, 136, 259
Crossbow, 282–3, *282*, 284–5, 299,
306
Cruisers, *216*, 226, 227, 232
Albany guided missile cruisers
(Am.), *250*, 253
Birmingham (Am.), 238, *240*
Boston (Am.), 252
Canberra (Am.), 252
Columbus (Am.), 252
guided missile, 253

in battle, 226–7, 228, 230, 231,
246–7
Long Beach (Am.) guided
missile ship, *250*, 253
Pennsylvania (Am.), 238, *238*
Crusaders, 282, 283, 290
Cugnot, James, 331
Cuisse, 280
Cuniberti, Italian engineer, 222
Cushing, Lieut, 198

Daggers, 254, *255*, 256
Dardanelles, 297
Darius I, 352, 353
David and Goliath, 256
Da Vinci, Leonardo, 40, *40*, 299,
304, *304*, 330, 336
Davis, Commander, U.S.N., 344
De Mole, Australian, 334
Destroyers, 202, 228, 230, 231,
246–7
Diesel engine, 208, 209
Diesel, Rudolph, 209
Dionysius I, of Syracuse, 260
Dirigibles, 38, 39, *39*
Donahue (of R.A.S.C.), 334
Dönitz, Admiral Karl, 212
Douhet, Brig.-Gen. Giulio, 66
Drake, Sir Francis, 161, 163, 164
Drebbel, Cornelis, 204
Dromon, Byzantine warship, 146–7,
146
Dunlop (tractor inventor), 331
Duquesne, Abraham, 168

Edgeworth, John, 360
Edward I, 284, 292, *293*
Edward III, 294, 299
Egyptians, 254, 256, 257, 258, 284
boats, of, 135–37, *135*, *136*
Electric engines,
in airships, 28–9
in submarines, 208
Electronic warfare, 132
Elephants, 292, 330
Engineers, of Alexander the Great,
260
Ericsson, John, 180, *181*, 182, 190
Etruscans, 268, *284*

Falcons, falconets (field artillery),
301
Farman, Henri, 49, *49*
Ferguson, Capt Patrick, 313
Feudal structure, 276
Fighter direction, 100, *101*
Fighting towers, on warships, 153;
see also forecastle
Fire, as weapon, 148, 149, 354; *see
also* Fire-ship, Flamethrower
Firearms, at sea, 158
Fire control, naval, 196
Fire-ships, 142, 145, *145*, 165, 340
Fitch, John, 178
Flame-throwers, 145, 354, *354*
Flankers (field artillery), 301
Fleets,
Byzantine, 304
Dutch, 166–7
English, 160, 161, 163, 165,
166, 167, 170, 172, 173
French, 168, 232
Roman, 144, 146
Spanish, 158, 161, 163–5
see also Navies (Modern)
Flettner, Anton, 108
Flint, 254, *256*
Flintlock, 311, 313, 316
Flying bombs, 123
Queen Bee, 123

Queen Wasp, 123
see also VI
Fokker, Anthony, 53
Foot-soldiers, 258, 266, 274, 280,
282, 324
arms for, 306
seaborne, 141
Forecastle, 151, 153, 158, 160
Forester, C. S., 297
Forsyth, Rev. Alexander, 313
Forsyth's gunlock, *312*, 313
Fortifications, 260, 270, 272, 288,
292
Forts, 188, 260, 264, 288
Fowler (of armoured road loco),
332
Francis B. Ogden, screw-driven
launch, 180
Franklin, Benjamin, 17, *18*
Friction lock, 311
Frigate, sailing, 174, *175*, 224
Frobisher, Martin, 163, 164
Fuller, Col J. F. C., 335
Fulton, Robert, 178, *179*

Gal, Major Uziel, 324
Galea, Byzantine reconnaissance
boat, 147
Galeass, 156, 157, *157*, 163
Galleon, 156, 158, 160–1, *161*, *163*,
165, 166, 168
Galley, 156, 161, 163
Gas, poison, 356, *356*, 357, *357*
Gas turbine 111–112
Gatling, Richard, 320
see also Machine guns
Gee radar navigation system, 100,
100, *102*
Genoese, 282, 285
Geodetic construction of aircraft, 84
German Air Force, 52–7, 60, 72,
75–7
Germanic tribes, 271
Germans, Germany,
and airship development, 32–5
arms and armour in mediaeval,
280, *310*, 311
in World War I, 50–7, 326, 327,
328, 356
In World War II, 335, 336, 337,
357, 358
Landsknechts mercenaries, 287
Giffard, Henri, *26*, 28
Gladius, Roman sword, 268
Gliders, 45, 46, 47, 48, 50
Goddard, Professor R.H., 119–20
Goering, Reichsmarshal H., 76, 77,
84
Gokstad ship, 150, *151*
Gomper (tractor inventor), 331
Grant, Gen. Ulysses S., 321
Grape shot, *184*
Grasse, Comte de, 172
Great Britain, S.S., 180, 186, *186*,
187
Greaves, leg armour, 266, 268
Greek fire, 148, 149, 354
Greeks, ancient, 140–3, *255*, 259,
266, 267, 268, 280, 284
city states, 139, 142, 266
Grenades, 344
hand, 350
rocket-assisted, 351
Gun carriages, 294, 304
Gun carts, 299–300
Gun mountings, 159, 172
Gunnery, central battery, 182
Gunpowder, 156, 158, 159, 280,
294, *294*, 354, 364
prismatic powder, 216

Guns,
American 120mm, 346
anti-aircraft, 224, 324, 342, 344, 346
anti-tank, 324, 342
Bofors 40mm, 346, *347*
British 2 pdr, 342
British 6 pdr, 342
British 13 pdr, 346
British 17 pdr, 342, *342*
British 3 in, 346
British 3·7 in, 346, *347*
French 75 mm, 346
German 20 mm, 346
German 28 mm (Squeezegun), *342*, 343
German 37 mm, 346
German 77 mm, 346
German 88 mm, 342, *342*, 346, *347*
German 105 mm, 337, 346
long range, 327, 328, 329
machine guns, *see* Machine gun
mortar, *see* Mortar
naval, 158, 182, *183*, *184*, 190, 194, 216, 218, 222, 224, 232, 327
Oerlikon 20 mm, 346
rail-borne, 326, 349
recoilless, 344, 345
rifle, 324; *see* Rifle
Russian twin 57 mm, 346
Russian 122 mm, 337
Russian 152 mm, 337
self-propelled, 337
siege guns,
420 mm 'Big Bertha', 326, *329*, 349
Paris gun, 327, 328, *329*, 349
Gustavus Adolphus, *300*, 302
Gyro instruments, 70

H2S, radar navigational aid, 102, *102*
Hackbutt, 310
Hadrian, Roman emperor, 264
Hadrian's wall, 264, *264*
Haig, F–M Sir Douglas, 334
Hale, William, 118, 119
Handgun, 286, 306, *306*, 309
multiple, 309
Hannibal, 352
Hargrave, Lawrence, 9, 10
Harold II, 284
Harris, Air Chief Marshal Sir Arthur, 84, *86*
Hart, Clive, 6
Haute-piece, 280
Hawker, Major L. G., 56–7
Hawkins, Sir John, 160, 163, 164
Helicopter, 40, 105, 107, 116
armament for, *107*, *108*, 109
autogiro, *104*
Bell Huey Cobra, *108*, 109
Breguet, 108
Focke-Acheglis Fa-61, *104*, 108
Pescara 4S, *104*
Sikorsky VS-300, *107*, 109
Sioux, *107*
synchropter, 108
torpedo-delivering, 253
Whirlwind, *107*
Helmets, 266, 268, *269*, *274*, 276, *276*, 280
Henry VIII, 159, 299
Henson, William, 43
Heraldry, 280
Hittites, 254

Holland, J. P., 208
Hoplites, 266, 267, *267*, 268
Horses, 256, 257, 258, 274, 276, 330
Hussites, 300
Hydraulic loading system, 196
Hydrogen, in airships, 14, 24, 25, 27, 29, 37
Hyksos, 258

Immelman, Max, 56, *56*
Indians, American, 284, 312, *314·*
Infantry, 258, 264, 266, 268, 300, 302, 309, 312, 315, 324
Swiss, 286, 287
Interrupter gear, 52, 53
Iron, 254, 256, 300
for cannon shot, 294
for guns, 159
for ships, 186
Iron-tipped weapons, 268
Ironclad, 186; *see also* Warships
Israelis, 324, 345, 346
Israelites, 256

Japan and Japanese, 218, 241, 246
Air Force, 80–1
Javelin, 268, *269*, 272
Jet propulsion, 111–6
Jouffroy, Marquis de, 178
Julius Caesar, 144, 269
Justinian, Emperor, 274

Kale, George, 331
Kamikaze aircraft, 340
Kites, 6–11, *7*, *8*, 50
aerodynamics, 6, 8, 10
and Romans, 9
Chinese, 6–7, 8, *8*
Japanese, 6, 8
kite-carriage, 9, *9*
Korean, 6, 8
Malay, 6, 8
man-lifting, 8–11
Knight, armoured, 274, 276, *279*, *280*, 282, 284, 285, 286, 288, 306, 330
'Ko' (early Chinese dagger), 254
Kondor Legion, 75
Kremlin, the, Moscow, *293*
Kremlins, fortified citadels, 292

Lake, Simon, 208
La Mountain, John, 20
Lana-Terzi, Father Francisco de, 13
Lance, 274, 276
Lanchester-Prantl theory, 66
Landsknechts, 287
Langley, S. P., 44
Laser guided bomb, 132
Laser target marker, *133*
Lavoisier, Antoine L., 13
Lead, for shot, 294
Lebaudy brothers, 31, *31*
Legions, Roman, 268, 270, 271
Levavasseur (of French Artillery), 334
Lilienthal, Otto, 44, 45, *45*, 46, 48
Lôme, Dupuy de, 182
London Naval Treaty (1930), 234
London, aerial bombing of, 36, 37, 77
by V2, 121
London, Tower of, 288, *288*
Longboat, Viking, *276*
Longbow, 256, 282, 283, 284–5, *284*, 306
Lonship, 150–1, *150*, 152
Lorica, Roman mail armour, 268
Lowe, Thaddeus, 20, 21, 24

Luftwaffe, *see* German Air Force
Luppis, Capt, 198

Mace, 274
Macedonians, 260, 272, 274, 284
Machine guns, 320–323
automatic, 322
Browning, *321*
for aircraft, 52, 54, 83, 84
Gardner, *319*, 321
Gatling, 319, 320–1
Lewis, 54, 323
Maxim, 322, 322–3, *323*
Montigny mitrailleuse, 321, *321*
Nordenfelt, 321–2
'Pom-pom' (Maxim), 323
portable, 324; *see also* Submachine gun
Puckle, *319*, 320, *320*
Spandau, 55
Vickers, 54, 57
semi-automatic, 333
Williams, 320
Mahomet II, 291, *291*, 296, 304, 356
Mail armour, 268, 274
Manpads (Man-portable Air Defence system), *130*
Marc Antony, 144–5, *145*
Marco Polo, 8
Marlborough, Duke of, 312
Masts and rigging, 153, 157, 194
Matchlock, 306, 309, 311
Maurice of Orange, 286
Maurice Tiberius (Byzantine emperor), 274
Maxim, Hiram S., 44, 322, *323*
Maximilian I, Emperor of Austria, 287, 301, *306*
Mercenaries, 282, 286–7, 303
Messerschmitt, Willy 72
Metals, early use of, 254, 259
Meusnier, French engineer, 26, *26*
Miller, Patrick, 178, *178*
Minelayer, 231
Mines, 350, *350*
anti-personnel, *350*, 351, *351*
anti-tank, *350*, 351, *351*
naval, 198, *201*
Minoan civilization, 259
Missiles, guided, 116, 123–32
Atlas, 124, *124*
Harpoon, *130*
Honest John, *126*
ICBM, 124–32
Minuteman, 125, *125*
MIRV, 125
Phoenix, *130*
Poseidon, *131*
Polaris, 253, *253*
Quail, 130, 132, *133*
rocket-propelled, 120
SAM (Russ.), 346, *358*
Savage (Russ.), *131*
Scarp (Russ.), 125
Spartan, 128
Sprint, 128
SUBROC, *253*
Talos, 253
Terrier, 253
with nuclear warheads, 125, 253
Mitchell, Colonel Billy, 66
Mitchell, R. J., 76
Mohne and Eder Dams, 94, *95*, 96
Monk's gun, 311
Monoplane, development of, 69, 73, 76
Monroe, Monroe Effect, 344
Montford, John de, *280*
Montgolfier, Etienne and Joseph, 14, 16, 26

Morse code, 361
Mortars, 302, 304, *304*
    French 370 mm, 326
    naval use, 168
Murderers (cannon), 302
Muskets, *308*, 311
Muzzle loading, 194, 216
    of mortars, 304

Napalm, *97*, 98, 354
Napoleon Bonaparte, 18
Narses, Byzantine general, 147
Nasal (nose protector), 276
Navigational aids to aircraft, 37, 70,
    100, *100*, 102, *102*
Navies, modern, development of,
    160, 218, 232, 234, 235, 241
    American (1776 and 1812),
        174, 204
        in Civil War, 189—90, 198,
            204
        in 20th Cent., 39, 232, 233,
            238, 244, 248; 252, 253
        in World War II, 39, 246—7
    British
        in 19th Cent., 188, 194, 196,
            197, 202, 203, 217
        in World War I, 224, 226,
            227, 228, 229, 230, 231,
            232, 233
    French, 38, 188
    German
        and submarines, 210, 211,
            212, 214
        in inter-war years, 234—5
        in World War I, 211, 224,
            226, 227, 228, 229, 230,
            231
        in World War II, 93—4, 212,
            213
    Italian, 232
    Japanese, 218, 220, 233, 235,
        244, 245—7
    Russian, 182, 188, 218, 219
Nef (early mediaeval vessel), 152
Nelson, Admiral Horatio Lord, 170,
    170, 174
Neolithic age, 256, 284
Newcomen, Thomas, 176, *176*
Nordenfelt, Torsten, 209
Normans, 276, *279*, 284, 288
Nuclear power, 248, 252—3
    for aircraft carriers, 248
    for battleships, 252
    for submarines, 214, *250*, *252*
    turbine, 252
Nuclear warfare and warheads, 90,
    90, 125

Oarsmen, 136, 137, 140, 141, 142,
    147, 150, 151, 156
Oberth, Hermann, 120
Oboe, bomb sighting system, 100,
    102, *102*
Octavian, Roman emperor, 144, *145*
Ohain, Hans von, 96
Onagen (Roman catapult), 272
Organ guns, 320
Outer Space Treaty (1966), 129

Paddle propulsion, 178, 180—1
Paleolithic age, 284
Palgrave (Scandinavian axe), 254
Parachute, 40
Paris,
    bombardment of (1918), 327,
        328, *329*
    siege of (1871), *321*
Park, Air Marshal Sir Keith, 77
Pauldrons (armour), 280

Pénaud, Alphonse, 44
Pennington, E. J., 332
Pentekonter, 138—9, *139*
Periscope, 208—9
Perinthes, siege of, 260
Perriers, 157, 301
Persians, *141*, 142, 266, 267, 274,
    284, 352
Pescara, Marquis Raul, 106
Petronel, 310
Phalanx, 266—7, 268
    Swiss, 286
Philip of Macedon, 260, 267
Philip II, of France, 291
Philip II, of Spain, 161, 163
Philistines, 256
'Phlogiston', 13
Phocaeans, 140
Phoenicians, 136, 138—9, *139*, 140
Phrygians, 274
Pickard, James, 177
Pikemen, 286, 287, 309
Pilum (Roman javelin), 268
Pistol, 286, 311, 316
    'pepperbox', *316*
Plate armour, 276, 280
Pocket battleships, 234, *234*
    Deutschland, *234*, 235
Pocock, George, 9
Pompey, Roman general, 269, 270
Pot-de-fer (early cannon), 294
Priestley, Dr J., 13, *13*, 14, *14*
Prod (stonebow), 283
Propellor, variable pitch, 68—9, 74,
    76
Prussia, 313, 348
Pyroscaphe, S.S., 178

Quarrel (crossbow shaft), 283
Quinquireme, 142, 144

Radar equipment, 52, 100, 102, 128,
    129
    for guided missiles, 252
Railways, 348, *348*
Ram, warship feature, 138, *139*,
    140, 141, *141*, *142*, *146*, 147,
    189, 190, 194
Rameses II, 258
Rameses III, 135, 136, 137
Ram-jet, 252
Rating system for men-of-war, 167
Rattler, S.S., 180—1, *181*
Recoil of guns, 159, 172
Reed, Edward, 194
Rerebrace, 280
Revolver, 314, 316—7
    Adams', 317
    Colt, *316*, 317, 317
    pepperbox, 316
    Smith and Wesson, *317*
    Tranter, 317
    Webley, 317
Ribaudequins, 299, 300
Richard II, 282, 290, *291*
Richborough, Roman camp at, 270
Richelieu, Cardinal, 168
Richthofen, Manfred von, 56—7
Rifle, 312—4
    Baker, 312
    Chassepot, 313, *313*
    Henry, 314
    Lee-Enfield, 315
    Lee-Metford, 315
    Martini-Henry, 313
    Pennsylvania (Kentucky), 312,
        312, 313
    repeating, 314
    Von Dreyse, 313, *313*, 315, 321

Winchester, 314, *314*
Rifling, 182, 312
River-crossing, 352
Rocket-launcher (Panzerschreck),
    345
Rockets, 117—21, *117*, 122, 252—3,
    341, 358, *358*
    anti-submarine (ASROC), 253
    Baka bomb (Jap.), 252
    bazooka, 122, 344
    Chinese, 116
    helicopter-borne, *107*, *108*, 109
    Katyusha (Russian), 122, 358
    Okha (Jap.), 122, *122*
    16th Cent., *116*
    See also VI, V2
Rodney, Admiral Lord George, 170,
    172—3
Roland, *276*
Romans, 9, 142, 144, 264, 268—70,
    274, 280, 282, 284, *352*
    army organisation, 268, 274
    chariots, 258
    fleet, 144, 146
    fortified camps of, 270, 288
    missile throwers, 256, 282
    siege equipment, *263*, 272
Rommel, F-M Erwin, 342, *351*
Royal Air Force, 64, 76, 241
    Pathfinder Force, 102
Royal Aircraft Establishment,
    Farnborough, 11, 123
Royal Naval Air Service, 333
Royal Navy, *see* Navies, British
Rudder, introduction of stern
    rudder, 152

SAC (Sensor aided combat), 132
Saddles, 274, 276
'Safeguard' Anti-ballistic missile
    system, 128
Sail, development of, 152, 156, 157,
    158, 208
Sakers (field artillery), 160, 301
Santos-Dumont, Alberto, *28*, 29, 31,
    31
Sappers, early use of, 260
Saracens, 148, 149, 282, 283, 284,
    290, 291,
Satellites, 361
Saulnier, Raymond, 52
Savery, Thomas, 176, *176*
Scale armour, 274
Schnorkel, in submarines, 210
Schwartz, Bernard, 294
Schwarz, David, 32, *32*
Screw propulsion, 180—1
Scutum (Roman shield), 268
Scythians, 274
Semaphore, 360
Sennacherib, 263
Septireme, 142, 144
Serpentine (field artillery), 301
Serpentine gunpowder, 158, 159
Serpentine matchlock, 308, 309, 311
Serpentinelles, 301
Shang dynasty, China, 254
Shells, *184*, *185*
    armour-piercing, *185*, 343, 344
    for modern cannon, 326, 327
    high explosive, 182
    hollow charge, 344
    shrapnel, *184*
Shields, 274
    Greek, 266, *267*
    Roman, 268, 269
Shih Huang Ti, Chinese emperor,
    264
Ships of the Line, 167, 170
Shot,

armour piercing, 343, 344
    for cannon, 157, 301, 304, 326
    for hand guns, 310
    for naval guns, 157, 168, 172, 190
Shrapnel, *184*, 304
Shrapnel, Lieut, 304
Shrimp (guncart), 300
Siege machines, 272–3, 288, 296, 330
    Assyrian 260, *260*
    Roman, *263*, 272
Siege warfare, 272, 296, 297, 299, 304
Siege cannon, 294, 296, 324
Sieges,
    Boulogne (1544), 299–300
    Byzantium, 260
    Constantinople (717–18), 148–9
    Constantinople (1453), 272, 291, 296, 297, 329, 356
    Kai Fung-fu (1232), 116
Sikorsky, Igor, 62, *105*, 106
Simms, F. R., 332
Slings, 254, 256
Smith, Francis Pettit, 180, *181*
Snakes (mounted cannon), 300
Snaphaunce (early flintlock), 311
Solerets (armour), 280
Spanish Armada, 158, 161, *162*, *163*, 163–5, *164–5*
Spartans, 266, 267
Spearheads, *256*
Spearmen, 260, 266
Spears, 254, 258, 266, 267, 272, 274
Spear-sticks, 256, 257
Steam, development of, 176–8, 194, 208
Steam carriage, 331
Steam engine,
    applied to ships, 178, *178*, *179*
    early industrial, 176–7, *176*
Steam power for aircraft, 26, 28, 43, 44, *44*
Steam turbine, 203, 223
Stirrups, 274, 276
Stone age, *257*
Stone fortifications, 272, 288
Stone-tipped weapons, 256, *256*, 257
Stonebow (prod), 283
Stones, 254, 256, 272
    for cannon, 294
Strategic bombing, 60, 61, 64, 65, 66, 80, 82, 93
    by Zeppelins, 36
Strategy in sea warfare, 198
Streamlining, of aircraft, 66, 68
Stressed skin airframe construction, 67–8
Stringfellow, John, 43
Submachine gun, 324
    AK-47 (Russian Kalashnikov assault rifle), 324
    Bren, *325*
    Galil (Israeli), 324
    M-3, 324
    MP-18 (German), 324
    Sten-gun, 324, *325*
    Thompson (Tommy gun) (Am.), 324, *324*
    Uzi (Israeli), 324
Submarine, 204, 206, 207, *207*, 209, 210, 228, 231, 235, 246
    Drzewiecki's, *204*, 205
    Garrett's, 205
    H. L. Hunley (Am.), *199*, 204
    Holland (Am.), 208, 209

Nautilus US atom-powered, 214, *252*
Nautilus (Br.), 208, *208*
nuclear-powered, 214, *250*, *252*
Turtle (Am.), 204, *205*
U-boats, 210, 211, *211*, 212–4, *215*
Submarine warfare, 212, *213*, 214, *215*
Submarines, mini-, 94
Submersibles,
    David (Am.), *204*; see also Drzwiecki's, *H. L. Hunley*, *under* Submarine
Suleiman
    (8th Cent.), 149
    (16th Cent.), 292
Sumerians, 254, 256, 257, *259*
Sutton Hoo, 276
Swinton, Lt-Col, 334
Swiss, 286
    mercenaries, 286–7, 303
Swords, 254, 274, 309
    German, 287
    Greek, 266
    Roman, 268, *269*
Symington, William, 178

Taces (armour), 280
Tactics,
    fighter aircraft, 76
    land battle, 269, 284, 286
    naval, 164, 172, 174
    tank, 335
Tank,
    amphibious, 341
    bridge-laying, 340
    flame-throwing, *340*, 354
    mine-destroying, *336*, 337, 340
    origin and first use, 334, 335
    remote controlled, 340, 341
    rocket-launching, *340*
Tanks, *334*, 351
    American,
        M-60, 336
        Chieftain, 336
    British
        Centurion, 336
        Churchill, 336, 340, *340*
        Crusader, 336, *336*
        Matilda, *336*, 337, 340
        Mk IV, 335
        Valentine, 336, 340
    French AMX-13, 341
        AMX-30, 336
        Char B, 336, 337
    German,
        A7V, 87, *87*
        Leopard, 336
        Panther, 336, *336*
        PzKw Mk III, 335
        PzKw Mk IV, 335, *337*, 347
        Tiger, 336, 337, *337*, 342
        Renault, 335, *335*
    Russian,
        PT-76, 341
        T-34, 335, 336, *336*, 337, *337*
        T-37, 341
    St Chamond, 335
    Schneider, 335
    Swedish S-tank, 336
Tassets (armour), 280
Temple, Felix du, 44
Templer, Capt J. L. B., 24, 25
Tirpitz, German battleship, 93, 94
Torpedo,
    acoustic homing, *250*
    development, 94, 198, 200, *201*, 203, 209, 218, 253

'Harvey', 198
    Whitehead, 209
    Whitehead-Luppis, 198
Torpedo boats, 197, *199*, 200, 202, 218, 220, 322
Torpedo boat destroyer, 202
Torpedo tubes, 197, 200, 202, 209, 224
Torque catapult, 272
'Tortoise' (Roman device), 270
Tracked vehicles, early, 334
Traction wheel, 331
Train, armoured, *348*
Trebuchet (catapult), 272–3, 296
Trenchard, Marshal of the R.A.F. Lord, 66
Triple expansion engine, 196
Trireme, 140–2, *141*
Tritton, William, 334
Trunnions, 300, 304
Tsiolkovsky, K. E., 119
Turbo-electric engine, 232
Turbo-fan engine, 114, 115, 116
Turbo-jet engine, 114, 116, 252
Turks, 148, 292, 314
Turret, armoured, 182, 190, *190*, *191*, 192, *192*, 194, 217, 218, 222

United States Air Force, 80, 83, 109, 115, 132
United States Army, see Armies, American
United States Navy, see Navies, American
Ur, Standard of, 257, *259*

V1 rocket, 116, 123, *123*, 358
V2 rocket, 116, 120–1, *121*, 124, 358
Vambrace (armour), 280
Varus, Roman general, 271
Vauban, Sebastian, 312
Verdun, siege of (1916), 326, 327
Vienna, siege of (1529), 292
Vikings, 150–1, *151*, *276*, 284
Visor, 274, 280
V/STOL (Vertical and Short Take Off and Landing) aircraft, 116

Walled cities, 264, 288
Wallenstein, Count, 303
Wallis, Dr Barnes, 84, 93, 94, *95*, 96
Walls, 272
    Great Wall of China, 264, *264*
    Hadrian's, 264, *264*
Walter de Milemete, 294
Walther, Helmuth, 211, 212
Wars,
    American Civil, 20, 21, 189, 190, 198, 317, 320, 321, 348, *348*, 349, 351
    American Independence, 174, 312
    Anglo-Dutch, 167
    Arab-Israeli (1973), 324, 345, 346
    Boer, 9, 25, 323, 332
    British-American (1812), 118, 174,
    Crimean, 186, 188, 198, 317, *317*, 351, 356
    Crusades, 290
    English Civil, 280, 286, 311
    Franco-Austrian, 348
    Franco-Prussian, 23–4, 321, 349
    French Revolutionary, 18
    Greek-Persian (5th Cent. BC), 266–7
    Hundred Years', *280*, 284
    Italian 16th Cent., 302
    Korean, 109, 115, 354
    Libyan, 61

Mexican, 119, 317
Napoleonic, 118, 132, 304, 311, 312,
Peloponnesian, 142
Roman Civil, 268–70
Russo-Japanese, 218–20
Sino-Japanese, 80
Spanish Civil, 75, 84
Thirty Years', 280, 286, 302, *303*
Vietnam, 105, *107*, 109, 115, 132, 350, 354
World War I,
  artillery in, 323, 326, 327, 328, 346, 349
  at sea, 224–31
  firearms in, 315, 317, 323, 324
  in the air, 35–7, 50–4, 62, 64, 346
  tanks in, 332, 334, 335
  submarines in, 209, 210
World War II,
  artillery in, 342, 346
  at sea, 235, 241, 245
  in the air, 65, 71, 72–7, 80, 82–4, 89, 90, 93–4, 96, 108, 116, 122, 235, 238, 245
  machine guns in, 324
  submarines in, 210, 21·2, 214
  tanks in, 335, 336, *336*, 337, 340, *340*, 341
  Zulu, 321
Warship
  Byzantine, 146–7
  development of, 156, 157, 159–60, 166, 168, 174, 186, 188, 190, 196
  Egyptian, 135–7, *135*, *136*
  Greek, 140–2
  ironclad, 186, 188, *197*
  Phoenician, 138–9, *139*, 140
  Roman, 142, *142*, 144–5
  Viking, 150–1
Warships,
  Albemarle (Am.), 198
  Constitution (Am.), 174, *174*
  Couronne (Fr.), 168
  Cumberland (Am.), 189
  Demologos (Fulton) (Am.), 178, *179*
  Devastation (Fr.), 188
  Devastation (Br.), 194, *194*, 196
  Eagle (Br.), 198, 204
  Gloire (Fr.), 188, *189*
  Havoc (Br.), 202
  Henry Grace a Dieu (Eng.), 158
  H. L. Hunley (Am.), *199*, 204
  Hornet (Br.), 202
  Housatonic (Am.), *199*, 204
  Husacar (Peru), 198, 200
  Iris (Br.), 217
  Lightning (Br.), 200
  Lave (Fr.), 188
  Mercury (Br.), *216*, 217
  Merrimac (Am.), 189, 190, *190*, *191*, 192, *192*
  Monitor (Am.), 190, *190*, *191*, 192
  President (Am.), 174
  Re d'Italia (Ital.), 189
  Shah (Br.), 198
  Sovereign of the Seas (Eng.), 166, *167*
  Thunderer (Br.), 196
  Tonnante (Fr.), 188
  United States (Am.), 174
  Victory (Br.), 170, *170*
  Viper (Br.), 203
  Warrior (Br.), 188, *188*, 189
Washington Naval Treaty, 232, *233*,
234, 244
Water-tube boiler, 202
Watson-Watt, Sir Robert, 100
Watt, James, *176*, 177
Welsh, 284, 292
Wheel-lock, 310, *310*, 311, 316
Whitehead, Robert, 198, 200
Whittle, Sir Frank, 111, 112, *112*, 114
Whitworth, Sir James, 182
William, Duke of Normandy, 284
William III, 311
Wilson, Lt W. G., R.N.A.S., 334
Window, anti-radar device, 102, *103*
Windsor Castle, 288, *288*
Wireless, 9, 20, 21, 223
Wise, Lt H. D., 10
Woelfert, Karl, 29, *29*
Wright brothers, 45, 46, *46*, 47, 48, *48*

Zeppelin, Count Ferdinand von, *32*, 33, 34, 35
Zeppelins, *35*, *36*, 62, 344
  construction and development, 33, 34
  defence against, 37
Ziska, John, 300, 356

Acknowledgments

The publishers would like to thank the following organizations and individuals for their kind permission to reproduce the photographs in this book:

Aerofilms 270–271; American History Picture Library 314, 316 centre right and below right, 324–325, 348 left, (Imperial War Museum) 323, (Smithsonian Institution) 314–315, (Vickers) 336 centre; Associated Press 33, 37; British Tourist Authority 264 below left; Camera Press 46–47, 54–55, 66–67, 74 above left, 106 above and centre, 355, 359; J Allan Cash 265; Cooper Bridgeman Library 170–171; Crown Copyright, Permission of the Controller H M S O 251 below, 296 above and below, 310–311 below, 312, 319 above; Mary Evans Picture Library 10–11, 13 below, 14 below, 15, 18 above left and below, 32 above left, 43 below right, 135, 142, 145 above right and centre right, 158, 158–159, 178 centre right, 184 above and centre, 185 above and centre, 187 below, 188, 189 above left, 192, 192–193, 198, 199, 200 centre left and centre right, 201 above right and below, 204 above, centre and below, 205 above, centre right, and below, 218, 218–219, 220–221, 221 above, 280, 294, 297, 308 below left, 310 above 320–321, 332 above left, 353 above, 354; Ferranti 132, 133 below; Flight International 68, 69; Sonia Halliday Photographs 261 above, 291 right above and below; Michael Holford 139, 174, 222–223, 254–255, 255 above and below, 258–259, 262–263, 266–267, 274, 277, 278–279, 288, 290–291, 295, 352 left, 358, (Courtesy of the Ministry of Defence) 230–231; Anne Horton 28, 299 right, 305 above and below; Robert Hunt Library 329 above and below left, 338–339, 344–345, 351 right, (Associated Press) 350 centre right, (Imperial War Museum) 325 above; Illustrated London News 189 below right, 196–197, 200 right above and below, 201 above left, 208–209, 217, 226 below right, 238–239, 240–241, 245 below left and right; Imperial War Museum 58–59, 86 above left and right, 86–87 below, 92 below, 94, 100 left, 100–101, 101 above and below right, 103, 210–211, 213, 215 below, 216, 224 above and centre, 226 above right and centre right, 226–227, 228, 235 above and below, 244 below, 245 above left, 321 right, 324, 325 below, 332 above right, 333 above left and right, 336 above, 336–337 above, 337 centre and below, 336–337 below, 340 above and below left, 340–341, 345, 346, 349, 353 below, 356–357, 357, 360 left, above centre and below, 360–361, 361; Jane's Weapon Systems 133 above; Keystone Press Agency 91 above, 246, 248 right, 249, 270 below; Mansell Collection 104, 184–185 below, 201 centre left, 212, 236, 238, 239, 240, 241, 244, 245, 248–249, 249 below, 260, 276, 281, 284, 300, 300–301, 301, 302–303, 308 below, 308–309, 352–353; 372–373 National Gallery London 286–287; National Maritime Museum 154–156, 162–163, 166–167, 167 right, 186–187; Novosti Press Agency 293 above, 336 below; Popperfoto 56 above, 60 above, 112, 202, 214–215, 214 below, 229 above and below, 242–243, 244 above, 247, 250 above left, 251 above, 252, 253 left and right; RAC Tank Museum 333 below right; Radio Times Hulton Picture Library 348–349, 356; John Rigby 50–51 below, 87 above; Ronan Picture Library 14, 16, 16–17, 20–21, 23, 24, 25, 29, 31 above right, 32 below, 46 above left, 116, 117 left and right, 241 above right, 261 below, 284–285, 304; Science Museum, London 136, 150, 168–169, 178 centre left, 179, 180–181, 189 centre, 203, 204–205 centre, 236–237, 248 left; Spectrum Colour Library 74 below left, 74–75, 106 below, 107 above and below, 114–115, 115 below, 126–127, 289, 292–293; John W R Taylor 50 left and above right, 52 above and below left, 52–53, 56 below, 57, 60–61, 61 above, 64–65, 72–73, 76–77, 80–81, 85 above and below, 88–89, 90, 92–93, 96, 97 above and below, 104 centre left and right, and below, 105, 108–109, 109, 112–113, above and below, 120–121, 122, 124, 125, 128–129; Wadsworth Atheneum, Hartford, Conn. 316 above; Weidenfeld Archiv 306, 307, (Waffensammlung des Kunsthistorischen Museums, Vienna) 313 (Bildarchiv der Oesterreichischen Nationalbibliothek, Vienna); Derrick E Witty 316 centre and below left, 317, 318–319, 319 below, 320 left.

Illustrations by Hildegarde Bone, Wilf Hardy, Peter Jackson, Bill Robertshaw, George Tuckwell and John Young.

PDO 84-0027